INDUSTRY AND INNOVATION

INDUSTRY
AND
INNOVATION
Selected Essays

W.H. CHALONER

Edited by

D. A. Farnie and W. O. Henderson

FRANK CASS

First published 1990 in Great Britain by
FRANK CASS AND COMPANY LIMITED
Gainsborough House, 11 Gainsborough Road,
London E11 1RS, England

and in the United States of America by
FRANK CASS
c/o Rowman & Littlefield Publishers, Inc.
8705 Bollman Place, Savage, MD 20763

British Library Cataloguing in Publication Data

Chaloner, W.H. (William Henry), *1914–1987*
Industry and innovation: selected
essays/W.H. Chaloner
1. Great Britain. Social conditions, 1714–
I. Title   II. Farnie, D.A. (Douglas Antony)
III. Henderson, W.O. (William Otto), *1904–*
941.07

ISBN 0-7146-3335-6

Library of Congress Cataloging-in-Publication Data

Chaloner, W.H. (William Henry)
    Industry and innovation : selected essays / W.H. Chaloner ; edited
by D.A. Farnie and W.O. Henderson.
        p.   cm.
    "Select bibliography of professor Chaloner's writings (by Douglas
Farnie)": p.
    ISBN 0-7146-3335-6
    1. Technological innovations—Great Britain—History. 2. Great
Britain—Industries—History. 3. Great Britain—Economic
conditions—1760–1860. 4. Industry—Social aspects—Great Britain–
–History. 5. Entrepreneurship—Great Britain—History. I. Farnie,
D.A. II. Henderson, W.O. (William Otto), 1904–   . III. Title.
HC260.T4C47   1989
338'.06—dc19   88–31684
                                                              CIP

Printed and bound in Great Britain by
BPCC Wheatons Ltd, Exeter

CONTENTS

III Manchester as a Regional Metropolis

IV Social Aspects of the Industrial Revolution

V Monetary Standards and Imperial Trade

VI Select Bibliography of Professor Chaloner's Writings

To John, Timothy and David

LIST OF ILLUSTRATIONS

ACKNOWLEDGEMENTS

Chapter 1 reproduced by permission of the Presses Universitaires de Nancy; Chapter 2, the *Agricultural History Review*; Chapter 3, the Royal Historical Society; Chapter 4, *Business History*; Chapters 5 and 7, the Council of the Newcomen Society; Chapter 6, the Lancashire and Cheshire Antiquarian Society; Chapters 8 and 9, the John Rylands Library; Chapter 10, the British Association; Chapters 11 and 18, Manchester University Press; Chapter 13, the Institute of Economic Affairs; Chapters 14 and 15, the Historical Association; Chapter 16, *Victorian Studies*; Chapter 17, Professor John Yudkin. Roy Fuller's poem is reproduced by permission of *The Spectator*.

W. H. Chaloner on Economic History

A distressing cleavage has arisen of recent years in the attitude of economic historians towards their subject. The cleavage is between those whom we may label the traditional economic historians, who regard economic history as a branch of historical studies, and those (often economists sporting the cloak of economic history for the occasion) who seem to consider economic history as a collection of impersonal, even inhuman, 'trends' or 'forces', plus a body of historical statistics of varying trustworthiness. From these, by selective extraction, the popular economic theories of the day may be illustrated and tested. This cleavage is as yet less pronounced in Great Britain and France than in the United States of America, where, owing to the humble position occupied by economic history in university curricula, the teachers of the subject often appear to their British counterparts to be economists and sociologists who have either strayed from their true vocation, or have been directed, more or less gently, away from it, rather than historians.

The author of the present collection of essays belongs to those who consider economic history as a branch of what the French call the historical sciences, and believes that it is impossible to treat usefully of the rise, decline and metamorphosis of industries and economies without some consideration of the part played by the efforts of individual men and women in these processes.

W. H. Chaloner, *People and Industries*
(Frank Cass, 1963), pp. 6–7

INTRODUCTION

EDITORS' PREFACE

This volume commemorates one of the most notable historians of his age. The editors have brought together a selection of his writings in order to make them more widely available. Mrs Chaloner has consented to the publication of this volume and has given the editors every assistance. In particular she has made available the manuscript of the lecture on 'Working-Class History and Middle-Class Historians'.

The task of selecting the most appropriate essays presented its own challenge as they were so many and so varied. Since Chaloner's writings were distinguished by their range and their number it was difficult for even two editors to prepare a proper selection. At this point the editors were greatly helped by the advice of three of Chaloner's most distinguished pupils and associates – Professors Barker, Harris and Musson. They carefully considered our initial selection and improved it in various ways. They also helped to ensure the most effective grouping of the essays. Professor Harris gave invaluable aid in the translation of one essay from the original French. The editors are grateful to these scholars for their unstinting cooperation which has helped to make this volume better than it would otherwise have been.

There can be no doubt as to the substantial amount of Chaloner's researches. Between 1938 and 1985 he published the 136 items (including four books) listed in the bibliography at the end of this volume. The publication of his doctoral thesis was delayed by his wartime service in the Ministry of Information and by a heavy load of teaching after the war. It was published in 1950 by the University of Manchester Press. This was followed by *People and Industries* (Frank Cass, 1963), a collection of 17 articles which (with one exception) had already appeared in print and had reached a much wider readership than his monograph on Crewe. In addition Chaloner wrote two slim volumes of business history – *Vulcan 1859–1959* (1959) and *National Boiler 1864–1964* (1964) – which were published privately. Chaloner came to prefer the article to the book as the most appropriate vehicle of publication. His articles were generally published in one of two forms – either in the transactions of learned societies (such as the Newcomen Society and the Lancashire and Cheshire Antiquarian Society) or in the 1950s in the

Manchester Guardian and *History Today*. It is articles from the first group which have been chosen for inclusion in this volume, partly because many articles in the second group had already been reprinted in 1963. The editors thank the societies which have permitted articles from their proceedings to be reprinted.

Certain types of articles have been excluded such as essays written jointly by Chaloner and Henderson, unpublished manuscripts (with one exception) and bibliographical articles and prefaces whose contents may have dated more than that of other articles. The editors have however printed a brief review of Chaloner's bibliographical prefaces by Mr Harry Horton.

In making their final selection of 18 of his best and most typical essays they have sought to illustrate those themes which interested Chaloner most. During the course of a long and productive career his interests expanded to include the industrial revolution with particular reference to iron and steel, engineering and transport; the growth of Manchester as the centre of a great industrial and commercial region; changes in food production and in the Englishman's diet. Above all Chaloner was interested in people both as individuals – as inventors, entrepreneurs or workers – and as members of groups such as trade unions, social clubs, and chambers of commerce.

Throughout his career Chaloner was deeply concerned with the social consequences of the industrial revolution for the workers. This interest impelled him to examine changes in the workers' standard of living. He studied the workers' diet, health, housing, education and wages. He ranged himself with the 'optimists' (led by Clapham and Ashton) who held that the standard of living of the workers had shown a marked rise in the nineteenth century and he was highly critical of the 'pessimists' (such as the Hammonds) who argued that the industrial revolution had been an unmitigated disaster for the workers.

Chaloner rarely expressed in print his own views on economic history, though his book reviews are a rich mine of penetrating judgments. A brief extract from the introduction to *People and Industries* has been used as an epigraph because it embodies sentiments to be found nowhere else. The editors trust that the following essays include the most typical as well as the most important of Chaloner's writings. They believe that the articles illuminate a distinctive and independent-minded personality as well as a large tract of history.

W. H. Chaloner: Memorial Address

Rev. Benjamin Drewery[1]

William Henry Chaloner was born at Crewe in 1914. His family – not only Welsh, but Welsh-speaking – had come to Crewe, where his grandfather, and later his father, found work on the railway. He was one of four brothers, of whom the survivor, Gordon, is present with us today.

The father of Bill, as we must call him, was a Congregationalist and his mother a Baptist – a mixed marriage indeed, but all within the great flowering of the Nonconformist Conscience. In 1947, Bill produced a 22-page history of Crewe Congregational Church at its Centenary, and he never lost interest in the churches or (more especially) in churchmen. It is entirely fitting that his funeral service should be in a church built on land given in 1855 by John Platt, of Platt Bros., Oldham, then the greatest textile engineers in the world.

Bill's family life as a boy was close and affectionate. Money would not be plentiful, and his mother actually made him the suit of clothes he wore when he first went to university. This was preceded by eight years at Crewe Grammar School, from 1925. The whole of the rest of his life, except for the war, was given to Manchester University: when he retired in 1981, only one man – a porter – out of the whole academic and administrative staff, had served the University longer than he. On that very day I said to the Registrar[2] in the Staff Coffee Room – 'It's Bill's last day. The University will never be the same again.' 'Have no fear', said the Registrar, 'he'll be back tomorrow' – and he was!

His First Class Honours in history, followed by an M.A. in 1937 and a Ph.D. in 1939, were inevitable. His Ph.D. thesis on the history of Crewe from 1780 was expanded into a book published in 1950, which pioneered the study of urban history from an economic and social perspective. He had been brought up in the great traditions of Unwin, Ashton and Redford, and his tutors had included Professors Jacob and Namier and the young A.J.P. Taylor. Bill once told me with regard to the said A.J.P. Taylor, that Professor Jacob once sent for him and said – 'Taylor, there's a Senior Lectureship in History going at Trinity College, Dublin. I am prepared to recommend you for it. Are you interested?' And Taylor drew himself up and replied: 'No, Professor. Until Oxford is ready, Manchester will suffice!'

Bill's academic career was interrupted by the war, in which he served as Chief Photographic Censor within the Ministry of Information in London. Typical of him was the delight with which he met the original of Sir John Betjeman's 'A Subaltern's Love Song' – named by the poet as Miss Joan Hunter Dunne.

> Miss J. Hunter Dunne, Miss J. Hunter Dunne,
> Tarnished and burnished by Aldershot sun,
> What strenuous singles we played after tea,
> We in the tournament – you against me!

In 1945 he returned to Manchester University as Assistant Lecturer in History, rising through all the grades to a Professorship in 1976. And it is here that the humble preacher stands helpless before his mass of material. Bill was Director and Chairman of the Higher Degrees Committee in the Faculties of Arts, Music and Theology, where he was of inestimable value to me when I brought him Ecclesiastical History students aspiring to a Doctorate. How he dealt with the musical aspirants I never knew, because his knowledge of that art was limited to the 'Pirates of Penzance' – but there were no complaints! Within the University his greatest contributions, along-side his specialist productions, were to the life of Dalton Hall, to the development of the Library (where he and Dr. Fred Ratcliffe[3] were both zealous searchers for books), to the University Press, to the many outside bodies on which he represented the University, such as the Oldham Area Health Authority and the North Western Museum of Science and Industry, to the publications of the Chetham Society – and on a wider level to the Transactions of the Lancashire and Cheshire Antiquarian Society, the Economic History Society, and the Agricultural History Society, on whose Councils he served for many years. Here in Oldham, which almost stole the place of Crewe in his affections, he long served as a governor of the Hulme Grammar Schools: the music master of the boys' school, Stanley Baty linked to Bill by marriage, is here on the organ today.

Nor may one omit his overseas travels, from 1949 to the end. Bill became a regular envoy to the International Economic History congresses; he lectured at the Sorbonne, and addressed a world congress at Salt Lake City on 'Three Centuries of Emigration from the British Isles'; he was external examiner to the University of

Khartoum, visiting Kenya and the Sudan several times. How he contrived to write a single book during this ocean of activity is a deep mystery: but the list of his publications is so formidable that I can only mention one or two of them – and here, as in so much else, I am wholly indebted to his colleague and our great friend Dr Douglas Farnie, who is also with us today.

In 1957 he demolished the legend of the 'hungry forties' and contributed to the Festschrift for Dr. Henderson in 1975 a pioneer survey of 'the currency problems of the British Empire 1814–1914', which reflected an interest in numismatology for which he became locally an oracle. In 1958 he and Henderson submitted Engels' *The Condition of the Working Class in England* to a severe scrutiny, undermining its claims to canonicity as a sacred text of Socialism, and being later flattered by a hostile Russian review of one of his essays on British miners. Dr. Farnie rates as his most notable unpublished article the famous lecture on 'Working-Class History and Middle-Class Historians: the Webbs, the Hammonds and the Coles'. His essay on 'The Skilled Artisans during the Industrial Revolution 1750–1850' anticipated much of the later interest in artisan culture. In *People and Industries* (1963) he created a revisionist portrait of what has often been thought to have been the 'unacceptable face of capitalism' during the industrial revolution. Undergraduates revered his 'Trends in Fish Consumption' (1966) which linked the Lancashire cotton industry and the town of Oldham to the history of fish and chips. His *People and Industries* (1963) was translated into Japanese.

What shall I say more? His knowledge and love of books placed him on the same celestial level as that of the legendary Arthur S. Peake,[4] the virtual founder of the Faculty of Theology at Manchester, of which Bill was always a great friend. In 1976 he published with R.C. Richardson a bibliography of British economic and social history, which reached 5,800 entries by its second edition in 1984. He was Chairman of the Portico Library and the Manchester Bibliographical Society. 'His interests', says Dr. Farnie, 'ranged from agriculture to iron, from skilled artisans to the Cheshire gentry, from biography to genealogy, from food and drink to education':[5] as a son of Crewe he was an expert on transport. More than any other man, he put economic history on the map for his contemporaries, bringing it before a wider public through the Workers' Educational Association and his Extra-Mural Lectures, himself building up a Himalayan range of knowledge that was the awe of his colleagues and students alike. Perhaps the unsolved problem of Professor Chaloner's intellectual development was what I might call a political mystery. He was brought up as a stout liberal Nonconformist in an area where William Gladstone was not merely a statesman but a demigod, whose brooding presence would regularly crystallise in nearby Hawarden. In later life Bill loved to pose as the 'hammer of the left', to a degree which would have brought the great Liberal patriarch bounding from his chair. Whence, why and how? Here is a wonderful theme for the Ph.D. thesis of a future W.H.C. at Manchester!

But when all this is said and done, one has left out the most vital element in the personality of our honoured friend – his unfathomable generosity and friendliness, his salacious wit, his humanity, his eternal 'sense of fun'. I have been told that when his three sons were boys he would read them at night stories of Noddy and Rupert, with textual emendations supplied by his own imagination and innocently mistaken by his audience for the original text. By the express permission of his family, I am authorised to give you two anecdotes of him, which reveal the real Bill as truly as the forbidding tally of his publications.

A year ago there was a most unfortunate burglary at Bill's house. While the family was sitting at Sunday lunch, the burglars stole some silver plate from another room. Of course the police arrived and valuable data such as fingerprints were taken. But then came the moment when the Inspector opened Bill's study door, took one look inside, and said – 'By Jove, they've made a mess here!' – and the point was that they'd never been in it!

In January 1975, two carloads of us went from Manchester University to Cambridge for a dinner in Honour of Prof. Gordon Rupp's 65th birthday *Festschrift* presentation. (I must add that, by a sombre coincidence, I am speaking on Saturday at Wesley's Chapel, City Road, London, in a memorial service to the same Gordon Rupp who died in December.) He had earlier been for ten years Professor of Ecclesiastical History at Manchester, and a dear and honoured colleague of Bill himself. I myself went with the convoy but could not return with them, so I gave them directions for coming home via Melton Mowbray, where they could buy pork pies for their wives.I said – 'Park at the station, walk through the town centre, and the shop is next door to the Ladbroke's betting shop corner.' So we picture some seven or eight eminent Manchester men advancing in single file up the narrow pavement, led by the saintly Rev. Dr. Gordon Wakefield[6], editor of the standard *Dictionary of Christian Spirituality* and an old school friend of Bill's from Crewe days. Suddenly a voice rang out from half-way down the file to a passer-by: 'Can you tell us the way to Ladbroke's betting shop?' It was, of course, Bill, and they say the face of the Rev. Dr. Wakefield was a beautiful study!

Even Bill could not go on for ever. A serious operation on March 2nd led to three months' illness of growing severity which was never truly diagnosed until two days before the end. We do not dwell on those weeks of increasing helplessness, or on the crippling suspense of his family as they tried to minister to him. He died on May 25th, and for many of us a light has gone out which none can ever re-kindle.

We think above all of his wife Joan, married in 1949, in many ways the unseen power-house behind the multifarious range of her husband's achievements. She has been reminded of the words used by Winston Churchill when A.J. Balfour was dying: 'the tragedy which robs the world of all the wisdom and treasure gathered in a great man's life and experience, and hands the lamp to some impetuous and untutored stripling, or lets it fall into fragments upon the ground.' Her three sons – John, Timothy and David – and the four grandchildren, deserve our proud and sorrowful affection. Myriads of students and friends will hardly believe that Bill has gone: nor will his old colleagues at the University. For what we shall miss most of all will be his presence at the coffee-table after lunch, when among half-a-dozen close friends he would truly be the life and soul of the party – so full of humour and understanding, so unfailing-ly generous and kind. For as the Registrar said to me yesterday – we did not merely look on him with the respect and admiration that his gifts as a scholar and administrator evoked, but with something more: with very deep affection. The souls of the righteous are in the hand of God: no torment can touch him now.

NOTES

1. The text reprinted here by kind permission of the author is that of the memorial address delivered by the Rev. B. Drewery at Professor Chaloner's funeral service held in the Church of St. Thomas, Werneth, Oldham on 4 June 1987. The lesson was taken from Proverbs 8.vv.1–21.
2. Mr K.E. Kitchen, University Registrar since 1980.
3. Dr F.W. Ratcliffe, University Librarian (1965–80) and Librarian to the University of Cambridge since 1980.
4. A.S. Peake (1865–1929), the first Rylands Professor of Biblical Criticism and Exegesis in the University of Manchester and editor of a standard *Commentary on the Bible* (1919).
5. The *Daily Telegraph*, 2 June 1987.
6. G.S. Wakefield, author of *Puritan Devotion: its Place in the Development of Christian Piety* (1957), *The Life of the Spirit in the World of Today* (1970) and *A Dictionary of Christian Spirituality* (1983).

SOURCES OF INFORMATION ON W.H. CHALONER'S CAREER

Who's Who in Greater Manchester, 1985–86, Manchester Literary and Philosophical Society, 1985, 63.
The Daily Telegraph, 2 June 1987
The Times, 2 June 1987
The Guardian, 3 and 6 June 1987
The Independent, 9 June 1987.

I.m. W.H. Chaloner ob. 25.v.1987

Professor Chaloner linked the history
Of fish and chips to the cotton industry,
My native town of Oldham especially.

– This in the legendary final section
Of the work entitled *Trends in Fish Consumption*,
Reached by students with sudden stupefaction.

– Moreover, lived and died in that damp place,
Among green moors and roseate factories;
By then the deafening spindles more or less

Mere things historical, and even (perhaps
According to his thesis) fish and chips,
Among vile dens of hamburgers and kebabs.

Roy Fuller

The Spectator, Vol. 260, no. 8346, 25 June 1988, p.41.

Memoir of a Partnership

W.O. Henderson

In 1949 Redford asked Chaloner and myself to translate Werner Schlote's *British Overseas Trade*. At that time neither of us could have foreseen that this was to be the beginning of a partnership that was to last for over a quarter of a century. Altogether we translated five German books and an article by Drescher on agricultural production in England. We also wrote two introductions and 7 joint articles. Our last article, written in 1975, was on Marx and racialism. But during our long partnership we were also pursuing our own independent researches.

Academic collaboration may run into difficulties if each partner thinks that the other is not pulling his weight. We never experienced any such difficulty as we soon worked out a satisfactory division of labour. When we translated a book I would dictate the first draft and Chaloner would suggest amendments paragraph by paragraph. The final version was, I am sure, always a distinct improvement on the first draft. When it came to the footnotes and the bibliography Chaloner was in his element. He had a quite exceptional knowledge of the printed and manuscript sources of British economic and social history in the eighteenth and nineteenth centuries. (His only rival in that respect was my former supervisor H.L. Beales.) Chaloner supplied a bibliography to all our translations. The 'Note on recent Published Work' added to Schlote's book set a precedent that was maintained in later translations.

One of Chaloner's most important contributions to the collaboration was his uncanny ability to track down documents relevant to our enquiries. For example, when we were engaged in the 1950s on research on Friedrich Engels' life in Manchester it was Chaloner who found – in a solicitor's office – four contracts between Engels and Godfrey Ermen. Those of 25 September 1862 and 30 June 1864 throw light on Engels' financial position as a junior partner in the cotton firm of Ermen & Engels while an examination of two agreements of 1869 shows that Engels secured a handsome competence on which to retire to London. Again it was Chaloner who discovered the existence in private hands of a complete set of the *Volunteer*

Journal for Lancashire − a find which enabled us to reprint a selection of Engels' writings on military affairs (*Engels as Military Critic*, 1959).

When we had translated Friedrich Engels' *The Condition of the Working Class in England* (1958) and reprinted his articles on the volunteers (1959) I hoped that we might go on to write a new biography of Engels. Chaloner however said that he had had enough of Engels and that he had other research projects in view. But when I carried on with my life of Engels Chaloner was always ready with helpful advice and suggestions concerning possible new lines of research.

Chaloner had six other collaborators besides myself. He collaborated with Musson to produce the well-illustrated book on *Industry and Technology* (1963) − with Barrie Ratcliffe to translate and edit Gustave d'Eichthal's journal of his visit to England in 1828 − and with R.C. Richardson in compiling a bibliographical guide to British economic and social history.

W. H. Chaloner's Bibliographical Introductions

Harry Horton

The range of W.H. Chaloner's published work – books, articles, bibliographies, reviews – produced over almost a half-century of study and teaching – compels our admiration. In respect of one particular group of writings, Negley Harte – in his obituary notice of Chaloner in *The Independent*, 9 June 1987 – remarked with perspicacity that 'much of his work, unassumingly hidden, lies in his bibliographical introductions to many seminal works reprinted by Frank Cass and the Manchester University Press'. It is with these 'introductions', growing naturally, as it were, out of Chaloner's lifelong love of books, that this short contribution is largely concerned.

I was never a formal pupil of Chaloner, beyond membership of his essay class in 1945 when he returned to the Manchester University History Department after the war. But his coming to live in Oldham after marriage, and my joining the staff at Manchester Central Library in 1952, afforded contact with him occasionally on journeys, by rail and bus, to and from the city, quite apart from serving him in the course of duty at the Reference Library counter. I write, 'never a formal pupil' – but I must be only one of many who over the years learned from even casual conversation with him.

A feature of these conversations, if they turned to historical themes, would be the range of literature referred to in passing. He had perhaps just received a new book for review; or had read of a new study in progress (often producing the appropriate cutting from that capacious brief-case); or he advised you that the latest issue of a particular journal contained a valuable correction or expansion of some subject. Casual discussion, as much as the essay class, the lecture, or the published work was so well-informed; and it is little to be wondered at that the 'bibliographical introductions' should be singled out by Negley Harte as especially noteworthy.

An examination of the subjects of the 'seminal works' to which, when reprinted, Chaloner supplied an introduction provides an indication and a confirmation of the range of topics which remained particularly central to his own studies and writings. Great themes of the Industrial Revolution – iron and textile industries and transport – are in the books by Ashton [83], Baines [91], Priestley [95], Jackman [79] and Dendy Marshall [117].* The two last-named were exactly right for attention from the historian of Crewe, his home railway-town. Books which have become illuminating contemporary texts of nineteenth-century industrial history fell naturally within his scope – Cooke Taylor [105], Dodd [103] and Head [104]. Chaloner's concern with the history of the Manchester area made it appropriate for him to serve Bamford [94] and Prentice [101] with his scholarship.

The titles by Unwin [106], Ashton [83] and Redford [88] have special significance, not only to the subjects of the books but because Chaloner followed resolutely in the succession and tradition of those distinguished teachers. Of course after the war he became a colleague of Arthur Redford in the History Department. From the work of all three Chaloner evidently drew inspiration and it seems fitting that in the fullness of time the 'disciple' should ensure the continuing usefulness of writings from an older generation of Manchester scholars, so keeping their books close by the desk of both student and teacher.

There are over a score of 'introductions' and in one or two instances a second edition of the reprint enabled Chaloner to revise or to add to his first essay. For example, the reprint of Jackman [79] appeared in 1962 with 15 pages by Chaloner; the 3rd edition in 1966 included three further pages of references. The introduction to Redford [88] in 1964 was considerably revised to incorporate new material when a 3rd edition was published in 1976.

The introductions vary from a couple of pages as in Priestley [95] and Cooke Taylor [105], to substantial pieces in Ashton [83], Redford [88], Bamford [94] and Prentice [101]. Taken all together, they comprise a considerable achievement in size alone, whether reckoning by the total number of pages or by the sum of individual references. Obviously the nature of some subjects demanded a list of separate articles and studies, such as the 70 or so citations on roads in the two editions of Jackman [79]. For other subjects a note of a single significant study might be the only requirement, either necessary or possible. It seems right to emphasise from this that comprehensiveness (where needed) and an appreciation of what is really important find equal expression in these introductions.

Valuable biographical sketches appear here and there, exhibiting

*The figures in square brackets identify Chaloner's writings listed in the Bibliography.

a familiarity with appropriate sources and a facility for blending stray facts gleaned from registers, directories and obituary notices. The piece on Priestley, 'a shadowy figure', exemplifies this approach at its best [95]; and for a later writer Chaloner's note on C.F. Dendy Marshall presents succinctly the man and his achievement [117].

The introductions are never merely listings of titles.The narrative woven around the references draws attention to the merits – and the shortcomings – of books and articles; passages from them are occasionally quoted at length to illuminate the theme under consideration; individual references are placed firmly within the wider context of the subject. A sentence from the introduction to Ashton can stand as the leit-motif for this body of work: 'The purpose of the following bibliographical note is to guide the student through recent work, and to indicate its significance' (Ashton [83], p.vii).

Throughout is demonstrated Chaloner's enviable familiarity with the material he is referring to and evaluating. We find for H.R. Schubert, *History of the British Iron and Steel Industry from c.450 B.C. to A.D. 1775* (1957) that 'it is unfortunate that the book contains such a large number of misprints': – Ashton [83, p.vii]. In the essay in Prentice [101, p.xiv, note 2], C.R. Fay's *The Corn Laws and Social England* (1932) is referred to thus: 'Fay's somewhat neglected book is a store of exact information on the technical aspects of the operation of the Corn Laws.' The concern for wholly trustworthy references (not *always* a feature of bibliographies) is revealed in a telling note on the first page of Cooke Taylor [105] – 'see N. McCord, *The Anti-Corn Law League 1838–1846* (1958) pp.185–6, where the title of the book [i.e. Cooke Taylor] is incompletely given ...' Chaloner rightly looked for, and expected accuracy in descriptions, as I can testify when compiling indexes (under his editorship) for the *Transactions of the Lancashire and Cheshire Antiquarian Society* and (at Chaloner's invitation and under the editorship of Finberg) for the *Agricultural History Review*.

These bibliographical introductions are certainly 'a store of exact information' and often direct us to a 'somewhat neglected book' – to take Chaloner's own words out of context. To study these pieces and consider their contents is to draw upon a great source of learning and be led in our own reading in a plain path. This characteristic work of a fine scholar is worthy of our grateful tribute.

PART ONE

THE WILKINSONS
AND
THE IRON TRADE

1

The Brothers John and William Wilkinson and their relations with French Metallurgy, 1775–1786

The activities of the Wilkinson brothers in France between 1775 and 1786 form an important chapter in the history of the development of the French iron industry and in the history of Franco-British relations towards the close of the eighteenth century as well as an example of the progress of the coke smelting of iron in two neighbouring countries.

In about 1770 John Wilkinson (1728–1808) and his brother William (? 1744–1808) – joint owners of an important ironworks at Bersham, near Wrexham in North Wales – had succeeded in replacing charcoal by coke in their blast furnaces. However in July–August 1775, Marchant de la Houlière, a brigadier in the infantry of Louis XVI, in the course of a 'metallurgical journey' through the main regions of the English iron industry, had studied for himself the processes of coke smelting, with which he himself had experimented, not without success, in 1773. He had secured a subsidy for this journey from the Estates of Languedoc and on his return he prepared an official report which is preserved in the *Archives Nationales* in Paris.[1]

Provided with a letter of introduction from Messrs. Boulton & Fothergill of Soho, near Birmingham, and accompanied by the Irishman MacDermott, chaplain to the French ambassador in London, he met John Wilkinson at his second ironworks near Broseley, in August 1775.[2] Wilkinson had a long conversation with him and gave him a letter of introduction to his brother William at Bersham. Later in his report de la Houlière described the two interviews in the third person and without identifying his hosts:

He [Marchant de la Houlière] ventured to drop certain vague hints to an eminent ironmaster who owns four foundries and has brought the casting of cannon to the highest pitch of perfection, to the effect that an Englishman who would come to France and cast them in a similar manner, would make a large fortune. This gentleman replied that an Englishman could have no confidence whatever in our Government and our Ministry, when they had the power to dismiss him at any moment, but if it were a question of a private arrangement between individuals, then he saw a tidy profit was to be made, with all the benefits accruing from an assured market on a long-term basis. [He also said] that he would send his younger brother, who is unmarried and manages quite a large cannon foundry on his [elder] brother's behalf. I replied that I would willingly go into an equal partnership with him, that I would give him suitable security, and that on my return I would lay this before the Ministry. He told me that he would want a guaranteed market for twelve years at least, absolute certainty of exact payment for goods supplied, exemption from all taxes on coal, and above all, the freedom to export, to wherever he could find a market for them, all cannon, cannon balls, and bombs manufactured in excess of service requirements, for these Englishmen never set a limit on their field of trade. I told him that this might do very well in times of peace, but should war break out, the most that he could expect would be permission to export to allied or neutral powers. At this stage we parted, I promising to write to him.

Next day I was at Bersham foundry near Wrexham, which is managed by this younger brother of his, a man from 30 to 35 years of age. I gave him an account of my conversation with his brother. He appeared to me to agree with all the views expressed, and had a great desire to see France. I assured him that he would hear from me.

The Ambassador is in a position to seek out and verify that the persons with whom I had ventured to open negotiations have a capital of more than £80,000 invested in their foundries, that they are entrusted by their Government with the supply of naval cannon, that they have made many for the Dutch, and sent considerable supplies to Constantinople, that they are no mere speculators, but persons of good breeding, actuated solely by that spirit of gain which is all too common in their nation. I do not think that we can make a better arrangement in order to be sure of having cannon as good as the English. At least we must fight with equally good armaments.[3]

The results were not long delayed. William Wilkinson made an initial journey to France in the autumn of 1775 and de la Houlière wrote on December 3 that 'M. le comte de Guines[4] has brought here the Englishman mentioned ... He has requested six cannon from his foundry as samples.'[5] While waiting for the arrival of the cannon[6] and of material ordered at the same time, William visited the ironworks of de la Houlière at Alais as well as other sites where deposits of iron and coal lay close together. He declared himself convinced that France could undertake coke smelting and proposed the establishment of a cannon foundry on the isle of Indret, in the Loire, near Nantes.[7] On his return to England, William Wilkinson remained at the Bersham works until the winter of 1776. It was undoubtedly during the spring of 1777[8] that he left for a second stay in France which this time was to be of long duration.

He probably travelled in the company of Jacques-Constantin Périer of the *Compagnie des Eaux de Paris*, the eventual purchaser of water pipes.[9] An agreement was soon signed between William Wilkinson and de Sartine, minister and secretary of state for the navy, naming Wilkinson as the 'director' (*régisseur*) of a royal foundry for the casting of cannon on the English model, to be established on the isle of Indret, near Nantes, at the mouth of the Loire.[10] His emoluments were fixed at £600 (12,000 *livres*) per year and were raised on May 29, 1779 to £2,500 (50,000 *livres*). Wilkinson was to supply the plans, whilst the task of construction itself and the assembly of the machines was to be entrusted to two French naval officers, de Serval and Magin. Very soon the two officers were at loggerheads with Wilkinson, who was already proving difficult to get on with. They were replaced by another naval officer, belonging to the naval foundry at Ruelle, Pierre Toufaire (1739–1794).[11] Toufaire arrived on September 29, 1777 and the two men set to work to make the enterprise a success. 'These two rare spirits soon understood one another and established a close friendship which was never broken.'[12] Toufaire sent his first report in 1777 on the choice of the site of the foundation works for the boring mill. A second report followed at the end of the month. Construction began effectively on December 1, 1777 and was actively undertaken in 1778–79, benefiting from the ease of sea and river transport. If the building and equipment of the works made rapid progress, the installation and operation of the foundry remained dependent upon a major supply of water power. Moreover, the War of American Independence increased the needs of the French government, whose orders for cannon became increasingly urgent: it was necessary to work quickly and at the same time to solve intricate technical problems. The topography of the isle (of Indret) was altered by abandoning an incomplete mole and by constructing a second mole parallel to the first and at right angles to the left bank of the Loire. The moles thus formed a 'tidal basin', forerunner of the factories driven by a tidal mill. The whole foundry with its reverberatory furnaces as well as a forge were completed and ready to begin operations by August 1778 but according to Toufaire, an initial tapping had been made on December 20, 1777. A railed way (with iron rails of the most modern English type) covering the 1,100 metres between foundry and forge, was built in 1779. Wilkinson also created an excellent firing range in order to test his cannon, which he began to produce in small numbers in 1778. Unfortunately their price was very high: no belligerent would have agreed to buy them at such a price even in wartime. In May 1779 William Wilkinson, undoubtedly feeling somewhat frustrated, informed M. de Sartine of his intention of returning to England.

Then he changed his mind, probably under the influence of the second agreement which raised his salary to £2,500 per annum (May 29, 1779). M. de Sartine nevertheless remained afraid that Wilkinson might leave without notice, taking with him those 'secrets' which he should, according to the terms of his contract, impart to the French workmen and technicians.[13] According to Ballot, the Indret works, although unfinished, had already cost two million *livres* by the beginning of 1779.[14] For de Sartine this was one more reason to request a report on the progress of the works. On the recommendation of Gribeauval, the director of naval ordnance, he entrusted François Ignace de Wendel (1741–95),[15] the son of the ironmaster Charles de Wendel, owner of the Hayange works in Lorraine, with the task of reporting on the state of the works at Indret. François de Wendel, an artillery captain, had practical and personal knowledge of the iron industry.[16] It was moreover essential to be tactful in dealing with Wilkinson. In De Wendel's own words:

M. de Sartine was embarrassed by the belief that the English method of cannon-founding was a secret and by the fear of losing the person who had brought the secret to France before he had divulged all the mysteries of its operation. On the other hand, the exigencies of war constrained him to secure an establishment whose construction was – in the hands of a foreigner and above all of an Englishman – taking an unduly long time. In order to satisfy his wish to know the condition of the works without antagonising M. Wilkinson he decided to send me to Nantes without any other authority than a letter from M. de Gribeauval ... in which I was introduced as an artillery officer interested in seeing the works at Indret. After a stay of two months (July–August 1779) in that district I returned to Versailles.[17]

The detailed report of De Wendel has been published[18] and surveys with remarkable confidence as well as an exceptional authority the financial and technical aspects of the question. It shows that the three main innovations of the British engineer were:

(a) refining in the reverberatory furnace of the pig iron intended for the manufacture of cannon,

(b) casting in dry sand,

(c) boring of the cannon according to the English patent granted to John Wilkinson in 1774, which was no real secret.

De Wendel paid homage to the indisputable ingenuity of William Wilkinson and replied to critics by referring to the shortage of supplies of coke pig iron. The English 'artist', as De Wendel termed him, was compelled sometimes to use the product from the melting down of old cannon sent to Indret by the French arsenals in inadequate quantity and sometimes to use pig iron smelted with charcoal, which was costly and unsuitable for refining in the reverberatory furnace.

For a long time the English have been smelting iron ore with desulphurized coal which they call 'coke'. That pig iron is peculiarly suitable for use in the reverberatory furnace.[19] It is known that pig iron smelted by charcoal – which is the only sort used in France – is much more refractory and gets harder the more frequently it is remelted. By this means French pig iron, unless it should be excessively 'grey' (which seldom occurs except in old cannon) goes 'whiter' and harder in the reverberatory furnace. British pig iron, on being remelted, can still be filed and it remains completely free from blow holes.

Under such conditions half the cannon cast by Wilkinson were defective because of blisters and flaws in the metal. De Wendel nevertheless estimated that the four existing forges – working 360 days in the year – could easily produce at least 1,200 twelve pounders. He criticised the lack of finish which turning would have avoided. The moulding process which was employed necessitated rectification by hand chiselling, which was a very expensive task. But the faults were largely due to the inadequacy of supply of materials and to the poor quality of the moulding sand. Four reverberatory furnaces had been built for melting as well as a fifth for the needs of the workshops and Wilkinson was actually engaged in establishing two more.

The conclusion of the report of 1779 was that

Indret is a very fine works, but it can be used only with blast furnaces to smelt iron ore either with coke or with charcoal. Such are the blast furnaces which supply the foundry at Indret when the supply of old cannon dries up.

There in essence is the justification for Le Creusot. The central conclusion of the report of 1779 may be divined from these words: 'Until this time everything had to be created. Now it only remains to perfect everything.'

In September 1788, eight years after Wilkinson had broken off all relations with Indret, the countryside still resounded with echoes of his fame, according to the account of the agriculturalist traveller Arthur Young:

Messrs Espivent had the goodness to attend me in a water expedition, to view the establishment of Mr Wilkinson, for boring cannon, on an island in the Loire below Nantes. Until that well-known English manufacturer had arrived, the French knew nothing of the art of casting cannon solid, and then boring them. Mr. Wilkinson's machinery for boring four cannons is now at work, moved by tide wheels; but they have erected a steam engine, with a new apparatus for boring seven more ... [23]

It is hardly surprising that Young, after a visit to Le Creusot, notes this feature:

The French say that this active Englishman is brother in law of Dr Priestley and therefore a friend of mankind; and that he taught them to bore cannon in order to give liberty to America.[24]

During this period Wilkinson and Toufaire continued to work amicably and on March 17, 1780 M. de Sartine was visited by Toufaire. During the interview the officer handed to the minister 'his fine description of Indret in a rich binding'. In return he received the most flattering of compliments with the promise of the title of chief engineer.[25] Sartine then invited De Wendel to take charge at Indret. After discussion De Wendel accepted a fifteen-year lease for the new cannon foundry under certain conditions (April 7, 1780) and left for a new inspection of Indret, in the course of which he noted that 'many things are lacking in this establishment and that the construction works are still not finished'. He also declined to take immediate charge of the business and 'M. Wilkinson continued to direct until September 15 (1780)'.[26]

De Wendel admitted that Wilkinson's experience would be valuable to him in fulfilling one of the most delicate conditions of the contract i.e. the installation of blast furnaces to smelt iron ore with coke by the English method and of reverberatory furnaces, in order to supply the works with pig iron. During the year 1780 Wilkinson seems to have sought for a favourable site for the establishment of such blast furnaces. Amongst other sites he visited Le Creusot in Burgundy, where coal mines were operated by the Renard Company whose concessionaire since August 8, 1776 had been François de la Chaise. De la Chaise extolled the advantages of Le Creusot to Wilkinson and abrogated the contract with the Renard Company (May 13, 1780). He was always ready to take part in a new venture. For his part De Wendel suggested the Rhône valley, near Saint-Etienne, but the Englishman wished to visit other sites before taking a decision. Wilkinson then strove to regularise his own position in relation to the French government. Believing himself to be irreplaceable, he decided to exploit to the full the circumstances of the war and of the strategic needs of France. He insisted upon negotiating in person with the minister, demonstrating great self-confidence. Discussions were already under way when the minister wrote to him on March 9, 1781 proposing a new contract 'to smelt iron ore with desulphurized coal by means of a fire engine'.There are in existence two drafts of this 'treaty'. The first draft, undoubtedly drawn up by Wilkinson, was sent to the minister on March 29, 1781.[27] The second draft,[28] drawn up by De Wendel, comprises sixteen articles. Its significance lies in the annotations where one may easily recognise the handwriting of William Wilkinson, by means of which he expressed his profound disagreement upon many points. In the absence of the definitive text one must rely upon the draft of March 28, 1781 in order to gain an idea of the final provisions – Wilkinson having conceded nothing that he deemed essential and the minister having confirmed his acceptance of the terms. Wilkinson demanded £3,000 (60,000 *livres*) per annum, a renewable contract for at least three years and a subsidy for board and lodging of £50 per month from February 1781, or a total of £3,600 (72,000 *livres*) per annum. In addition any travelling expenses necessitated by his post would be refunded. He also reserved the right to take leave in order to look after his own business, whilst agreeing not to leave France without special permission, except in the case of the death of his brother or of his recall by the British government.[29] In return for these very favourable terms, he agreed to remain for at least three years, or for longer if he could, to supply plans and machines and to teach the new methods of coke-smelting. Toufaire was entrusted with the construction of the buildings, whilst Wilkinson supervised the equipment of the interior, with full power over the workmen. De Wendel was nominated 'royal commissioner' to a 'royal manufactory', still in the state of projection, constituted by letters patent dated April 1, 1781. The choice of a site still remained a topic of keen discussion between the two men.[30] Wilkinson's opinion tended to prevail, but on July 29, 1781 he left Paris in the company of De Wendel and of Toufaire, on the order of de Castries, successor of de Sartine as minister for the navy. Their mission was to 'survey various provinces of the kingdom in order to choose an appropriate site for the establishment of blast furnaces and forges'.[31] A letter of July 29[32] sent by De Wendel to M. de la Porte, Intendant-General of the ministry of the navy, clearly shows that the choice of a site had not yet been made:

I leave today with this ironfounder (William Wilkinson) and M. Touffaire [sic] for Montcenis where M. Wilkinson wishes the projected establishment to be located. Nevertheless, Monsieur, since various reasons may favour the province of Forez I have thought it necessary to confer with M. de Flasselles.[33]

Nevertheless he must have been convinced by what he saw of Montcenis and by Wilkinson's arguments, since the three men decided to build the blast furnaces in the valley of Le Creusot. On October 5 De Wendel signed an agreement with de la Chaise by the terms of which de la Chaise agreed to supply De Wendel with 24 million pounds weight of coal. On November 1 de Castries informed the Intendant of Burgundy of the wishes of the King in the affair, notifying him that De Wendel, Wilkinson and Toufaire were at Montcenis 'engaged in preparing the plans of this new establishment and in assembling the material necessary for the immediate starting of construction works.'[34] The difficulties proved to be considerable. The Charolais Canal (canal du Centre) linking the Saône and the Loire and (by means of the Rhône) the Mediterranean to the Atlantic, was not completed and transport costs remained high. The sparsity of population and the poverty of the region soon created problems of supply of labour and of provisions for men and for animals for transport purposes. Wilkinson was also compelled to import skilled workmen from England. Finally, relationships were difficult with the owners of land, mines or quarries.[35]

The original plans envisaged the construction of a single blowing engine for the blast furnaces, but because of the shortage of water power at that spot De Wendel, Wilkinson and Toufaire wanted to instal a second engine for the forge.[36] The two steam engines had to be manufactured in England by John Wilkinson who discussed the plans for them with his brother during William's sojourn in the Austrian Netherlands between December 1781 and January 1782. The first engine[37] cost £6,500, an exorbitant price if one remembers that the same machine would have been sold for about £1,000 in England.[38] De Wendel intended to buy altogether five engines from the Wilkinson brothers for £30,000 but apparently only three reached Le Creusot. William also imported from England 'a wagon of English make', intended for the carriage to Montcenis of the machines brought via the Loire and the canal to the port of Digoin as well as a boring rod to explore the terrain for minerals, iron tubes for the forge's blowing engine and connecting tubes for the foundry.[39]

Until recently one might see in the courtyard of the old offices of the firm one of these iron objects bearing the inscription 'Wilkinson, 1782' and during the demolition of the old buildings a copper plaque was discovered bearing these words:

IN THE YEAR OF OUR LORD 1782
THE EIGHTH IN THE REIGN OF LOUIS XVI
DURING THE MINISTRY OF M. DE LA CROIX-CASTRIES
M. IGNACE DE WENDEL OF HAYANGE, ROYAL COMMISSIONER
M. PIERRE TOUFAIRE, ENGINEER
THIS FOUNDRY, THE FIRST OF ITS KIND IN FRANCE
WAS CONSTRUCTED TO USE COKE FOR THE PRODUCTION OF IRON
FOLLOWING THE METHOD INTRODUCED FROM ENGLAND AND
ESTABLISHED BY M. WILLIAM WILKINSON

As often happens in affairs of this sort the project soon appeared to be more difficult and costly than had at first been thought. Very soon De Wendel had to appeal to the minister of the navy for financial help. At first an agreement was reached by the terms of which one third of Wilkinson's salary (rising to £3,600) would be paid by the Treasurer-General of the Navy, whilst the manufactory of Le Creusot became the property of De Wendel (May 1782). De Wendel then met Jacques-Constantin Périer and a consortium was formed, comprising the most powerful financiers of Paris, under the name of Périer, Bettinger et Cie (December 18, 1782). Among the members were Sérilly, Treasurer-General of the War Ministry, Nicolas Bettinger, his chief clerk and confidential adviser, Baudard de Saint-James, Treasurer-General of the Navy, and Palteau de Veymeranges, friend of De Wendel, investigated for his relations with Calonne, the future Comptroller-General of France. The De Wendel–Sérilly group subscribed two-thirds of the capital, Périer and de Saint-James the remainder. Work was resumed and was practically finished during 1785. Wilkinson's attitude to Le

Creusot was not above criticism since if his technical knowledge was essential to the undertaking in his own opinion, it was Toufaire who seems to have played the key role in the construction works. A document of November 9, 1786 relative to the 'bonus' which Toufaire was to receive contains the following phrases:

M. Wilkinson, who has received 216,000 *livres* (£10,000) for having spent nine to ten months at Montcenis during the period of three years (1781–1784) has not imparted the knowledge of any mode of procedure relating to the trade and as for the buildings he has only suggested certain dimensions. On the contrary it is M. Toufaire who has conceived the whole of the establishment, who has created all the details and who has helped and often directed M. de Wendel in their execution.[40]

William spent a large part of his time visiting the blast furnaces and the centres of the French iron industry. He brought back from his travels enough material for a small memoir entitled *Mr William Wilkinson's Account of the Iron made in France*, dated February 5, 1787, preserved in the Boulton and Watt Collection in Birmingham, which reveals an expert understanding of the question. At the same time he tried to drive bargains with the French government. In October 1783, 'expecting that the establishment which the King is creating here [at Montcenis] may place that of Indret in a position to subsidise our needs',[41] he proposed to the Intendant-General of the Navy to supply three million pounds weight of English coke-founded cannon per annum. That offer rivalled that of the Carron Company of Scotland, whose Paris agent M. Alexander had been authorised to propose to the French government the supply of 1,000 tons of Scottish cannon per annum, with a five-year contract (September 1783).[42] The return to a peacetime economy in Great Britain had reduced the sale of munitions of war and this explains these two attempts which proved fruitless.

Wilkinson does not seem to have played an important role at Montcenis after 1784, although he stayed there until June of that year,[43] since about that time a dispute arose with De Wendel.[44] Thereafter the expensive equipment ordered by the Englishman from his brother John nevertheless continued to arrive at Le Creusot up to July 1785, coming through Honfleur.[45] These arrivals created difficulty with the accounting service of Le Creusot, Wilkinson having given only slight information over the orders and the mode of payment.[46]

Le Creusot nevertheless was almost completed and the works could begin production. A foundry, reverberatory furnaces, a boring mill with four boring rods for boring cannon, a railway linking the colliery to four blast furnaces, forges driven by water power, and two steam-powered blowing engines were established and formed the first great centre of iron manufacture outside Britain to smelt iron according to the method invented by the Quaker Abraham Darby in 1709. The first blowing machine began operations on October 15, 1785.[47] The two great blast furnaces had been finished a year earlier and the first smelting of coke pig iron took place in furnace No. 1 on December 11, 1785. De Wendel immediately sent the *Journal de la mise à feu de la fonderie royale du Creusot* to his friend De Givry at Strasbourg, with whom he had made a metallurgical journey to England in 1784. During this journey they had visited the blast furnaces of John Wilkinson. William Wilkinson had recently met De Givry during a study tour in the Vosges and De Givry had replied to De Wendel in these words:

I am not surprised that [William] W[ilkinson] seeks to denigrate your activity: you should reply to him in the best possible way, by achieving the greatest success.[48]

As for William Wilkinson, he returned to England in April 1786. In 1788 and 1789 he paid several visits to Scandinavia and to Prussia, where he gave advice to the King of Prussia on the exploitation of the State lead mines at Tarnowitz in Silesia. His work did not go unrewarded. The King of Prussia presented him with a golden snuff box.

APPENDIX[49]

Mr William Wilkinson's Account of the Iron made in France
February 5, 1787

Mr Degros of Châlons-sur Saône in Burgundy has for several years past had the care of receiving the iron from the interior part of France and forwarding it down to Lyons and the South of France. He has frequently told me that there has for many years previous to 1782 passed through his hands 30,000,000 pounds or 15,000 tons shortweight of bars. This iron comes chiefly from the provinces of Franche Comté, the northern part of Burgundy and the southern parts of Alsace and Champagne, and serves to supply Lyons, Languedoc, Dauphiné, Provence and Marseilles, as there are no iron forges south of the latitude of Lyons on the East part of France.

The iron sent is nearly half cold-short, and is chiefly consumed in Forez in the nail and iron manufactories of St. Etienne and St. Chamond and I have always been informed from the director of the *Farmes* [sic] at St. Etienne who received the duties on it that they consumed in these fabrications 6,000 tons yearly. There prices were at Châlons until [17]82 about 260 to 280 livres the ton Fr[ench] weight or from £10.16/– to £14.10/– English, common Merchant Iron from £13.16/– to £14.10/– and fine drawn ½ inch squares &c £15.10/– to £16.10/–. Since that time I am informed the prices have rose considerably and the quantity lessened ... owing to the quantity of woods which have been destroyed. All this iron has paid the *Mark de fer* of 17/– English per ton.

I have been informed from the officers who receive the *Mark de fer* that almost 30,000 tons are consumed of home made iron, but as the Provinces of Alsace, Lorraine or Roussillon do not pay for what they consume at home and as they smuggle their manufactories into France it is difficult to say what they may furnish Luxembourg, in which there are several forges, chiefly supply[ing] the manufactory of Charleville and neighbourhood; that iron is supposed to pay the duty on coming into France but I am told by some capital men in that trade that they do not pay the half.

Charleville consumes in every line about 6,000 tons, not 1/6 of which is made in France, but comes from the Pays Messin and Luxembourg.

Champagne supplies Paris [with] iron tender and coldshort: a few forges in the [district] about Joigny and Montbard in the North of Burgundy do the same for coldshort entirely. The castings of all sorts used in Paris come from Champagne and Normandy and Perche. Berry supplies along the Loire as well as Nivernois: this last is chiefly coldshort – the former is of a good nature but improperly treated as such does not keep up its ancient credit. Périgord, Angoumois supply Bordeaux and Rochelle with bars and castings of which last great numbers of sugar pans are yearly sent to the West Indies – Iron chiefly tough.

Roussillon works are all bloomeries. I have seen 8 of them: they make about 2 tons a week each: this iron is very good and tough. What is more than sufficient to supply the Province and which Perpignan and Port en Vendin takes. Much is smuggled into Spain in small articles manufactured in the provinces as nails and articles of husbandry &c.

I have a particular detail of Nivernois and Berry Works (in Wales at present). I do not recollect it. Very few works in Brittany and those coldshort. The duty on importing into that province from France and its situation and trade to the North renders Swedish and Russian iron much in use there and cheaper than the French as the duties are only 5/– per ton. Anjou and Touraine have not one ironwork that I ever heard of – Maine and Perche a few, Picardy none and Languedoc or Low Gui[e]nne the same.

In Dauphiné they have about 28 fineries for making of steel from pig iron which they get from Allevard and other furnaces on the side and from Savoy which work from a white spathic ore. This steel is reputed good for small articles but not for heavy strong tools.

NOTES

This paper was submitted as a communication to the International Colloquium 'Le fer à travers les âges' held at Nancy (3–6 October 1955) under the auspices of the Fédération Historique Lorraine and published in a special issue of the *Annales de l' Est* of the Faculté des Lettres de l'Université de Nancy: Mémoire no. 16 under the title *Actes du colloque internationale: le Fer à travers les âges: hommes et techniques*, Université de Nancy, Faculté des Lettres, 1956, pp. 285–99, 'Les frères John et William Wilkinson et leurs rapports avec la métallurgie française, 1775–1786'. It is reprinted here in an English translation by kind permission of the Presses Universitaires de Nancy, 25 rue Baron Louis, 54000 Nancy, France.

The editors are grateful to Professor J.R. Harris of the University of Birmingham for supplying a copy of the original paper and for expertly guiding them through the minefield of the translation of a highly technical treatise.

1. Archives Nationales (AN) F^{12} 1300: English translation with notes, by W.H. Chaloner, 'Report to the French Government on British Methods of smelting iron ore with coke and casting Naval Cannon' in *Edgar Allen News*, Sheffield, December 1948–January 1949.

2. M. de la Houlière to Boulton and Fothergill, August 31, 1775, originally preserved in the Birmingham Assay Office but now transferred to the Birmingham Reference Library.
3. Document cited above in note 1.
4. The French ambassador in London.
5. AN. F^{12} 1300 (cited by C. Ballot, *L'introduction du machinisme dans l'industrie française*, Lille–Paris, 1923, pp.449–50). That first visit by William Wilkinson to France is also mentioned in a letter of M. de la Houlière to M. de Sartine of June 10, 1780 (AN. D^3 32. Document 162).
6. In order to carry out William Wilkinson's wishes the comte de Givry wrote on December 23, 1775 to Viscount Weymouth, the Secretary of State for the Southern Department, requesting authority for the export to Rouen of 8 cannon of different calibre. See T.S. Ashton, *Iron and Steel in the Industrial Revolution* (1924), p.46. The export permits were granted by the Privy Council in 1776. The cannon were eventually shipped via Brest and not via Rouen (*Privy Council Register*, June 1, 1775–May 31, 1776) pp.350, 375–6.
7. According to Ballot (*op.cit.*, p.450) this site was chosen in 1775–76.
8. French historians give different dates: March 11 of the same year according to Moutard, *La Fonte* No.8 (1933), p.265 or May 17 according to Ballot (*op.cit.*, p.450, note 2).
9. According to Boulton: letter of May 2, 1777, cited by J.P. Muirhead, *Origin and Progress of the Mechanical Inventions of James Watt*, Vol.II (1854), pp.104–5.
10. There is an abundance of printed material available upon Indret, e.g. C. Ballot, *L'introduction du machinisme ...* (1923), pp.60–3; B. Gille, *Les origines de la grande industrie métallurgique en France* (1947), pp.193–5; P.M.J. Conturie, *Histoire de la Fonderie Nationale de Ruelle: 1750–1940, Part 1: 1750–1855* (1951), pp.259–90; three articles by M.T. Moutard – 'Une vieille fonderie de la Marine: Indret' in *La Fonte*, VIII (1933), pp.265–76, IX, pp.303–19, and X, pp.342–58; G. Bourgin, 'Deux documents sur Indret' in *Bulletin d'Histoire économique de la révolution:* Années 1917–19(1921), pp.467–89 and 'Deux documents sur l'introduction en France des techniques anglaises au xviiie siècle' in *Techniques et Civilisations*, Paris, II, No.2; P.J. Wexler, *La formation du vocabulaire des chemins de fer en France* (1955), pp.20–2; J.H. Viez, *La corporation des fondeurs, organisation professionelle de la fonderie en France* (1946), pp.145–7; and a 'Mémoire sur la fonderie d'Indret' (1788) in AN. F^{14} 4505.
11. On Toufaire see P. Rondeau, 'Un grand ingénieur au xviiie siècle, Pierre Toufaire, ingénieur en chef de la Marine à Rochefort (1774–1794)' in the *Bulletin de la Société des Archives historiques de la Saintonge et de l'Aunois*, IV, January 1883–4. Toufaire left a diary in seven volumes (1777–1794) which has recently been discovered by Mr P.J. Wexler, to whom I am very grateful for the help he has given me concerning Wilkinson.
12. P. Rondeau, *op.cit.*, p.368.
13. Jean Vial, 'L'invention en métallurgie' in *Revue d'Histoire économique et sociale*, XXVII (1948–49), iii and iv, p.259 note 109.
14. C. Ballot, *op.cit.*, p.45. This figure, derived from an unknown source, seems to be exaggerated. Le Clerc-Labourée gives the following figures in 'Notes historiques sur la fonderie impériale d'Indret' (*Bulletin ...* 1917–19 (1921), pp.287–9 – 1777 ... 78,807 *livres*, 1778 ... 307,509 *livres*, 1779 ... 577,499 *livres*, and 1780 ... 381,603 *livres*.
15. See Jean Chevalier, *François Ignace de Wendel* (Soc. d'Histoire et d'Archéologie de Lorraine, Metz, 1939).
16. François de Wendel was also associated with Sérilly in the lease of the royal armaments factory at Charleville (cf. B. Gille, p.189).
17. *Mémoire sur Indret* in AN. Marine D^3 24, a.d. The memoir has been reproduced without acknowledgement in *Techniques et Civilisations*, II, August 1952, pp.63–7: 'Deux documents sur l'introduction en France des techniques anglaises du xviiie siècle'. This memoir is printed on pp.65–7.

18. *Bulletin d'histoire économique de la Révolution*, 1917–19, pp.467–89. There exist then two 'memoirs': the most important (a) of 1779 reproduced in the *Bulletin*, and (b) of 1780 reproduced in *Techniques et Civilisations*.
19. The inventory of December 31, 1780 reveals the existence of an important stock of coke-smelted pig iron of English origin: estimated at 43,500 pounds in weight (*La Fonte*, IX, 1933, p.314).
20. AN. Marine D^3 34.
21. The text of the memoir of 1779 remains unclear: five boring drills (p.468) were working 20 hours daily, but on p.482 one reads that 'only four boring machines are used for all the cannon: one of these machines is used only to round off the base of the bore'.
22. *Bulletin* ... (1921), p.469.
23. Arthur Young, *Travels in France* ... (ed. C. Maxwell), 1929, p.117. The truth of this description has been confirmed by the research of Moutard (*La Fonte*, IX, p.316). From the beginning of the undertaking the number of boring machines was never enough to permit the manufacture of massive cannon.
24. Arthur Young, *op.cit.*, p.199.
25. See Rondeau, *op.cit.*, pp.370–1.
26. AN. Marine D^3 34.
27. AN. Marine D^3 32 (document k60): 'Conditions under which M (William) Wilkinson agrees – for himself and for his brother (John) – to establish a plant which will use desulphurised coal to smelt iron, using a fire engine.'
28. De Wendel to M. de la Porte, July 29, 1781 in AN. Marine D^3 32: De Wendel to M. de Castries, February 26, 1782 in AN. F^{14} 4504 (de Castries had replaced de Sartine at the Admiralty). For the date see Toufaire's diary.
29. He visited the Austrian Netherlands during the winter of 1781–2, in the company of his brother John, in order to meet Dom Nicolas Spirlet, the abbot of Saint-Hubert about the manufacture of cannon (R. Evrard, *Dom Nicolas Spirlet* ... Liège, 1952), pp.47–8 and p.53.
30. See the letter from De Wendel to M. de Sartine of April 7, 1781 in AN. Marine D^3 33.
31. AN. Marine D^3 33.
32. *Ibid.*
33. Intendant of the Généralité of Forez to the west of Lyons.
34. AN. F^{14} 4505.
35. On Le Creusot see especially C. Ballot, *L'introduction du machinisme dans l'industrie française* (1923), pp.452–69; J. Chevalier, *Le Creusot* (second edition, 1946); H. Chazelle and P. Marchand, *Le Creusot: histoire générale* (1936); J. Chevalier, *François Ignace de Wendel* (Soc. d'Histoire et d'Archéologie de la Lorraine, Metz, 1939); P.M.J. Conturie, *Histoire de la fonderie nationale de Ruelle, 1750–1940, Part I 1750–1855* (1951), pp.248–58; B. Gille, *Les origines de la grande industrie métallurgique en France* (1947), pp.185–9, 197–9 and 207–9.
36. Toufaire to de la Porte, September 20, 1781 in AN. Marine D^3 33.
37. The customs at Honfleur held it up for over three months: AN. F^{14} 1504.
38. See 'Situation de l'établissement de la fonderie royale du Creusot', August 1784 and 'Mémoire sur l'établissement d'usines à la manière anglaise, Montcenis', July 1785. The memoir mentions the price paid for two English steam engines as 250,000 *livres*.
39. AN. Marine D^3 33: 'Objets sur lesquels Monseigneur est prié prononcer' s.d. (November–December 1781?).
40. AN. F^{14} 4504.
41. AN. Marine B^1 98. Fos 124 and 126–7.
42. AN. Marine B^1 98. Fos 55–57.
43. H.C. Bolton, *Scientific Correspondence of Joseph Priestley* (New York, 1892), pp.71–3.
44. A probable reason for the dispute is given by De Wendel in *Mémoire* ... (AN. F^{14} 4504): the stacks of blast furnaces I and II were of poor quality and could be used only for six months 'because the stones which form their interior, where smelting

takes place, had been poorly chosen by the English artist who presided over their construction. Although this defect in the quality of the stonework was apparent from the start of production, it was decided to use the furnaces in their existing condition.'

45. Notably the second and third steam engines (AN. F^{14} 4504: document dated January 17, 1785).

46. 'Most of the machines which he [Wilkinson] had to supply are arriving here daily: yet we have no knowledge of this order, we cannot discuss its details nor can we verify the price: possibly the prices are too high: possibly the defects in some of the parts included in the order may cause difficulty in assembly, for which no remedy would be available' (De Wendel, Montcenis, to M. de Castries, July 1785 in AN. Marine D^3 34: Indret).

47. AN. T 591 (i) reproduced by B. Gille, op.cit., pp.207–9. The second blast furnace began operations in June 1786 (AN. F^{14} 4504: 'Mémoire sur l'établissement d'usines à la manière anglaise à Montcenis en Bourgogne' (A.D. 1787?)).

48. AN. T 591, 4 and 5: draft of a letter of January 8, 1786.

49. William Wilkinson's report is preserved in the Boulton and Watt Collection in the Birmingham Public Library.

2

The Agricultural Activities of John Wilkinson, Ironmaster

It is not generally known that besides being a large-scale industrialist, John Wilkinson (1728–1808), the celebrated ironmaster, was also one of the 'spirited proprietors' who appear so frequently in agricultural history during the latter half of the eighteenth century. His youthful background was semi-rural, but his career as a large-scale landowner does not appear to have begun until the War of American Independence (1776–83), when it became difficult to satisfy public and private demands for cannon. Consequently his profits as an ironmaster accumulated rapidly, and some of them were invested in agricultural improvement. About 1777–8 he bought the bleak hill of Castlehead, near Grange-over-Sands in north Lancashire, then surrounded by a peaty marsh, and the adjacent Wilson House estate, with the double purpose of building a country residence on the former site, and 'with a view of making iron from the peat with which the country so much abounded' on the latter.[1] The peat-smelting of iron, although technically successful, was however not an economic proposition, and his thoughts turned 'to consider what other uses could be made of so extensive a tract, in particular whether it could not be made capable of cultivation'.

The general nature of the tract Wilkinson undertook to improve was extremely discouraging. According to Sir John Sinclair, Bt., M.P., President of the Board of Agriculture, who honoured Wilkinson with a visit to Castlehead in 1805, it would have been called in Scotland a 'flow moss'. On the average about five feet of the first stratum consisted of a soft, spongy kind of peat, which made very poor fuel. Below this, however, the black peat was deep (15 feet and over) and of excellent quality. After these two layers the bottom was 'a fine strong blue clay', capable of being used as a top dressing after being burnt in small heaps with peat, but otherwise 'unfriendly to vegetation until it has been long exposed to, and ameliorated by the atmosphere'.[2]

Wilkinson's first attempts to improve about four or five acres of this waste marsh, on which animals could be pastured only in frosty weather, began in 1778 and were unsuccessful. The surface was breast-ploughed and then burnt. But the drainage trenches were cut too far apart and the 'proper management' of the sod-kilns in which lime for spreading on the moss could be produced 'was not then understood'.[3] Later Wilkinson tried a more complex system of drainage trenches which proved more successful.[4] Special spades and ploughs were used, and the great ironmaster's inventive brain even produced a special 10-inch circular patten for the hind-feet of the horses used in the reclamation, so that they could be employed even in the soft parts of the moss.[5] 'Before this invention', remarked Sir John Sinclair, 'the ploughs were wrought by the strength of men until the moss had consolidated.' By 1805, after an elaborate rotation of crops and a considerable and costly spreading of clay, sand or mould on the surface, the reclaimed moss had produced hay, turnips, oats, winter rye, barley and potatoes, the latter being 'of a quality peculiarly excellent'.[6] It is typical of the man that he threw himself whole-heartedly into this new sphere of activity, for in 1787 he was the only person who took the trouble to send the Royal Society of Arts samples of Chinese hemp fibre in 'a state fit for the purpose of manufactures' after that Society had distributed the seeds of the plant to a large number of persons for experimental growth.[7]

The extent of land that Wilkinson reclaimed was variously estimated at 500 Lancashire acres and 1,000 statute acres.[8] In 1778 the moss was with difficulty let to local farmers at a penny per acre; by 1805 those portions of the moss which Wilkinson had only recently improved were worth between 30s and 40s an acre per annum, while land which he had reclaimed in the 1780s produced an annual rent of between £3 and £4 per acre.[9] Nevertheless critics said 'that Mr Wilkinson might have bought, at a cheaper rate, the best land in Lancashire'. Sir John Sinclair commented: 'Perhaps so. But Mr Wilkinson must derive much higher satisfaction from the plan he has pursued. By so doing, he has furnished employment to numbers of industrious people; he has raised great quantities of food for man, where nothing, but for his exertions, would have been produced ... and ... he is justly entitled to be ranked among the best friends to the agricultural interests of the country.'[10]

In 1791 Wilkinson was busy finishing off a big programme of tree-planting at Castlehead which had extended over a number of years.[11] In 1796 the landowners of Cartmel parish obtained an Act (36 Geo III, cap 64) for enclosing commons, waste lands, and mosses in the constituent townships of the parish, a process, which lasted until the final award in 1810. Both John Wilkinson (Castlehead was in Allithwaite Upper township) and his brother William, who then had a house at Flookburgh, had interests in the enclosure. They were in fact the third (£1,880) and fifth (£1,415) largest recipients respectively of the

Cartmel common land divided out by the Commissioners appointed under the Act.[12] According to Stockdale, on the 12th of October 1798 William Wilkinson bought 8 acres for £685 'behind and upon Newton Fell' in Upper Allithwaite township at a public auction, while three days later, John, not to be outdone, requested the commissioners 'that he might have an allotment at or upon Wilson Hills, as it would be an advantage to his estate'. Besides the 51 acres allotted to him at Wilson Hills John came into possession of over 40 acres at Blawith and Castlehead Moss in Broughton township, while William received allotments at Holker Bank and Winder Moor in Lower Holker township.[13] The Commissioner's award under the Act shows that the two brothers received other allotments by virtue of their status as local landowners: it is interesting to note that William Wilkinson bought out a number of small proprietors.[14]

Not content with these acquisitions, 'Mr Wilkinson of Castlehead, a gentleman of fortune, patriotism, and universal knowledge', became interested during 1786 in a vaster design put forward by John Jenkinson of Yealand. Jenkinson's plan was for 'recovering from the dominion of Neptune that extensive tract called Lancaster and Milthrop [i.e. *Milnthorp*] Sands' by diverting the Kent and other lesser rivers.[15] After a survey of the area, which seemed to him to present few obstacles to the execution of the plan, Wilkinson proposed the opening of a subscription list and offered to lead it with £50,000 if the neighbouring landowners would raise the remaining £100,000 between them. But even though his estimate of £150,000 for reclaiming over 32,000 acres was considered to be unduly pessimistic by 'many well-informed gentlemen', the plan never materialised, being 'defeated, by a difference of opinion amongst individuals, claims of the lords of the manors, etc.'[16]

It was not only at Castlehead that Wilkinson undertook agricultural improvements. In 1792 he bought the Brymbo Hall estate, and later added to it a number of smaller estates and farms in the bleak township of Brymbo in Denbighshire, north Wales. On his death in 1808 the whole concentration amounted to about 872 acres.[17] The original soil was naturally poor, 'being a hungry clay on a substratum of yellow rammel or coal schist'.[18] By good tillage and heavy manuring with lime (10 tons to the acre) Wilkinson so improved crop-yields that the township's corn-tithes increased by £40 per annum in value. 'A crowned head had assisted him in making his compost manures. Offa, King of Mercia, had employed men to bring together the soil; and Mr Wilkinson went to the expense of lime, to be mixed with it. Large cavities, of the shape of inverted cones, were cut at convenient distances, in Offa's dyke, which runs across Brymbo farm. The cavities were filled up with limestone and coal and then burnt.'[19]

At Brymbo, too, he experimented with powdered 'sweet coal', i.e. coal with a very low sulphur content, as a top dressing for grasslands. As compared with land manured with a compost of soil and lime, the area so treated produced the best and earliest grass.[20]

His lime-making activities in north Wales were not, however, confined to the township of Brymbo. At some date before 1798 he had secured a lease for forty-two years of land containing limestone adjacent to Lord Derby's estate at Hope in Flintshire. Here he had erected large lime kilns, of which he wrote: '... my present lime works being so near coal of my own ... enables me to sell it on easy terms to the country and to meet any competition whatever.'[21]

Wilkinson's last will and testament provides some evidence that his investments in agriculture extended to south Staffordshire. '... The late William Johnson's cash account with me is not settled, and the same cannot be adjusted without reference to the cash-book and diary of the said William Johnson ... it is supposed they contain the transaction of my farm at Bradley blended with an adjoining one ... held by William Johnson ... and the produce of both farms were [sic] received for by said William Johnson.'[22]

Attention has often been called to Wilkinson's role as a pioneer in the use of agricultural machinery. In 1798 the six counties of north Wales contained only two threshing machines. One of these, 'of a cumbersome and expensive construction', was employed by Wilkinson on his Brymbo estate. Even more remarkable was the fact that his machine was driven by steam power. The use of agricultural machinery was stimulated by the high wage rates typical of war-time conditions, and by 1810 improved threshing machines had become 'too common to be enumerated' in north Wales.[23]

The general impression derived from a study of Wilkinson's farming and reclamation activities is therefore of large-scale, long-term 'ploughing' of industrial and mining profits into agriculture on marginal lands at a time when a rapidly expanding population and Government expenditure in connection with a series of wars (1776–83, 1793–1802, 1803–15) resulted in a rising price-level, a buoyant economy, and, towards the end, a considerable degree of inflation. Wilkinson was perhaps fortunate in that he did not live to see the depression in agriculture during the years immediately after 1815.

NOTES

This article is reprinted from the *Agricultural History Review*, V (i), 1957, pp.48–51.

1. *Communications to the Board of Agriculture*, V, Part 1, 1806, p.2; John Wilkinson to James Watt, 6 May 1776 (Boulton and Watt Coll., Birmingham Public Library).
2. *Communications*, p.2.
3. *Communications*, p.3; Sir John Barrow (1764–1848), who visited the Castlehead area about 1781–2, states that Wilkinson had met with success 'mostly and simply by driving in stakes to obstruct the tide both in its flow and ebb', *An Autobiographical Memoir*, 1847, p.229.
4. *Communications*, pp.3–5. Wilkinson also narrowed and altered the courses of some brooks in the Castlehead area 'by which the flux of the tide, in the space of about eight years, has raised the lands near six feet'. – J. Holt, *General View of the Agriculture of the County of Lancaster*, 2nd ed.,1795, p.88.
5. *Communications*, pp.4–5 ('Mr Wilkinson's Horse Patten').
6. *Communications*, p.6. Wilkinson also grew chicory at Castlehead, presumably for horse fodder – Holt, *op.cit.*, p.72.
7. *Trans. Royal Society of Arts*, V, 1787, pp.171–2. It is not clear whether this hemp was grown at Broseley in Shropshire or on one of his other estates. Wilkinson's report on the product was unfavourable.
8. *Communications*, p.7; Holt, *op.cit.* p.105. The Lancashire acre varied. One, based on $7\frac{1}{2}$ yards to the rod, was equal to 1.86 statute acres; another, based on a 7 yard rod, was equal to 1.62 acres.
9. *Communications*, pp.2, 7. The great rise in the value of the land during the early 1790s is shown by the fact that in 1795 Holt had noted: 'Mr Wilkinson's improved moss land was, before draining, worth from 7 to 10 shillings per acre, is now worth from £4 to £5 per acre of the large measure.' *op.cit.* p.47*n*.
10. *Communications*, p.8. Wilkinson's method was later applied to Trafford Moss in south Lancashire (Holt, *op.cit.*, p.105). His schemes altered the landscape of the Furness wastes: 'before the drainage, the windows of the third story of Mr Wilkinson's house just appeared from a certain point; but from that place, at present, the windows on the first floor are plainly seen ... the fall of the moss is about four feet and a half.' Holt, *op.cit.*, p.106 *n*.
11. Draft letter of 10 October 1791, John Wilkinson to Dr Priestley. – Warrington Public Library, Priestley–Wilkinson Correspondence.
12. For an account of the enclosure, see J. Stockdale, *Annales Caermoelenses*, 1872, pp.326–84. Stockdale had access to the Commissioners' minute books, and one of them, covering the period from 25 July 1796 to 3 July 1803, has been deposited in the Lancashire Record Office, Bow Lane, Preston.
13. Stockdale, *op.cit.*, pp.334, 340–1.
14. Award of 8 February 1810 (Lancashire County Record Office, Preston), pp.76, 100, 105, 431 ff., 434, 455.
15. Holt, *op.cit.*, pp.88–94; *Gentleman's Magazine*, LVI, 1786, pt.ii, p.1140.
16. Holt, *op.cit.*, pp.88–90.
17. For details of these see A.N. Palmer, 'John Wilkinson and the Old Bersham Ironworks', *Trans. Hon. Soc. of Cymmrodorion* (Session 1897–8), 1899, p.40.
18. Davies, *Agriculture of North Wales*, 1810, pp.281–2. Of Wilkinson's Brymbo estate about 150 acres were originally 'wild heath, till then abounding only in springs and furz'. Palmer noted that the Waen Farm ($76\frac{1}{2}$ acres) was 'enclosed from the common'. *op.cit.*, p.40.
19. Davies, *op.cit.*, p.282.
20. *Ibid.*, pp.297–8.
21. Wilkinson to Mr Alty, Knowsley, Lancs, 9 May 1798 (Lancs County Record Office, DDK 447/9). When Wilkinson was granted a seven-year mining lease of land at

Hope by Lord Derby in 1798, it was agreed that he was not to burn any of the limestone brought out of the lead ore diggings: 'he must be bound that he will not root and mangle too much of the rocks to the disadvantage of his Lordship ... the old tenants ... complain heavily that if Mr Wilkinson will take all the rocks they will be entirely deprived of their living'. Edward Jones, Hope, Flintshire, to Mr Alty, Knowsley, Lancs, 3 July 1798, Lancs County Record Office, DDK 447/8/3 and 447/8/5.

22. Document A, date-lined Bradley, 26 July 1804, subjoined to will dated 29 November 1806, General Register Office, Somerset House, London. William Johnson's widow, Mrs Mander, was to be compelled by Wilkinson's executors to produce the accounts.

23. Davies, *op.cit.*, pp. 121–2.

3

Dr. Joseph Priestley, John Wilkinson and the French Revolution, 1789–1802

Like Jacobitism and Chartism, the study of the influence of the French Revolution on British politics and public opinion has attracted a good deal of sentimental interest, but it is a curious fact that with the exception of Professor Alfred Cobban's anthology (*The Debate on the French Revolution, 1789–1800* (1950)), A.H. Lincoln's *Some Political and Social Ideas of English Dissent, 1763–1800* (1938), and a few scattered articles comparatively little appears to have been published since 1926 on the subject.[1] It has therefore never been examined in the light of those trends in historiography associated with the names of Unwin and Namier.[2]

This paper is based primarily on a collection of letters, sixty-nine in number, mainly from Dr. Joseph Priestley (1733–1804) to John Wilkinson (1728–1808) the ironmaster, which have been for many years deposited in Warrington Public Library.[3] They range in date from 1789 to 1802 and therefore cover that period of Priestley's life which is of most interest to modern historians. They do not, however, give a complete picture of his closing years; references to Priestley's scientific work are purely incidental, although there are many valuable details of the Birmingham riots of 1791 in which Priestley lost his house and much of his personal property. Wilkinson's interests in the correspondence were primarily those of a businessman. He was no Wedgwood, although he occasionally attended the Lunar Society's monthly dinner-meetings as a guest, and seems to have read some, at any rate, of the books and pamphlets which his illustrious brother-in-law so regularly sent him. Therefore the letters relate mainly to economic and personal matters. Wilkinson's replies, with one exception, a draft, appear to have been among the papers destroyed by Joseph Priestley, jun., after his father's death in 1804.[4] There is on this account not much evidence of his reactions to Priestley's opinions about the progress of the French Revolution. Wilkinson was essentially 'independent', a man of means, able, if not always willing to provide a career for a young man or to subsidise dependants; the kind of patronage which is the central theme of these letters.

The connection between the Wilkinson family and Dr. Joseph Priestley began in or shortly after 1758 when John Wilkinson's father, Isaac, ironmaster, of Bersham furnace near Wrexham, sent his youngest son William Wilkinson to the excellent school conducted by Priestley at Nantwich in Cheshire where he was minister to the Presbyterian congregation. Isaac and his wife were Nonconformists, being members of the Dissenting congregation, then of the Presbyterian persuasion, meeting at the Chapel in Chester Street, Wrexham.[5] John Wilkinson himself had been educated at Dr. Caleb Rotheram's Dissenting Academy at Kendal in the early 1740s.[6] When Priestley left Nantwich in 1761 to become tutor in languages and *belles lettres* at the recently-founded Warrington Academy, William Wilkinson, then about 17 years old, is stated to have followed him thither as a pupil, and shortly afterwards became his brother-in-law. For on June 23, 1762, Dr. Joseph Priestley and Mary Wilkinson, one of Isaac Wilkinson's three daughters, were married in Wrexham parish church.[7]

Priestley characteristically lamented the fact that he had received 'little fortune' with the ironmaster's daughter, 'in consequence of her father becoming impoverished, and wholly dependent on his children, in the latter part of his life', but equally characteristically added: 'I unexpectedly found a great resource in her two brothers [John and William], who had become wealthy, especially the older of them.'[8] By the 1780s John Wilkinson had built up an industrial empire with ironworks at Bradley in Bilston, Staffordshire, and at Broseley and Snedshill in Shropshire, while William Wilkinson, after a period as managing partner at Bersham furnace, had emigrated to France in 1776–7, to take service with the French Government, first as the builder and *régisseur* of the state ironworks and cannon foundry on the island of Indret in the River Loire near Nantes (1777–80) and later (1781–5) as technical adviser in connection with the state ironworks of Le Creusot at Montcenis (Saône-et-Loire).[9] William Wilkinson bore the reputation of having been tainted with French modes of thinking. C.J. Apperley ('Nimrod') described him later as 'one of those no-God, no-devil, no-king sort of men, which prevailed to a certain extent, even in England' at the height of the French Revolution.[10]

The two brothers 'acted the part of kind and generous relations' to Priestley in 1780, when his employment with Lord Shelburne came to an end, and his affairs consequently 'wore rather a cloudy aspect'.[11] John Wilkinson's proposal that his sister and his now famous brother-in-law should settle near him in the Black Country was instrumental in leading Priestley to decide upon a permanent residence in Birmingham, where his election to the position of junior minister of the New Meeting took place in 1780. John soon provided a house for him at

Fairhill in Birmingham, and as the *Gentleman's Magazine* noted in its issue for 1787, Priestley was thereby rendered 'independent of the patronage of the great; Mr. [John] Wilkinson being in possession of a fortune of 80,000 *l.*, all acquired by his own industry.'[12]

In 1786 John Wilkinson suffered a severe blow from the loss of his only child, Mrs. Mary Houlbrooke.[13] His quest for someone to succeed to his concerns led him to adopt as his heir Joseph Priestley, jnr. (1768–1833), the doctor's eldest son. Young Priestley began to learn the trade of ironmaster at Bradley ironworks in South Staffordshire, but after nearly four years' apprenticeship John Wilkinson decided that he was unsatisfactory and the two men parted in 1790,[14] much to Dr. Priestley's disappointment. Wilkinson also refused to employ William Priestley, another of the doctor's sons.[15]

It must be remembered that Priestley was one of the founders of the Unitarian faith, which aimed at making Christianity 'rational' (a typical eighteenth-century endeavour) by purging it of such unscientific accretions as the Virgin birth and the divinity of Christ. Unitarians were therefore widely regarded as little better than deists, who in turn were considered to be almost atheists, and Unitarianism came to be looked upon, in spite of the obvious material respectability of its adherents, as theologically the least respectable Nonconformist sect. At the time when the correspondence begins Priestley had already begun to take a prominent part in the renewed agitation for the repeal of the legislation imposing civil disqualifications on Nonconformists, in particular the Test and Corporation Acts. In 1787 he had published *A Letter to the Right Honourable William Pitt, First Lord of the Treasury and Chancellor of the Exchequer; on the subject of Toleration and Church Establishments; occasioned by his speech against the repeal of the Test and Corporation Acts, on Wednesday, the 21st March 1787.* The defeat of Fox's motion of March 2, 1790, on the same subject is said to have been brought about in part by the injudicious publication of Priestley's *Familiar Letters* of 1790.[16] In these letters Priestley called upon the clergy of the Established Church to avert revolution in England by introducing reforms, and, letting his imagination run riot for once, he described his unpopular theological efforts as 'grains of gunpowder' for which his opponents were furnishing the lighted match.

The obvious contrast to these proceedings was provided by the proclamation of the removal of religious disabilities in France (August 1789), and considerable sympathy with the French Revolution naturally existed in the Priestley–Wilkinson family circle, combined with general hostility towards the established order in Church and State, although the degrees of feeling naturally varied from individual to individual. William Priestley (1771–*c.* 1835), the doctor's second son, wrote home enthusiastically from Paris about the fall of the Bastille in 1789, and while the doctor himself later refused a seat in the national Convention of 1792, he told William in June of the same year to 'go and live among that brave and hospitable people, and learn from them to detest tyranny and love liberty'.[17] On June 8, 1792, William was granted letters of naturalisation as a French citizen by the National Assembly, and on the following August 26th his father also had the same honour conferred upon him, and did not reject it.[18] In Wilkinson's case a disgruntled and anarchistic attitude towards the British Government on matters connected with his business affairs, can be traced back to the years of the American War. His general maxim was:

'Manufacture and Commerce will always flourish *most* where Church and King interfere least.'

Early in 1791 Dr. Priestley published a reply to Burke's *Reflections on the Revolution in France*,[19] about which he wrote to John Wilkinson on January 20 of that year: 'I am pleased to hear that you liked my *Letters to Mr. Burke*. We are printing the third edition; one thousand for each of the two first and fifteen hundred for this.' About a month later he asked Wilkinson to repay a £600 loan in order that he might set Joseph up in life.[20] Wilkinson did so,[21] and between 1791 and 1793 Joseph tried unsuccessfully to make a living in business at Manchester. Although he failed, he took an active part in Radical politics in the town, helped to found in 1792 the institution known as the Manchester Reading Society or the New Circulating Library,[22] and became a close friend of Thomas Cooper. Joseph had just settled in Manchester when his father's house in Birmingham was sacked and destroyed by the Church and King mob (July 14, 1791). The details of this episode are so well known that it is not proposed to do more than mention it here. Dr. Priestley fled to London and sat down to write his *Appeal to the Public on the Subject of the Riots in Birmingham.*[23] John Wilkinson gave his brother-in-law £500 and offered to buy him a house. A letter written by Wilkinson from Wrexham to James Watt on August 16, 1791, shows that the ironmaster's property had been in danger too, but he had the resources with which to take adequate if rather alarming precautions. He wrote:

'Church and King' as a watchword has been very near bursting out into a Birmingham flame in this town ... I have ordered 6 swivels to be mounted on the engine galleries at Bradley, also 2 howitzers for the millyard on carriages with a view to kill a few as you direct if necessary. We shall also prepare for a defence of like nature at Bersham. W[illiam]. R[eynolds]. by about 20 firearms and bayonets saved his life and house. There is more safety in a gun well manned than will be found in a careless Justice.[24]

Meanwhile Dr. Priestley had become more and more involved in the affairs of Benjamin Vaughan (1751–1835) who had been one of his students at Warrington Academy. The Vaughan family, too, was Unitarian, and Benjamin Vaughan had been in Lord Shelburne's service as private secretary in the 1770s, although he had resigned this post in 1778 in order to study medicine at Edinburgh for three years. In 1781 he joined the London firm of Manning and Sons as a partner and married a Miss Manning, an aunt of the Cardinal. He visited Paris and Nantes in 1790.[25] In the autumn of 1791 Priestley placed £500 in Vaughan's hands to be invested in French Government bonds and advised his brother-in-law to do the same with the £5,000 Wilkinson wished to place at his disposal. During these months Priestley was even fuller of optimistic delusions about France than usual. In an undated letter, very probably written about September 13, 1791, he informed Wilkinson:

... I consider my stay in this country as very uncertain. Many of [my] friends seriously think of going to France, and the neighbourhood of Dijon, in Burgundy, has been pointed out to them as convenient for their manufactures. If this should take place, and my son William get a settlement in France, which I hope my friends there will find for him, I shall probably emigrate from Manchester ...[26]

He wrote again to John Wilkinson on October 4, 1791:

I am glad you approve of my views with respect to France. *Now*, I think it must be evident to everybody, whether they will acknowledge it or not, that *that* country must rise, and that *this* cannot well go higher ... I think I told you I had the offer of a completely furnished house near Paris. Today I have received a very flattering address from a society at Thoulouse [*sic*], ... inviting me to reside in the South of France, and intimating that one of the now vacant monasteries will be destined for my use. I have now, however, absolutely taken a house at Hackney ...

On the subject of Vaughan he continued:

There is no person, I believe, in England who is better acquainted with France and French affairs than he is ... He has already placed a considerable sum in the French funds, and many, I doubt not, will soon do the same, as was the case with the American funds, which have risen thirty per cent per annum by some money that he happened to have in their funds at a very critical time.[27]

Wilkinson took the advice and accordingly lodged £5,000 in the French funds in his own name for Priestley's benefit (he was to draw the annual interest). In 1793 the Committee of Public Safety discovered these securities among the possession of J.C. Perregaux, a Paris banker of Swiss origin, and listed them under the heading of property belonging *aux anglais, écossais, irlandais, et hanovriens*. Priestley then held 13 *billets de l'emprunt de 125 millions*, the accumulated interest on which was 650 *livres*. William Wilkinson also held 97 *billets* of the same loan;

John Wilkinson's 121 *billets de l'emprunt de 125 millions* had been placed at the disposal of the *Caisse de l'Escompte*.[28] At some time between October 1791 and the autumn of 1793 Wilkinson purchased a second £5,000 worth of French public bonds and promised to transfer the ownership of the whole £10,000 to Priestley.[29] The investment soon proved to be an unproductive one and, when Priestley decided in the winter of 1793–4 on emigration to the U.S.A., Wilkinson agreed to allow the doctor to draw a bill on his banker, Sir Benjamin Hammet, for £200 every year 'till the money in the French funds came to be productive'.[30] This arrangement lasted until 1800, according to the evidence of these letters,[31] although Alexander Gordon in his article on Priestley in the *Dictionary of National Biography* states that Wilkinson did not withdraw this pension until 1804.

In the early 1790s Wilkinson made a present of some property to those of the doctor's children who had emigrated to the U.S.A. (Joseph, William and Henry), including a considerable sum in shares of the 'old' French East India Company.[32] By 1796 both the *emprunt de 125 millions* and these *actions des Indes* had been 'taken out of the hands of their respective proprietors and placed in those of the [French] Government', with the result that the value of the first was 'much diminished' and that of the second 'nearly annihilated'.[33] Well might Priestley lament in a letter of 1798: 'If the ten thousand pounds had been in the American funds, instead of the French they would have yielded more than twenty thousand.'[34] Towards the end of 1797 the French Directory made an *arrêt* in Priestley's favour allowing him 1,200 *livres* a year in specie, but he had not received any payments under this arrangement as late as 1800. In addition, 'owing to the act of transfer being useless from the want of some legal formality', the £10,000 worth of French Government stock was still in John Wilkinson's name in the French Treasury's book in 1801,[35] and remained so until the iron-master's death in 1808, in spite of efforts to get him to move in the matter. Under the terms of the Peace Treaty of 1815 John Wilkinson's trustees eventually received 510,099 francs, 10 centimes (over £20,000), for the investment in the *emprunt de 125 millions*, although their claim on account of the *actions de la compagnie des Indes* was rejected. It is noteworthy that a claim made by Joseph Priestley, jun., was rejected, although details are lacking.[36]

On February 7, 1792 Benjamin Vaughan was elected M.P. for the borough of Calne in Wiltshire by means of Shelburne's influence and soon began to make use of his parliamentary privileges by franking Priestley's letters to Wilkinson. It is not surprising that Vaughan soon became extremely critical of the British Government's foreign policy, and of the struggle which the British Government, in his opinion, was so foolish as to prosecute after the French had declared war on February 1, 1793. The following passage indicates the general line of argument and thought which Priestley's circle found comforting. Wilkinson was informed by Priestley on February 10:

I dined on Saturday in company with Mr. Sheridan and some other politicians. It appeared very evident that our Court had no expectation of the French declaring war in consequence of the dismission of M. Chauvelin,[37] and it is now a general opinion that they are now endeavouring, in some circuitous way, to make peace before any considerable blow is struck. That the French do not fear the war is evident enough, though it is as evident that they wished to avoid it and were sincerely desirous of our friendship.[38]

Priestley grasped eagerly at any evidence, however slight, that the French wanted peace or that the British Government was tiring of the struggle.

Meanwhile, the *Morning Chronicle* was printing, between July 20, 1792, and June 25, 1793, a series of letters from Benjamin Vaughan, under the pseudonym of 'A Calm Observer'. A number of them were reprinted in 1793 as *Letters on the subject of the Concert of Princes and the Dismemberment of Poland and France*. A second edition, enlarged and corrected, appeared later in that year. The general tone of the book can be gauged from the title of letter VII: 'Positive Arguments for negociating a Peace with France'.[39] Priestley sent a copy of it to Wilkinson in July 1793 and wrote: 'If you should have any guess about the writer, I have a particular reason for desiring you would not give any intimation of it to Mr Vaughan.'[40]

On May 8, 1794, however, Vaughan, in company with Lord Lauderdale, Sheridan, William Smith, M.P., and Major Maitland, was summoned before the Privy Council and questioned regarding a letter he had written to that 'wicked and seditious traitor'[41] John Hurford Stone (1763–1818) who was then in Paris. Vaughan had sent this letter to William, John Hurford Stone's younger brother, for delivery. William Stone was arrested two days later and committed to Newgate on a charge of high treason.[42] The letter offered some advice to the French on the subject of invading England, combined with information about British morale. According to Alger it 'dwelt on ... the readiness to enlist in the navy, the approval of the war by Parliament, and the temper of the nation, as proofs of the expediency of France making a peace on fair terms'.[43]

After the interview with the Privy Council Vaughan lost his nerve and fled to France, where he fell foul of Robespierre. After Robespierre's fall he was arrested by the Committee of Public Safety, but eventually liberated. After his release he made for Switzerland, still

M.P. for Calne. Finally, in 1796 he settled down on the extensive family estates in Maine, U.S.A., where he died peacefully in 1835.[44]

Mention of the Stone brothers leads to another curious episode in the Priestley–Wilkinson financial transactions. During the period of commercial depression in 1792–3 Wilkinson had made use of his creditworthiness among the tradespeople of the Wrexham area by putting into circulation notes of small denomination in order to pay his workmen at Bersham furnace. This practice was not uncommon among industrialists in the 1790s.[45] In Wilkinson's case these small notes were countersigned French *assignats* and on December 19, 1792, the Rev. Peter Whitehall Davies, J.P., of Broughton Hall, near Wrexham, reported as follows to Lord Chief Justice Kenyon:

My Lord
I take the Liberty to trouble your Lordship with another Letter in which I have inclosed an assignat, made payable at Bersham Furnace, endorsed Gilbert Gilpin; – I am informed he is the first Clerk of Mr Wilkinson, whose Sister married Doc[r]. Priestly. with what view Mr Wilkinson circulates assignats is best known to himself. – It appears to me that good Consequences can not arise from their being made currant, & that very pernicious Effects may. – Mr Wilkinson at his Foundry at Bersham (where I am informed he has now a very large number of Cannon) & in his Coal, & Lead Mines employs a considerable Body of Men. – They are regularly paid every Saturday with Assignats. – The Presbyterian Tradesmen receive them in Payment for Goods, by which Intercourse they have frequent Opportunities to corrupt the Principles of that Description of Men, by infusing into their minds the pernicious Tenets of Paine's Rights of Man, upon whose Book I am told, publick Lectures are delivered to a considerable number, in the neighbourhood of Wrexham, by a methodist – The bad Effects of them are too evident in that Parish ...[46]

That these effects were lasting may be gauged from Sir Frederick Morton Eden's description of the population of Wrexham parish about 1797, when it was, he stated, composed of '... shopkeepers, inn-keepers, agriculturists and miners; the last are chiefly employed in the lead-mines, smelting lead and casting iron, etc., for Messrs. Wilkinson and Co. Here is one congregation of Methodists, one of Free-thinkers, one of Anabaptists, and one of Presbyterians.'[47]

Lord Kenyon lost no time in reporting the matter to the Government, which was, by this time, seriously alarmed at the spread of French revolutionary doctrines throughout the country, and inclined to see in the circulation of the *assignats* an insidious attempt to foster the propaganda of what was soon to become an enemy state. On December 24, 1792, the law officers of the Crown were given leave to introduce a bill into the Commons 'to prohibit the circulation of promissory or other notes, orders, undertakings, or obligations ... created and issued under or in the name of any public authority in France'. The bill was passed rapidly through both Houses and received the royal assent on January 8, 1793.[48] All such notes in circulation were to be redeemed in current money immediately.

From references in the Priestley–Wilkinson correspondence it is possible to trace the subsequent history of the ironmaster's unfortunate foreign exchange speculation. After the passing of the act Wilkinson called in and repatriated some of the *assignats*. On February 10, 1793, Priestley wrote to his brother-in-law thanking him for the gift of some of them, which he promised to send to his second son William, who was still in France. Wilkinson's endorsement on the back of this letter shows that on February 22 he sent ten more of them to Priestley who replied on March 19, 1793, 'I sent William twenty-seven of the *assignats* you were so good as to send me, and he was very grateful for them; but as I can make no particular use of any more you had better keep those you have till better times.'

Wilkinson evidently hoped to recoup his losses even after Britain and France had been at war for nearly a year, for Priestley wrote on the following December 13, to say that he had an opportunity of sending to France any *assignats* that Wilkinson might have in hand. He also warned Wilkinson that as the *assignats* bore the head of Louis XVI they would have to be presented in Paris 'before Christmas next'. Shortly afterwards a parcel addressed to Priestley and containing 898 *assignats* arrived at his publishers, Joseph Johnson, 72 St. Paul's, besides 14 more which Wilkinson sent separately.[49] Their face value was 4,750 *livres*, or about £240 at par. Priestley handed them over to William Stone, who sent them to his brother John Hurford Stone in Paris. By the time he received them they had already lost more than 4/5th of their original value.[50] The Stone brothers were Unitarians and carried on a business with their uncle as wholesale coal merchants in London. John Hurford Stone was a member, first of Dr. Price's, then of Dr. Priestley's congregation at Hackney, but his philosophical speculations soon ranged far beyond Unitarian doctrine. In October 1790 he presided at a dinner given by the Society of Friends of the Revolution (of 1688) to a French deputation from Nantes. He numbered Samuel Rogers the poet among his friends, while Fox, Sheridan, Talleyrand and Mme de Genlis were guests at his dinner table in 1791.[51]

Later in 1791 he went to Paris, where in September 1792 he presided over a dinner of British residents to celebrate the victories of the French armies. He also presided over a second dinner of this kind on November 18, 1792, at which the toasts were 'The coming Convention of Great Britain and Ireland' and 'The English patriots, Priestley, Fox, Sheridan, Christie, Cooper, Tooke and Mackintosh'. This resulted in the promotion of the British Revolutionary Club of Paris in the following month.[52] He returned to England in somewhat humiliating circumstances after war had broken out in February 1793, but soon went back to France. After the arrest of his brother William Stone by the British Government on May 10, 1794, he dared not set foot in England, as he had been named as the principal in the indictment. William Stone was charged with high treason for 'treacherously conspiring with his brother, John Hurford Stone, now in France, to destroy the life of the King and raise rebellion in his realms'.[53] He prospered in France by securing the confidence of the Directory, became one of the chief printers in Paris on Government contracts and eventually (1817) acquired French nationality.[54] After 1795 Priestley, then safe in the U.S.A., kept up a correspondence with him about Wilkinson's precious *assignats* until at least 1798, by which time they had depreciated from their original value of about £240 to 20 shillings.[55] John Hurford Stone proved to be almost as embarrassing a correspondent to Priestley in America as he had been to Benjamin Vaughan in Britain, for one of his letters to the doctor in 1798 was intercepted and printed by William Cobbett, who was then conducting pro-British propaganda in the U.S.A. Its publication elicited from Priestley a repudiation of any desire on his part for a French invasion of England in the pamphlet, *Letters to the Inhabitants of Northumberland*. George Canning also took up the case and gave the episode a dubious immortality in his poem *The New Morality*, which contains the line:

Priestley's a Saint, and Stone a patriot still.

There was also a biting cartoon from Gillray.[56]

In the course of 1793 Priestley turned his thoughts more and more towards emigrating to the U.S.A. He read Jedidiah Morse's *American Geography* and sent his son Joseph on ahead, accompanied by Thomas Cooper and two other associates, with definite instructions to make a study of the United States on the spot, to decide on a suitable place for the settlement of English 'friends of freedom' and to buy the tract of land selected. The chosen land proved to be in the backwoods of Pennsylvania,[57] on the banks of the River Susquehanna. The scheme is closely linked with the better-known project of Coleridge, Southey, Wordsworth and others to found their Pantisocracy[58] in the U.S.A., a 'social colony in which there was to be community of property and where all that was selfish was to be proscribed'.[59]

In January 1794 Dr. Priestley told Wilkinson that the scheme of buying a tract of land originated with one of Benjamin Vaughan's younger brothers, John Vaughan, who had set up as a merchant in Philadelphia. In the same letter he announced his firm decision to emigrate to the U.S.A. Thomas Cooper was on his way back to

England with the report and Priestley suggested that Wilkinson might like to take the opportunity of investing in American lands.[60] The little book which Cooper published in London later in the year, *Some Information respecting America*, was largely an advertisement for the proposed settlement, but Miss Park's assumption that Priestley was the 'Friend' to whom Cooper addressed the book, although likely, is not proven. There can be no doubt, however, that the book helped the Pantisocrats to choose the exact spot for their project.

Priestley himself arrived in New York on June 4, 1794, when the land scheme still appeared to be promising. From the Priestley–Wilkinson correspondence it is clear that Joseph Priestley, jun., John Vaughan and Abel Humphries had persuaded the reputedly powerful firm of Morris and Nicholson to back them.[61] Robert Morris (1734–1806) and John Nicholson (d. 1800) were Philadelphia merchants of Welsh origin and formed one of the three firms which were reported in 1794 to be 'buying up all the lands in Pennsylvania that they can meet with'.[62] Briefly, the syndicate floated a land company with a capital of 300,000 dollars divided into 100 shares of which Morris and Nicholson were to take up 34. The object of the Company was to purchase, settle and manage 'a quantity of land situate on the waters of Loyalsock, Muncy and Fishing Creeks, in the county of Northumberland in the State of Pennsylvania', the whole of which was to be known as 'Liberty'. Joseph Priestley, jun., hoped to sell plots on the instalment plan by inviting subscriptions in money or the proceeds of the sale of goods dispatched from Britain by intending small purchasers. The syndicate paid the State of Pennsylvania $1 per acre and the first fifty settlers were to get their land at this price. Latecomers had to pay more.[63] But the scheme failed soon after Dr. Priestley arrived to join his sons. It turned out to be the usual story of speculation in virgin lands. He wrote to the Rev. Theophilus Lindsey on September 14, 1794:

What brought us here is the expectation of it being near the settlement that my son and Mr. Cooper were projecting, and behold, *that is all over*. When the lands came to be viewed, they appeared not to be worth purchasing or accepting of ... They were deceived by the proprietors ... I now advise my son to get a farm for himself, near me, and think no more of large partnerships, which seldom answer ... What Mr. Cooper will do I cannot imagine. We must all live on our means for some time to come.[64]

This in fact, is what the new immigrants finally had to do. Nevertheless, as the documents recently discovered by Miss M.C. Park in the Ridgeway Library in Philadelphia and the Pennsylvania Land Office of the Department of the Interior at Harrisburg show, Joseph Priestley, jun., resumed land speculation in the same area early in February 1795 and continued on an extensive scale until the end of 1796,[65] so that eventually lands held by him and his associates amounted to some 700,000 acres.[66]

The bankruptcy of Morris and Nicholson during the general financial crisis of 1796 (they paid only 2*s*. 6*d*. in the £, presumably Pennsylvania currency)[67] finally put an end to Joseph Priestley, jun.'s hopes of a fortune in land speculation and he settled down with moderate success to become a farmer in Northumberland, Pa., where his father had had a house built in 1796. According to Rochefoucauld-Liancourt, Robert Morris generously agreed to take back a large part of the lands which Joseph had contracted to buy: '... celui-ci s'est défait de la presque totalité de ce qui lui restait, et a acheté autour de la ville [Northumberland] quelques terrains qu'il s'est occupé à mettre en valeur'.[68] Much of the land young Mr. Priestley had hoped to acquire for $1 an acre actually fetched $3.50 an acre when sold off during the liquidation of Morris and Nicholson's assets, a fact which Dr. Priestley did not fail to record.[69]

An interesting parallel and contrast to the Priestley family's misfortunes in this affair is provided by the adventures of William Russell (1740–1818), the head of Dr. Priestley's congregation in Birmingham. Until he retired from business in 1791, Russell had been senior partner in the Birmingham family firm of W. and G. Russell, export merchants. He decided to emigrate to the U.S.A., where his firm had many connections and thousands of pounds' worth of bad debts, about the same time as Priestley and for similar reasons. He set sail with his family and servants from Falmouth on April 14, 1794, on board the U.S. merchant vessel *Mary*. The ship was intercepted and taken into Brest by the French frigate *Proserpine*. The Russell establishment was released from detention on December 23, 1794, and William Russell decided to visit Paris, where he purchased a valuable property on the Quai Voltaire, and also acquired a confiscated monastery, the Abbaye Ardennes, near Caen, together with its dependent estate worth about £800 a year. The family then resumed its journey to the U.S.A. and arrived in New York on August 22, 1795. Russell hastened to visit Dr. Priestley at Northumberland, and settled down for five years at Middletown, Connecticut, from which centre he collected several thousand pounds' worth of the bad debts. He left the U.S.A. for France in 1801, lived an idyllic life for the next thirteen or fourteen years in the converted Abbaye Ardennes, and returned quietly to England after the Peace of 1814.[70]

Priestley continued to plan a visit to France from the depths of the Pennsylvanian backwoods. The *Moniteur* of November 21, 1796, contained a reference to the 'projet du docteur Priestley de s'établir en France',[71] and in April 1797, cheered by the 'great success of the French in Italy', as heralding an early peace, he announced to Wilkinson: 'I am about to go to France, to see what I can make of the property you were so good as to give me there. I shall probably sail in about a fortnight'.[72] But Joseph opposed the idea[73] and for some obscure reason he never set out. Six months later the doctor informed Wilkinson of his growing money difficulties:

Mr [John] Vaughan, to whom, on his brother's joint bond and promise of land security, I transferred all my property in the American funds (by which I got 8 per cent, instead of 6), I hear does not pay all demands upon him though he has not hitherto refused mine.[74]

In the winter of 1797–8 hope of a domicile in France revived, particularly as Priestley was by then, under the administration of President Adams, more grossly calumniated as a supposed friend of France 'in the newspaper that has the greatest currency of any in this country' than he had been in England.[75] Yet again he hesitated,[76] waiting for an interval of peace, and meanwhile growing older and more 'comfortably fixed' in America.[77] Then, in the winter of 1800–1, his friend Thomas Jefferson became President, and the scurrilous attacks to which he had been subjected in the American press ceased. This 'determination to visit France in the first interval of peace', although still expressed,[78] was growing weaker. President Jefferson had assured him that 'Yours is one of the few lives precious to mankind, and for the continuance of which every thinking man is solicitous'.[79] Soon afterwards a letter from Priestley was received by the President with 'the pleasure which the approbation of the good and the wise must ever give'. There was, too, the President's personal assurance:

It is impossible not to be sensible that we are acting for all mankind; that circumstances denied to others, but indulged to us, have imposed on us the duty of proving what is the degree of freedom and self-government society may leave its individual members.[80]

Bearing these flattering remarks in mind, it is hardly surprising that, in spite of the Peace of Amiens, Priestley never revisited Europe.

NOTES

'Dr Joseph Priestley, John Wilkinson and the French Revolution, 1789–1802' is reprinted from the *Transactions of the Royal Historical Society*, 1958.

1. Mary C. Park's dissertation on 'Joseph Priestley and the problem of Pantisocracy', *Proceedings of the Delaware County Institute of Science*, Media, Pa., xi, no.1 (1947), 1–60; a chapter in A. Temple Patterson's *Radical Leicester* (1954) on 'Leicester politics and the French Revolution, 1789–96'; H.J. Collins's chapter on 'The London Corresponding Society' in *Democracy and the Labour Movement*, ed.

J. Saville (1955), pp. 103–34; Eric Robinson's articles on 'The English "Philosophes" and the French Revolution', *History Today* (Feb. 1956), 116–21, and 'An English Jacobin: James Watt, jun. 1769–1848', *Cambridge Historical Journal*, xi (1953–5), 349–55; and F. Knight, *The Strange Case of Thomas Walker* (1957).

2. Among the older works may be cited: J.G. Alger, *Englishmen in the French Revolution* (1889); W.T. Laprade, *England and the French Revolution, 1789–1797* (1909); S.H. Jeyes, *The Russells of Birmingham in the French Revolution and America, 1791–1814* (1911); H.W. Meikle, *Scotland and the French Revolution* (1912); W.P. Hall, *British Radicalism, 1791–1797* (1912); G.S. Veitch, *The Genesis of Parliamentary Reform* (1913); H.N. Brailsford, *Shelley, Godwin and their Circle* (1913; repr. with bibliographical postscript, p.254, in 1942); P.A. Brown, *The French Revolution in English History*, (1918); Robert Birley, *The English Jacobins from 1789 to 1802* (1924); E. Colby (ed.), *The Life of Thomas Holcroft* (2 vols., 1925); Dumas Malone, *The Public Life of Thomas Cooper* (1926); and F.K. Brown, *The Life of William Godwin* (1926).

3. Two, for example, are copies of letters from Thomas Jefferson to Priestley.

4. M.C. Park, *op.cit.*, 15.

5. A.N. Palmer, *History of the Older Nonconformity of Wrexham* (1888), p.135; J. Hall, *History of the town and parish of Nantwich* (1883), pp.388–90.

6. *Commercial and Agricultural Magazine*, i, no.4 (Nov. 1799), 229.

7. Rev. H. McLachlan, *Warrington Academy: its history and influence*, Chetham Soc., new ser., cvii (1943), 18; *The Athenaeum* (ed. Dr. J. Aikin), iii (Jan.–June 1808), 393.

8. *Memoirs of Joseph Priestley to the year 1795* (1806), p.15.

9. W.H. Chaloner, 'Les frères John et William Wilkinson et leurs rapports avec la métallurgie française, 1775–1786', *Le Fer à travers les Ages: Hommes et Techniques, Annales de l'Est* (Nancy, 1956), 285–301, translated on pp.19–32 of the present work.

10. *Fraser's Magazine* (April 1842), 411: 4th instalment of 'My Life and Times' by 'Nimrod'.

11. *Memoirs ...*, p.96. Priestley had for seven years (1773–80) been librarian and political research assistant to William Fitzmaurice-Petty (1737–1805), second earl of Shelburne, and first marquis (1784) of Lansdowne, who as First Lord of the Treasury (1782–3) conceded independence to the U.S.A. After leaving Shelburne's service Priestley continued to receive a pension of £150 a year from him and remained on friendly terms with Benjamin Vaughan, who became a member of Shelburne's group in the House of Commons (see above, p.44).

12. lvii, pt.ii, 1161.

13. Parish Registers, Market Drayton, Salop, *sub anno* 1785 and Moreton Say, Salop, *sub anno* 1786.

14. *Christian Reformer*, xix (1833), 499–50.

15. Dr. J. Priestley to John Wilkinson, Nov. 3, 1790, Jan. 20, 1791.

16. *Familiar Letters, addressed to the Inhabitants of the Town of Birmingham, in Refutation of several Charges advanced against the Dissenters, and Unitarians, by the Rev. Mr. Madan, – Also Letters to the Rev. Edward Burn, in Answer to his on the Infallibility of the Apostolic Testimony concerning the Person of Christ. And Considerations on the Differences of Opinion among Christians, in Answer to the Rev. Mr. Venn* (1790).

17. J.G. Alger, *op.cit.*, 14.

18. J.T. Rutt, *The Theological and Miscellaneous Works of Joseph Priestley* (25 vols., 1817–1831), i, pt.ii (letters of June 17 and 22, 1792, xxi, 87, 594).

19. *Letters to the Right Honourable Edmund Burke, occasioned by his 'Reflections on the Revolution in France'* (1791).

20. Dr. J. Priestley to J. Wilkinson, Feb. 17, 1791.

21. Dr. J. Priestley to [Cornelius Reynolds], Feb. 25, 1791.

22. *Manchester Guardian*, Oct. 23, 1844, p.6, cols. 2–3, Nov. 9, 1844, p.5, col.5; P. Handforth, 'Manchester Radical politics, 1789–1794', *Trans. Lancs. and Ches.*

Antiq. Soc., lxvi (1957).

23. Dr. J. Priestley to John Wilkinson, Aug. 20, 1791: 'I thank God I never enjoyed better health or spirits than I have done since this affair ...'
24. Boulton and Watt Coll., Birmingham Public Library.
25. Alger, *op.cit.,* p.91.
26. Dr. J. Priestley to John Wilkinson, Sept. [? 13], 1791.
27. Dr. J. Priestley to John Wilkinson, Oct. 4, 1791.
28. Archives Nationales, Paris, F 4774/68.
29. Dr. J. Priestley to John Wilkinson, Dec. 2,1793, Nov. 3, 1796. It was expected that the £10,000 would produce £600 per annum (Dr. J. Priestley to John Wilkinson, March 15, 1798).
30. Dr. J. Priestley to John Wilkinson, Nov. 3, 1796.
31. Dr. J. Priestley to John Wilkinson, June 14, 1800.
32. Thomas Cooper, Manchester, to John Wilkinson, April 16, 1794.
33. Z. Walker to Dr. J. Priestley, Sept. 15, 1796; Dr. J. Priestley to John Wilkinson, Nov. 30, 1797; J.C. Perregaux to Dr. J. Priestley, Aug. 16, 1797.
34. Dr. J. Priestley to J. Wilkinson, Jan. 21, 1798.
35. J.C. Perregaux to Dr. J. Priestley, Aug. 16, 1797; Dr. J. Priestley to John Wilkinson, June 14, 1800; H.C. Bolton, *Scientific Correspondence of Joseph Priestley* (1892) pp.157–8 (letter from Dr. J. Priestley to J.C. Perregaux, April 12, 1801).
36. Pub. Rec. Off., T 78/IND 8818 (1) – claims; T 78/268–awards (1816–1817).
37. The French ambassador.
38. Dr. J. Priestley to J. Wilkinson, Feb. 10, 1793.
39. 1st ed., 119–34.
40. Dr. J. Priestley to J. Wilkinson, July 15, 1793. Priestley later showed the greatest anxiety that Wilkinson should read such pamphlets as *A Convention the only Means of Saving us from Ruin,* by the notorious Joseph Gerrald of the London Corresponding Society, and the anonymous *Peace and Reform against War and Corruption* (Dr. J. Priestley to J. Wilkinson, Jan. 9, 1794).
41. The description was Sir John Scott's (later Lord Eldon).
42. *Gentleman's Magazine,* lxiv (1794), 572; Alger, *op.cit.,* 95.
43. Alger, *op.cit.,* 92–5.
44. See *Dictionary of National Biography* and *Dictionary of American Biography sub nomine.*
45. T.S. Ashton, *Iron and Steel in the Industrial Revolution* (1924), 75–6; G. Unwin and others, *Samuel Oldknow and the Arkwrights* (1924), 176–93. John Wilkinson to Boulton and Watt, June 26, 1792 (Boulton and Watt Collection, Birmingham Public Library).
46. Ashton, *op.cit.,* 228–9.
47. *State of the Poor*(1797), iii. 891.
48. 33 Geo. III, cap. I; *Journals of the House of Commons,* 1792–3, 51–91 *passim.* No record of the debates on the bill appears to have survived.
49. Dr. J. Priestley to J. Wilkinson, Jan. 25, 1794.
50. Z. Walker to Dr. J. Priestley, 15 April, 1796.
51. Alger, *op. cit.,* 63–4.
52. Alger, *op. cit.,* 64, 98.
53. Alger, *op. cit.,* 66. After being two years in prison, William Stone was acquitted in 1796.
54. Alger, *op. cit.,* 67. Lord Kenyon pointed out that he definitely identified himself with the French as early as 1794, referring to them as 'we' and to the British as 'you' in his correspondence.
55. Nov. 3, 1796, Oct. 7, 1797, Jan. 21, 1798; Z. Walker to Dr. J. Priestley, Sept. 15, 1796.
56. Priestley's letter of Sept. 4, 1798, on the subject to Cobbett is reprinted in his *Works* (ed. Rutt) i, pt. ii, 406. See also British Museum: *Catalogue of Political and Personal Satires,* vii (1942), 468–72, and *Copies of Original Letters ... by Persons in Paris*

[Helen M. Williams and J.H. Stone] to *Dr. Priestley in America, Taken on Board a Neutral Vessel* (1798).

57. M.C. Park, *op. cit.*, 12–16.
58. For the Pantisocracy, see P.A. Brown, *The French Revolution in English History* (1918), pp.108–9; A.E. Bestor, *Backwoods Utopias*, 1950, pp.36–7, and footnotes; M.W. Kelley, 'Thomas Cooper and the Pantisocracy', *Modern Language Notes*, xlv (April 1930), 218–20, and references listed by M.C. Park, *op. cit.*, 58–9.
59. Joseph Cottle, publisher to the Pantisocrats, quoted by H.N. Brailsford, *Shelley, Godwin and their Circle* (1913), p.53.
60. Dr. J. Priestley to John Wilkinson, Jan. 25, 1794.
61. *Purchase of American Lands* (printed folder), 4 pp.; MS. Conditional articles of agreement ... between Robert Morris and John Nicholson ... and Joseph Priestley, Abel Humphries and John Vaughan (both documents bound up in Priestley–Wilkinson, MSS.).
62. H. Wansey, *Excursion to the United States* (2nd ed., 1797), p.125. *Dictionary of American Biography*, *sub* Morris, Robert and Nicholson, John.
63. MS. Conditional articles of agreement ... between Robert Morris and John Nicholson ... and Joseph Priestley, Abel Humphries and John Vaughan (Priestley–Wilkinson MSS.).
64. Quoted in William Vaughan to John Wilkinson, Oct. 25, 1794. See also Dr. J. Priestley to John Wilkinson, Nov. 12, 1794.
65. Park, *op. cit.*, 52–7 (appendix).
66. Park, *op. cit.*, 17–18.
67. *The Autobiography of Benjamin Rush*, ed. G.W. Corner (1948), pp.236–237. Before the crash the two men were estimated to be worth ten million dollars.
68. *Voyage dans les États-Unis d'Amérique*, i (1798–9), 131.
69. Dr. J. Priestley to John Wilkinson, Jan. 21, 1798.
70. S.H. Jeyes, *The Russells of Birmingham in the French Revolution and America 1791–1814* (1911), *passim*.
71. *Ancien Moniteur* (*réimpression* of 1843), xxviii, 493.
72. Dr. J. Priestley to John Wilkinson, April 1, 1797.
73. Dr. J. Priestley to John Wilkinson, April 11, 1797.
74. Dr. J. Priestley to John Wilkinson, Oct. 7, 1797. Later Vaughan's assignees in bankruptcy agreed to make Priestley an annual allowance of $500 for 5 years (Dr. J. Priestley to John Wilkinson, June 14, 1800).
75. Dr. J. Priestley to John Wilkinson, Nov. 30, 1797.
76. Dr. J. Priestley to John Wilkinson, March 15, 1798.
77. Dr. J. Priestley to John Wilkinson, June 14, 1800.
78. Dr. J. Priestley to John Wilkinson, Dec. 15, 1800.
79. Thos. Jefferson to Dr. J. Priestley, March 21, 1801.
80. Thos. Jefferson to Dr. J. Priestley, June 19, 1802.

APPENDIX

In addition to the first four articles reprinted in this book Chaloner wrote the following ten essays on the Wilkinsons:

1. 'New Light on John Wilkinson's Token Coinage', *Seaby's Coin and Medal Bulletin*, July 1948, pp.306–8.
2. 'John Wilkinson as Note Issuer and Banker' in *Seaby's Coin and Medal Bulletin*, December 1948, pp.550–3.
3. 'An English Ironmaster's Visit to Sweden in 1788', *Daedalus Year Book of the Swedish Technical Museum*, Stockholm, 1948, pp.152–4.
4. 'Marchant de la Houlière's Report to the French Government on British

Methods of smelting Iron Ore with Coke and casting Naval Cannon in the Year 1775' in *Edgar Allen News*, December 1948 and January 1949.

5. 'Early Iron. iii, Notes on Wilkinson', in the *Architectural Review*, November 1949, p.333.
6. 'Builders of Industry (i) John Wilkinson, Ironmaster' in *History Today*, May 1951, pp.63–70 reprinted in *People and Industries* (1963).
7. 'Isaac Wilkinson, Potfounder' in L.S. Pressnell (ed.), *Studies in the Industrial Revolution* (Athlone Press, 1960), pp.23–51.
8. 'The Life of Gilbert Gilpin, Chief Clerk at Bersham Ironworks near Wrexham, 1786–96' in *National Library of Wales Journal*, Winter 1960, pp.383–4.
9. Bibliographical introduction to T.S. Ashton, *Iron and Steel in the Industrial Revolution* (1924, third edition, 1963).
10. 'The Stockdale Family, the Wilkinson Brothers and the Cotton Mills at Cark in Cartmel, c 1782–1800' in *Transactions of the Cumberland and Westmorland Antiquarian and Archaeological Society*, 1964, pp.356–72.

PART TWO

ENTREPRENEURS AND INNOVATION IN BRITISH INDUSTRY

4

Hazards of Trade with France in Time of War, 1776–1783

Much is known of the difficulties besetting eighteenth-century merchants trading overseas in time of peace and of the hazards facing shipping at the hands of men-o'-war and privateers in war-time. Little or nothing seems, however, to have been written about the legitimate trade carried on between belligerent countries under the protection of passports during the same period. Fortunately a good deal of material on certain voyages made under these conditions during the War of American Independence has survived in the Boulton and Watt papers.[1] From the mid-1770s onwards Boulton and Watt were selling numerous steam pumping engines to Cornish mine proprietors; their chief supplier of cylinders and other heavy castings, John Wilkinson, operated at Bersham ironworks near Wrexham, only twelve miles from Chester, and the three men became heavily involved in the shipment of engine parts from the quays at Chester round Wales and the Land's End to the 'copper kingdom'.

This entry of the 'Steam Engine Parliament' into the shipping business inaugurated a period of active interest in maritime problems during which arose the much-repeated legend that 'John Wilkinson supplied cannon to the French'. As this legend has had a long run and can therefore be expected to die hard, it is necessary to examine in some detail how it originated in order to discover how untrue it is when taken in the literal sense. At the same time it is proposed to indicate what element of truth this over-simplification contained. John Randall appears to have been the first to print these accusations.[2] 'From the work at Bersham, guns were sent off to the South[3] for the purpose of being smuggled into France, and at Willey a great number of cast pipes, under the name of water piping, were got up for the purpose of supplying, in reality, the French with good gun metal ... Some of these pipes were no doubt *bona fide* transactions. They were for the Paris Water Works; but others it is said were not; and Wilkinson's pipe-making was stopped by the Government, and numbers of pipes remained for years at the warehouse at the bottom of Caughley Dingle.'

The legend appears to have arisen for four main reasons. First, John's brother William was working for the French Government during the War of American Independence (1776–1783) setting up a State ironworks where guns could be cast and bored in the English manner.[4] Secondly, John had agreed in 1777 with Jacques Constantin Périer to supply iron pipes for the new Paris waterworks. Thirdly, Boulton, Watt and Wilkinson had contracted in November 1778 to supply Joseph Jary of Mort, near Nantes, with the parts for one of the Soho firm's patent engines. Finally, in the winter of 1781–2, John visited the Liège district with his brother William to advise Dom Nicolas Spirlet, the Abbé of St Hubert, how to make iron and cast cannon in the English fashion.[5] It should be remembered, too, that in spite of the fact that war broke out between Great Britain and France in March 1778 on the issue of the latter's aid to the rebellious American colonists, French industrialists and businessmen continued to visit this country.

On 7 February 1777 the brothers Jacques-Constantin Périer and Augustin Charles Périer had been granted Royal letters patent giving them the privilege of erecting steam engines to pump water from the Seine and establishing a network of pipes for distributing it to customers. They formed the 'Compagnie des Eaux à Paris' (27 Aug. 1778),[6] but long before this event J.C. Périer had been busy in England. Boulton wrote on 2 May 1777: 'The sum of intelligence concerning Perrier [sic] is ... that W. Wilkinson went over to solicit orders for the pipes, &c.; that Perrier, when he went to Broseley, was resolved to have common [i.e. Newcomen-type] engines; that afterwards he was convinced that ours were much superior, and then wanted [John] Wilkinson to make them for him, as he did not see the use of applying to us, being out of our jurisdiction; that W. represented he would be liable to prosecution and that he was bound by honour and interest not to do it but through us; that W. thought, that being out of our jurisdiction, we should serve Perrier upon moderate terms, should take out our premium in *actions*, which would be saleable as bearing 6 per cent interest; that W., if employed for pipes, &c. takes 100 shares at 50*l.* each'.[7]

Louis XVI's *Conseil* granted Boulton and Watt a 15-year patent on 14 April 1778, through the intervention of the Comte d'Hérouville, on condition that tests were carried out either on Dunkirk meres or at Paris to prove their engine superior to others 'pour l'effet et l'économie'.[8] J.C. Périer now made another journey to England in November 1778 to treat with Boulton and Watt 'de l'acquisition de deux machines à vapeur pour [l']entreprise des eaux à Paris dont les travaux sont déjà commencés'.[9] Accompanied by MacDermott,[10] chaplain to the French Ambassador, as interpreter, Périer, finding that Boulton was away in

Cornwall, 'came down to me [Wilkinson] at Wilson House [in Furness] and induced me to return from thence sooner than I intended. He is engaged here [Bersham] in giving me the needful instructions for the articles he wants – after which we go to Broseley.'[11] A few weeks later (Jan.–Feb. 1779) Périer visited Soho, where the partners agreed to supply him with two engines on very moderate terms.[12] Wilkinson began to make the pipes in December 1778,[13] and by June 1779 Boulton and Watt informed Périer that the iron-master was casting one 24-inch and three 12-inch pipes every day at Willey furnace, near Broseley in Shropshire, besides making many more at Bradley in South Stafford-shire. In all he had over 300 12-inch pipes ready and hoped to step up production to 300 a month.[14]

Another French industrialist, Joseph Jary, 'Concessionaire du roi pour les mines du Nord près de Nantes en Bretagne', who toured Shropshire and South Staffordshire in April 1778, already possessed a Newcomen-type steam engine at his coal mine at Mort and became 'very pressing' in his desire to have one of Boulton and Watt's improved machines: 'he must remove his engine in the course of this year and his wish is to have a new one in 4 months'. Boulton and Watt, on the other hand, were then awaiting the *arrêt du Conseil* granting them a patent for their engine in France and were by no means eager to accept orders before this had been secured. Jary was 'a knowing hand'[15] and con-sidered that as the first French purchaser of a Boulton and Watt engine he should 'be put on a better footing than others as regards paying for it'.[16] There is some evidence which suggests that William Wilkinson had been busy surveying the openings for engine sales in Brittany. According to John Wilkinson there was another colliery, the Montrelais Company, about 20 miles from Jary's mine 'about which my brother wrote some time ago. Mr Jary's [proposed new] engine would soon set the other Co. upon the same plan.'[17] John Wilkinson took up Jary's cause with considerable enthusiasm and suggested to Soho that he should get the castings ready to ship immediately news of the *arrêt* was received. Boulton and Watt remained more cautious.[18] Indeed, Watt looked upon 'his being the first in France as nothing'.[19]

Jary, in England on a second visit, continued to importune Wilkinson, who wrote on 1 November 1778: 'I am most terribly pestered with Jary. Some time ago I had a letter requesting I would give him direction where to come to me, which he said he was determined on let me be where I could. I wrote … That I would have no concern in anything that imitated your invention. He had laboured hard to convince me that as a founder I might execute any orders he gave me, etc., etc.'[20]

The Frenchman thereupon followed Boulton and Watt down to

Redruth in Cornwall where his importunities and Wilkinson's reasoning prevailed upon them to supply him with an engine at his own terms.[21] He appeared to be very jealous of the Périers.

The engine was put in hand immediately, but the problem arose of how to ship the Périer and Jary orders to France despite the war-time controls on trade and a growing shortage of shipping. As early as April 1779 small vessels could not 'be prevailed upon to go round the Land's End'. Freights were very high and ships scarce.[22] Boulton and Watt were allotted the task of securing the British, French and American passports, while Wilkinson carried on a herculean and complicated correspondence arranging the details of shipment, insurance, etc. In fact we can say that his initiative sustained the enterprise throughout. The position was complicated by the fact that Jary wished to charge the vessel bringing his goods with contraband 'red copper in sheets',[23] which would necessitate a separate shipment of copper from London to Ostend in the then neutral Austrian Netherlands. Périer also wanted copper sent in cake form.[24] After fruitless attempts to charter a Spanish merchantman Wilkinson and his Chester wharfinger, Hugh Jones, formed the following plan of campaign:

To fix upon the *Mary*, Capt. Jno. Williams, whom we expect back at Chester the next month as the vessel that must at all events carry these articles as well as Mr Perrier's – that he loads all Mr Jary's goods and so much of Mr Perrier's as can then be got ready – having taken in all at Chester, to proceed coastways to Chepstow[25] and there take in what pipes are ready from Willey and Bilston, or any other articles you have to send from Soho.

That passports be solicited for the *Mary* brigantine, Jno. Williams, Master, burthen 160 tons, 14 men and boys, the vessel square sterned with a figure head, clears out from Chepstow with cylinders and castings and fire engines for Havre de Grâce and returns to Liverpool with burrstones or in ballast.

Resolved that Mr Boulton is the properest gentleman to solicit this passport in England.[26]

Irritation over war-time controls, danger and delays led to an interesting exchange of views between Watt and Wilkinson at this time which illustrates very well their real feelings about the widening struggle in which Britain was becoming ever more deeply involved. Watt wrote on 26 June 1779: 'I understand that this cursed Spanish War has created a devil of a hot press and bill brought into the House of Commons on the 23rd to support it and suspend the Habeas Corpus Act on that point. The Devil take the Dons and the [?Yankees] both, and lock them up in the same Chamber which will be a hell enough for both of them'.[27] Wilkinson agreed even more heartily: 'This cursed war will be the ruin of the engine branch in France ... While the Impress Act attacks by the sea the Militia Bill operates by land. I can sincerely join in your wish of the 26th, but beg leave to add what I think an amendment, which is that our Min[ister]s be added to the crew, which you consign to one chamber. The harmony cannot be completed without them'.[28] By this time news had arrived that a passport would be granted, and Watt begged that the irascible ironmaster 'would not consign the Ministry to the hot chamber, while they continue in the humour of granting us passports'.[29] The cleavage of Wilkinson's interests between the demands of war and the development of the steam-engine meant that difficult decisions about the allocation of his resources of workers and manufacturing capacity had to be taken in 1781–2.

Watt's contact in Government circles was William, second earl of Dartmouth (1731–1801) of Sandwell Hall, near West Bromwich, Lord Privy Seal from 1775 to 1782 who replied on 6 April: '... I see no reason to discourage your application. The proper mode of making it, will be by memorial to the King in Council. The matter will then be considered at the Council Board ... If you will draw up such a memorial and let me have a copy of it, I will talk with the Lord President, and some of the members of the Council upon it. ...'[30]

Dartmouth informed Boulton on 5 July that the memorial had 'passed the Council office, and the order is gone to the Secretary of State's office to make out the passport,'[31] but not until the latter half of August did Boulton's efforts secure the actual issue of the Mary's passport and the lifting of the embargo from the vessel.[32] In the meantime the French and American passports had arrived, the latter granted by Benjamin Franklin from 'his Court at Passy'.[33]

While these essential preliminaries were being carried out further difficulties had arisen. Jary disliked Périer, and Périer objected to his order being shipped with Jary's. Jary also 'pointed out that it would cost him above double the freight from Chester to Havre to carry the goods from Havre to Nantes on account of the high insurance', and desired them to be landed at Nantes or failing that at the harbour of St Malo, only seventy-five miles from the coalfield.[34] Périer wished his goods to be delivered further up river, at Rouen rather than Havre.

By May the Mary was en route from London to Chepstow via Cork and a letter of Wilkinson to Watt suggests that the latter in making up her cargo planned to send additional materials to France: '5 cwt of shere [sic] steel is shipped thither [i.e. to Chepstow] from London, costs 57s. money in town. I think if some of Atwood's at 64s. was sent at same time it would not be amiss.'[35] This was intended for the Périers who wanted a ton, 'principally of those kinds which are used for turning metals'. Watt informed Périer that an application for a passport for a ship to carry his goods had been made to Earl Gower, Lord President of the Council, and continued: 'As the steel we know the character of is to be had only at London we have ordered only at London to avoid expense of carriage to Chepstow and have ordered double that quantity of the best sorts made at Bristol. If these should please you can have more of them next trip. The lead cannot be exported from England in time of war and we are uncertain if the copper can, but Mr Wilkinson thinks he can load out the ship without them'.[36] Périer also desired Wilkinson to load the *Mary* with 8 or 10 tons of pig iron of the best quality 'to cast the bent pipes for the mains as many [accidents] must occur'. Watt added a cautionary note: 'I apprehend if you judge proper to send this it must be run into some form such as gudgeon beds, thick plates or firedoor frames or other easy moulded pieces to avoid any demur at the Custom House, large grate bars etc.'[37]

By the beginning of June Wilkinson had enough of the 24-inch and 12-inch pipes and of the parts for Périer's two engines ready to load not only the *Mary* but another vessel, the *Severn* of Newnham, for which he proposed a separate passport should be sought, while Jary's goods could be sent to Nantes on the sloop *Peter*, in return for ninety guineas freight charge, the payment of port charges and an indemnity against the capture of the vessel by the French, the Americans and the Spaniards. Wilkinson then began to doubt whether the passport would operate as 'a licence to ship goods restrained by proclamation', and had to be reassured by Boulton that no further licence than the passport was necessary. No sooner had his fears been quietened in this respect than he began to worry about the adequacy of unloading facilities for the heavy engine parts at Le Havre and Rouen, because the two heaviest parts weighed about 6 tons each.[38]

The arrival of the *Mary* and her knowledgeable master, Captain John Williams, at Chester late in June[39] confirmed Wilkinson's worst forebodings:

He (Capt. Williams) says it is not possible for him to go up to Rouen under £5 per ton freight – nay, indeed, that his vessel cannot on any account go there without [being] discharged one half at Havre. He has been at both places and knows the river, ports, and custom well, and from what he says it would be madness going further than Havre; says charges in that river for going up, would he do so, would cost him £70 sterling, besides the delay which might be 2 months. His wages now stand in about £50 a month and on the most extravagant terms – men are not to be had at present ... Mr Perrier ... should also be apprised that the air vessel or two parts of it weigh 6 tons each and that there are no cranes at Havre to take out such weights.[40]

The loading of the *Mary* for the coastwise voyage to Chepstow, prior to her French trip, now began. She mounted 12 guns, as Capt. Williams 'might not like to be insulted by any long boat which otherwise might affront him ... you [might] as well strip the captain of his coat as his ship of the guns'.[41] Early in July the British Government laid a general embargo on British sailings to foreign ports,[42] and according to Watt this proved '... very distressing on trade in general, as no British vessel has been allowed to sail for foreign parts that we know of. We hope, however, that it will soon be taken off, as the Navy is sufficiently provided with seamen.'[43]

August was now well advanced and Boulton's efforts to secure the *Mary*'s passport had not yet succeeded, whereas the vessel was about to sail from Chester[44] with cylinders and other engine parts from Bersham and to load some of the water pipes at Chepstow. On 19 August 1779, however, Watt, still despondent, lest the embargo should 'entirely knock up our French business', reported to Wilkinson on 19 August: 'Mr Boulton has got the pass and licence ... and has written to Mr Stanley of the Custom House concerning ... the lifting of the embargo. This job has ... cost £19 and Mr B. says it would cost no more tho' 6 were wanted'.[45] About the same time Boulton reported that he could not secure a passport for the *Severn*, which put Wilkinson into a 'hobble' with the owner, who had been kept in suspense about the vessel's charter.[46]

Périer could now count on receiving at least one cargo, subject to the hazards of the sea. 'Poor Jary'[47] however, had some bad news and good advice from Watt, advice with which Wilkinson heartily agreed:

I much fear from the delay that the Court of France are not going to grant the passport for the *Peter*, particularly as they have not granted the second passport for Mr Perrier's goods [i.e. for the *Severn*] ...
Since we wrote to you last the price of freights and sailors' wages have increased prodigiously. But if the passport arrives in time we shall do all in our power to make the *Peter* perform your voyage, but we are not able to wage war against sovereigns, their embargoes, etc. Upon receipt of the French passport we shall petition the Privy Council for a passport for the *Peter* to Nantes, but do not choose to do it sooner lest the expence should be lost. If you find you are soon not likely to obtain the French passport for the *Peter* you had best determine at once to freight some neutral vessel either belonging to Ostend or Holland to take the goods in at Chester and run for Nantes directly ... You *must* send this vessel to us, and not depend on her being found here ... We are very much concerned at the state of your works, which nevertheless we can in no way assist you in at present further than by advice.[48]

The *Mary* had an unlucky start from Dawpool, the port of Chester, towards the end of August. The press gang seized all her hands as she was about to sail and Captain Williams had to comb Chester for a new complement – 'What with the embargoes, pressing and all the evils this war occasions, I see no end to disappointment in shipping', lamented Wilkinson.[49] A few days later he reported that the *Mary* had lost her crew three times, to the best of his belief, and was probably still delayed at Hoylake by contrary winds.[50] In actual fact she sailed on Sunday 29

August.[51] The crew then compelled Captain Williams to put in at Beaumaris in Anglesey 'where some of them run away and entered aboard others, notwithstanding a month's pay advanced'.[52]

A fresh alarm now arose. It had been decided to load the *Mary* at Chepstow with Périer's engine materials and the special orders only leaving behind 'nothing but pipes' on the quay. John Baldwyn, the Chepstow wharfinger, however, wrote late in August that nothing had come to him 'from Birmingham or Bilston' although these priority consignments had been despatched many weeks before.[53] Watt thereupon sent a sharp letter about the missing consignments to Baldwyn which forms an excellent comment on the Soho firm's careful business records and the slowness of inland water transport for heavy goods in the late eighteenth century: 'The goods arrived at Stourport on the 30th June, were put on board at Stourport the 24th July and fell down the river on the 17th of August, and were expected to arrive at Chepstow on the 29th.'[54]

When these articles turned up safely at Chepstow, fresh fears arose for the fate of the *Mary*: 'no *Mary* yet, perhaps Paul Jones[55] has taken her under his protection'.[56] She was also likely to lose £100 by the voyage to Havre 'unless she gets there and back like a carrier pigeon'.[57] In mid-September Motteux, Périer's London agent, ordered the *Mary* to Honfleur, not Havre.[58] Nothing can be discovered of the *Mary*'s loading and departure from the Boulton and Watt MSS for the following six weeks. On 3 November 1779, however, Wilkinson wrote to Boulton: 'I have heard nothing of the *Mary* since she sailed above a month ago. She had fair winds and fine weather and I was in hopes of her being back ere this time.'[59]

Captain Williams did in fact discharge his cargo safely at Honfleur in October and by 5 November was off Plymouth on his return voyage, confident of his ability to make a second trip to France in a few days 'had he the English licence ready'.[60] Unfortunately, although two further cargoes for France had been piled up at Chepstow, passports were not available, as the French Ministry would not grant any more 'for English bottoms'.[61] Later correspondence reveals that Thomas Vickers, one of Wilkinson's Bersham millwrights who specialised in erecting engines, had been aboard the *Mary* as ship's carpenter on this voyage, but was not allowed ashore at Honfleur. Wilkinson commented: 'The reason given by Mr P[érier] is that he could not obtain leave for his landing. This is a plain proof that he does not choose to have even an English workman employed in putting the engine together ... Such a jealous temper is a bane to undertakings of this nature and is a weed of luxuriant growth in France.'[62]

Périer now began to use his influence in French official circles and succeeded in securing a French passport for his second cargo to go by the *Mary*. Hope revived and on 19 February 1780 Wilkinson, then in London, received from Motteux a British passport for that vessel from Chester to Honfleur. He wrote to Boulton and Watt: 'As soon as Mr Perrier advised that the Minister would use his interest for the *Mary* I wrote my brother (under cover to Mr Perrier) who, I expect, is now with him, to use every means for permission of Jary's goods going by his conveyance ... tho' I know that Mr P. will not relish the proposal I intend to urge it again and through my brother by the next mail.'[63]

By the end of March, Wilkinson was busy despatching the *Mary* from Chester,[64] to which port some of the material accumulated at Chepstow now had to be shipped. Fresh difficulties then arose. William Wilkinson wrote that Jary 'did not approve' the plan of sending his goods with Périer's; 'the expence coastways from Havre or Honfleur [to Nantes] would be more than to get them from Chester'. John was therefore glad that Périer's consent for the goods to go had not then been received: 'It does not appear that there is any way to get his [Jary's] engine conveyed unless he can get a licence and as that rests with him, I do not know what we can do for him on this side. No opportunity offers for Ostend and if it did I suppose that must be liable to the same objections made to a French port, where they must afterwards go coastways'.[65]

Further enquiries at Liverpool appeared to show that Hugh Jones of Chester had been unenterprising and negligent. Writing to John Turner, Wilkinson's manager at Bersham, on 8 July 1780, Watt informed him with apparently justifiable irritation:

I am now in terms with a person to carry them [Jary's goods] to Nantes ... I am also informed that opportunities frequently occur from Liverpool to Ostend, that two vessels sailed lately for that port, one of which would have taken the goods had they been at Liverpool and that another vessel is expected to go from Liverpool soon. If we had not depended upon H. Jones for information we should have sooner made [delivery] ... part of M. Jary's goods ... have been suffered to be out upon the open quay in the rain at Chester and ... they are much damaged ... it is a matter of serious consequence ... that after much labour has been spent in filing and finishing goods that they should not afterwards be spoilt by bad usage.[66]

Wilkinson's reaction to this letter was strong. He pointed out that he had reason to suspect that the main obstacle to Jary's efforts to get a passport for the sloop *Peter* to go from Chepstow to Nantes was Périer's sinister influence in French official circles: 'I have taken such measures through my brother William as I hope will remove it.' William had also obtained Périer's permission for Jary's goods to go to Havre in the next loading from Chepstow in case the plan for using the *Peter* proved abortive. With regard to criticisms of Hugh Jones, he was particularly severe:

I have for some time past desired Mr Rathbone of Liverpool to keep a look out upon all vessels from thence to Ostend and to offer these articles at any reasonable freight, and I have not heard of any but salt ships, which would greatly injure the goods ... and even those could not be obtained on account of terms or time.

It happens also [to be] inconvenient at that port to lodge such articles beforehand, nor is there any vessel in the coasting trade between those ports [i.e. *Chester and Liverpool*] (except one) that can take them.[67]

Watt thereupon managed to secure a neutral vessel to take Jary's 28 tons of goods from Chester to Nantes. In an attempt to avoid the seizure of the articles they were to be sold to the neutral captain, who was to take all risks from Chester to Nantes for a payment of 6 per cent *ad valorem*. The bill was therefore to be:

Freight of 28 tons @ 4 guineas	£117	12s.
Primage on 28 tons @ 10 per cent ton	£11	14s.
6 per cent on £750, the value of the goods	£45	0s.
	£174	6s.

Watt only consented to this arrangement, because it would 'bring the affair to a crisis', and awaiting an answer from Jary, he wrote gloomily that the shipping agent with whom he had made the deal probably did not 'rightly understand the port of Chester' and the difficulties attending it.[68]

This project fell through, for nothing more is heard of it. Instead Watt wrote to Jary again (26 July 1780) outlining three courses of action. Jary could renew his application for a passport for the *Peter*, which was about to sail for Chepstow via a Cornish port carrying his goods. If this could not be secured, the goods were to be landed at Chepstow to await a neutral vessel, for which Watt thought the British Government would grant a passport to Nantes. If these two plans failed they were to be shipped as part of Périer's second cargo to Honfleur.[69]

On 30 August, John received a letter from his brother William, heralding the arrival of a French passport for the *Mary* dated 10 July 1780 (to cover the shipment of Périer's goods). But it was valid for a voyage from either Chester or Chepstow to Nantes and not to Honfleur or Havre. Jary had the last laugh. Wilkinson immediately sent it off to his London agents 'to show at the Council Office' and to apply for its British counterpart.[70] He wished to send some extra pig iron, but Watt commented: 'It is a doubt if our Court will grant him passport for that purpose; however let him see to that.'

The British passport arrived in mid-October, but getting the *Mary* to Chepstow and loading her took until the end of December. It seems probable from John Wilkinson's letter to Watt of 28 December 1780, that the pig iron was shipped clandestinely: 'Last post brought me the *Mary*'s bill of lading etc. advising that she was cleared out and ready to fall down the river. I hope she is now on the passage and that this disagreeable business will soon have an end. I have been obliged to enter into securities of indemnification to procure the usual bonds, which with 5 guineas to the off[ice]r has removed the difficulties at Chepstow.'[71]

Watt's qualms about the cargo were well expressed in a letter to Jary after its safe arrival: '... In relation to the copying machine I would have sent one by the *Mary* but durst not. There was enough difficulty without it, and after all I wonder she was let go with such a cargo – *Quid non mortalia pectora cogis auri sacra fames*? I rejoice, however, that it happened.'[72]

Although little evidence about this voyage appears to have survived, it proved successful, for by 27 February 1781 Wilkinson was expecting the *Mary* to dock at Chester after a safe return from France.[73] Jary reported to Boulton about the same time that his goods had been safely landed.[74] But the *Mary*, considered as a productive investment, had lost more than £300 on the voyage, besides losing two ladings to London, a further clear loss of nearly £200.[75]

It remains now to consider the fate of Périer's second cargo, consisting mainly of 12-inch water pipes. Not only were Boulton, Watt and Wilkinson heartily sick of the whole business of despatching cargoes to France, but they were coming to distrust Périer more and more. 'By the way', Watt asked Wilkinson on 20 September 1780, 'how stands your cash account with the Parisian? He never condescends to take the least notice of us.'[76] Wilkinson had heard from Périer: 'He craves time for my balance of near £9,000 after paying my shares and begs I will not draw but that when they are in a situation he will remit ... I have replied to this with as much Temper as an Englishman is possessed of and have referred him to my broker for a conference on this disappointment to me, which I have stated to be as great as it was unexpected.'[77]

Wilkinson had acquired 30 shares in the *Compagnie des Eaux de Paris* in part-payment for his goods, and as the Company had 175 shares remaining on its hands, the proprietors at a meeting on 21 September 1780 had recommended that shareholders should take up these to the extent of one-fifth of their existing holdings. Wilkinson therefore had to purchase 6 more shares: 'I always had a suspicion that the ship hung rather heavy, tho' Mr P[érier] was not willing to own it, and your fixing upon money rather than shares was a fault he could not forgive.'[78]

In February 1781 Wilkinson received a remittance of unknown amount from Périer. A year later while in the Austrian Netherlands with his brother William, he wrote to Boulton: 'My brother informs me there was a motion made in the Assembly[79] to stop any further payment to you, but that Mr Perrier opposed an attempt so unjust, and by his interest overruled it. It was then resolved that the mony due on your agreement should be paid when the finances of the Company will permit ... We have too many Dukes and courtiers concerned in this enterprise, which will in the end ruin it.'[80]

It is small wonder then, that little attempt was made to ship Périer's second cargo. The pipes remained rusting on the wharves near Chepstow, helping to create the legend that Wilkinson exported cannon to the French in time of war. The Hon. John Byng saw them there on 16–17 June 1781: 'On the quay were ... incredible numbers of iron water pipes (like cannon) each 9 feet long and weighing about 800 weight which are going to France (by permission) ... Near 21 miles of them are sent: Judge the weight and expense.'[81]

Other observers had seen the pipes and heard of the *Mary*'s two French trips, and on 5 March 1782, John Robinson, secretary of the Treasury, wrote to the Board of Customs at the command of the Lords Commissioners enclosing the copy of the following information received at the Treasury and directing an enquiry into the facts and circumstances behind the statements contained in it:

Davies Shopkeeper of Colebrook dale, Co. of Salop, on Xmas day last declared the following at Mr Thos Booth's, that a Mr Wilkinson who had a very considerable Iron Foundery for Casting Cannon Balls Cylinders &c. situate between Chester and the Isle of Anglesea employed thereat 3 or 400 people who are the only Inhabitants in that Part of the Country. That he Wilkinson had been in France since the Commencement of the present War and settled a Correspondence for furnishing Iron pipes for conveying Water into the City of Paris, that for this purpose he applied to Government for Leave to export Iron pipes free unmolested and unexamined which was granted him – under so coulerable a pretext it was notoriously known, that he Wilkinson exported Cannon Balls, Cylinders of most unusual Thickness, and that Ball to the amount of twenty four thousand tons in Six Weeks supposed for France as all were put on Board those Vessels employed by Wilkinson for exporting the Iron pipes. That the most lucrative profits were made for each article of Iron. He Davies was asked how it happened that no persons were impressed to his Country's Good, as not to inform Government of such Infamous proceedings the more especially as it answered the most essential purposes of our Enemies. He replied the affair was publick enough in the Country, that at the place of Exportation none but his own people lived at, and that the other Iron Founders connected with Government was enabled therefrom to derive a far greater price for Cannon Ball &c. than otherwise they possible could do, but for this Circumstance.

The most immediate steps ought to be taken to interrupt (if real) the iniquitous practice of Wilkinson, & if detected bring him to the most condign punishment.

The Commissioners of Customs immediately ordered their clerk,

George Robinson to write to the collector and comptroller of Beaumaris in Anglesey (7 March 1782) asking them to make 'a full and particular enquiry' into these astounding allegations. Naturally these two customs officials could not help (21 March): 'We find there is a considerable Foundery at Harding[82] in Flintshire belonging to Mr John Rigby and another Foundery at Bersham belonging to a Mr Wilkinson, both of these Founderys are in the Port of Chester. If any thing has been exported, we presume it must be from that Port, there has not been anything exported from hence.'[83]

Unfortunately the records from the Custom House at Chester which might throw light on the proposed investigation do not appear to have survived. No legal action was taken against John; William remained unmolested on his return from France, and bearing in mind the evidence marshalled earlier, it would seem that the Lords of the Treasury quietly let the affair drop. In the absence of Wilkinson's business records, it is unfortunately impossible to assess the profitability of the above ventures. Some of Wilkinson's frustrated export water-pipes may still be seen supporting farm buildings in the Furness district of Lancashire. It is to be suspected that the profits were not commensurate with the enormous efforts expended, and that Wilkinson was speaking both from the heart and from knowledge of his account books when he wrote to Watt on 25 September 1780, on the shipping of Jary's engine goods: 'For my own part I only wish that I had never wrote a line or spoke a word further than that "His goods were ready at Chester".'

NOTES

This article is reprinted from *Business History*, Vol VI (ii), June 1964, pp.79–92.

1. Referred to hereafter as A.O. (Boulton MSS., Assay Office, Birmingham) and P.L. (Boulton and Watt Collection, Birmingham Public Reference Library).
2. J. Randall, *The Wilkinsons* (1876), 16.
3. Randall's lack of general background knowledge is shown by the fact that there was no outlet for the carriage of heavy articles south from Bersham to the Severn in Wilkinson's lifetime. Guns were carted north to Chester.
4. W.H. Chaloner, 'Les frères John et William Wilkinson et leurs rapports avec la métallurgie française, 1775–1786', *Le Fer à Travers les Ages: Hommes et Techniques, Annales de l'Est*, Mémoire no.16, Nancy (1956), 285–301; Marchant de la Houlière, *Report to the French Government on British Methods of Smelting Iron with Coke and Casting Naval Cannon, 1775* (ed. W.H. Chaloner, 1949).
5. R. Evrard, *Dom Nicolas Spirlet ...*, (Liège, 1952).
6. J. Bouchary, *L'eau à Paris à la fin du XVIII siècle: La Compagnie des eaux à Paris* (1946), 42–7.
7. Quoted in J. Muirhead, *The Life of James Watt, with selections from his Corres-*

pondence (1858), 265–6. Shares in the Paris Waterworks Co. were 1,200 French *livres* or £50 sterling each.

8. Boulton to Jary, 12 Oct. 1778 (P.L.); C. Ballot, *L'introduction du machinisme dans l'industrie française* (1923), 397.
9. Périer, London, to Boulton, 24 Nov. 1778 (P.L.).
10. Suspicion of the Wilkinsons' activities seems to have been aroused as early as 1777 (*Archives Etrangères*, Paris, Esp., t.528, fo.22).
11. J. Wilkinson to M. Boulton, 23 Dec. 1778 (P.L., copy in A.O.).
12. J. Watt to Dr J. Black, 13 Jan. 1779 (quoted in Muirhead, *Origins and Progress ...*, 113). Boulton and Watt accepted 24,000 *livres* in shares of the Waterworks Company (J. Bouchary, op. cit., 44).
13. J. Wilkinson to M. Boulton, 23 Dec. 1778. (P.L., copy in A.O.).
14. B. & W. to Périer, 5 June 1779; B. & W. to Motteux, 9 June 1779 (P.L.). Boulton and Watt saw these pipes at Willey at the end of May.
15. A later judgement of Jary was: 'He seems to be very fair and honest, and although a Grumbletonian has been punctual in his remittances' (J. Watt to J. Wilkinson, 20 Sept. 1780 (P.L.)).
16. J. Wilkinson to Boulton and Watt, 13, 14 April (letters 1 and 2), 1778 (P.L.).
17. John Wilkinson to B. & W., 14 April 1778 (P.L.).
18. Boulton to John Wilkinson, 16 April 1778 (P.L.).
19. Watt to Boulton, 6 August 1778 (P.L.).
20. (?) to Watt (P.L.). The letter is misdated 1 October.
21. Watt to J. Wilkinson, 7 Nov. 1778 (P.L.). Watt got a good impression of Jary: 'He seems an understanding man and has been honest enough to confess his proposals to you of his own accord ... We have parted with him upon the most amicable footing with a high opinion of his integrity ... he thinks that you and us together are more powerful engine makers than the *Grand Monarque*'.
22. Watt to John Williams, 13 April 1779 (P.L.).
23. Jary to B. & W., 12 Dec. 1778 (A.O.).
24. Boulton to Jary, 26 Jan. 1779 (A.O.). See also J. Wilkinson to J. Watt, 17 May, 25 June 1779, and J. Watt to J. Wilkinson, 27 June 1779 (P.L.).
25. Wilkinson's wharfinger and shipping agent at Chepstow was John Baldwyn (J. Wilkinson to B. & W., 8 June 1779 (P.L.).
26. J. Wilkinson to Boulton and Watt, 1 April 1779 (P.L.): J. Wilkinson to J. Watt, 10 May 1779 (P.L.).
27. P.L.
28. J. Wilkinson to Watt, 2 July 1779 (P.L.).
29. 5 July 1779 (P.L.). When the combined fleets of France and Spain swept the Channel in August 1779 Wilkinson lamented: 'We have been aiming too much for mastery by land and have neglected our proper element. Poor old England!' (Wilkinson to Watt, 24 Aug. 1779 (P.L.)).
30. Dartmouth to Watt, 6 April 1779 (P.L.). See also Dartmouth to Boulton, 22 June 1779 (A.O.), stating he had delivered the memorial into the hands of the Lord President.
31. Dartmouth to Boulton, 5 July 1779 (A.O.). There is an undated draft of the memorial in the Boulton MSS in the Assay Office, Birmingham.
32. Vincent Litchfield, Council Office, Whitehall, to Boulton, 7 July 1779 (A.O.); Watt to Périer, 12 Aug. 1779 (P.L.); Watt to Jones, 25 Aug. 1779 (P.L.).
33. Watt to J. Wilkinson, 14 June 1779 (P.L.).
34. Watt to Jary, 6 April 1779 (P.L.); Watt to Turner, and to J. Wilkinson, 6 May 1779 (P.L.). It appears from this last letter that 'quelques tuyaux de fonte' for the Montrelais Company were also to be included in the cargo. (See also Boulton & Watt to Jary, 12 June 1779 (P.L.)).
35. J. Wilkinson to Watt, 10 May 1779 (P.L.). Cf. 'If you get 5 cwt of Atwood's shear steel at 46s. and blistered at 33s. [that] will, I think, be enough the first shipping, with the 5 cwt. shear steel coming to Chepstow from London. Another ½ton may be sent the next time, when Mr Perier has determined on the quality sent as a sample' (J.

Wilkinson to Watt, 17 May 1779 (P.L.)).
36. Watt to Périer, 19(?) June, 1779 (P.L.).
37. Watt to J. Wilkinson, 13 May 1779 (P.L.). Wilkinson replied: 'As to the cast iron pigs there will be no room this voyage – and French metal is most excellent' (J. Wilkinson to Watt, 17 May 1779 (P.L.)).
38. Watt to Jary, 21 June 1779; Boulton & Watt to Jary, 19 July 1779 (their channel of communication by this time was via Messrs. Frédéric Romberg et Fils of Ostend); J. Wilkinson to Boulton & Watt, 18 June 1779, J. Watt to J. Wilkinson, 26 June 1779, J. Wilkinson to J. Watt, 2 July 1779. The entry of Spain into the war made an application for 'a Spanish protection' necessary.
39. J. Wilkinson to Watt, 25 June 1779 (P.L.).
40. J. Wilkinson to Watt, 4 July 1779 (P.L.).
41. Ibid.
42. J. Wilkinson to Watt, 4 July 1779 (P.L.). Watt to Harris, Wheal Chance, 6 July 1779 (P.L.).
43. Watt to Périer, 12 August 1779 (P.L.).
44. Wilkinson had been put to 'no little trouble and expence to get her cleared out of the Custom House at Chester' (Watt to Périer, ?25 Aug. 1779, (P.L.)).
45. P.L.
46. J. Wilkinson to Watt, 21 Aug. 1779.
47. He was 'likely to be drowned out of his mine altogether ... he must let the water rise 100 feet as the engine cannot keep it [?in check]'. Watt to J. Wilkinson, 28 Aug. 1779 (P.L.)
48. Watt to Jary, 25 Aug. 1779 (P.L.). For Wilkinson's agreement with this letter, see J. Wilkinson to Watt, 14 Sept. 1779 (P.L.) and Watt's letter to Jary of 15 Sept 1779 (P.L.) in answer to one of 21 Aug. It is an interesting sidelight on postal communications that this letter of 21 August, presumably posted in France, was in Watt's hand as early as 11 Sept.
49. To Watt, 27 Aug. 1779 (P.L.).
50. To Watt, 31 Aug. 1779 (P.L.).
51. To Watt, 1 Sept. 1779 (P.L.).
52. J. Wilkinson to Watt, 12 Sept. 1779 (P.L.).
53. J. Wilkinson to Watt, 1 Sept. 1779 (P.L.).
54. Watt to J. Baldwyn, Chepstow, 4 Sept. 1779 (P.L.).
55. The celebrated captain of an American privateer. (See *Annual Register*, 1778 (*Chronicle*), 177.)
56. Watt to J. Wilkinson, 11 Sept. 1779 (P.L.).
57. J. Wilkinson to Watt, 12 Sept. 1779 (P.L.).
58. J. Wilkinson to Watt, 17 Sept. 1779.
59. P.L.
60. J. Wilkinson to Boulton and Watt, 21 Nov. 1779 (P.L.).
61. J. Wilkinson to Watt, 5 Dec. 1779 (P.L.).
62. J. Wilkinson to Watt, 11 July 1780 (P.L.).
63. P.L., Watt ('... poor Jary. I pity that man because he has been so disappointed' – Watt to Wilkinson, 27 Feb. 1780) put the facts to Jary in a letter of March [?] 1780 (P.L.). It would have been expensive to export them via Amsterdam as there were import and re-export duties of 2 per cent *ad valorem* and, besides, Boulton and Watt placed 'no faith in neutral captains'.
64. J. Wilkinson to Watt, 31 Mar., 18 April 1780 (P.L.).
65. J. Wilkinson to Watt, 21 April 1780. Watt wrote to Jary, 1 June 1780 (P.L.): 'I have at many repeated times independent of Mr Wilkinson and unknown to him caused [?my agent to] make enquiries at Liverpool about neutral vessels for Ostend without success ... There have been none gone from that port this last year.' Watt had even written to the Danish consul, and promised to go personally to Liverpool to see the goods shipped in the event of securing a vessel.
66. P.L.
67. J. Wilkinson to Watt, 11 July 1780 (P.L.). Watt's fears for Jary's goods on Chester

quay appear to have been exaggerated. See also J. Wilkinson to Watt, 26 Sept. 1780 (P.L.).

68. Watt to J. Wilkinson, 14 July and 15 July 1780.

69. P.L. See also Watt to J. Wilkinson, 16 Aug. 1780 (P.L.) and J. Wilkinson to Watt, 20 Aug. 1780 (P.L.).

70. J. Wilkinson to Watt, 31 Aug., 4 Sept. 1780 (P.L.). There is a defective copy of this passport in the Boulton and Watt Collection, Birmingham Public Library.

71. P.L. Watt informed Jary that at Chepstow 'from some scruples of the Custom House officers I expected no other than that she would not be suffered to go the voyage. However ... by a proper dose of the golden powder their eyesight has been cleared and they have seen matters in a very different light,' 9 Jan 1781 (P.L.).

72. 26 March 1781 (P.L.). 'Accursed thirst for gold, what do you not tempt men to attempt?' (Virgil).

73. To Boulton & Watt (P.L.).

74. Boulton to J. Wilkinson, 28 Feb. 1781 (P.L.).

75. 'My anxiety to forward that business has been more out of my way in point of interest than the whole amount of his bill,' J. Wilkinson to Boulton & Watt, 4 March 1781 (P.L.).

76. P.L.

77. J. Wilkinson to Watt, 26 Sept. 1780 (P.L.). For Wilkinson's financial dealings with Périer see also J. Wilkinson to Watt, 8 July 1779 (P.L.) and Watt's reply, 13 July 1779 (P.L.).

78. J. Wilkinson to Watt, 6 Nov. 1780 (P.L.). The Company promised to pay interest on its blocked debts. Boulton and Watt had been paid 24,000 livres on 25 February 1779, but had to wait until 1786 for a second instalment of the same amount (Bouchary, op. cit., 44, n.10).

79. I.e. the general meeting of proprietors of the Compagnie des Eaux.

80. J. Wilkinson, Brussels, to Boulton, 16 Jan. 1782 (A.O.).

81. The Torrington Diaries (1934) i, 26. In 1788 John 'Wilkinson secured a further order, this time for 40 miles of iron pipes, from the Compagnie des Eaux de Paris' (D. Macpherson: Annals of Commerce (1805), IV, 176). See also Archives Nationales, O^1 1596 (Examen ... des comités ... des eaux de Paris, 1778–9).

82. I.e. Hawarden.

83. Beaumaris Custom House MSS (Caernarvon). I am greatly indebted to Mr David Thomas of Bangor for copies of these documents.

5

New Light on Richard Roberts, Textile Engineer (1789–1864)

At the present moment the standard authority on the life of Richard Roberts (1789–1864) is the article by Dr. H.W. Dickinson (*Trans. Newcomen Society*, vol. XXV, 1945–47 (1950), 123–37). In that paper Dr. Dickinson wrote (p. 128): 'In 1826 Roberts was induced to go to Alsace, France to plan and arrange the machinery for a new factory built at Mulhouse by André Koechlin et Cie, well-known cotton spinners. He spent a couple of years there and as it was his first introduction to a foreign country and language we should have liked to have known his reactions to his new surroundings as well as details of the actual work he did, but we have no record.' The purpose of this paper is to enlarge and to some extent correct the account of the years 1826–28 in Richard Roberts's life, using material not available to Dr. Dickinson.

Briefly, Roberts was a Welshman, born in the township of Carreghofa in the parish of Llanymynech, Montgomeryshire, about seven miles from Oswestry in 1789, the son of a shoemaker and turnpike tollkeeper. He soon showed an aptitude for things mechanical, but in fact worked in a local quarry until about 1809, when he is said to have migrated to the Black Country and taken service with John Wilkinson's executors at Bradley and later at the Horseley Ironworks. From there he moved into Lancashire, working in foundries and engineering workshops in Liverpool, Manchester and Salford, and finally, in 1814, going to London where he worked in Henry Maudslay's world famous engineering works until 1816. He then returned to Manchester and set up a small engineering works in Pool Fold, New Market Buildings, off Deansgate in that town, where he began the invention and construction of the great series of machine tools and textile machines which is headed by his metal-planing machine of 1817. In his advertisement in the first number of the *Manchester Guardian* on 5 May 1821, he described himself as 'lathe, screw, screw-engine, screw-stock, etc., etc., manufacturer'.

He was among the founders of the Manchester Mechanics' Institution in 1823 and in the same year was elected to ordinary membership of the

Manchester Literary and Philosophical Society which had been founded in 1781, and of which in 1823 John Dalton was President. At some time between 1821 and 1823 Roberts entered into partnership with one James Hill for the additional purpose of making patent machinery for the manufacture of the reeds used on weavers' looms. Neither Hill nor Roberts appear in *Patents for Inventions: Abridgments of Specifications relating to Weaving* in connection with reed-making machinery, but it is clear that either Roberts himself or Roberts and Hill had secured control of patent 4162 of 23 August 1817 taken out by Jeptha Avery Wilkinson of New York for 'certain improvements in the application of machinery for the purpose of manufacturing weavers' reeds by water or other power'.[1] This is confirmed by the description of Roberts's Manchester works (where he employed 'about 12 or 14 men in rather a crowded shop') given by Joshua Field on 30 August 1821, an account which was printed in our *Transactions* for 1932–3.[2] Field wrote: 'Mr R[oberts] took us to see the reed machines now at work. The invention is quite new, invented by a Mr. Wilkinson. The two pair of half sticks are put through holes in the machine perpendicular. The wire is sent between them, cut off and the wax end tied round them. It is hardly brought to perfection. The 2 machines now at work are very different in form and the one now making is to do everything. Upstairs in the same building the wire is prepared first by rolling flat, then hav[ing] the edges cut smooth by passing between cutters. It is then burnished. ...'

Just over a year after Field's visit Richard Roberts took out patent no. 4726 (14 November 1822) for improvements, grouped under six headings, in power looms for weaving,[3] and this improved version of William Horrocks's patent power loom of 1803–05 was considered so important by Dr. Andrew Ure that he gave it nearly 16 pages and many diagrams in his book, first published in 1836, on *The Cotton Manufacture of Great Britain*,[4] i.e. only a little less than the amount of space[5] he devoted to Richard Roberts's more famous self-acting mule (1825, 1830). The point here is that Roberts's improvements to the power loom were probably, from the industrial standpoint, just as important as his later spinning inventions (Plate I (a)).

In Edward Baines's *History, Directory and Gazetteer of the County Palatine of Lancaster* of 1824–25 Roberts and Hill were described as machine makers and power loom makers operating from 33 Faulkner Street,[6] off Mosley Street, in what is now the business centre of Manchester, but from no. 34 Faulkner Street another partnership operated: Sharp, Hill and Co., reed manufacturers by patent machinery, i.e. the three Sharp brothers. This partnership had acquired the rights in the patent reedmaking machine. Richard Roberts's private house was also in Faulkner Street, at no. 23, so that it looks as though

James Hill and the Sharps had provided the capital, while he provided the engineering skill and oversight. James Hill had his private address at 39 Ormond Street, Chorlton Row, about a mile away.[7]

The Swiss industrialist J.C. Fischer of Schaffhausen visited the workshops of Sharp, Hill and Co. on 20 June 1825. At that time the firm was employing another famous Swiss, Johann Georg Bodmer. Bodmer introduced Fischer to James Hill, but Fischer was taken over the works by Richard Roberts himself. He noted the high quality and large output of the firm and also admired the patent reed-making machine. He seems, in fact, to have become somewhat confused by the existence of the two separate establishments, since he recorded that power looms were being turned out at a rate of 80 a week (i.e. roughly 4,000 a year) and, as we have seen, this formed the business of Roberts, Hill and Co.[8]

We do not know with certainty what eventually happened to James Hill,[9] but it is quite clear that, probably in the latter part of 1825, and certainly by 1826, Richard Roberts had become partner in what was effectively an amalgamation of the two previous concerns, under the style of Sharp, Roberts & Co., which made the power looms and reed-making machines.[10] The other two main partners were the brothers Thomas Sharp, jun., of Birch Cottage, Rusholme, a village suburb of Manchester, and Robert Chapman Sharp of Fallowfield Lodge, Rusholme, who were also principals in the separate and old-established partnership of Thomas Sharp & Co., wholesale iron merchants. This firm had a counting house at 84 Market Street, Manchester, and a wharf on the canal in Oxford Street, named Wilkinson's wharf, a relic of the late Thomas Sharp senior's agency for the famous John Wilkinson's North Wales iron during the Revolutionary and Napoleonic Wars.

In 1825 Roberts became an innovator in spinning machinery when he took out a patent (no. 5138, 27 March 1825) for improvements in the spinning mule which eventually had the effect of automating the backwards and forwards motion of the hand-mule frame, and making the 'self-acting mule' an economic proposition. It must be remembered that other inventors had been working on the problem soon after the end of the French Wars in 1815, e.g. William Eaton of Wiln in Derbyshire, Maurice de Jongh of Warrington, Archibald Buchanan of the Catrine works in Scotland, Dr. Brewster of the United States of America, and Thomas Knowles of Manchester,[11] and indeed they continued working on the problem until well into the 1830s. For example, Joseph Whitworth took out a self-acting mule patent in 1835.[12]

It has not been possible to trace a strictly contemporary account of the circumstances which turned Roberts's attention to the making of a self-acting mule, but Dr. Andrew Ure, in *The Philosophy of Manufactures: or an exposition of the scientific, moral and commercial economy of the factory system in Great Britain* (1835) gave an interesting and triumphant account of it ten years later:[13]

In the factories for spinning coarse yarn for calicoes, fustians, and other heavy goods, the mule-spinners have also abused their powers beyond endurance, domineering in the most arrogant manner, as we have shown, over their masters. High wages, instead of leading to thankfulness of temper and improvement of mind, have, in too many cases, cherished pride and supplied funds for supporting refractory spirits in strikes, wantonly inflicted upon one set of mill-owners after another throughout the several districts of Lancashire and Lanarkshire, for the purpose of degrading them into a state of servitude. During a disastrous turmoil of the kind at Hyde, Stayley-bridge, and the adjoining factory townships, several of the capitalists,[14] afraid of their business being driven to France, Belgium, and the United States, had recourse to the celebrated machinists Messrs. Sharp and Co., of Manchester, requesting them to direct the inventive talents of their partner, Mr. Roberts, to the construction of a self-acting mule, in order to emancipate the trade from galling slavery and impending ruin. Under assurances of the most liberal encouragement in the adoption of his inventions, Mr. Roberts, who was then little versed in spinning-machines, suspended his professional pursuits as an engineer, and set his fertile genius to construct a spinning automaton.
    The drawing, stretching and twisting of the yarn had been rendered in a great measure the result of self-acting mechanism by the labours of Crompton and Kelly, the first inventor and the first improver of the mule; but to back off the spiral-coil from the tip of the spindle, and then wind the thread upon it in a shapely conoid, was the Gordian knot left for Mr. Roberts to untie. The problem did not puzzle him long, for to the delight of the mill-owners who ceased not to stimulate his exertions by frequent visitations, he produced, in the course of a few months, a machine apparently instinct with the thought, feeling, and tact of the experienced workman – which even in its infancy displayed a new principle of regulation, ready in its mature state to fulfil the functions of a finished spinner. Thus, the Iron Man, as the operatives fitly call it, sprung out of the hands of our modern Prometheus at the bidding of Minerva – a creation destined to restore order among the industrious classes, and to confirm to Great Britain the empire of art. The news of this Herculean prodigy spread dismay through the Union, and even long before it left its cradle, so to speak, it strangled the Hydra of misrule. It is to be hoped that the manufacturers who received this guardian power from mechanical science, will strengthen with grateful patronage the arm which brought them deliverance in the day of their distress. I have heard, on good authority, that no less than 12,000 *l.* sterling were expended by the enterprising partners of Mr. Roberts in bringing the self-actor to its present perfection. Had the inventor been less ably seconded, he might have shared the sad fate of many a man of genius, have seen the offspring of many toilsome days and sleepless nights carried off by piratical marauders, and disfigured in order to make it pass for their own.

Roberts's device of 1825 required a good deal of improvement, covered by another patent in 1830 (no. 5949, 1 July 1830), before it became commercially successful, but during the 1830s and 1840s the use of the self-acting mule spread rapidly, and the skilled mule spinners rapidly became redundant. As early as December 1834 Sharp, Roberts & Co's patent mules, containing between 300,000 and 400,000 spindles, had been established in more than 60 mills.[15] The patent of 1825 was extended for seven years, i.e. until 1846, in 1839. John Sharp stated on 18 July 1842 that his firm had not been sufficiently remunerated for its development of the self-acting mule: 'It was full seven years before it was introduced into the trade,' i.e. 1832.[16]

The fertility of British inventors and the rapid fortunes being made in the textile and engineering trades of Britain during the post-war period naturally attracted attention at a time when the laws relating to the export of machinery and the emigration of skilled artisans from Britain were being relaxed. It is important to remember that there had never been a ban on exports of steam engines. The famous Select Committee of the House of Commons on Artizans and Machinery of 1824 issued six reports, and in 1825 the subject was reopened by the Select Committee on the export of tools and machinery, all controls on the emigration of skilled artisans having been abolished in the meantime. However, under the Customs Regulation Act of 1825, 6 Geo.IV, cap. 107., certain classes of tools and machines might be freely exported, but there were schedules of prohibited tools and machines in the Act, Section 99 ('A table of prohibitions and restrictions outwards'), and the Board of Trade continued to have the power to issue licences for export.[17] There was also the problem for the Customs service of deciding what a machine was for, or what the parts of a machine were. John Martineau, the London engineer, told the Committee of 1824 that customs officers could not easily identify a scientifically dismounted machine and Alexander Galloway, another London engineer, stated:

There is no place to which our custom-house officers have been so rigid as in their examination of goods [consigned] to France and North America[18] ... as to other countries, as far as my experience extends, I must do all the superior officers of the Customs the justice to say, that the utmost liberality has been invariably exercised by them, and it was only in cases where it was impossible to shut their eyes, that they have even ventured to keep them open.[19]

It is important to remember that drawings of all machines, new and old, could easily be exported in spite of the ban which existed on the export of working drawings of some machines. The new material on Sharp, Roberts & Co. must be considered against this background. It consists of a series of letters written in 1826 and 1827 on behalf of Sharp, Roberts & Co. (mainly by Robert Chapman Sharp, but with one from Thomas Sharp junior) and by Rothwell, Hick & Rothwell of the Union Ironworks, Bolton, to André Koechlin et Cie of Mulhouse (Haut

Rhin), France. Unfortunately the other side of the correspondence has been lost. I must here express my gratitude to the Société Alsacienne de Constructions Mécaniques of Mulhouse, and to M. André Brandt of Mulhouse for permission to copy the correspondence and also for help and hospitality at Mulhouse. André Koechlin (1789–1875) had decided early in 1826, together with his associates Mathias Thierry (1782–1844) and Henri Bock (1797–1879), to build a large textile engineering works at Mulhouse which would rival those of the Northern textile districts of England. (Plate II).They turned to Sharp, Roberts & Co. for guidance, and in their quest they were helped by the fact that Bock was the London agent of the Alsatian firm of Dolfus-Mieg et Cie.

The earliest document in the new material is a letter from Thomas Sharp, jun., of Birch Cottage, Rusholme, near Manchester, dated Sunday 11 June 1826, to Henri Bock, who at that moment was in London with Richard Roberts. In fact it looks as though Bock and Roberts had just left Manchester. From a letter written on the following day (12 June 1826) by R.C. Sharp on behalf of Sharp, Roberts & Co. to André Koechlin et Cie, it is clear that Koechlin was planning to manufacture mules, carding engines and looms, and the letter from Manchester warned them to prepare a proper supply of timber as early as possible, 'of the sorts which will be required for the machinery you contemplate making, with a view to its being properly seasoned, which is a matter of the greatest importance … we … should rather propose that timber should be prepared for 200 looms, and for 20 (instead of 10) dressing machines, and 10 (instead of 2) warping machines.'

By July Koechlin's plans had expanded further and he now wished to purchase 'a series of lace machines constituting in general what is termed "one preparation",' which would have cost £2,223. It is not clear whether these were to be used for actual production or as models for copying, but this plan was eventually given up. The same letter[20] disclosed that Sharp, Roberts & Co.'s thoughts had been moving in the same direction during the great trade boom of 1824–5:

Having for some time been strongly urged to undertake the making of lace machinery, in the spring of last year [1825] we commenced arrangements for that purpose, and were endeavouring to procure specimens of the best machines. The fire at our works, however, and the very depressed state of the trade in the Autumn, induced us to relinquish the idea of going into the business until some more favourable opportunity presented itself. We shall now make more enquiry, and give the idea further consideration … as the trade is flat, the deliveries would be prompt. The greatest difficulty seems to be, to meet with a man who makes the best principle of machines for sale.

The letter then went back to the subject of the proposed 'mechanical establishment at Mulhouse': Koechlin was urged to get the best Danzig timber for the lathe frames and reminded that Sharp, Roberts and Co. had now almost completed work for him to the value of between £1,000 and £1,200: 'as money here is becoming daily more and more valuable, we shall feel obliged if you will arrange for us to value [i.e. draw on you] for £1,000 on account.'

A list of the tools and other equipment completed by mid-July gives some idea of the variety of the order and a fortnight later, 24 July 1826, Sharp, Roberts and Co. were able to report: 'The plans of the blowing machine and pit, and of the roof of the foundry will be forwarded on 31st inst.,'[21] and the letter added: 'Mr. Roberts still contemplates visiting France towards the end of next month, and will be glad to find the buildings in a forward state.'

It has been mentioned before that no ban could be enforced on the export of drawings of machines. In addition the French Customs regulations laid it down that all imported machines should be accompanied by drawings. Sharp, Roberts and Co. expressed some surprise on hearing this (August 1826), but agreed to comply: 'We have, however, prepared drawings of every thing forwarded to Melley and Schmid.'[22] Even so, difficulties at Le Havre, the French port of entry, did occur in November and had to be smoothed out by the representations of Mathias Thierry in Paris. Sharp, Roberts and Co. wrote:

... we hope that the good sense, and a proper regard for national benefit, on the part of the French Government, will render so much trouble unnecessary ... In respect of the patterns, which may fairly be considered as parts of machines, there should be a clear understanding as to whether they can be admitted openly into France, or whether they must be smuggled. From hence [i.e. from Liverpool], of necessity the latter plan must be adopted.[23]

At this time Sharp, Roberts & Co. did not make steam engines, and that part of the equipment was to be furnished by the Union Foundry of Rothwell, Hick and Rothwell at Bolton.[24] The managing partner and driving force in this firm at the time was Benjamin Hick senior (1790–1842), then a very active man of just over thirty-six years of age, who was to leave the firm in 1832 or 1833 to establish the Soho Foundry, also in Bolton, later known as Hick, Hargreaves & Co. Ltd. On 10 August Sharp, Roberts & Co. reported to Koechlin: 'We saw Mr [Benjamin] Hick ... on Tuesday last and he says the engine will be ready in three or not exceeding four weeks.'

They were able to get 5 per cent. discount off the prices Koechlin would have to pay for the engine, after some hard bargaining with Hick. The letter continued:

An annoying circumstance has occurred, in Mr. Roberts having been subpoenaed to the Assizes at Lancaster, to give evidence about the machinery broken in the late riots.

– a reference to the smashing of power looms in East Lancashire during 1826. This again delayed matters, for on his return from the Assizes on 16 August Roberts 'was a good deal indisposed, not having quite recovered when he was summoned to attend.'[25]

Problems of shipment now came to the fore. By 10 August much of the material was being packed into 10 or 11 cases 'excepting the slide lathe, the screw of which Mr. Roberts found to be defective, and ordered another to be cut, which will be done in three or four days ... The blowing machine, cutting engine, large lathe, planing and spindle making machines and several others, are in progress; and as we shall have *one* large planing machine on Monday next, we shall be able to give great despatch.'[26] Messrs. Melley and Schmid of Liverpool were to ship the goods, and Mr. Melley 'appeared very intelligent' to Sharp, Roberts & Co.[27] when he came over from Liverpool to make final arrangements. On 16 August the 12 packing cases were shipped down the River Irwell in the charge of the Old Quay Company, together with two foundry cupolas which were sent loose: 'The whole of the bright parts have been well smeared with rot tallow, and wrapped up in smeared paper.'[28]

Koechlin's new enterprise was legally formed in August 1826 and his ambitions appear to have increased. He made enquiries about more textile machinery and received the following reply:

Our present prices of power looms, warping and dressing machines ... we annex ... If an order is likely to be given, we shall be glad to receive it, and we pledge ourselves to send the most approved machines [constructed] upon the experience of the principal manufacturers and of ourselves, during three or four years.[29]

In early September 1826 Sharp, Roberts and Co. were visited by Henri Bock who left most detailed instructions about shipment. Once the steam engine had been sent all further articles were to be shipped from Liverpool by Messrs. H. Castellain, Schaezler & Co.[30] but 'any doubtful or confidential' shipments were to be made through Charles Lewis Bahr of 6 and 7 Chapel Walks, Pool Lane, Liverpool[31] who, not to put too fine a point on it, was an expert in smuggling. Richard Roberts accompanied Bock on the latter's return to France in September 1826 and reported from Paris in early October on his way back to England 'that everything is going on extremely well in respect of the new establishment at Mulhouse'. Roberts was expected back in Manchester on 13 October and R.C. Sharp commented: 'We do not know what interest it may excite in your country, but we can assure you, that *here*, it is much talked of, and not much relished.'[32] This may not have been Roberts's first visit to France, but it is the first of three separate visits mentioned in the letters: he did not therefore spend two years in France, as is sometimes stated. Meanwhile Sharp, Roberts & Co.'s efforts had been 'increasingly devoted to expediting the various machines, and preparing patterns'.[33]

Koechlin now (October 1826) wanted two new steam engines for collieries in France; the original engine ordered had meanwhile been loaded at Liverpool on the French brig *Susannah*. Unfortunately the customs authorities most vexatiously detained the *Susannah* for two or three weeks, 'in consequence of malicious information', because one of the patent reed machines was found on board, and Thomas Sharp had to make two journeys to London before the cargo was finally allowed to sail on 15 November.[34] As Sharp, Roberts & Co. wrote to Koechlin: 'Some days ago Mr. Bahr called upon us, and we had a good deal of conversation respecting the shipping of such machines or other articles as are at present prohibited.'

Koechlin and Sharp, Roberts & Co. had to face the problem of training someone to go out more or less permanently in order to supervise the erection of the machinery in France, and to take with him a team of skilled workers. The man chosen was, in Henri Bock's words, 'a real treasure', a Mr. Golling, who arrived at Sharp, Roberts & Co.'s works at the end of June 1826. One would like to know more about him. He had previously operated a foundry somewhere in the vicinity of Manchester and was described to R.C. Sharp by 'one of our first-rate spinners' as 'the most clever spinning machine maker in the country'.[35] By mid-July Golling was busy, with the help of a workman, in 'proceeding with drawings and patterns for carding engines'.[36] By the end of the month Golling, with his assistants, was 'going on very well', and had been over to some works in Derbyshire 'about a plan of an improved blowing machine'.[37]

Mr Golling is very assiduous, and appears to understand the business. Mr. Roberts and he frequently confer about the form, etc. of patterns, from which, and the opportunity he has of seeing the general character of ours, we venture to think he will ... prove valuable to the concern.[38]

Golling gradually collected a team of artisans to take out to France, who were in training for various departments in the new works and their arrival in France was to be planned as far as possible to coincide with the arrival of the mill gearing at Mulhouse.[39]

We should not wish that any workmen should go over to Mulhouse, until there is employment for them, as we are convinced their moral characters would be much impaired by it. Our nation cannot encounter idleness at home with impunity, much less abroad, where novelty, cheap living, and above all, cheap brandy, might have too many charms for them.[40]

During November 1826 the export of this gearing gave rise to some trepidation:

In respect of the mill geering by sending it all at once, with a declaration or certificate that it belongs to the steam engine, already sent but could not be prepared in time, we hope the admission of it will be granted.[41]

We are pleased to hear that our ideas of the mill geering being permitted as part of the steam engine are likely to be realized and we will be careful that it is so particularized when shipped from Liverpool.[42]

Meanwhile Sharp, Roberts & Co. had secured an improved blowing machine for Koechlin, but it is not absolutely clear whether it was a second blowing engine for the foundry at Mulhouse or a new cotton blowing machine, but in any case, Sharp, Roberts & Co. were very pleased with it: '... we may with safety declare it is the most complete and beautiful piece of workmanship which we ever saw of the same description.'[43] Later the Manchester engineers wrote about its 'entire success' in France and regretted not having taken out a British patent for it.[44]

In addition Sharp, Roberts & Co. reported early in the New Year (4 January 1827):

Messrs Castellain & Co. having arranged to ship by the *Jeune Adèle* to the extent of 20 tons, we have this day forwarded about 7 tons weight, and on Saturday and Monday shall make up the quantity to be in time for that vessel.[45] We shall observe the necessary precautions in respect of the drawings on the lot last advised of.

The letter went on:

We have purchased for you a bobbin and fly frame upon the very best construction after a difficult negotiation for two to three months; but that, with the patterns of spinning and weaving machines, will have to be entrusted to Mr. B[ahr], at such time as we think will be most advantageous.[46]

This *Jeune Adèle* and its cargo were later in the month described in the following terms: 'we are assured that no vessel ever left this country with a superior lot of machinery.'[47] By this time Golling had very nearly completed all the patterns which it was thought advisable for him to make in England '... and we have', wrote Sharp, Roberts & Co. 'made a liberal supply of loom patterns. These with the bobbin frame, and other matters, we shall take a suitable opportunity of forwarding through Mr. B[ahr].'

Sometimes Koechlin overreached himself in his desire to secure the best English machinery. He sent Sharp, Roberts & Co. a 'neat sketch' of a bobbin and fly frame, which on inspection in Manchester turned out to be

one which has been in use here for ten or twelve years, and upon which several improvements have been made, and especially in course of last year, for which a patent was taken out by Mr. Henry Houldsworth.[48] The opinion of its value [i.e. of Houldsworth's improved model] is such, that numerous orders have been given by parties, who had machines upon the former principle. We think it therefore very desirable, that you should possess [? such] a machine, the more so because we know that Messrs. Risler Frères and Dixon[49] have made great exertions, not only to procure a machine, but also to engage a workman, who had been employed in making similar machines, in either of which attempts we do not learn that they have yet succeeded.[50]

Risler Frères and Job Dixon of Cernay (Sennheim) in Alsace were, of course, keen rivals of the Koechlins in the cotton trade and in the textile engineering business.

By January 1827 Sharp, Roberts & Co. felt justified in despatching an engineer (not Golling) from Manchester, *via* Paris, to Mulhouse, presumably to erect and start the steam engine: 'His employers give him an excellent character for steadiness and talent, having had proofs of both, on a similar occasion to that of his present mission.'[51]

Koechlin showed great concern about getting possession of the drawings of the machinery in the *Jeune Adèle*'s cargo, but had to be told that, from the 'very great particularity now observed by the Customs House officers in Liverpool', they had to be sent to Messrs. Castellain and Schaezler to produce if required. Then a disaster occurred:

On Wednesday evening last, we received a letter from Messrs. Castellain, Schaezler & Co. stating that the *Jeune Adèle* had been on the point of sailing [from Liverpool], but was stopped, in consequence of information having been given at the Surveyor's office, that power looms were contained in some of the packages. Mr. [Thomas] Sharp therefore went down to Liverpool on Thursday morning, and ... had an interview with the Collector, and afterwards with the Surveyor, when it proved, that the information did not refer to any packages sent by us, but by some other houses, and shipped under the agency of Mr. Bahr.[52]

Nevertheless in spite of the assurances of the Collector and Surveyor that no suspicion attached to Sharp, Roberts & Co.'s cases 'nearly the whole of them have been opened, and exposed to wet ... We have now prepared a remonstrating memorial to the Privy Council on the subject, which we purpose transmitting on Mr. Sharp's return [from Liverpool]'[53]

Naturally this incident at Liverpool led to general consternation:

We begin to fear some difficulty in getting over any of the prohibited articles, as Mr. Bahr seems to be much alarmed at the increased vigilance of the Custom House officers; on which point strong orders have been issued by Government to all the ports. At any rate, no attempt must be made for some weeks.[54]

Mr. Bahr later (29 March 1827) 'expressed his full determination to be quiescent for six or eight weeks after the last adventure'.

When Thomas Sharp interviewed the Collector and Surveyor at Liverpool on 5 February he was told that owing to orders received from the Board of Customs in London 'no other course was left to them, but to examine a certain part of the cases'. They had, however, 'found everything so correct and satisfactory' that the whole of the machinery was at liberty, and the *Jeune Adèle* could be released to proceed on her voyage.[55] It is interesting to note that the *Jeune Adèle* then took on an extra cargo, three cases of files from Peter Stubs & Co. of Warrington. The same letter gives a list of tools sent: 'cutting engine, screw engine, bolt screwing machine, 6ft. slide lathe, squaring, fluting and punching engines for rollers, and cast iron patterns for spinning and weaving machines' (Plate I (b)).

The vessel reached Le Havre during March.[56] Sharp, Roberts & Co. experienced great difficulty at this point in securing payment from Koechlin and complained as follows:

... at your earnest entreaty we have for months held back the completion of machines for other connexions, to the amount of from £3,000 to £4,000 in respect of which we have long been in advance of cash, and should otherwise long ago have received the balance of payment.[57]

The departure of Richard Roberts, Golling and their team of workmen was then unavoidably delayed because Roberts fell seriously ill in the middle of February 1827. This illness prevented him from devoting any attention to business for three weeks and even by the end of March, although he was considerably recovered, his doctors would not allow him 'to undergo any fatigue'. Complete recovery would take another three or four weeks. This, and other evidence of his illnesses in 1826 and 1847–48, suggests that, as in the case of James Watt, much of his work was hampered by ill-health, and that he almost certainly overworked himself.

In preparation for the first of his two expeditions to France made in 1827 Roberts had visited 'three or four spinning and weaving mills, in order to inform himself of the best arrangements for the various departments', and by 15 May Golling and his family had arrived safely in Mulhouse, escorted from Manchester by Henri Bock. From the *Arbeiterbuch* in Mulhouse we know that Golling's son Samuel stayed from 15 May 1827 to 20 May 1829. He had worked on account of A. Koechlin et Cie for 28 weeks before going to Mulhouse. Richard Roberts himself left Manchester later, probably on 28 or 29 May, accompanied by M. Thierry, jun. Koechlin by this time was exceedingly disturbed by the non-arrival of Roberts and wrote an angry letter to Sharp, Roberts & Co. on 28 May, to which Sharp, Roberts & Co. replied very coldly[58] and after some delay on 27 June:

We regret to observe that it [Koechlin's angry letter of 28 May] was written under the influence of a feeling or opinion that by the protracted departure of Mr. Roberts, we manifested an indifference to your interests as well as to our own.

R.C. Sharp recommended Koechlin to question M. Mathias Thierry as to the true facts:

... we can confidently and truly declare, that our exertions in the execution of your orders, and the attention we have devoted to the business in various ways has proved injurious to *our interests here* to a degree very far exceeding any benefit we have *hitherto* received; and which can only be repaid to us by the success of your concern.[59]

Once he had got Roberts at Mulhouse, Koechlin wanted to keep him there until the 'whole of the mill geering be erected, and all the machinery be put to start'. R.C. Sharp replied that such an idea was never contemplated, 'either in our contract or any subsequent arrangement'. He continued:

When the main points of the mill geering, and the situation of the various machines are determined, the fitting up of the works can, or ought to, proceed with all due speed, under the direction of Mr. Thierry and Mr. Golling, with the knowledge which Mr. Ogden[60] possesses of the use and situation of the whole; when that is done, a second visit from Mr. Roberts would be consistent and available. For the purposes above referred to, we consider his staying one clear month will be ample; but at any rate his stay should not, and indeed must not, be prolonged above five weeks, which will make his absence from our concern two months. Before the expiration of that time, three or four machines of the highest present and future importance, will be certainly at a stand for want of his personal instruction. A few weeks here [in Manchester] will enable him to put them into a train for completion, and then he would be at liberty to go over again to Mulhouse and complete arrangements for a proper commencement.[61]

In a letter to Koechlin from his hotel in Paris on 21 April 1827 Thomas Sharp had commented on the 'very great difficulties [which] have lately presented themselves, in respect of exporting machinery, and most specially of those sorts requiring *secrecy* and *management*'; and towards the end of June Sharp, Roberts & Co. had to report another disaster:

On the 8th inst. those gentlemen [Messrs. Castellain and Schaezler of Liverpool] advised us of the seizure of the [ten] cases [containing the latest machines] by the Custom House officers at Liverpool, who refused to state to which, or what part of the machinery suspicion attached.

In consequence, on the 10th inst. we transmitted a strong memorial to the Lords of the Privy Council, complaining of the proceedings, contending that the machinery is not of any prohibited class, and praying for the immediate release of the machinery.

After some further delay, the Customs officers agreed to release the seized goods on payment of two guineas, but stated that they might not be exported. Sharp, Roberts & Co. protested and proposed to send a further memorial to the Privy Council 'contending for the right to export'.[62] The cases themselves seem to have contained a punching engine, £400 worth of miscellaneous patterns, a cutting engine, a bolt screwing machine, a squaring machine, a fluting engine and 'driving apparatus'.[63]

What eventually became of this consignment is nowhere explicitly stated in the correspondence, although Thomas Sharp, after paying the two guineas, told the Customs officers rather cryptically at Liverpool that 'such proceedings would be adopted in the business as might appear desirable', and then:

> Mr. S. saw Mr. B[ahr] twice in Liverpool – the first time in great alarm about the fate of a boat with some cases on board – the second time relieved, from having just learnt that all was right. Mr. S. urged him to expedite the whole to the utmost of his power.[64]

Then in August 1827 the Prime Minister died, and R.C. Sharp reported:

> Nothing has yet been decided respecting the seized machinery as to exportation, owing to the disarrangements and confusion in all Government departments consequent on the illness and death of Mr. Canning. Mr. Huskisson's absence is also a drawback in the business, as he principally took cognizance of, and decided upon all applications of that nature.

Later in the same letter, which was begun on 18 August and completed on the 20th, came the welcome tidings that 'the whole of the articles entrusted to Mr. B[ahr] have been forwarded. That he has had much difficulty to contend with owing to the increased vigilance of the Custom House officers and the activities of agents otherwise appointed to watch after any packages suspected of containing machinery.'[65]

Weeks passed, and early in September Thomas Sharp was informed on another visit to the Custom House at Liverpool that the Privy Council had issued instructions to 'detain all machines of the classes of lathes, drills, fluting engines, screw or cutting engines, etc.' He was also shown in the Custom House 'a slide lathe, planing machine, and vertical drill, which we had sold to the Polish Government seven months ago, which had been seized under the last orders',[66] and intended to seek an interview with Charles Grant, President of the Board of Trade, in London, if no reply was received soon. If, however, the Government persevered in prohibiting export in the regular way, 'as the machines are of such indispensable necessity and importance, we think the only plan will be, to submit to the charge of forwarding them through Mr. B[ahr]; if indeed the packages are not too bulky for him.' In any case essential loom parts could be sent via Mr. Bahr immediately if necessary.

Richard Roberts arrived home in Manchester 'in good health, which the journey seems to have improved', probably in late July. Roberts had had the benefit, before his departure from Mulhouse, of consultation with Benjamin Hick, who had come out independently on the business of supplying a 20 h.p. steam engine. He reported that the 10 h.p. colliery engine supplied from Bolton had already been set to work, and the archives at Mulhouse contain a number of letters and other documents from Rothwell, Hick & Rothwell of Bolton, including a good autograph of Hick himself written in Mulhouse on 14 July 1827.

The question now arose of sending out a further team of men – John Leatherbarrow, a moulder,- another man, William Bower, 'who has worked with Leatherbarrow – he is well reported of, as a good blast tenter, and as full as steady as men of that class are', and a second moulder, a young man named John Varley.[67] R.C. Sharp noted: 'We have a good deal of difficulty in arranging their wages; as in consequence of the recent increase of business in the foundry trade, wages have much improved.'[68]

In view of 'a reduction of the coach fares to London', R.C. Sharp had calculated 'that £40 sterling will be sufficient to pay the whole of the expenses including passeports [sic]'; the men were strongly cautioned 'on the absolute necessity of observing steady conduct'. In the event they reached Mulhouse after spending only £32 14s. between them as a result of their 'prudent conduct' on the road.[69] At the same time Sharp, Roberts & Co. were training a crank turner for Koechlin, had a fitter-up of looms 'in view but not yet engaged', and a pattern maker 'ready if wanted', but could not find a grinder or a fitter-up of mules. Koechlin wanted a green-sand moulder who understood dry sand and loam moulding as well, but Sharp, Roberts & Co. thought that a mere journeyman 'clever in the three branches' would not easily be met with as in Britain 'the men who attempt all [classes of work], are often "good at none".'

Richard Roberts's third visit to France was now being arranged, but had to be delayed to await the outcome of Thomas Sharp's visit to London concerning the release of the machines for export. In the meantime Roberts had been very busy attending to Koechlin's interests by visiting the Union Foundry at Bolton, when another letter dated 21 September arrived from Mulhouse accusing Sharp, Roberts & Co. of neglecting the interests of their French customers. Robert C. Sharp returned a forthright answer:

> We further can state, with èqual candour, that could we have foreseen the claims upon our time and attention, and the sacrifice of our interests here, which our arrangements with you have caused ... we should not have been induced to enter into the existing arrangement.[70]

Worse followed: '... we yesterday received a letter,' wrote R.C. Sharp on 16/18 Oct. 1827, 'directed by the Lords of the Privy Council, containing a peremptory refusal to our prayer for permission to export your machinery. ...'

Sharp, Roberts & Co.'s mortification was increased, R.C. Sharp told Koechlin,

... by the accompanying certainty that the Lords of the Council have been influenced in their decision, from being informed, that the machinery is intended for a mechanical concern, establishing in France, either on our own account, or in which we are partners. This is one of a train of evils, which we have apprehended would result, from the course you have unfortunately pursued, of publicly declaring that we are partners in your concern.

Sharp, Roberts & Co. had wished for secrecy not publicity, 'until at least your works were matured', for two reasons. First, 'if it became known, that we had any connexion with your concern, the jealousy of the manufacturers of this country, would lead them to abstain from giving us their orders for machinery', and secondly, Koechlin's source of early information of improvements in machinery would dry up because Sharp, Roberts & Co. would be looked upon with suspicion 'and ... be denied access to those establishments [in England],which under other circumstances had been freely granted'.

Unfortunately it had been an active topic of conversation in the Manchester area for several months past that Sharp, Roberts & Co. were establishing 'a mechanical concern at Mulhausen' and very extensive orders were consequently withheld from the firm. In particular, in the second week in October an order for 300 or 400 looms had been lost for that reason:

We know also, that not only from the Chamber of Commerce in this town, but from various other sources, such information has been communicated to Government, and an active correspondence has been kept up. Consequently our movements have been strictly watched, every lot of machinery has been traced, and the result of the whole has been the peremptory decision of the Government now announced.

Sharp, Roberts & Co. had been assured that their exports of machinery would not have been interfered with if their name had not been linked to a particular firm on the Continent, and the machinery treated 'merely as an article sold to indifferent parties'.

In spite of this outburst, however, preparations went ahead for Roberts's French visit 'about the time of the departure of such patterns as we are about to forward through Mr B[ahr], or their arrival at Le Havre'. These were to contain pattern wheels for velveteen looms, a cutting engine and various other machines. R.C. Sharp stated: 'Not to possess them will be a most serious drawback upon the progress of your business as some of them are of a class entirely new to the Continent.'[71] Towards the end of October Roberts became 'so unwell as to be confined to the house', and there were further complaints about lack of remittances from Mulhouse: 'Even if there was any profit resulting to us from the transaction we should have expected a continuance of your former punctuality.' In the end Henri Bock had to travel up from London to smooth things over.[72]

By Christmas things looked somewhat better, although the necessity of completing two machine tools which were extremely important for Sharp, Roberts & Co.'s production programme for 1828, and involved orders worth many thousands of pounds, meant a further postponement of Roberts's departure. Roberts was working overtime on them, and in the case of one particular machine, R.C. Sharp wrote on Saturday 22 December: 'The men are to work tomorrow, Sunday and also on Tuesday, Christmas Day,' by which time it would be finished.[73]

The news about the prohibited cases of machinery was good. Some were already on their way 'at which we rejoice, as well as in the (almost) certainty, that the two important cases will also speedily be shipped'.[74]

It is almost certain, too, that Richard Roberts departed for Mulhouse on the evening of Boxing Day, 1827 'without stay in London', his mind set at rest by the completion of the machines referred to, in order, as R.C. Sharp pointedly wrote to Koechlin on Christmas Day, 'that he may be able to give the full and unencumbered force of his talents to the completion of your works'.[75]

At this point, rather tantalisingly, the file of correspondence ends. Roberts, it would seem, did go to Alsace, for arrangements had been made for him to pick up Mrs. Leatherbarrow in London. That lady wished to join her husband in Alsace (she had been sent on in advance in charge of the guard of the Manchester–London coach, and deposited at the Swan with Two Necks in Lad Lane in the City, 'as she is not accustomed to travel'). We do not know how long this visit lasted, but the great mechanical establishment at Mulhouse began production in May 1828, and Dr. Andrew Ure wrote in 1836:

Towards the end of the year 1829, M. Emile Dolfus, as chairman of their committee of mechanics, made to the Société Industrielle of Mulhausen an interesting report, replete with new and valuable experimental facts, upon the different power looms then employed in the cotton factories of Alsace. This report was published in the bulletin of the society for the year 1830, accompanied by several plates representing the ingenious power-looms of M. Josué Heilmann, M. Jourdain, MM. Risler and Dixon, and finally that of Messrs. Sharp and Roberts, as constructed in the great workshops of MM. André Koechlin and Company at Mulhausen.[76]

APPENDIX I

The reaction of the Manchester textile interests to the co-operation between Sharp, Roberts & Co. and André Koechlin et Cie is to some extent reflected in the memorial addressed by the Board of Directors of the Manchester Chamber of Commerce and Manufactures to the Lords Commissioners of the Treasury in November 1826.[77]
There was a clash of interest between the exporters of cotton cloth and yarns on the one hand, and the textile engineers on the other. The Manchester memorialists hoped that the free export of machinery would not be allowed, although they admitted

> to the full extent, the principles of free trade, [and] they would support no exclusive monopolies, either of raw produce or manufactures; they would sustain no unprofitable trade by bounties or prohibiting duties, they would draw their supplies from the cheapest and best sources, but nevertheless they would not indiscriminately export the machinery employed in our staple manufactures, to enable other nations to undersell us in foreign markets.

The memorial went on, pointing out: 'That such competition is no chimera; it has been felt in various markets, from the manufacturers of France, Switzerland, Saxony and the United States of America. The race is begun, and we would not wantonly throw away any advantages.'

> ... the machinery employed in our manufactures cannot be classed, either with raw produce or manufactured goods. It has peculiar properties and ought to be treated as an exception to the general rule, for the following reasons:

> Improvements in Machinery are effected by slow degrees and at great cost; and it is generally long before the inventors are reimbursed for the financial expense bestowed on making experiments. For every attempt that succeeds, there are a thousand failures; and when after many trials and unsuccessful efforts, a real improvement has at length been accomplished, if it is to be exported for the use of our competitors abroad, we shall give them advantages which we do not ourselves enjoy; the expence will be all our own, and they will partake equally with us in the advantage. It may also be stated, that the foreign manufacturer would possess superior advantages in regard to all patent inventions, which cannot be made use of in this Country, but with the consent of the Patentee.

> As an object of national commerce, the exportation of the finer and more valuable Machinery cannot be considered of importance – it cannot be of large amount, nor of long continuance. One complete Machine furnishes a guide for the construction of others. The power to use a Machine to advantage, implies and requires the power to keep it in repair, but as high a degree of mechanical skill is necessary for repairing, as for making anew – practice will give manual dexterity – subdivision of labour will attend upon the encrease of manufactories, and the greater the extent to which the exportation of Machinery is at first carried, the more certainly and speedily will that exportation cease.

... notwithstanding the present prohibitory law, Orders in Council are granted for the export of large quantities of printing machines, lathes, and other utensils essential to our staple manufactures ... your memorialists know as an undoubted fact that under cover of such Orders in Council, machinery of a very different description ... is fraudulently and surreptitiously shipped for exportation to foreign countries.[78]

Professor Redford concluded in 1934 that the persistent but illogical efforts of the Manchester merchant to maintain these export restrictions 'may most charitably be explained as arising from an irrational reluctance to surrender the advantages which British industrialists had gained by their own ingenuity and enterprise, at a time when the British agricultural interest was still sheltering behind the Corn Laws'.[79]

APPENDIX II

The following extracts throw interesting light on the development of Messrs Sharp and Roberts' business in the 1830s and early 1840s. The German traveller Friedrich von Raumer visited the works in 1835 and wrote from Manchester on 28 August of that year as follows:

I saw here the very extensive manufactory of machinery of Messrs Sharp and Roberts, where I had everything explained to me by a young country-man of mine; ...

The English workmen (I do not speak of the children) receive in proportion higher wages, and live better than those in Germany. In the manufactory of Messrs Sharp and Roberts, for instance, the average weekly wages is about thirty shillings, and the principal necessaries of life, food, clothing, and fuel, are now no dearer here than with us. The breakfast of the workmen consisted, as I saw, of the finest wheat bread, cheese of the best quality, and a considerable portion of ale or porter. Some save part of their wages, but the greater part spend all they get; and thus, considering the very great numbers of workmen, there arises, in case of a falling off of trade, much greater danger for England than for Germany. But, at the present moment, the market in England is so extended, that nothing is to be feared.

A very absurd remnant of the old system is the prohibition to export certain kinds of machinery. England would outstrip all other nations in this species of manufacture; whereas now no secret can be kept beyond a few years, and then other countries supply themselves. It is also very erroneous to imagine that the successful progress of manufactures depends only on the possession of certain machines.[80]

· Von Raumer made a second visit in 1841 and wrote from Birmingham on 21 August:

Early yesterday morning, we went to the manufactory of machinery of Messrs Sharp and Roberts [at Manchester], which I saw some years ago, but which has since much increased, both in extent and in the power of the machines. Thus a new machine cut in two, iron plates five inches broad and five-quarters thick, as if they had been as soft as butter. The manufacture of steam-engines affords by far the most employment: we saw many that

PLATE I

Power loom (from E. Baines, *History of the Cotton Manufacture in Great Britain*, 1835). Machine made by Sharp, Roberts & Co

Gear-cutting engine supplied to André Koechlin et Cie, 1826 (courtesy, Soc. Alsacienne de Constr. Méchaniques, Mulhouse). Machine made by Sharp, Roberts & Co

PLATE II

André Koechlin & Co.'s factory at Mulhouse: (top) 1835–40, (bottom) 1840–42

were to go to Germany, and one for Berlin had just been finished. In the end, it is an advantage to both parties that the exportation and importation of machines are no longer prohibited. The wages of a workman in Messrs Sharp's manufactory rise from eighteen shillings to £2 per week.[81]

NOTES

'New Light on Richard Roberts, Textile Engineer (1789–1864)' was a lecture read at the Science Museum, London on 6 November 1968 and is reprinted from the *Transactions of the Newcomen Society*, Vol.41, 1968–9, pp.27–44, by permission of the Council.

1. Ed. B. Woodcroft (1861), 63. There are no other patents of this kind from before 1810 to 1825.
2. *Trans*. XIII (1934), 24–7, 47.
3. Woodcroft (ed.), *Abridgements ... Weaving* (1861), 72.
4. Vol.II (ed. 1861), 228–43.
5. Ibid., 136–58.
6. Vol.II, 213 and 330.
7. Ibid., 213, 255, 260, 326.
8. C. Fischer, *Tagebücher*, 1951, ed. K. Schib, 264–7; W.O. Henderson, *J.C. Fischer and his Diary of Industrial England, 1814–51* (1966), 62, 76.
9. He may be identified as the James Hill, textile commission agent, living at 40, Ormond Street, Chorlton Row, noted on page 73 of the *Manchester and Salford Directory*, 1828.
10. *Manchester and Salford Directory* (1828), 134.
11. A. Ure, *The Cotton Manufacture of Great Britain*, II (ed. of 1861), 153–4.
12. Ure, *op. cit.*, 167.
13. *Op. cit.* 366–68.
14. Thomas Ashton, master cotton spinner of Hyde, is said to have been chairman of the deputation which waited upon Roberts.
15. Ure, *Cotton Manufacture*, II, 155.
16. *Anti-Bread Tax Circular*, III (94), 21 July 1842. Sharp added that he believed that it was owing to Lord Brougham that they got the patent extended in 1839.
17. A. Yoshioka, 'The problem of machine exportation at the time of the establishment of capitalism in England' in *Modernization and Industrialisation. Essays presented to Yoshitaka Komatsu*, Tokyo (1968), 188–211. I am grateful to my friend Dr. Y. Takei of Shinshu University, Japan, for a translation of this article. See also *A collection of the Public General Statutes passed in the Sixth Year of ... His Majesty King George the Fourth*, London (1825), 624–5.
18. An interesting confirmation of this statement is provided by the sad story of Luke Wagstaff, spindle maker, of Stalybridge, Cheshire, who also had in 1800 an office address at The Grapes, Oldham Street, Manchester:
    'On Monday, the 4th inst.,' says a Liverpool [news]paper of the 25th Oct. 1811, 'Mr. Miller, the Superintendent of police, took a man of the name of Wagstaff into custody, in the act of putting on board the ship *Mount Vernon*, bound to New York, twenty-three boxes containing about 140 gross of spindles used in the spinning of cotton. The prisoner has been proved to be a manufacturer of spindles and to have agreed with the captain of the *Mount Vernon* to take a passage to New York. He was examined before the Mayor and committed to take his trial at the next assizes.'
    Quoted in Thomas Midgley, *Samuel Crompton, 1753–1827* (1927), 22; see also Bancks's *Manchester and Salford Directory* (1800), 179.
19. *First Report from the Select Committee on Artizans and Machinery* (1824), 9 (*Martineau*), 20 (*Galloway*).
20. S.R. & Co., Manchester, to A.K. et Cie, Mulhouse, 10 July 1826.
21. In actual fact they were delayed by the illness of Roberts and an assistant. S.R. & Co. to A.K. et Cie, 31 July, 10 Aug. 1826.

22. To A.K. et Cie, 31 Aug. 1826.
23. S.R. & Co. to A.K. et Cie, 20 Nov. 1826.
24. The fullest account of the early history of this firm is to be found in the annotated account of Joshua Field's description of the Union Foundry (*Trans. Newcomen Society*, XIII, 29–33, 47–8). For the later history of the firm see E.L. Ahrons, 'Messrs Rothwell & Co., Bolton', *Engineer*, 129, 11 June 1920, 598–9.
25. S.R. & Co. to A.K. et Cie, 17 Aug. 1826.
26. S.R. & Co. to A.K. et Cie, 17 Aug. 1826.
27. S.R. & Co. to A.K. et Cie, 10 Aug. 1826.
28. S.R. & Co. to A.K. et Cie, 17 Aug. 1826.
29. From 18 to 20 looms could be driven by 1 h.p. and a 9/8 loom cost £10. 5s., a 7/8 loom £9. 15s., a 9/8 warping machine £15, and a 9/8 dressing machine £41 or £37, depending on whether it was a sweep or revolving motion.
30. Although this firm appears from the correspondence to have had an office or agent in Liverpool, it cannot be traced in the Liverpool directories of this period. In fact it was a firm of merchants with a City address, 3 Copthall Court, London (*The Post Office London directory for* 1823, 24th ed., 66). It seems to have been connected with the merchant bank of Frederick Huth & Co. (*Gore's Directory of Liverpool*, 1839).
31. Baines, *Lancashire*, I, 210, where his address is given as 31, Pool Lane. Since this paper was delivered Mr. Arthur Behrend has published *Portrait of a Family Firm: Bahr, Behrend & Co., 1793–1945*, (Liverpool, 1970), which gives some interesting details about Charles Louis Bahr (1786–1860), a Hanoverian, who joined the firm in 1814. He was sole partner from shortly after that date until 1835 when he took into partnership two other Liverpool shipbrokers, David Behrend and H.A. Stewart (p.9).
32. S.R. & Co. to A.K. et Cie, 19 Oct. 1826. See Appendix.
33. S.R. & Co. to A.K. et Cie, 11 Oct. 1826.
34. S.R. & Co. to A.K. et Cie, 9 and 20 Nov. 1826.
35. S.R. & Co. to A.K. et Cie, 7 Dec. 1826. This foundry, the exact site of which has not been discovered, was let to a Mr. William Vickers for a year from 24 June 1827 at £40 p.a. (S.R. & Co. to A.K. et Cie, 6 Aug. 1827).
36. S.R. & Co. to A.K. et Cie, 10 July 1826.
37. S.R. & Co. to A.K. et Cie, 24 July 1826.
38. S.R. & Co. to A.K. et Cie, 31 July 1826. This was in spite of the illness of a Mr. Rotch of Sharp, Roberts & Co.'s drawing department.
39. S.R. & Co. to A.K. et Cie, 9 Nov. 1826. An interesting commentary on public health is contained in the same letter: 'Our proceedings, as well as those of other establishments in town, have been much impeded for six to ten weeks, by numbers of our men having been attacked, from time to time, with a complaint (cholera morbus) which has been more prevalent than known for many years, and has in a number of cases proved fatal. Most of the men, however, are recovered, and at work again, but the unlooked for circumstance has thrown us back a fortnight at least.'
40. S.R. & Co. to A.K. et Cie, 7 Dec. 1826.
41. S.R. & Co. to A.K. et Cie, 27 Nov. 1826.
42. S.R. & Co. to A.K. et Cie, 30 Nov. 1826. See also 7 Dec. 1826.
43. S.R. & Co. to A.K. et Cie, 7 Dec. 1826.
44. S.R. & Co. to A.K. et Cie, 18, 20 Aug. 1827.
45. The total weight came to 31 or 32 tons.
46. S.R. & Co. to A.K. et Cie, 4 Jan. 1827.
47. S.R. & Co. to A.K. et Cie, 11 Jan. 1827.
48. Henry Houldsworth, jun., of Glasgow and Manchester, in January 1826 took out a patent for improvements in the bobbin and fly frame (Ure, *op. cit.*, II, 55).
49. For Risler Frères et Dixon, cotton spinners at Cernay (Sennheim) near Mulhouse, see A. Brandt, 'Apports anglais à l'industrialisation de l'Alsace au début du XIXe siècle', *Bulletin de la Société Industrielle de Mulhouse*, no.726, I (1967), 4–5.
50. S.R. & Co. to A.K. et Cie, 22 Jan. 1827.
51. S.R. & Co. to A.K. et Cie, 22 Jan. 1827.

52. S.R. & Co. to A.K. et Cie, 29 Jan. 1827.
53. S.R. & Co. to A.K. et Cie, 5 Feb. 1827.
54. S.R. & Co. to A.K. et Cie, 5 Feb. 1827. One effect of this incident may be noted. Sharp, Roberts & Co. set Mr. Golling to work: 'Mr. Golling has been assiduously engaged in making a set of patterns, (with what we hope will be considerable improvements), from the slubbing frame which we purchased, and which may probably prevent the necessity of sending the frame over' (S.R. & Co. to A.K. et Cie., 29 March 1827).
55. S.R. & Co. to A.K. et Cie., 8 Feb. 1827.
56. S.R. & Co. to A.K. et Cie, 29 March 1827.
57. S.R. & Co. to A.K. et Cie, 1 March 1827.
58. Part of the unpleasantness resulted from a visit by Thomas Sharp to France in April and May 1827 in order to sell the rights in the patent reed-making machinery (which had by then only 4 years to run, but had apparently been renewed in 1826 for a term of 14 years). Koechlin had been offered the machine under a choice of two methods of payment, but proved 'indifferent (one might almost say unwilling)', to include it in his arrangements at Mulhouse. (Thos. Sharp, Hotel Meurice, Rue St. Honoré, Paris to A.K. et Cie, 21 April 1827.) In the end the patent rights were sold, after some confusion, either to a firm in Ghent or possibly in Rouen (S.R. & Co. to A.K. et Cie, 23 May, 7 June 1827).
59. S.R. & Co. to A.K. et Cie, 7 June 1827.
60. 'We trust Ogden has conducted himself steadily, as where that is the case, he is a valuable hand' (S.R. & Co. to A.K. et Cie, 6 Aug. 1827).
61. S.R. & Co. to A.K. et Cie, 30 June 1827.
62. S.R. & Co. to A.K. et Cie, 30 June 1827.
63. R.C. Sharp to Henri Bock, Manchester, 28 April 1827.
64. S.R. & Co. to A.K. et Cie, 23 July 1827.
65. S.R. & Co. to A.K. et Cie, 18, 20 Aug. 1827.
66. S.R. & Co. to A.K. et Cie, 28 Sept., 1 Oct., 1827.
67. S.R. & Co. to A.K. et Cie, 23 July and 18/20 Aug. 1827.
68. S.R. & Co. to A.K. et Cie, 18/20 Aug. 1827.
69. This state of affairs continued throughout 1827: 'Indeed in any branch connected with mechanics, good and steady workmen have for several months been most difficult to meet with, either for home or abroad. The very great revival of all mechanical trades within the last six months, has caused work for good men to be very plentiful, and wages high, and consequently desirable men are unwilling to leave such a certainty, for the uncertainty of what they may experience abroad; and whatever sort we have spoken with, are very expectant as to wages' (S.R. & Co. to A.K. et Cie, 28 Sept., 1 Oct. 1827).
70. S.R. & Co. to A.K. et Cie, 28 Sept., 1 Oct. 1827.
71. S.R. & Co. to A.K. et Cie, 16/18 Oct. 1827.
72. S.R. & Co. to A.K. et Cie, 30 Oct. 1827.
73. S.R. & Co. to H. Bock, c/o Castellain, Schaezler, London, 22 Dec. 1827.
74. Ibid. These were sent either to Le Havre (Messrs Béranger) or to Calais (Messrs Riesenthal).
75. S.R. & Co., 25 Dec. 1827, to A.K. et Cie, c/o Javal Frères, Paris (redirected to Mulhouse).
76. Ure, *Cotton Manufacture*, II, 228.
77. A. Redford and others, *Manchester Merchants and Foreign Trade, 1794–1858* (1934), 132.
78. MS in possession of the author (copy of memorial of November 1826 sent to William Strutt of Derby by G.E. Aubrey, Secretary of the Manchester Chamber of Commerce, with covering letter dated 15 March 1827).
79. *Op. cit.*, p.133.
80. F. von Raumer, *England in 1835*, 3 (1836), 221.
81. F. von Raumer, *England in 1841*, II (1842), 301.

6

John Galloway (1804–1894), Engineer of Manchester and his 'Reminiscences'

During the latter half of the eighteenth century a steady stream of migration flowed from Scotland into England. Some of these migrants were sons of the manse; others were skilled craftsmen, while yet others were the sons of small farmers and landowners, anxious to make a career in the rapidly-expanding economy of South Britain. The best-known Scots migrants of this type are James Watt (1736–1819), the inventor of the rotary steam engine, and William Murdoch (or Murdock, as he began to spell it after he settled in England). Murdock (1754–1839) was, among other things, the inventor of gas lighting. Watt and Murdock settled in the Birmingham area, but many skilled Scots craftsmen and businessmen got no further south than Lancashire, e.g., the three Grant brothers of Ramsbottom, and John Kennedy (1769–1855) of Knocknalling, New Galloway, in Kirkcudbright, who became partner with McConnel in the famous Manchester cotton spinning firm of McConnel and Kennedy. Kennedy has left an entertaining description of how he came south in his fifteenth year and reached Chowbent in Lancashire on 8 February 1784 to be apprenticed there to two Scots, Messrs. Cannan and Smith, textile machinery makers. Cannan was himself from Kells parish in Kirkcudbright. Young John Kennedy was friendly with Adam and George Murray, again from Kirkcudbright, who also founded a famous Manchester cotton spinning firm. Adam Murray in fact negotiated the arrangements for Kennedy's apprenticeship to Cannan.[1] Chowbent was therefore a kind of information centre, employment exchange, and staging post for Scots on the way to work and sometimes fortune in England. Kennedy states: 'After dinner [on Sunday] all the Scotchmen of the establishment assembled at the Bear's Paw [in Chowbent], to hear the news from the native country.'[2]

Another of these Scots emigrants, William Galloway, a millwright by trade, was born at Coldstream on the north bank of the Tweed on 5 March 1768. It is not known whether he, too, came to the rapidly growing town of Manchester *via* Chowbent, but he is stated to have arrived in Manchester some time during 1790 at the age of 22 and to have set up in business as a millwright in Lombard Street, where he also had his private residence. Later he moved the business to 44 Great Bridgewater Street, 'the workshop being situated at the corner of Albion Street'.[3] In the 1890s a portion of the buildings of this Caledonian Foundry, as it came to be called, was said to be still in existence, but had been by then incorporated in Central Station.[4] In Scotland, William Galloway had a friend and fellow millwright, James Bowman (born 1769). Bowman had left Scotland to try his fortune in London about the same time as Galloway had arrived in Manchester. William Galloway wrote to him about 1806 'proposing that he should come to Manchester (where trade gave strong indications of its ultimate prosperity) and assist in the prosecution of the business. £200 was all the capital required.'[5]

Many years later John Galloway, William's son, wrote:

It was rather remarkable that nearly all the original millwrights in Manchester came from the neighbourhood of the Tweed ... All were Scotchmen – quiet, respectable and mostly middle aged, with experience, for in those days a man was not put to mind one machine year after year. He had to understand pretty nearly the whole process, from taking particulars and making patterns, to fixing the machinery in the mill.[6]

Actually the first *Manchester and Salford Directory* in which William Galloway's name appears is the issue of 1804 by Deans and Co., where he is described as a millwright of 37 Lombard Street, off Deansgate.[7] This was his private house. Not until the issue of Dean's *Manchester and Salford Directory* for 1808–9 was there any mention of the firm of Galloway and Bowman, millwrights of Great Bridgewater Street.[8] The exact date when the partnership was formed cannot therefore be ascertained. In Pigot's *Manchester and Salford Directory* of 1813 Galloway and Bowman were described as 'millwrights and engineers',[9] an indication that the firm had begun to manufacture and repair stationary steam engines. By 1817 the directory entry after Galloway and Bowman reads 'millwrights, engineers and ironfounders'.[10] It is obvious that the business expanded rapidly in the years immediately after the Peace of 1815, and in Pigot and Dean's *Manchester and Salford Directory* for 1819–20 the name of the third partner, William Glasgow, appears for the first time.[11] Like the other two, he came from the Tweed. Glasgow was a foundryman by trade and became the junior partner in order to supervise the new ironfounding section of the enterprise.[12] John Galloway later wrote: 'Up to this time we bought all our castings but now took a large plot of land in Bridgewater Street near Oxford Road'.[13] This brought the extent of the works up to Gaythorn Street. John Galloway states that Glasgow joined the firm 'about 1820' and had previously been manager for Messrs. Rothwell and Hick of

Bolton.[14] It is interesting to note that William Glasgow lived right on the job, for his private house was No.56 (later No.54) Great Bridgewater Street.[15]

At this period the principal activity of Galloway, Bowman and Glasgow was the manufacture of iron water-wheels and the gearing connected with them. John Galloway gives as examples work done by the firm about this time for the brown-paper mill of Smith and Inglis of Throstle Nest and the construction of a water-wheel for a cotton mill at Douglas Green, Agecroft.[16] Galloway, Bowman and Glasgow were already doing some foreign business: '... in 1820, we put up two corn mills at Lille, and a very large oil-cake mill in connection with which two French gentlemen came over.'[17]

The year in which George IV ascended the throne appears to have been particularly busy.[18]

Trade ran in cycles in those days as now, being busy at one time and then slack, – only in those days, as became our quieter life and the fewer means of communication, cycles were longer. 1820 was a busy time for us. In that year we made gearing and engines for some rice mills in Charleston in South Carolina for Lucas, Ewbank and Cordes, very wealthy people, owning about 1000 slaves. The two latter were sons-in-law of the former. Lucas, a fine old gentleman, came over with his son to have the latter with us for a couple of years training in engineering; he had a black slave as attendant, who went back with old Mr. Lucas. This was before steamers crossed the Atlantic. It took him 6 weeks. We were prepared in those days to undertake anything that was wanted, so we arranged to build a large threshing machine for them ... they insisted upon trying it. Evidently they were in advance of the times, as machine threshing afterwards became an accomplished fact. We did a lot of work for them of all sorts, in fact the sons-in-law went into Mexican silver mining, for which we made the machinery, mostly pumping, and sent men out to fix it. Mining in Mexico was then very popular.[19]

The John Lucas referred to was a pioneer of mechanisation in American agriculture and is mentioned in Professor Reynold M. Wik's recent work, *Steam Power on the American Farm*.[20] His unsuccessful attempt to thresh rice by steam took place in 1817. In the 1820s, however, overseas, as compared with home, orders were rare; even a job in Ireland in 1827 was considered 'very unusual'.[21] According to the evidence of the local directories and the endorsement of completion on the apprenticeship indentures of William Bowman, it is clear that by 1828 William Galloway and James Bowman had entered into a separate partnership to carry on the trade of machine makers. This partnership was legally a separate one from that of Galloway, Bowman and Glasgow, brass and iron founders, millwrights and engineers.[22]

John Galloway was born on 14 February 1804 at his father's house at 37 Lombard Street, which was then 'surrounded by smiling gardens instead of gin palaces', as he remarked in his 'Reminiscences'.[23] John

John Galloway (1804–1894)

Galloway had an elder brother William Galloway, jun. (1796–1873), who was trained as an ironfounder.[24] John was educated at a school in Mosley Street, kept by Messrs. Thomson and Albinson (or Albiston),[25] and connected with the Mosley Street Congregational Chapel, then under the pastorate (1801–26) of the Rev. Samuel Broadley.[26] The fees were $1\frac{1}{2}$ guineas a quarter, 'which was then thought very high'. He left school in 1818 and on his fourteenth birthday was apprenticed to his father and uncle for seven years to learn the art and mystery of the millwright and engineer's business. William Galloway, senior, undertook to provide his son with 'good wholesome meat, drink and lodging and also linen and washing, making and mending the same' while the two partners agreed to pay their apprentice 6s. a week for the first year of service, a payment which was to rise by stages to 16s. in the seventh and final year.[27] James Bowman's son William was apprenticed to the firm on similar conditions on 7 May 1821 to learn the trade of millwright.[28]

During his apprenticeship young John Galloway was an eye witness of the Peterloo Massacre of 1819, of which he has left a short but valuable account.[29]

In 1824, at the age of 20, he was sent to France to help in the execution of an order for the French Government:[30]

In 1824 I made a journey to Dunkerque in France. We had received an order for some large boilers, engines, and pumps, for the French Government, and in June I started to take charge of the work. A tour round the world at the present time is scarcely considered anything like such a bold adventure as a journey to the Continent at that time. All the apprentices went with me in a body to the Royal Hotel, and as the coach – the 'Telegraph' – passed under the archway out of the yard, they gave me a round of cheers. I started at 7 p.m., arriving at London at 8 p.m. next night, – but the journey was afterwards made in one day. Supper was taken at Derby at midnight, where coachmen were changed, breakfast at Leicester and dinner at Northampton. Another line went by Wilmslow and Birmingham, but the opposition was very mild, and probably both companies were doing very comfortably. I remained a day or two in London and sailed from the Tower Stairs by the 'Lord Liverpool' to Calais, and had a fine passage. On sailing down the Thames, I saw four men hanging in chains between high and low water marks – they had been executed for piracy. I had to return to England in about three months for some pumping machinery, and in the following November I went from London to Dover by coach on a Monday, a journey occupying from 6 a.m. to 6 p.m. Two lines of steamers, English and French, had just been put on. The weather was very rough so the boats would not start – Tuesday, Wednesday, Thursday and Friday were the same. By this time the town had become very full of people, and the Captains were occupied selling tickets and securing passengers. Saturday was a little better, so we set out and arrived at Calais without trouble. The hotel at which I stayed was not inviting, and no carpets could be seen anywhere. I had a passport which was examined at every town which we entered, and at Calais I proceeded to Dunkerque in a diligence, an enormous wagon drawn by five horses at about 6 miles an hour, just as at present in many parts of France. The natives lived very poorly, even compared with the backward state of our own peasants; bread and an apple or a piece of garlic was all they appeared to have to eat, and they were equally badly dressed. Our goods were sent to Liverpool and shipped thence direct to Dunkerque. Correspondence was only made use of under absolute necessity, writing once a fortnight, and a letter cost fifteen pence. The work we executed was in connection with a 'scouring' arrangement for keeping the river clear of sediment. An enormous expanse of shoreland, many square miles in extent, was enclosed and made into a pear-shaped lake in the neck of which five very large gates were placed which opened to receive the water of the flood tide, and which closed when the ebb tide set in, and remained closed till low water. The sluices or gates were then raised, and eventually the 'bar' which had been a most serious detriment to Dunkerque was cleared away. Then when the tide was quite low the locks were opened, and the water rushing out with great force, swept the bed of the river clear.

John Galloway came out of his time in 1825, but remained with the parent firm for another ten years. As early as 1830, however, he and his brother William 'began to consider the advisability of making a venture on our own account, as there were too many in partnership already, and conflicting interests began to present themselves'.[31] John Galloway in particular was very interested in the possibilities of the railway locomotive:[32]

I passed a great deal of my time at the railway terminus in Ordsal Lane, being very intimate with Fyfe, the Superintendent. I made many trips to Liverpool, a journey of 2 to $2\frac{1}{2}$ hours. The Railway Company proved very good customers to us, because an engine seldom came in without requiring some repairs, and they had no workshop of their own, though Mr. Fyfe later on got a lathe or two and a few men about the place. We then determined to make a locomotive, *the first made in Manchester*, which was not the heavy and trim looking piece of mechanism of the present day. It was named the 'Manchester'. The cylinders were vertical, and the whole affair was kept very light, as the rails were iron and only 34 lbs to the yard, instead of steel and 80 to 100 lbs as at present. Watt had commenced with vertical cylinders, and for a long time horizontal were not tried as it was considered certain that they could not be satisfactory, owing to the weight of the piston etc., which would wear the cylinder, so we made the engine with vertical cylinders. The wheels were of wood, made by John Ashbury himself, a young man just out of his time, who afterwards founded the great waggon works at Openshaw bearing his name – on to these we shrunk iron welded tyres. When we had completed it in the shop in Bridgewater Street, we were met by the serious difficulty of getting it down to the station. We could not put steam on, nor was there a wagon which would take it, so we had to 'bar' it down to Ordsal Lane, which took a gang of men with crowbars from 6 p.m. to 9 a.m. The road was not paved with sets as now, but very poorly and irregularly. The news got about that it was going to be tried, and a lot of friends gathered round to take part, so I got about half a dozen third-class carriages to run up to Chat Moss and back. A third-class carriage was not the luxurious affair of today, but worse than a cattle truck – there was no top and no seats, and as there was no law to prevent overcrowding, as many people were pushed inside as could be, and great inconvenience was suffered. Coke only was burnt originally

MANCHESTER LOCO-MOTIVE ENGINE.

The first locomotive to be built in Manchester – the 'Manchester', 1831

Galloway, Bowman and Glasgow's second locomotive – the 'Caledonian', 1832

in the engines – it was several years before coal was permitted as fuel. We started off about noon, about 200 in number, as every one was anxious for a ride, and pulled up at Chat Moss tavern – this was usual in those days and was continued for a long time afterwards, being sanctioned by the Company. We pulled up at Parkside, where we unhooked the waggons, the occupiers of which had quite a holiday in the country, while eight or nine of us ran a few miles further on the engine. We turned back on the same line, a proceeding which would not be countenanced for a moment now, as signalling was unknown, but we knew from the small number of engines and trains in existence that there was little danger of meeting another. A train from Liverpool on its own line was coming up and we ran alongside it for some distance, when, without expecting it, we ran against the points. One wheel remained on the line but the other ran off, straining the crank axle. The engine was quickly pulled up, and the passengers jumped or tumbled off in great excitement; – fortunately no one was hurt. It took us an hour or two to get back to Parkside, as the crank shaft being crooked, the engine 'wobbled' very much. The party were waiting, thinking we must have run on to Liverpool, and the question arose how to return. Old Fyfe, the first Superintendent on the railway, was with us and we waited for a train from Liverpool, which took him, and he brought another train back to take the party. Some had however gone on foot and walked the whole way, probably thinking it was safer, and as it was summer time it would not be disagreeable. I and a few others remained all night to get the engine back, which we accomplished by taking out the bent axle. We had no more trouble with this engine, nor with any other, but we did not make more than 4 or 5 altogether, as the trade did not seem likely to be remunerative, and we certainly did not foresee the immense possibilities of the railroad. It was generally considered that about 20 engines would be all that would be required, and competition was keenly felt at the beginning. An engine cost about £900 or £1000, the price fixed by the Railway Company. Sharp, Roberts & Co. made one at about the same time as we did, called the 'Experiment', with a vertical cylinder below working on to a crank, but it was not quite successful; still they kept to the trade and eventually became the noted firm of Sharp, Stewart & Co. Gradually the cylinders became inclined more and more until they were horizontal. As already stated, there was a great prejudice against horizontal cylinders,[33] and we made, I believe, the first horizontal engine to pump water by two vertical pumps from the River Irwell into a tank which we also provided to supply water to the tenders ...

Fortunately John Galloway's engineer's notebook containing entries from 26 May 1831 to 28 March 1833 has been preserved. Not only does it give a few details about the locomotive *Manchester*, but it also contains notes of the trials of a second and entirely different locomotive built by Galloway, Bowman and Glasgow in the early autumn of 1832, called the *Caledonian*. It was at one time believed that the *Manchester* was reconstructed soon after building, renamed the *Caledonian* and sold to the Liverpool and Manchester Railway under that name, but the researches of Messrs. Dewhurst and Higgins have shown that these two locomotives were quite different and separate machines.[34] The following details of the *Caledonian*'s trials in September and October 1832 are of great interest:

20 Sept. [1832]
Caledonian
25 Waggons for Liverpool
1134 lbs coke — started ½ past 5 o'clock a.m.
[Arrived] Park Side ½ past 6 [a.m.]
Stoped 8 minutes at foot of incline 2 min. past 7 at top
14 min. past — Goliah — 12 min.
Stoped 8 min. in consequence of losing a cotter.
Liverpool 8 min. past 8 [a.m.]
504 lb of coke left at Liverpool. ...

Caledonian   27 Oct 1832
Left Manchr. Station ¼ past 5 o'clock at Park Side
25 past 7 — stoped 6 mins at bottom of incline
10 mins. past 7 — at top second time
30 waggons = 150 tons — 1,400 lbs. coke[35]

John Galloway's notebook also reveals the extraordinarily varied types of engineering job the firm was carrying out in 1831–3. Besides water-wheel work, these included machinery for Wharton and Marston saltworks in Cheshire (1831–2), engines for the Strines Calico Printing Company at Disley in Derbyshire (1831–2), steam engines and driving gear for cotton spinning mills and weaving sheds in the East Lancashire and North Cheshire area, as well as in Manchester and the neighbouring townships (1831–3), colliery waggons of 2½ tons capacity for Hulton Park colliery (1831), lined with sheet iron and costing £30 each, machinery for silk mills at Leek (1831) and Macclesfield (1833), waggons and axles for the Liverpool and Manchester Railway (1831), a lead rolling mill for Mr. Gratrix of Alport Town (1831–2), and pipes for Benjamin Joule's Manchester brewery (1832).

In 1835 William and John Galloway made their great decision to hive off, as it were, from the parent concern and to enter into business on their own account. They went to a great deal of trouble in selecting a new site:

We tried hard for the land on which the Central Station now stands, which was a brickyard. Knott Mill was finally decided on as being the most likely. It was a busy spot then, as all the carrying from the [Bridgewater] Canal Wharf passed the gates.[36]

In this way the Knott Mill ironworks of W. and J. Galloway began its remarkable career. The first building erected was the foundry, and in digging the foundations the workmen struck 'many remains of a foundry which had stood there previously'.[37] This had been owned by a Scot named Alexander Brodie (1732–1811), ironmaster and armaments manufacturer, of Carey Street, Lincoln's Inn Fields, London, who also operated blast furnaces at the Calcutts, Broseley, Shropshire.[38] Brodie was in partnership with two men named McNiven and Ormrod; his foundry and steam-engine works flourished during the Revolutionary and Napoleonic Wars until shortly after his death on 7 January 1811.[39]

As events turned out the lack of continuity between Galloway, Bowman and Glasgow and the new firm of W. and J. Galloway was more apparent than real. William Galloway, sen., died aged 68 on 7 September 1836,[40] while James Bowman seems to have predeceased him, as his name appeared in Pigot and Sons' *Directory of Manchester and Salford* for 1832,[41] but not in the issue for 1836. On 5 May 1840 John Galloway wrote to old John Lucas of Charleston, South Carolina:

> We feel the most sincere pleasure on this our first communication with you, which we hope may long continue, it reminds us in a most lively manner of bygone days, and of your old friends in Manchester (Father and Uncle Bowman) who have both passed away, leaving friends, business and steam engines to others.

It is not clear what happened to the third partner, but a William Glasgow of 18, Gloucester Street, Manchester, was in business as an ironfounder in 1841.[42] Two long advertisements in the *Manchester Guardian* for 22 June 1839, announced the forthcoming sale of the stock, machinery, buildings and site of the Great Bridgewater Street works of the 'late firm' of Galloway, Bowman and Glasgow. It is known that William and John Galloway bought some of the stock,[43] but the buildings and site did not find an immediate purchaser in the depressed trade conditions of 1839–42. On 29 February 1840 John Galloway wrote to J.J. Cordes of Newport, Mon.: '... the man whom we still keep taking care of the premises in Bridgewater Street told the writer the other day that ... letters ... still occasionally drop in addressed to the old firm'.

Little is known of the first five years of William and John Galloway's new venture, except that the first steam engine they made was for Hayward of Yeovil, Somerset, and their second for a mill at Glossop.[44] But for the period January 1840 to the beginning of 1863 copies of about 800 out-letters and estimates relating to the firm's business survive, the vast majority in John Galloway's handwriting. This collection is second in importance only to the records of James Nasmyth's Bridgewater Foundry at Patricroft for the history of mid-nineteenth-century engineering in the Manchester area. The letters show that pig iron was obtained from South Wales, Derbyshire, Yorkshire, and the new Shelton furnace in North Staffordshire, set on blast in 1841.

In 1840 the two brothers made a determined attempt to secure as many orders as possible for gasworks equipment and gas pipes, possibly because these articles kept both the engineering side and the foundry side of the business occupied, although some of the resulting orders for pipes were sub-contracted to W. and G. Green of Oldham 'who receive and execute three fourths of the pipe orders for all the gas and water companies here and [in] the adjoining towns'.[45] The results of this campaign were excellent. England was rapidly becoming urbanised and the demand for gas installations to supply both towns and industrial firms appears to have been practically insatiable. By 22 October 1842 John Galloway could write: 'In the fitting up of gas apparatus we are more extensively engaged than any firm in this neighbourhood.'[46] Another important sphere of activity was indicated by the statement: 'We have erected the principal saw mills in this neighbourhood.'[47]

The two brothers were always anxious to adopt labour-saving devices. In 1842, for example, they backed Joseph Haley's patent rivet-making machine and by 1856, when the patent expired, their Knott Mill workshops contained six of these machines, operated by one man and 20 boys. A writer in the *Engineer* of 4 July 1856 stated:

The little fellows seemed to be in high spirits, whistling in chorus the un-mistakeable toodle-oddle [*sic* ? oodle] of the 'Ratcatcher's Daughter'. The rivets meanwhile were being struck off at the rate of two tons to each machine daily.[49]

The same observer noticed that the two brothers had installed Goffer of Dukinfield's machine for rivetting by steam-power in their boiler shop.[50]

In the early 1840s, too, W. and J. Galloway became pioneers of mechanical handling in industry by taking up the manufacture and sale of screw jacks for lifting heavy weights, again under a patent taken out by Joseph Haley.[51] The firm had one of these screw jacks on show in the Great Exhibition of 1851.[52]

It is as manufacturers of patent boilers, however, that W. and J. Galloway are now chiefly remembered:

... The railway also had a direct influence upon our particular trade of boiler making, for as the locomotives could not condense their steam, they had to be non-condensing, and consequently high-pressure, the terms becoming synonymous and continuing so to this day. Higher pressures, being more economical, came gradually into use, and the wagon boiler of Watt was no longer suitable. Boiler-making, of course, started with the engine making, and simply required to keep pace with it, that is, as the higher engine-pressures came into use, boilers had to be made accordingly. The wagon boiler (so called because of its shape) only carried about from 5 to 10 lbs. pressure per inch. As the work of the engine was principally performed by the vacuum, even with 'staying' it soon became evident that something stronger was wanted. They were provided with an apparatus which is never seen now, namely a vacuum valve to allow the entry of air should the pressure fall below that of the atmosphere, not an uncommon occurrence. The steam gauge consisted of a column of mercury in a bent tube open at one end to the boiler, and at the other to the atmosphere, with a wood peg sticking out and rising or falling with the pressure; when cylindrical boilers came in, these gave way to the present gauge. The Cornish or one-flue boiler was then adopted, and afterwards the Lancashire or two-flue.[53]

Unfortunately no detailed history of the important developments which were taking place in boilermaking in the nineteenth century appears to have been written. Most of the credit for the invention of the famous Lancashire boiler between 1840 and 1844 is given to the great Manchester engineer and rival of the Galloways, Sir William Fairbairn (1789–1874). He and John Hetherington took out patent No. 10166 for the Lancashire boiler on 30 April 1844.[54]

In the meantime the Galloway brothers had not been idle. On 12 May 1841 John Galloway informed J. and I. Colman of Norwich, starch and mustard manufacturers, that his firm had recently been paying 'much attention to the consumption of fuel', and later in the year informed J.J. Cordes of Newport, Mon.:

... we have lately introduced an improvement with a view of 'smoke burning' and of course a small saving of fuel, which answers well. You will perceive towards the far end of fire box a trough crossing it – this has the effect of obstructing the fire and direct passage of the flame or smoke into the flue, and bringing it into close contact with the red hot fire at far end of bars.

This was apparently an early form of the 'breeches' or 'double fire flue' boiler, a smoke-consuming variant of the Lancashire boiler, which the firm claimed to have registered in 1845 under the Designs Act of 1843 (6 and 7 Vict., cap. 65). This act extended registration to useful as well as ornamental industrial designs.[55] On 25 November 1845 John Galloway wrote to Messrs. James Lillie and Sons, a rival firm of engineers on the north side of Manchester:

Having lately seen a steam engine boiler of your manufacture made upon a construction of which we are the inventors and have acquired an exclusive privelege to make under the Act of Parliament for that purpose we beg to protest against the infringement of that privelege which you have been guilty of.[56]

John Galloway has left a general account of how his attention was drawn to the improvement of boiler efficiency:

The utility of smoke-burning was imperfectly understood, but as mills sprang up everywhere, the smoke nuisance became a real evil, and it struck me that if I could have two furnaces joining together immediately beyond the bridge, the hot gases from one would consume the green smoke from the other with alternate firing. The flues thus constructed had flat top and bottom, and as this must be strengthened I introduced a central row of vertical tubes; these at first were parallel, but afterwards, we made them taper so as to introduce them through the top hole. This also permitted the[ir] application to existing boilers, and made a great increase in our business. There was no machinery originally, but by and by plates were punched by machine; then as pressure increased, rivetting by machinery came into operation and now hard work is only made use of where machinery cannot well be brought in.

From 1848 onwards the two brothers took out frequent patents relating to improvements in boilers and other parts of the steam engine,[57] the most fundamental being that of 11 March 1851 (No. 13552) 'for the conical water-tubes so long known by their name, and which have been until recently [1905] almost universally used'.[58] The first 'Galloway' boiler is said to have been built in 1849 for Messrs. J. Leeming and Co of Salford, and the firm had a 30 h.p. specimen in operation at the Great Exhibition of 1851.[59] On 31 January 1854 the Galloways were forced to warn Messrs. William Fairbairn and Sons:

We are informed that you are putting into the boilers you are making the conical vertical waterpipes. If this is correct we beg to intimate to you that these pipes are patented by us, and that your use of them is an infringement.

Many other boiler makers are introducing them, but of course under our licence, which may also be granted to you if you desire it.

No reply had been received to this letter three weeks later,[60] and it is significant that the Galloways are not mentioned once in *The Life of Sir William Fairbairn, Bart.* by Sir William Fairbairn and W. Pole (1877), which contains much material on the history of the boiler in the mid-nineteenth century. Between 1848 and 1891 the firm made nearly 9000 Galloway-type boilers with a total indicated h.p. of 2 millions. During 1884 alone 388 boilers were constructed weighing 4000 tons.[61] A separate boiler works had been opened in Hyde Road, Ardwick, in 1872. This enabled the Knott Mill works to be devoted entirely to the manufacture of engines. In 1894 the Hyde Road works employed 800 men and the Knott Mill works 500.[62]

It is impossible to examine in a detailed fashion the overseas business of the firm within the compass of a short paper, but the out-letter book reveals that between 1852 and 1862 W. and J. Galloway were supplying gunpowder mills and steam engines for the Sultan of Turkey's State powder factories at Barrouthanna, San Stefano, near Constantinople. In connection with these orders the chief engineer and manager of the mills, Azakel B. Dadian, an Armenian,[63] visited Manchester in 1855. Shortly after the outbreak of the Crimean War, the Customs authorities at Liverpool seized some of this powder-mill machinery under an Order-in-Council prohibiting the unlicensed export of such goods to destinations east of Malta, lest they should reach Russian hands.[64] The *Engineer* of 4 July 1856 contains many details concerning a further six Galloway powder mills destined for Turkey.

From 1853 onwards W. and J. Galloway showed great activity in fulfilling Russian orders for steam engines and gearing to be used in setting up cotton spinning mills in and around St. Petersburg. One of the earliest of these mills was to contain 30,000 spindles.[65] During the Crimean War there was some question of sending machinery to Russia overland, presumably *via* neutral Sweden. There was nothing reprehensible in this, as the material was not contraband of war, but apparently the project came to nothing because of the high cost of transport. George and Alexander Chamot of St. Petersburg were Galloway's Russian agents for these sales, and only in one case does the name of the ultimate purchaser appear, i.e., P. Ponomareff, 1853–4, 1855.

From 1856 onwards the firm became deeply involved in the setting up of various early cotton mills in the Bombay Presidency. The first successful cotton spinning mill to operate in India was that established by James Landon and Ranchhodlal Chhotalal (later owned by the Broach Cotton Mills Company) at Umjad Bagh, Broach, in 1854–6. Landon's mill started working on 8 October 1855.[66] The second Indian cotton spinning mill was established by Cowasjee Nanabhoy Davar (1815–73), a Parsee financier of Bombay, who has been described as 'the Tata of the eighteen fifties'. On 7 July 1854 he and his associates (among whom was Edwin Heycock) floated the Bombay Spinning and Weaving Company. By January 1856 this Company had built at Tardeo, to the design of Sir William Fairbairn, a spinning mill containing 17,000 spindles supplied by John Hetherington and Sons of Manchester. This mill began production on 7 February 1856 under the supervision of British engineers and skilled cotton operatives.[67] Fired by this success, Cowasjee got into touch with the Galloways in 1855 through Henry Heycock, his Manchester agent (presumably a relative of Edwin), and William Whitehead, chief engineer of the Tardeo mill. It was proposed to build a duplicate mill containing 20,000 throstle spindles alongside the original building at Tardeo. This is almost certainly the reason why Cowasjee floated the Bombay Throstle Mill Company in 1857. This mill did not begin working until 1859.[68]

Simultaneously Cowasjee planned to set up a mill operated by a new firm called the Bombay Cotton Cleaning Company at Colaba, and on 1 October 1856 W. and J. Galloway undertook to furnish the necessary steam engines, boilers, cast iron columns and 'powerful presses for packing cotton into bales' for this mill as well.[69] Heycock was ordering further presses in 1859, and in the following year Cowasjee's Bombay Spinning and Weaving Company, which intended to instal 500 looms, was calling for estimates for two compound engines, mill gearing and 106 cast iron columns for the weaving shed.[70]

Besides making machinery W. and J. Galloway could turn their energies to what would now be considered civil engineering. For example, between 1855 and 1857 they undertook the contract for building the railway viaduct over the estuary of the Leven on the Ulverston and Lancaster Railway which was opened in 1857 (1563 ft.).

The Leven Viaduct in the late 1850s. John Galloway is the top-hatted figure in the centre foreground; the inscription on the trucks reads 'ULVERSTONE ORE WAGGON'

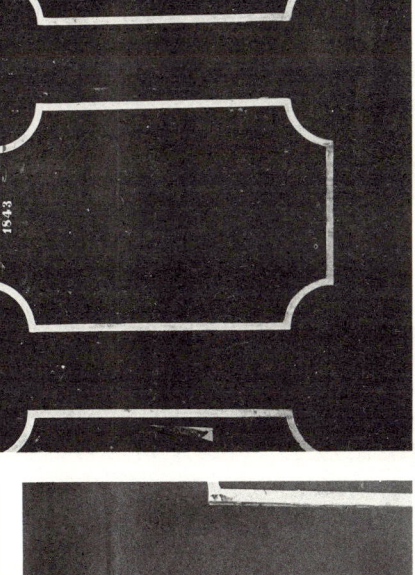

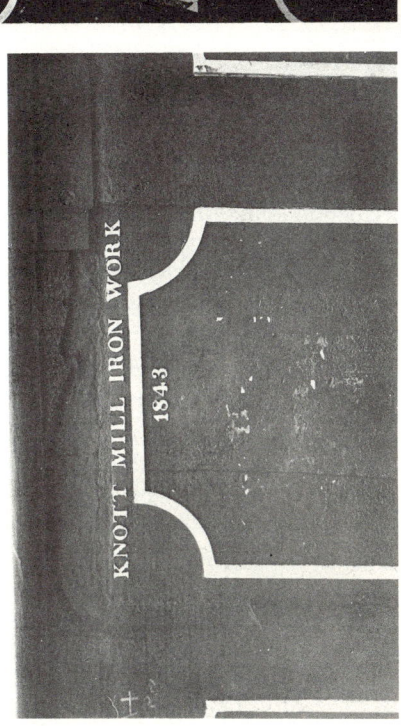

The cast iron bridge on Albion Street crossing the Rochdale Canal link with the Bridgewater Canal terminus. One side has 12 panels, the other 13. The central panel on each side bears the legend 'Knott Mill Iron Work/s, 1843.' W. & J. Galloway derived free publicity from the display of their insignia upon one of the main routes of entry into the city.

It cost £18,604[71] and John Galloway took up residence at Canal Foot near Ulverston during the operation, which made civil engineering history in that the piles were for the first time driven down into the sand with the help of a strong jet of water.[72] This loosened the sand so that the piles could be hammered in firmly with a tup. John Galloway's diary for part of the time he was engaged on this job has survived (24 March to 9 September 1856). The piling was completed by 25 October 1856 and the viaduct finished by 14 June 1857. On 4 September of that year W. and J. Galloway could write to the engineer, Brunlees: 'The trains are numerous and pass over without slackening speed'. The corresponding viaduct over the Kent estuary was built during the winter of 1856–7 by another Manchester contractor, James Featherstone.

The same method of pile driving found immediate employment in the lavish construction of those seaside piers which were so characteristic a feature of Victorian England. As early as 1835 John Galloway had paid a visit to Southport and, in his own words, 'noticed there was a great want of water, which was so far from the town ... as the water could not come we went to it. I considered a long time, and thought of a pier, but our project was delayed, because the pier would have to be so long.'[73] Finally, in 1859 a public limited liability company was formed with a capital of £8000 (later increased to £10,000) to build a 1200-foot pier, with James Brunlees and W. and J. Galloway as engineers and contractors respectively. They utilised the new method of pile-driving and the work stood complete for the opening ceremony on 2 August 1860.[74]

In conclusion something must be said about the Galloway brothers' association with Sir Henry Bessemer, who announced his new process of steel making in 1856. This prolific inventor had been a customer of the firm since 1843 and referred to William Galloway, jun., as 'my old friend' in his *Autobiography*.[75] It was apparently at the Knott Mill ironworks that Bessemer had the special equipment manufactured before embarking on his steelmaking trials at Baxter House, St. Pancras, London. Indeed John Galloway's statement on the subject suggests that during the production and testing of this equipment in 1855 the first ingot of Bessemer steel in the world was produced in Manchester at the Knott Mill works.[76] An added reason for accepting John Galloway's statement is that W. and J. Galloway actually took out a licence to manufacture the new steel in the Manchester area even before Bessemer announced his process to the world at Cheltenham on 13 August 1856.[77] Bessemer found great difficulty, however, in bringing his patent steel into commercial production. After three years of further experiments (1856–9) he founded a small but fabulously successful company, Henry Bessemer and Co., to erect a Bessemer steel works in Sheffield. The partners were Bessemer himself, Robert Longsdon and William Allen, his two brothers-in-law, and John and William Galloway, who had never lost faith in the eventual triumph of the inventor and his process.[78] Again the firm supplied the converters and other special equipment for the Sheffield works. Galloways also secured orders for Bessemer steel-making plant from firms which operated the process under licence from Bessemer, e.g., the Weardale Iron Company (24 March 1860), and John Brown of Sheffield (13 April 1860).

In 1856 John Galloway, jun., the son of William, and Charles John, the son of John Galloway, sen., entered the business as partners; the style of the firm thereupon became W. and J. Galloway and Sons. In 1889 the partnership was turned into a private company with a capital of £250,000 and ten years later became a public limited liability company. At the beginning of the twentieth century the firm already had a history which went back over a hundred years; the *Victoria County History* stated that it was then 'as far as we can ascertain the oldest of the large Lancashire engineering firms'.[79]

APPENDIX

Joseph Nadin (1765–1848), Deputy Constable, and the Administration of Justice in Manchester

About 1815 I saw two boatmen flogged for stealing brandy in transit from London to Manchester, they having tapped the casks on the way. Nadin's men were the operators, and the place by Dr. Mann's house at the corner of Deansgate and Great Bridgewater Street. The men, who had been brought in a cart from the New Bailey, were stripped, and tied to the triangle in the cart, and had 50 lashes each, one looking on quite coolly, as it seemed to me, while the other was being punished. When one had received the proper number, Nadin took up the man's coat and threw it over his shoulders. Nadin was a very important man in those days;[80] he was a strong, well-made man and at least 6 feet high, his long brown coat making him a conspicuous figure. His office was in Police Street, and the last time I (quite recently) passed it, I saw it just as it was then, one of two tall doors; the one nearest King Street. He was usually out a great part of the day and when he returned, his subordinates would have prisoners there waiting for him, charged with various offences, such as sheep-stealing, stealing from bleaching crofts, etc. He interviewed them in private and then they were taken down to the New Bailey, where the Salford Goods Station now is, and in due course were hauled off to Lancaster on the top of the coach or wagon. When a number of persons were hanged at Lancaster, they were brought out in front of the Castle and made to sit upon a form – sometimes it was too small and there was much pushing and struggling to get them all on at once, which seemed a necessary part of the function. All punishment was carried out without any regard to the feelings of the unfortunate criminals. Mr. Thomas Wright, the prison philanthropist, told me that the greatest number he had seen executed at once was eleven. Offences now considered practically trivial were then punishable by death, but I cannot say that it reduced crime. I also recollect when quite a boy, being lifted up to see a man in the pillory; it stood in the corner of the Market Place where the 'Bull's Head' juts out; this was an inn then, as there were no hotels, the name not having then been introduced from France. These inns however were patronized in quite a different way to the present; well-to-do people used to meet in the bar parlour in the evening, smoking their long clay pipes, drinking ale and discussing matters generally, including business, not forgetting to play practical jokes whenever an opportunity offered, for this was one of the main sources of amusement. The Crown Inn, Deansgate, was built in my early days and had a good bar parlour, while that at the 'Royal' was considered a very superior place. There was no restriction as to opening, but there never seemed to be any trouble on that account (J.G.'s MS, 7–9).

NOTES

This article is reprinted from the *Transactions of the Lancashire and Cheshire Antiquarian Society*, Vol.LXIV, 1954.

1. J. Kennedy, *Miscellaneous Papers* ... (privately published, 1849) – 'A brief notice of my early recollections', 1–18.
2. *Op. cit.*, 15. See also Professor T.S. Ashton's remarks in *The Industrial Revolution, 1760–1830* (1948), 19.
3. Typescript 'Transcript of some notes by Mr. John Galloway, engineer, Manchester, written about 1890' (copies in possession of Col. J.G. Riddick of Mobberley, Cheshire, his grandson, and Manchester Central Reference Library), 1. Hereafter referred to as 'J.G.'s MS'. See also the article by P.C. Dewhurst and S.H.P. Higgins, 'Galloway, Bowman and Glasgow, Caledonian Foundry, Great Bridgewater Street, Manchester' (*Journal of the Stephenson Locomotive Society*, XXIX, Nov. 1953, 327).
4. J.G.'s MS, 1.
5. J.G.'s MS, 1–2. James Bowman may have married a sister of William Galloway, for many years later John Galloway referred to him as 'Uncle Bowman' (J.G. to John Lucas, 5 May 1840).
6. J.G.'s MS, 10.
7. *Manchester and Salford Directory* (1804), 62.
8. *Op. cit.*, 67. James Bowman's private house was in Trumpet Street (*op. cit.*, 25).
9. *Op. cit.*, 88.
10. Pigot's *Manchester and Salford Directory* (1817), 93. This expansion after the Napoleonic Wars is confirmed by J.G.'s MS, 11.
11. *Op. cit.*, 51.
12. Cf. J.G.'s MS, 17: 'Our work for a long time consisted of millwrighting, and even after we commenced the construction of engines, we had no foundry of our own, though we supplied any driving machinery that was wanted.'
13. J.G.'s MS, 11.
14. *Ibid.*
15. *Manchester and Salford Directory* (1824–5), 66; *ibid.*, 1828, 59.
16. J.G.'s MS, 11.
17. J.G.'s MS, 30. In 1822 James Bowman visited St. Quentin and Lille on business (French passport dated 13 Nov. 1822 in Riddick MSS).
18. The firm experienced another busy spell in the general boom of 1824–5 (J.G.'s MS,

19).
19. J.G.'s MS, 18.
20. Philadelphia (1953), 8 (quoting *Southern Agriculturist,* VII (Nov. 1834), 580).
21. J.G.'s MS, 30.
22. M. Wardle's *Manchester and Salford Directory* (1829), 72; Pigot and Sons' *Manchester and Salford Directory* (1829), 117.
23. J.G.'s MS, 2.
24. Pigot and Sons' *Directory of Manchester and Salford* (1832), 106; *ibid.* (1836), 132 – William Galloway, jun., ironfounder, lived at 26, Jackson's Lane, Hulme, at this time.
25. Pigot's *Manchester and Salford Directory* (1813), 2.
26. B. Nightingale, *Lancashire Nonconformity* (1893), 137–47. Galloway calls it 'Dr. Halley's Chapel', but Halley was pastor from 1838 to 1857.
27. Indentures, 14 Feb. 1818 (Riddick MSS).
28. Indentures, 7 May 1821 (Riddick MSS).
29. J.G.'s MS, 5–7.
30. J.G.'s MS, 27–9.
31. J.G.'s MS, 19.
32. J.G.'s MS, 21–24.
33. But see J.G.H. Warren, *A Century of Locomotive Building by Robert Stephenson and Co., 1823–1923* (1923), 288–9.
34. Article quoted above (*Journal of the Stephenson Locomotive Society,* XXIX, Nov. 1953, 327–9.) The *Manchester* was on hire to the Liverpool and Manchester Railway in 1833, pulling coal wagons at William Hulton's Hulton Park Colliery (*ibid.* 328).
35. John Galloway's notebook (Riddick MSS); for the *Manchester* and *Caledonian* locomotives and the Liverpool and Manchester Railway Company, see J.G.H. Warren, *op. cit.,* 83, 288–9.
36. J.G.'s MS, 19.
37. J.G.'s MS, 19–20.
38. J. Aikin, *Description of the Country ... round Manchester* (1795), 177–8; J. Randall, *The Wilkinsons* (ed. 1917), 37. Brodie's foundry appears on William Green's 1794 map of Manchester, and in the Manchester directories from the 1794 issue (Scholes's, 22) to the 1813 issue (Pigot's). According to John Galloway, Brodie was the 'maker of a new stove for ships, and had a large connection, especially with Government' (MS, 20).
39. *Gentleman's Magazine* for 1811, Part I, 89. He was described as 'one of the most benevolent of human beings. His loss will be severely felt by the poor. He possessed an immense property.'
40. *Manchester Guardian,* 10 Sept. 1836.
41. P.46.
42. Pigot and Slater's *Directory of Manchester and Salford* (1841), 72.
43. John Galloway to J.J. Cordes, 20 June 1840: 'We purchased from the old concern all the patterns that had been made at various periods for your houses, ... at the time of sale by auction, ... a great number of promiscuous patterns we broke up previously, as valueless to sell.'
44. J.G.'s MS, 20.
45. J.G. to – Steele, 27 July 1840. See also letters 13, 23, 40, 79.
46. Letter to J. Kearsley, engineer, Midland Counties Railway, Derby.
47. J.G. to McGuirk, 18 Jan. 1842.
48. J.G. to T. and W. Pimm, 13 April 1842.
49. Pages 356–7.
50. *Ibid.*
51. Patent No.8768 of 31 Dec. 1840 for an improved lifting jack and compressor.
52. *Official Description and Illustrated Catalogue of the Great Exhibition* (1851), I, 224.
53. J.G.'s MS, 25.
54. H.H.P. Powles, *Steam Boilers: their history and development* (1905), 114–16.
55. *V.C.H. Lancs.,* II (1908), 371; K.R. Swan, *Law and Commercial Usage of Patents,*

Designs and Trade Marks (1908), 240–1.
56. See also Galloway to Sandeman, 9 Oct. 1845 and to D.W. Latham, Bolton, 5 Feb. 1846. Fairbairn had severed his connection with Lillie in 1822. The Patent Office, however, possesses no record of either the registration of a design or a patent by the Galloways in respect of a boiler during 1843–45.
57. E.g. in 1848, 1851, 1853, 1855, 1856, 1860, 1861, etc., etc.
58. Powles, *op. cit.*, 117.
59. *Official Catalogue*, I, 224; *Manchester Faces and Places*, V (1894), 127–8.
60. W. and J. Galloway to Messrs. Wm. Fairbairn and Sons, 20 Feb. 1854. For Fairbairn's activities in connection with boiler inspection (which led to the formation of the Manchester Steam Users' Association in 1854–55) and the subject of boiler insurance in general, see *A Century's Progress* (British Engine Boiler and Electrical Insurance Co. Ltd., Manchester, 1954).
61. D.A. Farnie, 'The English Cotton Industry, 1850–1896' (MS thesis for M.A., Manchester University, 1953), 71.
62. *V.C.H. Lancs.*, II, 371; *Manchester Faces and Places*, V (1894), 130.
63. For other members of the Dadian family and their activities, see Sir W. Fairbairn and W. Pole, *The Life of Sir William Fairbairn, Bart.* (1877), 168–76.
64. Copy of petition 'To the Lords of the Privy Council' from W. and J. Galloway, 26 Feb. 1855. In October 1855 the firm was working 'almost night and day' to fulfil the Turkish Government's orders (W. and J. Galloway to A.B. Dadian, 27 Oct. 1855).
65. W. and J. Galloway to G. Chamot, St. Petersburg, 23 March 1853.
66. S.D. Mehta, *The Cotton Mills of India, 1854 to 1954*. Textile Association of India, Bombay (1954), 9–13.
67. Mehta, *op. cit.*, 13–18, 26–7. Copies of three letters written by W. and J. Galloway to Cowasjee Nanabhoy Davar have survived (23 July 1857, 29 Nov. 1858, 1 July 1859).
68. W. and J. Galloway to W. Whitehead, Tardeo, Bombay, 9 Jan. 1856, 9 Feb., 25 May 1857; estimates for Henry Heycock, Manchester, 8 Aug., 16 Oct. 1856; Mehta, *op cit.*, 18–19. The textile machinery was supplied by Platts of Oldham.
69. Estimate by Galloways for Henry Heycock (on behalf of the Bombay Cotton Cleaning Co.) and receipt for £750 in part payment dated 1 Oct. 1856; W. and J. Galloway to Thos. Affleck and Co., Kandy, Ceylon, 23 July 1857.
70. Estimate for Henry Heycock, 30 June 1859; estimate for Bombay Spinning and Weaving Co., 1 May 1860; W. and J. Galloway to J. Freeborough, Bombay, 7 June 1860.
71. *Minutes of Proceedings of the Institution of Civil Engineers*, XVII, for 1857–8 (1858), 442–8 (James Brunlees, 'Description of the iron viaducts erected across the tidal estuaries of the Rivers Leven and Kent in Morecambe Bay, for the Ulverstone and Lancaster Railway'). See also W. White, *Furness Folk and Facts* (1930), 82.
72. For a good non-technical description of the process as applied to Southport pier see P. Mannex & Co., *Topography and Directory of North and South Lonsdale, Amounderness, Leyland and the Town of Southport* (1866), 251. See also F.A. Bailey, *History of Southport* (1955), chap.6.
73. J.G.'s MS, 30–1.
74. Mannex & Co., *op. cit.*, 250; E. Bland, *Annals of Southport and District* (1887), 128–9, 132.
75. Sir Henry Bessemer, *An Autobiography* (1905), 286–7.
76. J.G.'s MS, 32 and *Manchester Faces and Places*, V (1894), 130 ('A small piece of land adjoining the Knott Mill Ironworks was obtained, and a long series of experiments, lasting twelve months or more, was carried out to test the practical value of the process.').
77. Bessemer, *op. cit.*, 115–16.
78. For further details, see W.M. Lord, 'The development of the Bessemer process in Lancashire, 1856–1900', *Trans. Newcomen Soc.*, XXV (1945–7), 165–9; *Manchester Faces and Places*, V (1894), 130; and Sir John Clapham, *Economic History of Modern Britain*, II (1932), 53–6.

79. *V.C.H. Lancs.,* II (1908), 371. C.J. Galloway joined the board of the Steam Boiler Assurance Co. of Manchester (later the Boiler Insurance and Steam Power Co., Ltd.) on its foundation in 1859 and was chairman of the company from 1880 until 1904, by which latter date it was known as the Vulcan Boiler and General Insurance Co., Ltd. I am indebted to J. Eyers, Esq., for this information.

80. For Joseph Nadin, deputy constable of Manchester township from 1802 until 1821, see A. Redford and I.S. Russell, *History of Local Government in Manchester,* I (1938), 85, 90, 92, 97, 222–3, 225, 227, 234, 249, 253–8.

Was there a Decline of the Industrial Spirit in Britain 1850–1939?

Since the later 1960s a great deal of academic effort has gone into research purporting to show that the seeds of the relative decline of Britain in the world were sown during the period from the 1870s to 1914. The first large-scale publication on this theme appears to be that of the Canadian professor A.L. Levine, *Industrial Retardation in Britain, 1880–1914* in 1967. Levine's thesis can be summarised by saying that he noted shortcomings in the organisation and technology of British industries – failures to take greater advantage of mass production, mechanisation and the automatic principle, in the rate of electrification and in iron and steel technology. These failures were, he alleged, based on shortcomings in British educational institutions and social attitudes which resulted in a decline in the quality of British entrepreneurship and management, nepotism, the neglect of science and a lack of social mobility caused by what is loosely called 'class attitudes'. And of course the restrictive practices of the trade union 'labour aristocracy' also came under fire. Levine based much of his criticism on inadequate evidence and suffered from a sort of tunnel vision. He did not take into consideration the rôle of nepotism in American and German industry. For example, although the American economy was the product of a more business-oriented civilisation than the British, it was not unknown in American business for sons to refuse to enter their fathers' firms and to prefer more colourful careers as landowners, art collectors, literary men and playboys. Levine's views were reinforced on this side of the Atlantic by academics studying the so-called 'Great Depression' of 1873–96, now so neatly deflated by Professor S.B. Saul.[1] And quite recently there have appeared two influential texts which seem to reinforce the Levine thesis, M.W. Kirby's *The Decline of British Economic Power Since 1870* (1981), although it should be observed that Kirby devotes only 23 pages, approximately one-eighth of his book, to the period before 1914 and pays little or no attention to the damage and distortion inflicted on the British economy by the War of 1914–1918. The second offering, also published in 1981, was by a Texan professor, Martin J. Wiener, *English Culture and the Decline of the Industrial Spirit, 1850–1980,* which is on a somewhat different plane to Kirby's stodgy offering. It is also more likely to be influential because it is much more readable and therefore more persuasive. Essentially it perpetuates the myth of a 'Merrie England', where everyone in Britain, from industrialist to trade unionist, deep at heart, wants to live in a 'William Morrisy' rural Utopia. Again he blames the British class system and cultural values for Britain's decline, but relies in my opinion to an alarming extent on literary sources as economic evidence. These can be misleading, as the vapourings of Mrs. Frances Trollope in her weepy novel of 1840, *Michael Armstrong, the Factory Boy* or Charles Dickens in *Hard Times* show. Mr Bounderby's Coketown is not to be taken as anything more than a caricature of early Victorian industrial society. The quotations Wiener gives from the speeches and writings of Stanley Baldwin, J. Ramsay Macdonald and the popular writers and journalists of the early twentieth century cast a misleading glow over the realities of the interwar years.

By the 1860s what we may call the first stage of the Industrial Revolution in the classic sense was over. This had raised Britain to an unexampled world economic predominance. Great Britain, with a population in 1871 of only about 25 millions, produced in the early 1870s two thirds of all the coal used in the world, together with half of all the world's iron and steel. In addition she possessed some of the largest and most up-to-date textile industries (cotton, woollens and worsted, silk and linen, but above all cotton) backed up by the world's largest and most efficient textile engineering works. Her growing import and export trades were carried on by the largest mercantile marine in the world, almost wholly produced at home. This merchant fleet was rapidly being converted after the 1870s to metal-hulled steamships even for the long voyages to the Pacific, a process which was virtually complete by 1914. As Professor Headrick[2] has recently shown in detail, Britain's overseas empire was based on this advanced technology, which enabled her to produce the latest weapons of war both by sea and by land and to construct the railway, cable and telegraph networks so essential for controlling the overseas possessions.

By 1914, however, the position had changed greatly from a relative point of view, although the British economy had continued to grow in absolute terms at a satisfactory rate and indeed achieved some of its most spectacular productive triumphs in 1911–13. The increase in industrial motive power in the United Kingdom (excluding locomotives) between 1870 and 1907 was approximately tenfold, from just over one million horsepower in the former year to well over ten million horsepower in 1907, the year of the first British census of production. This hardly seems retardation and indeed presumes the existence of great engineering know-how and entrepreneurial ability.[3]

What were these relative changes in Britain's world economic position? Between 1870 and 1914 both Germany and the U.S.A. had risen to the front rank among the industrial powers. By 1914 Germany was producing twice as much pig iron as Britain and the U.S.A. three times as much. As late as 1875–79 Britain still produced 46% of the world's pig iron and 36% of the world's steel. By 1910–13 these shares had fallen to 14% and 10.3% respectively. Britain's share in the world's iron and steel exports declined rapidly, although she remained until 1913 the world's largest exporter of iron and steel, because Germany and the U.S.A. with their larger populations absorbed more of their outputs internally. But by 1914 Britain was also the largest importer of foreign iron and steel in the world, a situation which reflected the growth of the re-rolling and finishing sections of the British iron and steel industry – Britain imported the cruder and cheaper grades of foreign iron and steel to work up into more highly-finished and expensive products. This was the correct course to follow in a highly competitive world when trade barriers were lower than in the 1920s and 1930s. Three of Britain's basic industries in fact enjoyed the most successful productive periods in their histories just before the First World War – coal mining, cotton and shipbuilding, i.e. between 1911 and 1913. Let us examine them in turn.

Coal mining employed directly around one and a quarter million men, women and boys in 1914–21, out of a total population of about forty millions. When we consider the large families of miners, say five persons per family, this meant that around 10 to 12% of the population was directly dependent on the coal industry for a living. Between 1860 and 1913 coal output rose from 83 million tons to 287 million tons, of which 98 million tons were exported at a time when coal was a much more important source of industrial and transport power than it is today. In fact the coal industry of 1913 was the equivalent of today's oil and gas wells in the North Sea, contributing lavishly to the favourable balance of overseas payments. However, output per miner had been either declining or stagnant between 1888 and 1913. Recent research has shown that labour productivity in the British mines was roughly at the same level as in the German, Belgian and French mines. Productivity in the American mines was much greater than in Europe. Naturally there has been a debate as to why this should be so. Was it due to a lag in mechanisation and/or 'entrepreneurial failure'? It has been pointed out that in 1902 only 2% of British coal was cut mechanically, the rest being got out by pick and shovel, whereas 20% of U.S. coal was cut mechanically in the same year. It appears that British mine owners tended to introduce mechanical cutters only where their use was most appropriate, i.e. in the thinner seams. Given an adequate supply of efficient hand labour such as existed in the coalfields, it still paid British coal owners and managers to use the old methods in the thicker seams. Clearly the British coal industry was both highly successful and fairly efficient in 1913.

The British cotton industry reached the peak of its spectacular career in 1913. There was no other cotton industry in the world to rival it and in the record year of 1913 exports of cotton cloth totalled over 7,000 million linear yards (or over 8,000 million square yards). In that year one district of Lancashire alone – Oldham and its surrounding townships – contained no less than 29.4% of all the cotton spindles in the United Kingdom and 11.7% of all the cotton spindles in the world. British exports of cotton machinery foreshadowed what was to happen between the 1920s and the 1970s. These cotton machinery exports were going in 1913 to India, China, Japan and Russia. 45% of the output of the textile engineering industry went abroad in 1913. Cotton spinning, thanks to British engineering know-how and the industry's foremen, became one of the easiest mechanised industries to establish abroad. The claim that Lancashire millowners were backward in not adopting the wasteful American ring frame for spinning and held on too long to the mule spindle which spun finer counts of yarn has been shown to be unsound, thanks to the researches of Professor L.G. Sandberg. The Lancashire loom was more efficient in producing the finer cloths than the automatic loom pioneered in the U.S.A., but this latter was being built in Britain from the 1900s.

In shipbuilding the story is again of spectacular success just before the First World War. The wooden and iron sailing ships which had constituted the bulk of the British mercantile marine in the 1870s, were by 1913 being sold off to foreign buyers at the rate of 4% per year of the total fleet, which at 11.7 million tons easily outdistanced Britain's nearest rival, Germany (3 million tons), so that by 1914 85% of all United Kingdom registered ships were modern, having been built since 1895. In the 1890s British shipyards were supplying over 80% of the world's new shipping and the figure was still over 60% in 1913 in spite of foreign competition. Output from British shipyards in 1913 was a record 1.2 million net tons, the last of three good years.[4]

It should not be forgotten that during the opening years of the twentieth century Britain was investing capital abroad at a hitherto unparalleled rate so that the capital sum owned by individual British subjects and joint stock companies rose from about £2,400 million (in gold values) to £4,000 million in 1914; these brought in an annual return of £200 million or 5% on average for every £100 invested: this helped to offset the gap in our balance of payments made necessary by increasing imports of foreign manufactures and equally important, foreign food-stuffs and raw materials. About a quarter of this accumulation of capital assets was dissipated in 1917–18 to help pay for imports of vital raw materials, food and munitions, but investment abroad from Britain on a considerable scale was still going on as late as 1916. In fact the deficit in the pre-war total of £4,000 million was soon made up after the end of the First World War and on the eve of the Second World War the figure stood at about £3,800 millions with a slightly lower average rate of return; and of course, the price-level of 1938 was some 30% above that of 1914.

One of the foremost arguments of the critics of British industrial performance during the past hundred years has been the poor state of technical education as compared with Germany, although France, Switzerland and the U.S.A. are also held up as examples to backward Britain. This criticism will hardly hold water. The early promise of the mechanics' institute movement had, it is true, petered out in the 1850s and, except for a few institutes fostered mainly by the railway companies at Crewe, Wolverton, Derby and Swindon, the survivors did little to promote scientific and technical education. The pioneers in the mid- and late nineteenth-century drive to improve British technical education were Sir Bernhard Samuelson (1820–1905), M.P. for Banbury, who first developed the Cleveland iron ore deposits and Sir Henry E. Roscoe (1833–1915), professor of chemistry at Manchester who was one of the first 'politicians of science' of a species now so numerous in the modern world.

Great advances in scientific and technical education were taking place in the provinces from the 1860s onwards with the foundation of the nuclei of the civic universities, of Owens College at Manchester (1851), the Yorkshire College of Science at Leeds, Firth College at Sheffield, Mason's College at Birmingham, Liverpool College, and Armstrong College at Newcastle-upon-Tyne. All these institutions were supported in varying degrees by local businessmen and industrialists. The Germans had not only their universities but also their technical high schools which developed from the 1820s onwards. Some of them had developed technological specialisms – Stuttgart in engineering, Chemnitz in textiles and Freiberg in mining, much admired outside Germany. Dr. Michael Sanderson, however, in his under-appreciated book, *The Universities and British Industry, 1850–1970* (1972), considers that the British probably exaggerated their qualitative superiority: Sir William Siemens, who had a better right to an opinion than most on this matter, [having been born a German,] thought that the German technical high schools were not to be followed; they taught too much practice which their students mistook for unchanging principles; and in his view Cambridge, Owens College, [Manchester] and King's College, London, were far better places of higher scientific education. By the 1900s whatever advantages Germany may have had in possessing these institutions seems almost totally to have vanished.[5]

Kaiser Wilhelm II had decreed, at about the same time, that there should be no University in the Ruhr, to keep the workers' minds on practical matters rather than intellectual. This was not remedied until 1965.[6]

Germany, however, was undoubtedly superior in her capacity to turn out sheer numbers. In 1890 there were twice as many academic chemists in Germany as in Britain and in 1899 two thirds of the world's chemical research came from Germany. British industry overcame this disadvantage to a great extent by importing German chemists as Dr. D.W.F. Hardie in his *History of the Chemical Industry in Widnes* (1952) and Professor A.E. Musson in his study of the Crosfield soap firm, *Enterprise in Soap and Chemicals: Joseph Crosfield and Sons, Limited, 1815–1965* (1965), have shown. The phrase 'brain drain' had not yet been invented but it was a phenomenon well understood and practised in both British and American industry by 1900. Dr. Ludwig Mond's achievements on the Cheshire salt-field are well enough known and documented, as well as the achievements of Imperial Chemical Industries in the late 1920s and 1930s. Less well known are the achievements of the minor figures: Dr. Karl Markel, for example, from Stuttgart, who was borrowed from Ludwig Mond by John Crosfield, made works manager at Crosfields, and in the words of A.W. Tangye 'completely re-organized the old-fashioned and decadent firm and made it a great success',[8] one of many instances of the profitable transfer of chemical technology from Germany to Britain before 1914.

We must not forget that scientific teaching was by the end of the nineteenth century seeping down into the schools and technical colleges. It is doubtful whether in 1850 there was one science laboratory in any British school. By 1902 there were about 1,000 and when we hear of the deficiencies of the public schools in this respect it must be remembered that no serious research has been done into this aspect of the question. It came as a surprise to me to discover that there was in the early years of this century even a popular school of mechanics at Eton to which Richard O. Shuttleworth (1909–40), the car and aircraft pioneer, belonged in the early 1920s.[9] The firm which the Shuttleworth family had founded is a striking example of versatility. In 1907 Clayton and

Shuttleworth of Lincoln employed 2,700 workers making agricultural machinery – they were by no means the largest firm, or the most successful in the business – Marshalls of Gainsborough, also in Lincolnshire employed 5,000 in 1913 and Rustons of Lincoln 5,200 in 1911, but Clayton and Shuttleworth stand out because they sold their machines all over the Austro-Hungarian empire and had a subsidiary in Vienna employing 700 workers by 1914, and one in Budapest.

There has also been a good deal of discussion about the low social estimation of the engineer – as regards training, it is alleged, there was little difference between the seven-year apprenticeships of the artisan engineer in the workshop, and the training of the premium apprentice in the workshop and drawing office and destined for the professional bodies. This was contrasted with continental practice whereby apprentice engineers spent more time studying in the technical high schools and less time in workshop and drawing office. This has been disputed, and attention has been drawn to the fact that Royce (1863–1933), Bentley (1888–1971) and A.V. Roe (1878–1949) all served their time in railway workshops, while Herbert Austin (1866–1941) was trained in an engineering works in Melbourne. There have been too many sweeping generalisations about the alleged defects in British industry.

It is sometimes alleged that British industrialists did not seize new opportunities as swiftly as they might have done. Yet they began manufacturing pedal bicycles successfully in the 1870s and in 1913 Britain exported no less than 150,000 (Germany exported 89,000, the rest of the world none). A slump in the demand for bicycles in the mid-1890s led the small British workshops concerned to switch over to manufacturing components for the new petrol-driven motor cars, motor cycles and side cars. Here again, the Germans had been pioneers from the 1880s, but had met with production difficulties and the French manufacturers had easily outdistanced them by 1900. British manufacturers of motor vehicles met the French challenge and within seven years (1907) the value of British motor car and lorry production was £5.2 millions, rising three-fold to £15.6 millions by 1913. Had World War I not intervened, the British motor car and heavy vehicle industry would have been much larger in the 1920s and 1930s, when the world was flooded with cheap cars from the United States, which had seized its opportunity while Europe was at war. Nevertheless, once peace returned in 1919, the British motor industry, thanks largely to the future Lords Nuffield and Austin, did expand rapidly, although never on the American scale.

This brings me to the second part of my lecture on the war of 1914–18, its effect on the British economy and the inter-war years. Professor T.C. Barker has stressed the damage done to the British economy by this war. With one exception, merchant shipping, France suffered heavier losses in men and physical capital, but Britain suffered more seriously in the economic sphere. As they existed in 1914 the British economy and trade networks depended on the freest possible international exchange of goods and services. Britain in 1914 was still a Free Trade state and overseas tariffs and restrictions were, over large parts of the globe, relatively moderate, even in Russia, compared with what they were to become in the 1920s and 1930s. Foreign exchange restrictions were so unusual that they seemed to be a relic of the seventeenth century or even earlier, for the gold sovereign had established itself almost as a world currency. Not only was this system either modified or destroyed during the war and its aftermath, but the Japanese, Indian and Southern U.S.A. cotton mills and weaving sheds partially filled the gaps in Asian and American demand for cotton goods caused by the German U-boat campaign and these markets were never to be wholly recovered. The Lancashire cotton industry, dependent on a rather ramshackle system of financing, remained geared to the hope of continual expansion, an expansion which had proceeded since the 1780s and had only been seriously checked by the Cotton Famine of 1862–5 and the strikes of the mid-1890s. Once contraction started and the economies of long continuous runs of yarn and cloth production began to shrink, a downward spiral developed. By 1937 production of cloth was down to about 50% of what it had been in 1913 and worse was to come.

In the coal industry the process of shrinkage turned out to be roughly similar: total world demand for coal, which had increased on the average of 4% a year before 1913, now increased by only 1%, partly as the result of the switch to water power and oil and partly because of the greater attention being given to fuel economy in the production of electric power and coal gas. Newly-opened mines in Poland and Silesia produced cheap coal, the export of which was subsidised by governments. Exports of British coal fell from 104.5 million tons in 1923 to just under 50 million tons in 1938, and total production from 267 million tons in 1923 to 227 million tons in 1938. Direct employment in and around the mines fell by roughly 400,000, or one-third, during the same period, an indication both of increased mechanisation and the closing down of many inefficient and exhausted pits and the opening of new and more productive mines.

Professor Saul has shown that the British engineering and machine tool industries were reasonably efficient and innovative before 1914, although they did perhaps depend too much on the production of locomotives and textile machinery. No one can, however, blame those in charge of them for lack of hindsight. In the inter-war period the machine tool industry remained one of the bright spots of the economy, with Herberts of Coventry doing particularly well. In spite of the change and decay in the old staple industries new ones were arising – in radio and television, in the expansion of rayon headed by Courtaulds. The electrical engineering industry and power generation transmission industry in which British progress had been slow (British Westinghouse and British Thomson Houston were both subsidiaries of American firms) flourished particularly in the 1920s and 1930s, when Charles H. Merz's idea of a grid system, first tried out by his North East Power Company, was applied to the whole country by the Central Electricity Board from 1927 onwards.

The fact that British scientists and industralists were able during the First World War to build up the largest aircraft industry in the world from almost nothing within the space of four years indicates that the British economy did not lack enterprise and flexibility. That this industry had to be dismantled in 1919–21, only to be laboriously recreated in the 1930s and 1940s, illustrates both the elastic properties of the economy and the damaging effect of the First World War.

In the textile sphere, the rise of the rayon industry in Britain, dominated by Courtaulds, has been ably and amply chronicled by Professor D.C. Coleman. If any industry can be called science-based it is the rayon industry and Courtaulds dominated the home market by a skilful combination of industrial chemistry, the deployment of patents and an aggressive policy which widened markets through a constant lowering of prices throughout the 1920s and 1930s. Courtaulds had a profitable American subsidiary – the American Viscose Corporation – the sale of which to U.S. business interests in 1941 during Britain's hour of need is one of the most depressing economic stories of the Second World War.

Side by side with the rayon industry there came the growth of other new industries in Britain during the inter-war period, particularly during the 1930s. These have been ably investigated by Professor Harry W. Richardson in his book *Economic Recovery in Britain 1932–1939* (1967), and of this period even the pessimistic Professor Pollard has written:

probably never before or since has British production grown as fast. New industries were modernised and expanded, including motor cars, electrical engineering, aircraft, chemicals; old ones were brought up to date at least in part, including iron and steel; and Britain rapidly narrowed the gap between herself and the leading industrial nations.

NOTES

This paper, the 16th Dickinson Memorial Lecture, was delivered at Imperial College, London, on 9 May 1984 and is reprinted from the *Transactions of the Newcomen Society*, Vol.55, 1983–84, pp.211–18 by permission of the Council.

1. S.B. Saul, *The Myth of the Great Depression, 1873–96* (1969).
2. D.R. Headrick, *The Tools of Empire: Technology and European Imperialism in the 19th Century* (1981).
3. A.E. Musson, *The Growth of British Industry* (1978), pp.167–8.
4. J.H. Clapham, *The Economic History of Modern Britain*, Vol III (1938), p.62. In 1910–11 256,000 tons of old British sailing ships were sold abroad, in 1913, 448,000. In addition 225,000 tons of steamships were added to the British mercantile marine in 1913.
5. M. Sanderson, *The Universities and British Industry, 1850–1970* (1972), pp.22–3.
6. Dr. W. Kroker, in an informal address to the Summer Meeting of 1983, *Transactions of the Newcomen Society*, Vol.54 (1982–83), p.178.
7. M. Sanderson, op. cit., p.23.
8. A.E. Musson, op. cit. (note 3), p.79. For Sir John Brunner's munificent support to reform of the small grammar school at Northwich, Cheshire, along scientific lines, see Marjorie Cox, *A History of Sir John Deane's Grammar School, Northwich* (1975).
9. K. Desmond, *Richard Shuttleworth: an Illustrated Biography* (1982), p.27.

BIBLIOGRAPHY

Books
R. Floud and D. McCloskey (eds.), *The Economic History of Britain since 1700* vol.II: 1860 to the 1970s (1981)
A.L. Levine, *Industrial Retardation in Britain, 1880–1914* (1967)
D.H. Aldcroft (ed.), *The Development of British Industry and Foreign Competition, 1875–1914* (1968)
M.J. Wiener, *English Culture and the Decline of the Industrial Spirit, 1850–1980* (1981)
M.W. Kirby, *The Decline of British Economic Power since 1870* (1981)
A.E. Musson, *The Growth of British Industry* (1978)
T.C. Barker, 'History: Economic and Social' in C.B. Cox and A.E. Dyson (eds.), *The Twentieth Century Mind I: 1900–1918* (1972), pp.51–99 (a defence of the Edwardian economy)
A.S. Milward, *The Effects of the World Wars on Britain* (1970)
B.W.E. Alford, *Depression and Recovery: British Economic Growth 1918–1939* (1972)
M. Sanderson, *The Universities and British Industry, 1850–1970* (1972)
H.W. Richardson, *Economic Recovery in Britain, 1932–39* (1967)

Articles
D.N. McCloskey, 'Did Victorian Britain fail?', *Economic History Review*, 2nd ser., vol.XXIII, Dec. 1970, pp.446–59
N.F.R. Crafts, 'Victorian Britain did fail', *Economic History Review*, 2nd ser., vol.XXXII, Nov. 1979, pp.533–7
D.N. McCloskey, 'No it did not: a reply to Crafts', ibid, pp.538–41
S.B. Saul, 'The market and the development of the mechanical engineering industries in Britain, 1860–1914', *Economic History Review*, vol.XX, April 1967, pp.111–30
S.B. Saul, 'The machine tool industry in Britain to 1914', *Business History*, vol.X, 1968, pp.22–43
S.B. Saul, 'The motor industry in Britain to 1914', *Business History*, vol.V, 1962, pp.23–44

D.A. Farnie, 'The structure of the British cotton industry, 1846–1914', in A. Okochi and S. Yonekawa, eds., *The International Conference on Business History No. 8: The Textile Industry and its Business Climate*. University of Tokyo Press, 1982, pp.45–91
S. Pollard, *The neglect of industry: a critique of British economic policy since 1870*, Centrum voor Mattschappij Geschiedenis, Erasmus University, Rotterdam, 1984, pp.1–27

PART THREE

MANCHESTER AS A
REGIONAL METROPOLIS

8

Robert Owen, Peter Drinkwater and the Early Factory System in Manchester, 1788–1800

Robert Owen (1771–1858), cotton-mill owner, philanthropist and the 'father of British Socialism', came to Manchester about 1788 and left it soon after his marriage in September 1799, when he entered upon the government of his 'kingdom' at New Lanark in Scotland. The twelve years or so which he spent in Manchester were among the most formative of his life. He came to Manchester as a rather shy youth who was apt to blush and stammer in conversation, especially when talking to the opposite sex. He left it as a successful and self-assured cotton-mill manager, with a turn for public speaking, and as a man who had recently married the daughter of one of Britain's foremost cotton magnates, David Dale. His intellectual pursuits during his years in Manchester have already been dealt with by Miss E.M. Fraser, with particular reference to his membership of the Manchester Literary and Philosophical Society,[1] and it is proposed in the following pages to throw some new light on the economic side of his activities in the Manchester of the 1790s.[2]

Up to the present the chief source for Owen's economic activities in Manchester has been the first volume of *The Life of Robert Owen, written by himself.*[3] This was published in 1857, the year before his death, and was probably written down for the most part while its author was over 70 years of age. Statements of fact contained in it therefore require careful checking before acceptance, particularly in the account of his early life.

Owen came to Manchester from London, probably about 1788. He would, therefore, be about 17 years of age. He had already served his apprenticeship as a draper under James McGuffog, draper, of Stamford in Lincolnshire. Owen was a good judge of fine muslin (McGuffog had been an enthusiastic customer of Samuel Oldknow of Stockport).

A friend of Owen's secured him a situation with John Satterfield, who kept a draper's shop at No. 5 St. Ann's Square.[4] Owen received £40 per annum, besides his board, lodging and laundry. He did not stay long with Satterfield, as in the course of business in the shop he met a manufacturer of wire frames for ladies' bonnets, 'a mechanic with some small inventive powers and a very active mind'.[5] This man, a Mr. Jones, was almost certainly the John Jones who appears in the Manchester section of John Scholes's *Manchester and Salford Directory* in 1794 as a machine maker, of 58 Water Street.[6] Jones told Owen of

great and extraordinary discoveries that were beginning to be introduced into Manchester for spinning cotton by new and curious machinery. He said he was endeavouring to see and to get a knowledge of them, and that if he could succeed he could make a very good business of it.[7]

At last he succeeded in getting a sight of these machines and was convinced that he could make them himself. He persuaded Owen to write to his brother, William Owen, and borrow £100; the new partnership of Owen and Jones commenced business with this capital late in 1790 or early in 1791. It will be remembered that in 1779 Samuel Crompton had perfected his 'muslin wheel', or hand mule for spinning fine, strong cotton yarn capable of being woven into such superior fabrics as cambric and muslin. It was this machine or an improved version which was to form the main output of the new firm. The following advertisement appeared in the issues of the *Manchester Mercury* for 18 and 25 January 1791:

JONES and OWEN

Respectfully inform the Public, that they have opened a Warehouse near the New Bridge, Dolefield, for making WATER PREPARATION and MULE MACHINES, and flatter themselves from their strict Attention to Business, and the experienced Hands they employ, that they shall be able to finish work in such a manner as will merit the future Favours of those that employ them.

The above Machines are made upon the most approved Plans, and all orders punctually executed to the Time engaged for.

This 'large machine workshop' in what is now Bridge Street, was, according to Owen's account, specially built for the partners by a local builder, and also included some rooms for cotton spinners.[8] In a short time Owen and Jones had about forty men at work. Wood, iron and brass were purchased for their use on credit. Owen soon discovered that Jones lacked business ability, and took over the bookkeeping, all other financial matters and the superintendence and payment of the men. The firm also began to produce rovings (prepared cotton-wool in the stage immediately before it is spun into yarn) for sale to mule spinners and to buy their yarn back from them. It would seem, therefore, that the 'water preparation machines' were roving frames. The *Manchester Mercury* of 8 February 1791 contains the following advertisement:

TO MULE SPINNERS

GOOD MULE SPINNERS may be supplied with Roving Weekly, and the Twist bought in Return, by applying to Jones and Owen, Machine Makers, near the New Bridge, Dole Field, Manchester.[9]

Owen was only too glad to sever his connection with Jones after a few months, when a third party with capital came along and took Owen's place in the business. Owen was promised as compensation for his share in the partnership 'six mule machines such as we were making for sale, a reel, and a making up machine, with which to pack the yarn when finished in skeins into bundles for sale.'[10]

In actual fact he only received three out of the six mules, but, nothing daunted, he rented from a builder and land surveyor named Christopher Woodroofe[11] of Ancoats Lane 'a large newly erected building, or factory, as such places were then beginning to be called. It was situated in Ancoats Lane.'[12]

Here he started on his own 'in a small part of one of the large rooms in this large building'.[13] The separation of Owen from Jones cannot be dated with exactitude. There does not appear to be any announcement of the dissolution of the partnership in the *Manchester Mercury*, and Owen merely says that he did not stay with Jones for many months. Later, in April 1792, Owen was to tell Peter Drinkwater that he was making £300 per annum by his business as yarn manufacturer and dealer,[14] which suggests that he had at any rate between three and six months' experience of working on his own. This would fit in with a severance of his connection with Jones sometime during the latter half of 1791.[15]

Now the curious thing is that Owen states categorically that he became Drinkwater's manager early in 1791, a few months before his twentieth birthday (his birthday was on 14 May). It is possible to prove that Owen's account is a whole year out on this point.

We now come to Owen's connection with Peter Drinkwater. Drinkwater was almost certainly born in 1742.[16] When Mrs. Elizabeth Raffald brought out the third edition of her *Manchester Directory* in 1781, she noted Peter Drinkwater as a fustian manufacturer living in Spring Garden.[17] Seven years later, in Edmond Holme's *Directory* of 1788, there were two Peter Drinkwaters, presumably father and son, the elder still a fustian manufacturer, of Spring Garden, while Peter Drinkwater, jun.,[18] also a fustian manufacturer, had an establishment in King Street.[19]

Peter Drinkwater the elder subscribed 40 guineas in 1784–6 to the funds of the Committee of the Fustian Trade set up in Manchester to agitate for a repeal of Pitt's 'impolitic, odious and oppressive tax upon the cotton manufacture, and for preventing the ruin attendant upon passing the Irish Propositions [of 1785] into a law'. Drinkwater's importance in the cotton trade of the day may be judged by comparing the amount of his subscription with that of the great Sir Richard Arkwright, which was also 40 guineas, and that of Samuel Oldknow of Stockport, which was 5 guineas. No single individual or firm subscribed more to the fund than Drinkwater and Arkwright. It is not therefore surprising to find Drinkwater acting in November 1785 as chairman of a meeting held at the Exchange Coffee House 'to consider the best means of giving a proper and effectual support to that useful and highly necessary institution, the General Chamber of Manufacturers of Great Britain', and he became one of the earliest members of the Manchester 'Commercial Society of Merchants trading on the Continent of Europe' on its formation in 1794.[20]

Later he seems to have been a supporter of Pitt's Government at a time when there was considerable criticism of that Minister's foreign policy. For example, he was one of the signatories of a request to the boroughreeve and constables of Manchester to call a public meeting on 19 April 1791 to discuss the parlous state of Anglo-Russian relations. Several resolutions were passed at this meeting, and the chairman was instructed to pass them on to the two M.P.s for the county with a request that they should vote in accordance with the principles expressed in them. They were evidently of a pacifist tendency, for Peter Drinkwater was later one of several hundred persons who publicly protested against the proceedings of this meeting, in the following words: 'For although we feel ... the evils attendant upon a war, we think an interference of this nature highly improper, on a subject which the Constitution hath wisely lodged in the hands of the executive power.'[21]

In 1792 Drinkwater senior was appointed a J.P.[22] for the county of Lancaster (Salford Hundred) and from the list of J.P.s for 1794 it appears that he had a country residence, Irwell House, near Agecroft Bridge, where he lived in the summer, coming up to town on two or three days a week. In the 1790s he had a town house at 42 Fountain Street, Manchester, where he spent the winter season.[23] The *Gentleman's Magazine* for 1789 contains the obituary notice of his wife, Margaret, who died on 7 March of that year, and was described as 'sister to the late Mr. Serjeant Bolton'.[24]

In June 1785 this same Serjeant Bolton, Drinkwater's brother-in-law, had examined Thomas Highs as counsel for the Crown in the famous case of *Rex v. Arkwright* in the Court of King's Bench, when the Lancashire cotton-spinners successfully impugned, by writ of *scire facias*, the validity of Arkwright's second patent of 1775 for carding, drawing, and roving machines.[25] Highs (1719–1803) claimed that Arkwright filched both the idea of spinning by rollers and the device of cylinders in the roving frames from him. It is significant that Highs, according to Baines, 'was supported in his old age by the liberality of Peter Drinkwater,, Esq., of Manchester, and others'.[26] Owen refers to Drinkwater as 'a good fustian manufacturer and a first-rate foreign merchant', who was able on account of his great wealth to survive the commercial crisis of 1792–3 without very much loss.[27]

It is interesting to note that in Scholes's *Manchester and Salford Directory* of 1794, Drinkwater is no longer described as a fustian manufacturer, but as 'merchant and cotton manufacturer', of 29 York Street.[28] It appears that 29 York Street was his counting house, or business office. His town house, 42 Fountain Street, was, of course, just round the corner. For example, when the creditors of John Stopford, cotton manufacturer, of Oldham Street, who went bankrupt in 1790, desired to hold a meeting on 20 March 1792, it was 'at the Counting House of Peter Drinkwater in York Street' that they fore-gathered.[29]

It seems clear that in the course of the 1780s Drinkwater had begun to transmute some of the capital he had accumulated as a textile middleman and exporter into industrial capital. Wishing to cheapen the cost of his raw material by taking advantage of the improved methods of spinning which were spreading in the 1780s, he had purchased or set up a water-driven cotton factory at Northwich in Cheshire (the exact date of this event is unknown, but the evidence shows that it was probably before 1789). The Northwich mill 'was employed in what was technically called water-spinning, – or warp-spinning on machinery similar to Arkwright's at Cromford, Manchester, and elsewhere'. In 1792 it was under the management of an elderly man, who had been in charge of it for some years; its yarn was much coarser than that to be produced by Drinkwater's second mill.[30]

Early in 1789 Peter Drinkwater began to erect his second factory, a four-storied structure, popularly known as Bank Top Mill, and to those concerned in it as the Piccadilly Factory. It lay just off London Road, between Auburn Street and Upton Street.[31] Dr. Alexander Ure states that this Piccadilly factory was the first cotton mill in Manchester to be powered by a rotary steam engine.[32] According to Owen's account, Drinkwater had built the mill 'for finer spinning, and was beginning to fill it with machinery under the superintendance (*sic*) of a Mr. George [Augustus] Lee,'[33] when Lee rather shabbily decided to leave him in order to go into partnership with a rival Mr. (afterwards Sir) George Philips in a large cotton mill in Salford. In 1789, however, Drinkwater told Boulton and Watt that a gentleman named Richard Slack would have 'a very considerable interest' in the Piccadilly factory and the 'sole conducting of it'.[34] Lee had apparently been promoted from being a clerk in the Northwich mill to the management of the Piccadilly factory on the death of Slack early in 1791.[35] According to Owen, Drinkwater was 'totally ignorant of everything connected with cotton spinning'.[36] Indeed, Owen's picture of Drinkwater can scarcely be called a favourable one.

Fortunately there are other documents available which throw a great deal of light on Drinkwater's character and business concerns. In 1789 he became deeply involved in the installation of a Boulton and Watt steam engine in this 'rather expensive' new factory in Piccadilly and a small bundle of his letters, bearing various dates between 3 April and 13 December 1789, written to the famous Soho firm of engineers is preserved in the Boulton and Watt collection in Birmingham Public Library. The impression gained from reading these letters is of a good-hearted, if somewhat pompous and prolix gentleman.[37]

The first letter shows him meeting local opposition to the erection of the new steam engine:

I should have wrote you on this subject much sooner had I not been in-commoded on all sides by threats of a prosecution for erecting a nuisance and indeed, the prejudice is not yet much, if at all, abated. The fact is that we have already a great number of the common old smoking engines in and about the town,[38] which I confess are far from being agreeable and the public yet are not all inclined to believe otherwise than that a steam engine of any sort must be highly offensive.[39]

The contract with Boulton and Watt for the erection of the engine, ante-dated to 1 April 1789, shows that it was of the rotary type, with a 16-inch cylinder, had a piston with a 4-foot stroke, and was of the power of 8 horses. Drinkwater was to pay Boulton and Watt an annual premium of £40 and the engine was to be used for 'preparing and carding cotton and for such other purposes as may be required'.

In fact, Drinkwater mentioned in his letter of 3 April 1789 that he did not intend to use it for spinning cotton. In the same letter he frankly admitted that he was ignorant of the nature of steam engines of any kind, and asked Boulton and Watt to send him

as soon as possible a sketch for my regulation in digging over the foundations of the walls of the whole building, for which purpose I have now a considerable number of hands in waiting.

By following the correspondence we can watch the building rising and see the difficulties which beset the investor of capital even in the days of *laisser faire*. We can also note Drinkwater's eye for detail. By June 1789 he was reporting that no adequate foundations could be found until the labourers had dug down to a depth of over 9 feet, and accordingly cellars had to be added to the building. The thickness of the outer walls had also to be increased by half a brick to 23 inches. By June the bricklayers and well-sinkers had 'gone to the first floor nearly with one end of the factory'.[40]

Yet the engine was still not installed by the end of 1789 and Drinkwater wrote in November that he was 'much hindered in proceeding with my job by the uncommon wetness of the seasons, and now added to this I have had great difficulty indeed in sinking the well for the cold water pump by a quicksand which has caused several weeks' more delay'.[41]

He was insistent that the new factory should be as light and airy as possible. In his preliminary instructions to Boulton and Watt concerning the building of the engine-house he wrote:

I wish you to block up no more of my intended windows than you can help by either the width or the height of your brickwork or roof, for to give the building (I mean the factory part) its greatest possible convenience, it should have a continued series of windows – one and a pier introduced in the distance of every 8 or 9 foot or thereabout.[42]

Later, he complained that Boulton and Watt's plans would 'not only block me up 3 windows in the first factory floor, but also a good share of 3 in the 2nd floor'.[43]

Drinkwater's views on the sanitation and the lavatory accommodation in the new building were quite advanced, if not quite as modern as those of Boulton and Watt. The correspondence shows that he bestowed considerable thought on the whole question. In the preliminary instructions of April 1789, he wrote:

I would likewise wish you to introduce room for 4 small single necessaries – one for each room, to be placed nearly one over another, and so, if possible, to be so managed as neither to be offensive nor endanger the health of the people at work. To which purpose I shall be thankful for your advice, whether it will be proper to pass a current of water thro' them to a common sewer by help of the engine pump at nights and mornings before the works are set a-going, or whether to make air pipes or vents in the brickwork from the excrement in the bottom to the top of the roof will not answer the same end.[44]

A fortnight later he was seriously perturbed by the Soho firm's architectural suggestions:

Could not the necessaries be conveniently introduced in the angle [of the wall], not on the outside as you propose, for in that case it would block up 4 windows more, i.e. one on every story of the factory?

Boulton and Watt wished him to instal a flushing device consisting of watercocks to be operated from each lavatory, but he still thought that his original idea of 4 brickwork pipes about 14 inches square running right down the building to communicate with a common sewer 'would answer full as well and be less expensive than water closets'. He wanted to have the proposed piping flushed out once or twice a day.

Modern sanitary appliances are now taken so much for granted that we generally fail to realise when studying conditions during the Industrial Revolution that at one time the mass of the population did not know how to use them.[45] Drinkwater went on:

... the pipes of ... [water closets] ... I know from experience, would be apt to burst in frosty weather. Nor could, I fear, the poor ignorant workpeople and children be taught to turn and manage the cocks etc. without the closets running into a state of disorder and nastiness, a situation in which I have sometimes seen them, but in all these things your experience and better judgement will set me right.[46]

A further letter on 3 June 1789 shows that he had not only adopted Boulton and Watt's advanced sanitary arrangements, but had also fitted a stench trap and intended to flush the lavatories occasionally with 'a strong stream of water let out from the great wooden cistern of the engine ... when the rain collected from the roof into and through a leaden pipe does not do the business sufficiently'. And he added, very creditably:

... the object of keeping the factory sweet and wholesome at this point is a matter which I cannot help considering of the utmost importance, whether as regards decency, convenience or humanity.

It would be interesting to know whether Drinkwater's sentiments and the conditions in the Piccadilly Factory influenced Owen's later experiments at New Lanark.

If we may judge by Drinkwater's experience, it was not always an easy task for the rising cotton magnates to build factories, fill them with machinery and man them with trained, efficient workers. Drinkwater was worried about the capital expenditure to which he had committed himself and about the running costs of the new factory. In June 1789 he tried to secure from Boulton and Watt some reduction of the annual premium on his steam engine, and brought forward the example of what was described in 1836 as 'the oldest cotton mill in Manchester'. It stood on Shudehill, and had been built in the early 1780s by Messrs. Arkwright, Simpson and Whittenbury. It was noteworthy because the spinning machinery was not driven directly by steam power, but indirectly, by means of a single-stroke atmospheric pumping engine of the Newcomen type, which replenished the factory water-wheel's reservoir.[47] Drinkwater wrote:

... circumstanced as a cotton manufacturer is, it is *impossible to exercise its* [the engine's] *full power all at once* – the factory at Shude Hill which your Mr. Southern has seen has been more than 7 years in filling with machinery and I am doubtful whether with convenience it could have been filled much sooner. That I am now building will and must labour under the same inconvenience so far that I fear I shall not be able to use more than the power of 3 or 4 horses within the compass of two years or more after the engine is set agoing. Could you therefore be satisfied to receive a premium ... according to the power which the purchaser could bring immediately into use and so progressively till his buildings could be filled with machinery and people?[48]

Boulton and Watt remained unimpressed by this argument, which they had heard before. In the course of 1789, however, Drinkwater was favoured with a visit from the great Matthew Boulton himself, who promised, among other improvements, that the engine should be fitted with Watt's new governor, a device which would not 'permit 2 strokes per minute of increase of velocity though all the work were taken away at once'. This was particularly important where machinery had to run smoothly. Drinkwater was evidently a quick learner, both with regard to steam engines and the cotton trade, for in spite of his alleged ignorance on both subjects he wrote to Soho in November 1789, after Boulton's visit, with reference to the governor:

... among these inventions one, I understand, is of a nature solely calculated to secure more effectually an equable motion under different degrees of heat from the fire – a property so extremely essential in preparing cotton to work into *fine* yarn that I would on no account have you deny [me] the use of this instrument.

In his reply James Watt agreed to fit the governor or regulator to Drinkwater's engine, adding a strong warning against showing it to others.[49] As far as can be ascertained the engine was set to work in 1790,[50] and its newly-invented governor may explain some of Owen's later success as a spinner of fine yarns. Remember what Owen said about Drinkwater:

Mr. Drinkwater knew nothing about the mill. ... He never came to the mill, but almost always desired to see me at his counting house on the days he attended there, and that I should bring speciments of the manufacture week by week.[51]

For a short time before Owen entered into the picture, George Augustus Lee was the manager of the Piccadilly Factory, then employing about 500 people. Lee gave notice to leave Drinkwater's service and according to Owen's account, Drinkwater

... had to advertise for a manager to undertake the superintendance of this mill, now in progress; and his advertisement appeared on a Saturday in the Manchester papers, but I had not seen or heard of it until I went to my factory on the Monday morning following, when, as I entered the room where my spinning machines were, one of the spinners said – 'Mr. Lee has left Mr. Drinkwater, and he has advertised for a manager.'[52]

In Owen's well-known account of his interview with Drinkwater concerning the post, Owen alleged that he replied to Drinkwater's query 'How old are you?' by saying 'Twenty in May this year' which would place the affair in January–April 1791. In actual fact Drinkwater's advertisement appeared exactly a year after Owen's date. In 1792 Manchester had three weekly newspapers, the *Manchester Mercury*, each issue of which bore Tuesday's date, the *Manchester Chronicle*, published on Saturdays, and the short-lived *Manchester Herald*, which also bore Saturday's date. Drinkwater's advertisement first appeared in the *Chronicle* for 14 April 1792. The file of the *Mercury* in Chetham's Library shows that the advertisement was repeated in that newspaper on 17 April, and it also appeared in the advanced Radical *Manchester Herald* of Saturday 21 April, with certain slight alterations. This last insertion is date-lined 'King-street, 19 April', which shows that the vacancy was not then filled. It is impossible to state definitely which insertion Owen saw, but it may very well have been that in the *Manchester Herald*, which would place the date of this interview with Drinkwater on Monday, 23 April 1792. Unfortunately, if we take the terms of the advertisement as being correct, Drinkwater would not have been interviewing applicants for the post on a *Monday* morning, although Owen states that he had been doing so. The advertisement in the *Mercury* reads:

SUPERINTENDENCY OF A FACTORY

WANTED

A PERSON to superintend and conduct an extensive MULE FACTORY, to whom any salary will be allowed proportionate to Merit.

No one need apply, whose Character, in regard to Morals, as well as Capacity and Steadiness, is not every way respectable.

For Particulars apply to Mr. Drinkwater, at his Warehouse in Manchester, on Tuesdays, Thursdays or Saturdays from eleven to two o'clock.[53]

It is not proposed to go over the familiar details of how Owen persuaded Drinkwater to appoint him manager of the Piccadilly Factory at £300 per annum, after an inspection of the books of the small spinning factory off Ancoats Lane. Owen was rather abashed when he saw hundreds of workpeople and the new machines in Drinkwater's large modern establishment, but after keeping his eyes open and his mouth shut for six weeks he felt, as usual, 'ready to give directions in every department'.[54] The previous manager had succeeded in producing yarns and thread of what was then considered an extraordinary fineness, known technically as 'one hundred and twenty hanks in the pound', i.e. 120 hanks, each 840 yards in length, were required to weigh 1 lb., but it was of 'very indifferent quality'.[55] Owen soon succeeded in improving on this, according to his own story, and produced thread of the fineness of 300 hanks to the pound and above.[56] At the same time he reorganized the Northwich mill and kept it under regular personal supervision, riding over on horseback once a fortnight.[57] According to Owen, Drinkwater did not even take him down to the factory on his appointment, and during the period of Owen's management he seems to have visited it only three times, once in order to show it to Serjeant John Pemberton Heywood of Lincoln's Inn, his son-in-law,[58] and on another occasion, to Sir William Herschel (1738–1822), the famous astronomer.[59] Note that rather confusingly Owen states on three separate occasions, first, that Drinkwater 'never came to the mill' (p. 92), meaning that he was not in the habit of doing so, secondly, that 'he came only three times during the four years I retained the management of it' (p. 31), and lastly, 'Mr. Drinkwater ... for three years had once only been to his factory in Manchester' (p. 41).

In 1790, the year in which Drinkwater's Piccadilly Factory commenced operations, William Kelly, the manager of David Dale's cotton mills at New Lanark in Scotland,[60] applied water-power to Crompton's hand-mule, and in 1793 John Kennedy of Manchester made a successful attempt to spin fine yarn, say from 100 hanks to the pound and upwards, by using an improved mule driven by steam power. In connection with this Kennedy says of Drinkwater and Owen:

Mr. Drinkwater of Manchester, was the most extensive fine spinner at the time of which I speak. He was one of the early water spinners,[61] and in possession of the most perfect system of roving making. His large mill in Piccadilly was filled with mules of 144 spindles, each of which was worked by men's hands. Mr. Owen was then his manager and they came to see the new machine in 1793. They approved of it and thought it practical. Mr. Humphries[62] of Glasgow, who was a good mechanic, and succeeded Mr. Owen as manager ... got instructions to apply this system of power to his fine work produced by the mules in Piccadilly mill; and to make its advantages available he coupled these 144 [-spindle mules] together. ...[63]

It is not generally known that a number of short letters and several invoices written by Owen in his capacity as manager of the Piccadilly Factory have survived and are the earliest known documents in his handwriting. Two of them, dated 4 and 14 March 1793, are in the Boulton and Watt Collection in Birmingham. They are addressed to Boulton and Watt and give an order for a new boiler for the factory steam engine, which was to be made at John Wilkinson's ironworks at Bersham near Wrexham. It was transported by sea from Chester to Runcorn in the Mersey estuary and then brought up the Bridgewater canal via Preston Brook to Manchester.

An invoice made out by Owen, together with a short note was once in the Oldknow MSS.[64] It is dated 3 December 1793, and shows that Samuel Oldknow, the celebrated muslin manufacturer and cotton

One of the earliest documents in Robert Owen's handwriting (reproduced by kind permission of Birmingham Public Library) spinner of Stockport and Mellor (1756–1828) had ordered 5 lb. of 100 mule twist, 5 lb. of 105 mule twist and 19 lb. of 105 mule twist in cops. Owen added a short note:

> The yarn as above was this day sent by Jenkinson, hope you will receive it in good condition and find the quality to your satisfaction. Mr. D[rinkwater] has not positively determined upon the price: when he does, I will send you the account.
>
> Your obedt. servt.
>
> Piccadilly Factory.
> Robt. Owen.

The Jenkinson referred to was Aaron Jenkinson, carrier, of Meal Street, off Fountain Street, who maintained a service between Manchester and Stockport. The *Manchester Directory* of 1794 noted of Jenkinson that he 'comes in and goes out every day, Sundays excepted'.[65]

A search of the Oldknow MSS. in the John Rylands Library revealed a similar invoice, dated 20 July 1793, unsigned, but almost certainly in Owen's handwriting. This item is interesting in that it shows Owen producing twist of the fineness of 160 a year after taking over the management.[66]

Mr. Samuel Oldknow   Manchester, 20 July 1793.
Bot. of Peter Drinkwater.

		[s][d]			
$2\frac{5}{8}$ 5 lbs. Mule Twist No. 112		24/4	£6	1	8
$2\frac{3}{4}$ 5 lbs. Mule Twist No. 124		28/9	7	3	9
$3\frac{1}{4}$ 4 lbs. Mule Twist No. 150		40/2	8	0	8
$3\frac{1}{2}$ 4 lbs. Mule Twist No. 160		45/8	9	2	8
			30	8	9
	Deduct for reeling			8	9
			30	0	0
	Box			3	0
			£30	3	0

Another document, dated 30 October 1793, which was also at one time in the Oldknow MSS., is reproduced below.[67]

Manchester 30 Oct. 1793

Mr. Samuel Oldknow,
    Bought of Peter Drinkwater
    10 lbs Twist in Cops No.110
    10 lbs Do No.122

Mr. Saml. Oldknow,   D15
 Sir,   465

The above were intended for the exact nos. which you wanted, but upon trial found them to vary two hanks; if they are not sufficiently near to your order, on returning them, in a few days you shall have the Nos. required,

Remaining for
Peter Drinkwater
Your humble servant

Robt. Owen

Piccadilly Factory
 30 Oct. 1793

Samuel Oldknow's ambitious projects were responsible for Owen leaving Drinkwater's service. A match was in process of being arranged, presumably in 1794, between Miss Eliza Drinkwater[68] and Oldknow, who wished to have complete control over Peter Drinkwater's cotton-spinning interests.[69] Now when Owen had completed six months' service as manager by the autumn of 1792, Drinkwater sent for him and promised him £400 per annum during his second year as manager, £500 during his third year, and in the autumn of 1795 Owen was to become a partner in the business with Thomas and John Drinkwater,[70] the merchant's young sons. Owen and Drinkwater signed an agreement to this effect.[71] Owen's promised partnership, however, stood in the way of what Owen called Oldknow's plans for 'exclusive dealing with Mr. Drinkwater's property', for which he had 'extensive views and arrangements'.[72] In the course of 1794 Owen was accordingly summoned to Drinkwater's country residence, which Owen calls in his *Life* 'Newal House'. This is obviously a mistake for Irwell House. Whether the error was due to Owen or the printer it is impossible to say. At Irwell House, Drinkwater explained the position to him and asked Owen to cancel the agreement signed by both the men some time during the autumn of 1792. In return Owen was to name his own salary as manager. Owen replied by throwing his copy of the agreement in the fire and announcing his intention of quitting Drinkwater's service. He eventually relented somewhat, but only as far as promising to stay on temporarily until he had chosen a suitable successor in the management of the Piccadilly Factory. This was Robert Humphreys of Glasgow mentioned above.[73] According to Owen it was 'many months' or 'nearly a year' before Humphreys became available. Owen is vague on this point: 'I left Mr. Drinkwater in 1794 or 5',[74] but the evidence suggests that his departure took place in 1794.[75] It seems likely, therefore, that

Owen was in Drinkwater's service for about two and a half years, rather than the four years of his own statement. An alternative explanation is that he remained Drinkwater's manager well into 1795, but was at the same time actively engaged in the affairs of his new partnership with Scarth and Moulson.[76]

Of Drinkwater's later activities little is known. Owen states, for what it is worth, that 'Mr Drinkwater became dissatisfied with the business, sold the factory, and Mr. Humphries lost his situation'. Owen implied that these events occurred about 1800–1.[77] Drinkwater died on Sunday, 15 November 1801, either at Hayes, in Middlesex, near Uxbridge, or at St. Albans, Herts. (the newspapers differ). They are agreed, however, that he was on his way to London from Manchester at the time, and Cowdroy's *Manchester Gazette* adds: 'His death was awfully sudden.' Thus died Peter Drinkwater in the sixtieth year of his age.[78]

Owen found little difficulty in making a fresh start; it soon became generally known that he was leaving Drinkwater's service, and Owen writes:

Mr. Samuel Marsland, who with others had purchased the Chorlton Estate, near Manchester, with the view of building a new town upon it, applied to me and said he was going to build extensive mills upon this property, and if I would join him in partnership he would find the capital and give me one third of the profits.[79]

Owen, who now had more confidence in his abilities, declined this offer, because, according to his own story, he was not offered half the profits, much to his regret later on. Possibly the real reason was the fact that he would not have had sufficient power. Instead he entered into a much more unfavourable partnership with Jonathan Scarth and Richard Percival Moulson of Manchester, 'two young men, inexperienced in the business, although they had capital', as he was to write later. This partnership, which must be distinguished from the Chorlton Twist Company of 1796, was to undertake the erection of cotton mills on land purchased from Samuel Marsland and Company. Owen was to be the general manager and each partner was to have one-third of the profits. This arrangement appears to have lasted about a year.[80]

Again we are able to supplement Owen's account with material from the Boulton and Watt Collection. In the latter part of 1795 Owen visited Soho and agreed to purchase a Boulton and Watt rotary steam engine for £1,492, for the purpose of driving the machinery in the proposed new cotton factory in Cambridge Street, off Oxford Road. The steam-engine agreement, ante-dated to 2 October 1795 and signed by the three partners, may still be seen in Birmingham Public Library. The collection there also contains the following letter from Owen to Boulton and Watt:

Messrs. Boulton and Watt.

Gentlemen,

We have concluded to have an engine of 30 horses power and with the advice of Mr. Lowe to fix it at the end of all the buildings, within side the factory; we intend soon to send you a ground plan with the elevation of the buildings and a plan of the Chorlton Lands. We shall be much obliged by having the engine forwarded as early in the spring as you possibly can.

We are,

Respectfully yours,

Robt. Owen & Co.

Chorlton Hall,

Manchester. [27] Oct. '95.[81]

Contrary to what we should expect from Owen's account, Samuel Marsland had made the first approach to Boulton and Watt respecting the installation of the engines, and in addition was financing the industrial development of his 'trading estate' by finding half the cost of the engine. Indeed James Watt, jun., wrote to Marsland on 10 December 1795 asking him whether, in view of the fact that he was to guarantee half the cost of the engine, he wished his name to appear as a partner in the steam engine agreement. Marsland's connection with Messrs. Moulson, Scarth and Owen was, however, 'of a private nature' and his name was not included in the agreement.[82]

The engine was evidently not set to work until 1796 was far advanced,[83] by which time the financial crisis of the winter of 1796–7 loomed ahead. For Robert Owen and Company the trouble started with their Scots customers, who were eager buyers of the fine thread and yarn which Owen knew so well how to produce. The following letter tells its own story:

Messrs. Boulton and Watt.   Manchester, 15th Oct., 1796.

Gentlemen,

We should have answered yours of the 22nd. ult[im]o had we not been in daily expectation of Mr. Marsland paying us for his proportion of the engine which he at present does not find it convenient to do. From the great scarcity of money in Scotland we have been disappointed in getting bills discounted as usual and even prolonging the credit to six months, which lays us under the unpleasing necessity of remitting you a bill at that period drawn on W[illia]m and R[ichar]d[so]n Borradaile and Co. for £1,527. 10. 8. We, however, hope you will not find much inconvenience in paying it away.[84]

We assure you that nothing but the great scarcity of money in the commercial world would have induced us to ask for a longer credit than the time first mentioned, but if you think the bill at too long a date (though we did not expect your invoice would have been dated so early) we must allow you what you may deem adequate for the time.

Your acknowledgement per return of post will oblige,

Gentlemen,

Your obdt. Servts.,

Thomas Atkinson for

The Chorlton Twist Co.

The name Thomas Atkinson brings us to the last chapter in the story of Owen's business enterprises in Manchester – the Chorlton Twist Company, fine cotton spinners (1796–1800). This seems to have been a highly successful enterprise.[85] In his *Life* Owen wrote:

... while the mills were erecting, a new arrangement was made ... with those two rich old established houses, Messrs. Borrodale and Atkinson, of London, and Messrs. Bartons of Manchester, with whom and myself a new partnership was formed ... the 'Chorlton Twist Company', under my management, assisted by Thomas Atkinson, a brother of the one in the firm of Borrodale and Atkinson.[86]

Messrs. Barton were wholesale merchants and cotton manufacturers of No.6 Phoenix Street, Manchester.[87] The Borradaile connection is rather more complicated and certainly more interesting. Messrs. Borradaile and Atkinson were hat manufacturers of Greengate, Salford, in the 1790s, but the London headquarters of the firm operated from 34 Fenchurch Street (and, later, from 14 St. Helen's Place) as William and Richardson Borradaile and John Atkinson, merchants and hat manufacturers.[88] This was entirely concerned with dealing in furs and exporting hats; and we know from other evidence that in 1812 Messrs. W. and R. Borradaile of London were ship-owners and managing directors of at least one East Indiaman.[89] And so the wheel had come full circle. Drinkwater had entered the cotton industry with profits accumulated in foreign commerce. Later, in 1796, Owen, after trying unsuccessfully to carry on in the cotton industry with the backing of Marsland's real estate venture, was forced to fall back on the support of a firm which was securely based on the foundation of a profitable overseas trade.

NOTES

This paper is reprinted from the *Bulletin of the John Rylands Library*, September 1954, pp.78–102.

1. E.M. Fraser, 'Robert Owen in Manchester, 1787–1800', *Memoirs and Proceedings of the Manchester Literary and Philosophical Society*, vol. lxxxii:4 (1937–8), pp.29–41.
2. Such portions of Mr. Peter Gorb's 'Robert Owen as a Businessman' (*Bulletin of the Business Historical Society*, vol.xxv (Sept. 1951), no.3, pp.127–48) as deal with his Manchester activities depend almost entirely on *The Life of Robert Owen written by himself*, vol.i. Neither does R.H. Harvey in his recent biography of Owen (*Robert Owen, Social Idealist*, University of California Publications in History, vol.xxxviii, 1949) attempt to check Owen's statements. See, however, Margaret I. Cole, *Robert Owen of New Lanark* (1953), pp.19–34.
3. Pages 21–56 of the edition of 1857, referred to henceforth as *Life*.
4. P. Barfoot and John Wilkes, *Universal British Directory*, vol.iii (1790 ff.), p.840. In 1791 Satterfield, after waiting on George III, Queen Charlotte and the five

princesses with specimens of Manchester manufactures, was appointed Royal linen draper for the town of Manchester (*Manchester Mercury*, 12 April 1791, p.4 col.4).

5. *Life*, p.22.
6. See John Scholes, *Directory of Manchester* (1794), p.75. Professor G.D.H. Cole in his *Robert Owen* calls him Ernest Jones, but does not cite any authority (edition of 1925, p.48).
7. *Life*, p.22.
8. *Life*, p.23.
9. ... the principle on which the rovings were prepared had little chance of being known, being confined to the principal mill-owners [who were licensees] of Mr. Arkwright's patent process of spinning &c. But the demand for these machines after the decision of the Court of King's Bench ... [in 1785] ... soon found makers, and the perseverance of the mule spinner soon acquired the art ... The roving-making then became a distinct business, and in this state the cotton was sold to the little spinners. This was common till power was applied to the turning of the mule. Mills were then built of a suitable width, and in the course of a few years the hand-mule was entirely superseded' (John Kennedy, *A brief memoir of Samuel Crompton* ... (1830), p.21 and note, reprinted from the *Memoirs and Proceedings of the Literary and Philosophical Society of Manchester*).
10. *Life*, p.23.
11. For Woodrooffe's activities, see Woodrooffe Street and Factory Street, off Ancoats Lane, on William Green's *Plan of Manchester ... compleated in 1794*. Owen's establishment presumably stood on Factory Street. Owen called him 'Woodruff' (*Life*, p.24).
12. *Life*, p.24. See *Manchester Directory* (1788), p.94; (1794), p.151.
13. *Life*, p.25. He bought rovings from the firm of Sandfords, McConnel and Kennedy and engaged three men to work his mules, i.e. to spin cotton yarn or thread upon them from the rovings. 'When the yarn was spun, it was in the cop form, from which it was to be made upon the reel into hanks, each one [*sic* ?eight] hundred and forty yards in length. This operation I performed, and then made these hanks into bundles of five pounds weight each, and ... sold them to a Mr. Mitchell, an agent from some mercantile manufacturing houses in Glasgow, who sold the yarn to muslin weavers, or manufactured it themselves.' For the firm of Sandfords, McConnel and Kennedy (1791–5), machine makers and mule spinners, see J. Kennedy, *Miscellaneous Papers* (1849), pp.17–18 of 'Brief notice of my early recollections'.
14. *Life*, p.27.
15. The firm was advertising under the style of 'Jones and Co.' as early as September 1791 (*Manchester Mercury, 27 Sept. 1791*, p.4, col.2). Jones and his new partner appear to have carried on quite successfully without Owen, at least for a time. Owen wrote: 'I believe they ultimately stopped payment, and that Jones returned to his wire bonnet-frame making' (*Life*, p.26). However, the following advertisement appeared in the Manchester Mercury as late as 21 February 1792.

TO MULE SPINNERS &c
FOR SALE

EAST INDIA ROVINGS suitable to spin from 110 to 150 Hanks in the Pound. Likewise a sort of a better Quality, at Jones & Co.s, Machine Makers, in Water Street, Dolefield, Manchester. Spinners of the above Articles may be supplied Weekly and the yarn taken in Return, if agreeable, at market price.
Wanted: a good JOINER or two, accustomed to fit up Mules and Water Machinery.
Wanted, a good Turner, Iron Filer, and a Smith.
N.B. Mules and Water Machines made on the most approved Plan.

And, as noted above, Jones was still working as a machine maker in 1794.

16. Cowdroy's *Manchester Gazette*, Saturday, 21 Nov. 1801.
17. P.21.
18. P.35. Peter Drinkwater, jun., was presumably the son of the elder Drinkwater. He

went bankrupt in 1788 (*Manchester Mercury*, 8 July 1788, p.4, col.1). See also *Manchester Mercury*, 11 Sept. 1787, p.4.

19. This was also the address of the elder Drinkwater's warehouse.

20. A. Redford, *Manchester Merchants and Foreign Trade, 1794–1858*, pp.10, 20; *Report of the Receipts and Disbursements of the Committee of the Fustian Trade, 1786* (Assay Office, Birmingham). Drinkwater was a member of the small deputation appointed by the Manchester manufacturers in July 1784 to wait on the Lords of the Treasury with the object of preventing a rumoured plan to substitute a tax on raw cotton for the tax on printed goods (*Book of the Fustian Committee*, July 1784).

21. See *Manchester Mercury*, 19, 26 April, 3 May 1791.

22. He took his sacrament certificate on 1 July 1792, his oath of office on 19 July 1792, and made his first appearance at a Quarter Session on the same day. (Information kindly supplied by R. Sharpe France, Esq., of the County Record Office, Preston, Lancs.)

23. *Life*, p.29; John Scholes, *Manchester Directory* (1794), p.xiii; Gerard Bancks, *Manchester and Salford Directory* (1800), p.51.

24. *Gentleman's Magazine*, 1789, part i, p.279; C.H. Drinkwater and W.G.D. Fletcher, *The family of Drinkwater* (1920), pp.84–5.

25. A. Ure, *The Cotton Manufacture of Great Britain*. vol.i (1836), pp.221–2.

26. E. Baines, *History of the Cotton Manufacture* (1835), p.156 n.

27. *Life*, pp.26–7, 38–9. In 1794 he was in a strong enough financial position to buy the manor of Prestwich and Pendlebury, Lancs., from Thomas William Coke (Drinkwater and Fletcher, op. cit. pp.84–5).

28. P.40.

29. *Manchester Mercury*, 13 March 1792.

30. *Life*, p.39. For some further details about Drinkwater and the Northwich mill in 1797–8, see T.S. Willan, *The Navigation of the River Weaver in the eighteenth century* (Chetham Society, 1951), pp.126–7.

31. 'Mr. Drinkwater's Cotton Works' are prominently identified on William Green's map of 1794. No visible trace of the factory remains. It lay across what is now Aytoun Street.

32. Op. cit. vol.i, p.274.

33. *Life*, p.26; *Dictionary of National Biography*, vol.xxxii, p.360.

34. 18 April 1789 (Boulton and Watt Collection). According to James Butterworth (*The Antiquities of the Town, and the complete history of the Trade, of Manchester* (1822), pp.94–5) Slack was the 'overlooker of the spinning part only', while the superintendence of the engine and machinery devolved on Mr. I. Wakefield, who made 'great improvements in the machinery of the mule during his stay in that concern'.

35. For the death of Slack, 'certainly one of the first practical spinners of that day' (Butterworth), see *Manchester Mercury*, 22 March 1791, p.4, col.2, where the furniture in his house 'adjoining to the large New Cotton Factory, near Piccadilly, Manchester' was offered for sale. For George Augustus Lee (1761–1826), see also John Kennedy, *A brief memoir of Samuel Crompton*, pp.6–7. In 1816 Lee was examined by a Parliamentary Committee (17 June), Sir Robert Peel being in the chair:

Were you not a manager at Mr. Drinkwater's factory? [A.] I was, about six-and-twenty years ago [i.e. *c.* 1790]. What were the regular hours of work when you had the direction of that mill? [A.] From six [a.m.] to seven [p.m.], the same as Mr. Arkwright's; and another set of hands all night. I was a clerk there. The mill was in Northwich, in Cheshire. There was a mill in Manchester for mule-spinning, I think, where the hours were from six [a.m.] to eight [p.m.].

Did the children work all night there? [A.] No.

What mill was that? [A.] It was a mill in Piccadilly; I was there but a short time after it was erected.

The only instance of working there more than Arkwright's hours was confined to a mill in Piccadilly? [*A.*] No; I believe other mills in the town all worked from six to eight. I beg leave to observe that they worked by hand at that time in Manchester, not by a steam-engine.

The mule-spinning was by hand? [*A.*] Yes.

(*Report of the Minutes of Evidence taken before the Select Committee on the State of the Children employed in the Manufactories of the United Kingdom,* 25 April–18 June 1816, pp.355–6.)

36. *Life*, p.26.
37. See James Lawson, Manchester (one of Boulton and Watt's engine erectors) to J. Watt jun., Soho, 29 March 1796: 'I lost most of the morning by P. Drinkwater who wants a larger engine but determines nothing by his long harangue of nonsense. I have promised to dine with him on my return.'
38. These were pumping engines on Newcomen's pattern.
39. P.D. to B. and W., 3 April 1789. See also James Watt to William Thomson, Glasgow, 5 Aug. 1791: 'Mr Drinkwater at Manchester was threatened per advance with a prosecution if he made any smoke; he has, however, taken care not to do so, and has escaped hitherto.'
40. P.D. to B. and W., 3 June 1789; and James Watt to P.D., 6 June 1789. The nature of the subsoil in the township of Manchester noted here may account to some extent for the prevalence of those cellar dwellings which were to become notorious in the 1830s and 1840s.
41. P.D. to B. and W., 21 Nov. 1789.
42. P.D. to B. and W., 3 April 1789.
43. P.D. to B. and W., 18 April 1789.
44. P.D. to B. and W., 3 April 1789.
45. In this connection see D.M. Vaughan's remarks on 'Justice to the past in the teaching of social history' in *History*, vol.xxxii (March 1947), no.115, pp.52–5.
46. P.D. to B. and W., 18 April 1789.
47. Ure, op. cit. vol.i, p.273.
48. P.D. to B. and W., 3 June 1789.
49. James Watt to P.D., 25 Nov. 1789 in reply to P.D.'s of 21 Nov.
50. J. Watt to T. Cooper, 1 May 1790. Drinkwater installed a second Boulton and Watt engine in the Piccadilly Factory in 1799–1800. It was of 14 h.p. (Engine Book, Boulton and Watt Collection, Birmingham Public Library).
51. *Life*, pp.28–9.
52. Ibid. p.27. Lee actually left the factory the day before Owen took over the management (ibid. p.28).
53. 17 April 1792, p.1, col.3.
54. *Life*, p.29.
55. Ibid.
56. Ibid. p.34–5.
57. Ibid. p.39.
58. *Life*, p.31. Heywood married Drinkwater's daughter Margaret in 1797 (Drinkwater and Fletcher, op. cit. pp.84–5, *Manchester Mercury*, 18 April 1797, p.4).
59. *Life*, p.31.
60. One of Owen's first acts on taking over the managing partnership of New Lanark in 1799–1800 was to get rid of Kelly and the other co-manager, James Dale, David Dale's half-brother, because they 'were incompetent to comprehend my views, or assist me in my plans' (*Life*, p.59).
61. An obvious reference to the Northwich mill.
62. His full name was Robert Humphreys (R. Humphreys to B. and W., 14 Oct. 1797).
63. John Kennedy, *A brief memoir of Samuel Crompton...*, pp.27–8. Owen later gave Humphreys the post of manager at New Lanark (*Life*, p.59).
64. The author is greatly indebted to Mr. A.P. Wadsworth, Editor of the *Manchester Guardian*, for supplying a copy of this document from his notes.
65. John Scholes, *Manchester Directory* (1794), p.198.

66. Owen claimed to have been, in the early 1790s, the first British master cotton spinner to use United States Sea Island cotton (*Life*, pp.32–4). The Oldknow MSS. also show that mule twist was not the only commodity with which Drinkwater supplied Oldknow, as the collection contains a bill, dated 9 Nov. 1793, recording the sale to Oldknow by Drinkwater of 4 fat cows for £35 15s.
67. It is given here by the courtesy of Mr. J.R.L. Anderson of the *Manchester Guardian*, who owns a printed facsimile of it.
68. She eventually married, in 1809, Capt. (later Col.) George d'Aguilar, who became Deputy Adjutant-General, Dublin (*Manchester Mercury*, 19 Dec. 1809, p.4; Drinkwater and Fletcher, op. cit. pp.84–5).
69. *Life*, pp.39–41. Professor George Unwin was wrong in surmising that the Drinkwater–Oldknow partnership was being mooted in 1792 (*Samuel Oldknow and the Arkwrights* (1924), p.152). The partnership into which Oldknow entered in 1792 was with Peter Ewart (1767–1842). It was dissolved in 1793 (*Memoirs and Proceedings of the Manchester Literary and Philosophical Society*, 2nd ser., vol.vii (1846) – 'A biographical notice of the late Peter Ewart, Esq.', by W.C. Henry, pp.120–5).
70. R. and W. Dean, *Directory of Manchester* (1804), p.52; A. Redford, *Manchester Merchants and Foreign Trade, 1794–1858*, p.64.
71. *Life*, pp.31–2. Owen's unreliability is further shown by the fact that he refers to this event as taking place in 1790! (*Life*, p.32.)
72. *Life*, p.41.
73. *Life*, pp.41–2. According to Owen, Humphreys 'could not keep up to the quality of yarns' attained by Owen (op. cit. p.59).
74. Ibid., p.42.
75. See *Life*, p.68, where Owen refers to certain happenings towards the end of 1794 as taking place 'between my leaving Mr. Drinkwater and my commencement as a partner in the Chorlton Twist Company'.
76. Owen was definitely in close touch with Moulson by the end of 1794 (see *Life*, p.65).
77. Ibid., p.59.
78. *Manchester Mercury*, 24 Nov. 1801; *Manchester Gazette*, 21 Nov. 1801; *Gentleman's Magazine* (1801), part ii, p.1150. For further glimpses of Drinkwater, see *Manchester Mercury*, 4 Aug. 1795, p.4, col.4 and 6 Mar. 1798, p.1, cols.1 and 2.
79. *Life*, p.42.
80. Ibid., p.42. Moulson gave his address as Dolefield in 1792, when, together with Owen, he signed the declaration published by a numerous body of 'Protestant Dissenters, Inhabitants of the Towns of Manchester and Salford'. The gist of the declaration ran: '... we are steadily and affectionately attached to the British Constitution, consisting of King, Lords, and Commons ... fully confident that a Constitution, thus formed, will not fail to redress every real grievance, and effect every necessary improvement' (*Manchester Herald*, 29 Dec. 1792). Its purpose was to dissociate the moderate Dissenters from the extreme Radicals and the 'fellow-travellers' whose sympathies lay with the French Republicans.
81. This was 'of a larger size than the common run of rotative engines' (James Watt, jun. to Robert Owen and Co., 18 Dec. 1795). For Owen's residence at Chorlton Hall, see *Life*, pp.48–9. In John Scholes, *Manchester Directory* (1797), p.94, there is an entry: 'Owen, Robert, merchant and manufacturer, factory and warehouse, Cambridge Street, [off] Oxford Street; house, 2, Cooper Street.' See also ibid., p.27.
82. James Watt, jun. to Robert Owen and Co., 18 Dec. 1795. The 31-inch cylinder for the engine, cast and bored by John Wilkinson at Bersham, was 'one of the most perfect that ever passed through our hands' (ibid.).
83. M.R. Boulton to Owen, Scarth and Co., 18 Feb. 1796. According to Owen two or three years elapsed '... before the new Chorlton mill was at work' (*Life*, p.42).
84. The bill was drawn by Borradaile and Atkinson of Salford on William and Richardson Borradaile of London (James Watt, jun. to Chorlton Twist Co., 13 Oct. 1796). Boulton and Watt usually stipulated payment in bills at two months' date.
85. Soon after Owen left Manchester for New Lanark towards the end of 1799 or early in

1800 the Chorlton Twist Company's mill was bought by Messrs. Birley and Hornby of Blackburn, former customers of the firm (*Life*, p.64).

86. *Life*, p.42. On 13 Jan. 1798 Moulson withdrew from the Chorlton Twist Company, which then consisted of Owen, Atkinson and Scarth. Later in the year Matthew Chitty Marshall became a partner in the firm, but he and Scarth withdrew on 9 Aug. 1798 leaving Owen and Atkinson as the sole remaining partners in the concern (*Manchester Mercury*, 23 Jan., 18 Sept. 1798).

87. *Manchester Directory* (1794), p.11; (1800), p.13.

88. Barfoot and Wilkes, op. cit. vol.i, p.80; vol.iii, p.797; W. Lowndes, *London Directory* (1791), p.25; Critchett and Woods, *Post Office (London) Directory* (1816), p.37; Johnston's *London Commercial Guide* (1817), cols. 186, 425.

89. C.N. Parkinson, *Trade in the Eastern Seas, 1793–1813* (1937), p.188. According to Owen, John Barton, John Atkinson and Robert Owen agreed in the *summer of 1797* to purchase the New Lanark mills from David Dale for £60,000, payable at the rate of £3,000 *per annum* for twenty years (*Life*, pp.52–3).

9

Manchester in the Latter Half of the Eighteenth Century

The following 'delightful if somewhat ungrammatical' description of Manchester, as it has been called, is given at the base of an engraving entitled *The South-West Prospect of Manchester in the County Palatine of Lancaster*, published by S. and N. Buck in 1728:

Manchester is neither Borough nor Corporation, but a spacious, rich and populous Inland Town in the Hundred of Salford and South East part of Lancashire. Situate upon a Rocky Cliff, at the confluence of the Rivers Irk and Irwell, [?which] add much pleasure to its healthfull soil, which is most part Gravelly. It is a Mannour with Courts Leet and Baron; which at the decease of the present Lady Dowager Bland will devolve to Sir Oswald Mosley, Barrt. Tis governed by two Constables, annualy chosen in the Court Leet at Michlms: Tis famous for the Woollen, Linnen and Cotton Manufactories, whereby it's immensely enriched and many 100 poor Families employed from several Counties. This Town is adorned with many noted buildings ... and with handsom broad Streets both New and Old; And a large Bridge over the River Irwell which joyneth Salford, a populous, Beautiful Town, giving name to the Hundred, and seemeth as a Suburb thereto. The Exchange now building by Sir Oswald and the River Irwell falling into the Mersey, communicateth with Liverpool which (by their expence and labour) hath gained a considerable progress and is soon expected to be made navigable.[1]

What was the size of the urban community known as Manchester in the latter half of the eighteenth century? As the late A.P. Wadsworth remarked: 'the early estimates of the population of Manchester are remarkable for nothing more than their variety.'[2] Our difficulties are increased by confusion between the *ecclesiastical parish* of Manchester, which covered sixty square miles, and the *civil township* of Manchester which had a much smaller area. In addition, a distinction was sometimes made by eighteenth-century writers between the *township* of Manchester and the *town* of Manchester, i.e. the built-up area inside the township. Another frequent source of confusion is a reluctance to quote separate figures for Manchester and Salford. For example, in 1773 Dr. Percival quoted an estimate of 1717 which gave the population in that year as 8,000, but he was uncertain whether Salford was included or not. Certain returns made to the Bishop of Chester about 1717 suggest that Manchester had a population of 10,000 and Salford one of 2,500. In the latter half of the eighteenth century more trustworthy figures are available. In 1758 an enumeration of the population of Manchester took place as the result of a dispute about the manorial corn-mill rights and the figure of 17,101 was obtained for the township. The population had therefore roughly doubled in the previous fifty years. According to Percival, the rate of increase became more rapid after 1765 and in 1773–4 a further 'enumeration of the houses and inhabitants of the town and parish of Manchester' was taken 'by a person employed for the purpose, and at the joint expence of a few gentlemen in the town'. The manuscript volumes of this return are now preserved in Chetham's Library and John Whitaker expressed his belief in a note written in one of them that this enumeration was 'sufficiently accurate for every literary or political use'. The township of Manchester by then contained 24,386 persons in 5,678 families. In the period of recovery after the commercial crisis of 1771–2 'the town extended on every side, and such was the influx of inhabitants, that though a great number of houses were built, they were occupied even before they were finished'.[3] Manchester's rising prosperity had not therefore been seriously checked by the War of American Independence. Nevertheless, the war and its aftermath did aggravate certain social problems. Dr. Henry remarked on the increased incidence of fever during 1783–5 as compared with 1780–2, and considered that it was probably due to

... the crowded and uncleanly manner, in which the poorer people have been lodged, owing to the want of houses to accommodate them: for, though many have been erected, yet several causes have contributed to restrain the spirit of building. During the war, the high price of timber was a considerable obstacle; and since the peace, the frosts, which were, for two years together, very intense, and continued until the spring was far advanced, have prevented the making of bricks, and together with the tax, greatly enhanced their price.[4]

By Christmas 1788 the population of Manchester township had further increased to 42,821.[5] Less than thirteen years later, when the first nation-wide census was taken (1801), there had been another spectacular rise to 70,409. It was little wonder that on his visit to Manchester in 1784 Monsieur de Givry, member of a group of French visitors engaged in industrial espionage, could write that Manchester was a 'large and superb town ... which has been built almost entirely in the past 20 to 25 years'.[6]

We can distinguish three main direct causes of this spectacular rise. First of all there was immigration into Manchester. This influx consisted mainly of persons in the prime of life, with their young families. Most of them came from the districts immediately surrounding the town, attracted by the jobs on offer in one of the growing points of the British economy. But there was also an appreciable volume of long-distance immigration, particularly from Scotland and Ireland. The number of Scottish names in the Manchester and Salford directories increases rapidly after the 1770s[7] and many of the doctors and surgeons attached to the Infirmary were Scots.[8]

Secondly, there was a natural increase, the surplus of births over deaths. Although the death rate was high by modern standards, so was the birth rate, and there seems little evidence that the death rate was rising between 1750 and 1800. Towards the end of the eighteenth century a substantial excess of births over deaths appears to have occurred every year. For the three years 1765, 1766 and 1767 the Manchester and Salford bills of mortality (for what they are worth) show an annual average of 900 baptisms and 811 burials, whereas for the three years 1783, 1784 and 1785 the corresponding figures are 1,838 and 1,468.[9] The figures for 1791 are 2,960 births and 2,286 deaths.[10]

Thirdly, as the eighteenth century wore on, increasing supplies of food were available. This had not always been the case. 1756, 1757 and 1758, for example, were years of high food prices and food riots in Manchester, the price of oatmeal, the staple diet of the population, reaching a peak of 39s. 6d. per load of 240 lb early in 1757, compared with less than 20s. a load in 1753. There were food riots in the town in 1762.[11] The miseries of these years, however, do not seem to be paralleled again, in spite of the vastly increased population, until 1812 brought the notorious Shudehill potato riot.[12] The reasons can be sought in improved communications, which enabled food to be brought into the Manchester markets from an ever-widening area, and secondly the introduction of new foods, of which the most useful was the potato. But the potato was not alone – it was merely the most spectacular addition to the diet. Dr. John Aikin wrote in 1795:

The supply of provision to this populous town and neighbourhood is a circumstance well deserving of notice. Formerly, oatmeal, which was the staple article of diet of the labouring class in Lancashire, was brought from Stockport; ... Since that time, the demand for corn and flour has been increasing to a vast amount, and new sources of supply have been opened from distant parts by the navigations, so that monopoly or scarcity cannot be apprehended, though the price of these articles must always be high in a district which produces so little and consumes so much.

Early cabbages, and cucumbers for pickling, are furnished by gardeners about Warrington; early potatoes, carrots, peas, and beans, from the sandy land on and about Bowden downs. Potatoes, now a most important auxiliary to bread in the diet of all classes, are brought from various parts, especially from about Runcorn and Frodsham, by the Duke of Bridgewater's canal. Apples, which form a considerable and valuable article of the diet even of the poor in Manchester, used in pies or puddings, are imported from the distance of the cyder counties by means of the communicating canals, and in such quantities, that upwards of 3000*l*. in a year has been paid for their freight alone. The articles of milk and butter, which used to be supplied by the dairy-farmers in the vicinity, at moderate rates, are now, from the increase of population, become as dear as in the metropolis, and are furnished in a similar manner; viz. the milk, by means of milk houses in the town, which contract for it by the great, and retail it out; and the butter from considerable distances, as well as salt butter from Ireland and other places. Of butcher's meat, veal and pork are mostly brought by country butchers and farmers; mutton and beef are slaughtered by the town butchers, the animals being generally driven from a distance, except the milch cows of the neighbourhood, which are fattened when old. The supply of meat and poultry is sufficiently plentiful on market days; but on other days it is scarcely possible to procure beef from the butchers; nor is poultry to be had at any price, there being no such trade as a poulterer in the whole town. Wild fowl of various kinds are brought to market in the season.

With fish, Manchester is better provided than might be expected from its inland situation. The greatest quantity of sea-fish comes from the Yorkshire coast, consisting of large cod, lobsters, and turbots, of which last, many are sent even to Liverpool, on an overflow of the market. Soles, chiefly of a small size, come from the Lancashire coast. Salmon are brought in plenty from the rivers Mersey and Ribble, principally the latter. The rivers in the neighbourhood abound in trout, and in what is called *brood* which are young salmon from one to two years old, and not easily distinguished from trout, which they closely resemble in shape, but are more delicate to the taste. Salmon trout is also plentiful, and likewise fine eels. The Irwell at Manchester and for some distance below is, however, destitute of fish, the water being poisoned by liquor flowing in from the dye-houses. Many ponds and old marl-pits in the neighbourhood are well stored with carp and tench, and pike and other fresh water fish are often brought to market. The poor have a welcome addition to their usual fare, in the herrings from the Isle of Man, which in the season are brought in large quantities, and are sold at a cheap rate.[13]

The movement of foodstuffs into Manchester on this scale could not be effected without major changes in local transport facilities. Lancashire in the seventeenth, eighteenth and early nineteenth centuries was notorious for its bad roads, supplemented by the famous paved causeways of stones raised above the level of the fields, which were just wide enough for horses but too narrow for wheeled traffic.

Improvement began, however, as far as the Manchester area was concerned, in the early eighteenth century. In 1738 a local historian wrote that there were causeways 'everywhere about Manchester ... of a common breadth and kept in good repair by the extraordinary care of the proper officers'.[14] It is significant that the first road in Lancashire to be placed under the administration of a turnpike trust was the stretch from Manchester to Stockport. This road formed part of the Manchester to Buxton trust set up by Act of Parliament in 1725. In 1732 the Manchester–Ashton-under-Lyne–Mottram road was turnpiked, and this was followed three years later by the Manchester–Oldham–

Austerlands road. For most of the second half of the eighteenth century there was great activity in road improvement in south-east Lancashire and north-east Cheshire. But roads formed only a part of the transport facilities of the area. We have seen that S. and N. Buck remarked in 1728 on the work then in progress with a view to rendering the Rivers Mersey and Irwell navigable up to Hunt's Bank under an Act of Parliament passed in 1721. The men who directed and financed this task included members of the chief trading families of this area – John Lees of Clarksfield, Oldham, Joseph Byrom, a wealthy mercer, James Lightbowne, a woollen draper, and also the 'chief linen drapers' of Manchester.[15] Although the two rivers were rendered navigable as far as Manchester by the early 1730s, the project yielded no profit to its proprietors for many years.[16] Then in 1737 seven landowners and merchants from Manchester and the neighbourhood obtained a second Act empowering them to deepen and render navigable Worsley brook, down to its junction with the Irwell. Some, if not all, of this second set of 'undertakers' seem to have been connected with the Mersey and Irwell river navigation. But the scheme did not materialise and a plan put forward by a group of Manchester men for a canal from Manchester to Leigh and Wigan in 1753–4, i.e. five years before the Duke of Bridgewater's project, also came to nothing.[17]

The story of the third Duke of Bridgewater's canal enterprise, which brought his Worsley coal to Castlefield in the heart of Manchester by 1764,[18] has frequently been told. By reducing the price of coal, it certainly made Manchester a more comfortable place to live in. But more important was the extension of the Duke's canal across north Cheshire to Runcorn on the Mersey, opened throughout in 1776. Not only did this extension make it possible to send north Cheshire potatoes into Manchester, but it also provided a means of sending raw cotton from the West Indies, and later from the Southern States of the U.S.A., into south-east Lancashire via Liverpool. We must not, however, exaggerate Manchester's dependence on coal supplies from the Worsley pits. The Bradford colliery in East Manchester was sunk in the 1760s, and Dr. Aikin had this to say about the sources from which Manchester drew its supplies in the early 1790s:

The supply of coals to Manchester is chiefly derived from the pits about Oldham, Ashton, Dukinfield, Hyde, Newton, Denton, etc. ... The supply from the Duke of Bridgewater's pits at Worsley is less considerable, though a very useful addition for the poor.[19]

The industries of Manchester, and the fortunes of the merchants and wholesale manufacturers who directed them have only received fragmentary treatment at the hands of economic historians. It is true that we have that classic work *The Cotton Trade and Industrial Lanca-shire, 1600–1780* (1931) by the late A.P. Wadsworth and Miss Julia de Lacy Mann, and Professor Redford's *Manchester Merchants and Foreign Trade, 1794–1858* (1934). But it is curious that in a recent article on 'The Merchants in England in the Eighteenth Century'[20] by Mr. Walter E. Minchinton, the Manchester merchants are nowhere mentioned, although it was mainly through their efforts and those of their agents that the official value of British exports of cotton goods was pushed up from practically nothing in 1751 (£45,986) to £200,000 by 1764, and to nearly £5½ million by 1800, a figure almost equal to that for woollen and worsted cloth, linens, ribbons and mixed cloths of linen and cotton.[21] These men financed the spinners and weavers of south-east Lancashire by supplying them with raw materials and yarns. They also saw to the bleaching, dyeing and finally the printing of the goods they had made. Their activities tended to diminish the other local wholesale markets such as that of Bolton.[22] But this was not the whole range of Manchester's industries. Silk throwing and silk weaving flourished in the late eighteenth century and so did the manufacture of hats.

Then from the 1770s came the boom in cotton associated with the great inventions and the beginnings of the factory system. The first cotton factory in Manchester appears to have been that built in the early 1780s by the famous Sir Richard Arkwright, in partnership with Messrs. Simpson and Whittenbury. It stood on Shudehill and was noteworthy because the warp-spinning frame was driven by water power supplemented by a single-acting pumping engine of the New-comen type. This replenished the water wheel's reservoir by pumping back into it the water which had passed over the wheel. Some of the wholesale buyers who supplied goods both to home and overseas markets followed the example of Arkwright and began to invest profits made from merchanting in mechanised cotton spinning. Such a man was Peter Drinkwater (? 1742–1801) who in the 1770s was a wholesale fustian manufacturer, living in Spring Gardens, with a warehouse in King Street, and an extensive trade overseas. In the 1780s Drinkwater began to transmute some of the capital he had accumulated as a textile middleman into industrial capital. Some time in the 1780s he purchased or set up a water-driven cotton spinning mill at Northwich in Cheshire for the production of warps and in 1789 began to build his second factory, a four-storied building which lay just off Piccadilly between Auburn Street and Upton Street. This was powered by a Boulton and Watt rotary steam engine – the first in Manchester – which was used in the carding of cotton and the preparation of rovings. He also installed some 144-spindle mules worked by hand, and appointed good managers. From 1792 to 1794 or 1795 the famous Robert Owen managed Drinkwater's two mills and after Owen came Robert Humphreys, who applied steam-power to Drinkwater's mules according to Kelly's method of 1790.[23] By 1800 there were dozens of cotton spinning mills in the Manchester area and an unsuccessful attempt had even been made by the Grimshaw brothers in 1791 to try out, in a factory at Knott Mill, Deansgate, 500 of the clumsy power looms invented by the Rev. Edmund Cartwright. But the mill was burnt down in 1792 and not rebuilt. The Manchester handloom weavers continued to enjoy general prosperity during the period of the Revolutionary and Napoleonic Wars.[24]

The mechanisation of cotton spinning created a demand for textile machinery making and engineering industries. In the 1790s a number of Manchester firms arose to satisfy this demand. The most important of them was undoubtedly the partnership of James Bateman and William Sherratt, although their steam-engine factory was actually in Salford. Here they manufactured not only 'large cast wheels for the cotton machines' and old-fashioned Newcomen engines, but also pirated Boulton and Watt's patent rotary steam engine.[25] At Knott Mill, Alexander Brodie (1732–1811), London financier, Shropshire ironmaster and armaments manufacturer, set up a foundry and steam engine works about 1790 in partnership with two men named McNiven and Ormrod.[26] Apart from these two large firms there were many smaller concerns by 1800.

Auxiliary trades expanded in sympathy. Aikin wrote in 1795:

The making of paper at mills in the vicinity has been brought to great perfection, and now includes all kinds, from the strongest parcelling paper to the finest writing sorts, and that on which banker's bills are printed.[27] ... The tin-plate workers have found additional employment in furnishing many articles for spinning machines; as have also the braziers in casting wheels for the motion-work of the rollers used in them; and the clock-makers in cutting them. Harness makers have been much employed in making bands for carding engines ... whereby the consumption of strong curried leather has been much increased.[28]

The spectacular growth of the cotton industry naturally aroused much interest in France and Germany and from the late 1770s there was a trickle of foreign visitors to the town. The French geologist Faujas de St. Fond remarked during a visit to Manchester in 1784 that he could get no admission to the cotton factories because of the previous activities of visiting Frenchmen who had been engaged in spying out industrial secrets. And in 1792 another Frenchman, F.C.L. Albert, received and served a sentence of four years' imprisonment in Lancaster Castle for trying to secure specimens of cotton machinery and endeavouring to induce Manchester operatives to emigrate to France.[29] Gradually, however, the interest of foreigners in Manchester took on a different form. They came to stay as merchants and manufacturers. It is no accident that John Scholes's manuscript register of foreign merchants in Manchester begins in 1784,[30] and as early as 1799 a German, Carl Friedrich Brandt, was nominated as boroughreeve of the town.[31] Perhaps the most eminent of these 'new Mancunians' of the 1790s was Nathan Meyer Rothschild, the German-Jewish financier (1777–1836), although he did not stay for many years.[32] Aikin summed up the situation as follows:

Within the last twenty or thirty years the vast increase of foreign trade has caused many of the Manchester manufacturers to travel abroad, and agents or partners to be fixed for a considerable time on the Continent, as well as foreigners to reside at Manchester. And the town has now in every respect assumed the style and manners of one of the commercial capitals of Europe.[33]

In contrast with this exuberant economic advance, local government in the township of Manchester made only modest progress in the eighteenth century. Up to 1765 Manchester's local government status, as Defoe remarked in a hackneyed phrase, was indeed that of a village – it was governed by the Court Leet of the lord of the manor. Every year the Court Leet chose unpaid officers who were to see to the performance of the various municipal services such as they were understood at the time – the boroughreeve (a kind of mayor, but with little executive power), the day police, the market lookers or inspectors, the scavengers, etc. As the Court Leet met only twice a year long periods sometimes elapsed before offenders were summoned before it. Yet the eighteenth-century alternative to this system was to have an oligarchical municipal corporation which might try to control and warp the town's economic development in its own narrow interest, and would take just as limited a view as the Court Leet did of its sanitary functions. Aikin summed up eighteenth-century majority opinion when he remarked: 'With respect to *government*, it remains an open town, destitute (probably to its advantage) of a corporation, and unrepresented in Parliament.'[34]

But in 1765 would-be local reformers secured the passage of the Manchester and Salford Police Act, which set up a body of Cleansing and Lighting Commissioners empowered to provide, among other things, a more adequate fire brigade. Such local acts were the normal eighteenth-century method of securing better urban sanitation.[35] If the influential inhabitants named in the act had only used their statutory powers more vigorously they could have largely superseded the Court Leet, but they did not, and things went on much as before. Then in 1776 the first Manchester Improvement Act was obtained for widening and improving, in particular, Old Mill Gate and St. Mary's Gate, and also opening a new street between the Exchange and St. Ann's Square. The Act named the commissioners empowered to carry out the improvements and anyone who subscribed £20 to the good work could join their number. Having accomplished the purpose for which they were set up, the Improvement Commissioners naturally rested from their labours. In the 1780s there was much discontent with the Court Leet, which had in many of its functions become 'sluggish and inactive', and the setting up of the Manchester and Salford Police Commissioners by yet another Act of Parliament in1792 was the first substantial step towards a recognisably modern system of local government. Some of the clauses of the 1765 Act were re-enacted word-for-word in the measure of 1792,[36] but for the first few years the new Police Commissioners did little to justify their existence. They had the power to light and cleanse the streets and to maintain a police force during the hours of darkness, but none of these things had been done adequately by the winter of 1798–9. John Cross described the situation in 1799 as follows:

... during many wet and dark winter months, the streets have remained uncleansed and without lights; for some time no watchmen or patrols were appointed ... and none could pass through the streets in safety. Escaping personal violence, they were still in imminent personal danger, from the numerous unguarded cellars, pits and various obstructions that everywhere interrupted their passage ... the streets are still crowded with annoyances ... not a street has been widened or laid open.[37]

From 1799 onwards a new spirit of enterprise animated the Police Commissioners and, by the time they were superseded by the new Manchester Borough Council in the early 1840s, they had so extended their powers and functions as to become one of the most progressive local governing bodies in Great Britain.

It has recently been suggested by two eminent medical men 'that specific medical measures introduced during the eighteenth century are unlikely to have contributed substantially to a reduction in the death-rate'.[38] An examination of the work of the doctors associated with what is now the Manchester Royal Infirmary in the first fifty years of its existence suggests that this judgement may well be based on an inadequate appraisal of the histories of particular hospitals. What is now known as the Manchester Royal Infirmary was established in 1752 by a committee of philanthropists and medical men who opened a small hospital at No. 10, Garden Street, off Withy Grove. Within three years a permanent hospital had been built on land called the Daub Hole Field, purchased from Sir Oswald Mosley (now Piccadilly Gardens). The rural situation of the new hospital, which started off with fifty beds, is made clear from the fact that in 1762 Marsden Kenyon was given leave to make a gate at the West end of the Infirmary Garden into his field.[39] On the new site the number of persons treated both as in-patients and out-patients increased rapidly. From the first, the govern-ing committee (Weekly Board of Trustees) of the Infirmary laid what was, for eighteenth-century society, unusual stress on cleanliness: 'Nurses were expected to clean their wards by seven in the morning in the winter and by eight in the summer.'[40] The new building had contained some baths when originally opened in 1755, but in June 1779 the Trustees decided to erect 'a complete set of cold, warm and vapour baths' which, it was thought, would be of great utility to the hospital and of 'great public convenience to the inhabitants of Manchester'. The scheme aroused such enthusiasm that the original plans were at once enlarged, and two years later, in the annual report for June 1781, the Trustees observed with pleasure that 'the profits have greatly exceeded their expectations, whilst the public [of Manchester] at a very modest expense may have the use of one of the most complete and elegant sets of baths in the whole kingdom'.[41]

Progress could be very patchy, however. When John Howard, the prison reformer, inspected the Infirmary in 1788, he made certain criticisms, as a result of which the floors of all wards were washed more frequently with soap and warm water, the walls whitewashed, and the doors and other woodwork coated with turpentine varnish annually. The legs and arms of every patient had henceforth to be washed with soap and water immediately on admission. This was to 'be often repeated unless ordered to the contrary'.[42]

The Infirmary naturally did not admit those suffering from con-tagious diseases as in-patients, but in 1781 the hospital authorities started a most interesting and successful scheme for treating, in their own homes, patients suffering from infectious diseases such as small-pox and measles, provided they lived within the towns of Manchester and Salford. In 1784 the Trustees accepted a proposal by the hospital's doctors and surgeons to inoculate poor persons for the smallpox and to attend them, if necessary, at their homes while they were in quarantine. By 1786 the number of home patients treated annually had reached a thousand,[43] and in January of that year Dr. Thomas Henry noted that within the previous quarter of a century the mortality from smallpox in Manchester and Salford had sensibly diminished. He went on:

Perhaps there is no disease the medical treatment of which has been more improved than that of the small-pox; and, the improvements, suiting the dispositions and convenience of the lower class of people, have been more frequently adopted than might otherwise have been expected.[44]

Inefficient midwifery caused many deaths in the eighteenth century and midwives, like nurses, were notorious for dissolute character and drunken habits. During the eighteenth century, however, members of the medical profession took an increasing interest in gynaecology.[45] An important local manifestation of this movement occurred in Manchester in May 1790, when three members of the Infirmary's surgical staff and one physician, of whom the most famous was Charles White, met at the Bridgewater Arms, alongside the present Victoria Station, to discuss a scheme for delivering poor married women in their homes. Later they rented a private house in Salford for use as a maternity home. This was the ancestor of the present St. Mary's Hospital.

Dr. Thomas Percival, writing in 1773, twenty years after the foundation of the Infirmary, stated:

It is pleasing to observe, that, notwithstanding the enlargement of Manchester, there has been a sensible improvement in the healthiness and longevity of its inhabitants; for the proportion of deaths is now considerably less than in 1757. But this is chiefly to be ascribed, as Dr. Price has justly observed, to the large accession of new settlers from the country. For as these usually come in the prime of life, they must raise the proportion of *inhabitants* to the *deaths*, and also of *births* and *weddings* to the *burials*, higher than they would otherwise be. However, exclusive of this consideration, there is good reason to believe that Manchester is more healthy now than formerly. The new streets are wide and spacious, the poor have larger and more commodious dwellings, and the increase of trade affords them better clothing and diet than they before enjoyed. I may add too, that the late improvements in medicine have been highly favourable to the preservation of life. The cool regimen in fevers, and in the small-pox; the free admission of air; attention to cleanliness; and the general use of antiseptic remedies and diet, have certainly mitigated the violence, and lessened the mortality of some of the most dangerous and malignant distempers to which mankind are incident. The ulcerous sore throat, which prevailed here in the year 1770, is the only epidemic which has appeared in Manchester, with any fatal degree of violence, for many years. Miliary fevers, which were formerly frequent in this town and neighbourhood, now rarely occur; and if I may judge from my own experience, the natural small-pox (for inoculation is not much practised here) carries off a smaller proportion of those who are attacked by it, than is commonly supposed. Puerperal diseases also decrease every year amongst us, by the judicious method of treating women in child-bed: and as nature is now more consulted in the management of infants, it is reasonable to suppose that this must be favourable to their health and preservation.[46]

The Manchester doctors of this period also pioneered the cod-liver-oil treatment for rickets. It is often assumed that because rickets (a softening of the legbones due to vitamin D deficiency) was called 'the English disease' (*die englische Krankheit*), and because it appears to have been most prevalent in the early nineteenth century, this malady originated in the new factory districts. But rickets was well-known in many parts of England in the seventeenth century and it is noteworthy that rickets was first successfully treated by the administration of cod-liver-oil at Manchester Infirmary in the early 1770s. By the early 1780s between fifty and sixty gallons were prescribed annually.[47]

The very rapid rise in Manchester's population in the 1780s and 1790s appears to have resulted in increased local anxiety concerning contagious diseases. For example, typhus or 'putrid' fever, a louse-borne disease, had been a dangerous scourge throughout the eighteenth century. It was known by a variety of names, such as ship-fever, barrack fever and gaol fever, which indicates the frequency with which it broke out among persons massed together in close proximity. As might be expected, in the 1780s and 1790s, when the new cotton factories were being built and improvised in large numbers, frequent references are found to outbreaks of typhus in such establishments.[48] The best-known of these was the outbreak which began in Ashton-under-Lyne in 1795, but it had been preceded by an epidemic in Manchester in 1794. The Ashton outbreak spread rapidly to the Manchester area and on 7 January 1796 the Manchester Board of Health, including Dr. Thomas Percival and Dr. John Ferriar, was set up. Its promoters had great hopes that the Board's recommendations would be taken up and enforced by the Police Commissioners or by the magistrates in quarter session. Dr. Ferriar, for example, repeated his pioneer suggestion, made originally in 1791, that the common lodging houses in Manchester, notorious focal points of disease, should be licensed and supervised by the magistrates. The Board set up a temporary isolation hospital, the House of Recovery, in 1796, and by 1804 was able to erect a permanent hospital for infectious diseases, capable of holding a hundred patients. Yet in spite of their good intentions, the promoters of the Board never succeeded in 'playing a considerable part in improving the sanitation of Manchester'.[49] That was to be the task of the reformers of the nineteenth century.

Did Manchester's intellectual life between 1750 and 1800 match its economic growth? Unfortunately it is practically impossible to compare these two spheres of existence. Writing of conditions in the early nineteenth century Mr. Donald Read has repeated the generally received opinion that 'the intellectual life of Manchester was left in the hands of a very few. In things of the mind and spirit the town was very backward.'[50] The question arises: backward compared with what? The purpose of the following pages is to suggest that Manchester's intellectual development in this period, all things considered, compared favourably with other provincial centres such as Leeds and Leicester. Let us examine more closely a few of the outward manifestations of Manchester's intellectual life in the eighteenth century.

Although the history of the newspaper in Manchester goes back to at least 1719,[51] when Roger Adams of Chester started his *Manchester News-Letter* (later the *Weekly Journal*), these early publications generally led obscure and chequered lives, with frequent changes of title,[52] until the foundation of Joseph Harrop's *Manchester Mercury* on 3 March 1752. But it is important to remember that when Harrop (1727–1804), a young man of twenty-five, brought out the first number of the *Mercury* there were already two rival publications, *Whitworth's Manchester Magazine*, which had been in existence under various names since 1730 and the resurrected *Weekly Journal* (later known as the *Manchester Journal*), the first number of which was issued by Orion Adams in the January of 1752. The *Journal* does not seem to have lasted the year out, yet when Whitworth's newspaper (by then called *Manchester Advertiser*) came to an unprofitable end with issue no. 3414 on 25 March 1760,[53] Joseph Harrop's *Mercury* held the field alone for a short time only. In June 1762 the first number of the *Manchester Chronicle* or *Anderton's Universal Advertiser* appeared, and although it seems to have been short-lived, nevertheless John Prescott was confident enough to start Prescott's *Manchester Journal* less than ten years later, on 23 March 1771. This lasted until at least 1774.[54] By 1800 three weekly newspapers of respectable solidity were in circulation; the *Mercury,* Wheeler's *Manchester Chronicle*, founded in 1781, and Cowdroy's *Manchester Gazette*, established in 1795.[55] As in the general population and the business world, so it was with the newspapers: many were born but few lived long.

Closely allied to the rise of the newspaper was the growth of the postal service, through which an increasing number of newspapers were circulated. Until 1793 the establishment of the Manchester post office remained absurdly small. At the beginning of that year all postal services in Manchester were performed by an old woman, Mrs. Sarah Willatt, who held the office of postmaster, assisted by her daughter and a solitary letter carrier. The Manchester Post Office was the most profitable in the kingdom, producing £15,000 a year. Then, in April 1793, the old post-mistress was pensioned off on £120 a year. James Harrop, the son of the printer of the *Mercury*, was appointed in her stead and allowed a staff of four clerks and six letter carriers. A local penny post came into operation in July 1793 and functioned over an ever-increasing area around the town until the introduction of the general penny post in 1840.[56]

The Manchester Literary and Philosophical Society, founded early in 1781, of which Benjamin Franklin was an honorary member, arose quite naturally out of informal meetings for discussion held at Dr. Thomas Percival's house on the corner of King Street and Cross Street.

One of the first joint secretaries of the Society was Dr. Thomas ('Magnesia') Henry (1734–1816), visiting apothecary to the Infirmary and a successful manufacturing chemist.[57] In addition to furthering scientific education in the Manchester area, he lectured and published works on chemistry, dyeing and calico printing. Other honorary members of the Society included Dr. Erasmus Darwin, Dr. Joseph Priestley, the French chemist Lavoisier (some of whose works Henry translated) and the Italian Volta. Another of the founder members was Dr. Thomas Barnes, who later became principal of the Manchester Academy on its formation in 1785–6. The subjects discussed were extremely varied – social improvement, political economy, many aspects of the cotton and woollen trades, metaphysics and medicine. In 1793 Robert Owen, the 'father of British socialism', became a member, followed in 1794 by John Dalton, the propounder of the atomic theory.[58]

In the early 1790s public opinion in Manchester became seriously divided on the subject of political reform and the French Revolution. The controversies of these years have recently been discussed by Miss Pauline Handforth and Mrs. F. Knight, with particular reference to the career of the Radical Thomas Walker and the pro-French newspaper, the *Manchester Herald* (1792–3).[59] The split even had echoes in the Literary and Philosophical Society's proceedings in 1791, when Samuel Jackson, a noted sympathiser with what was happening in France, moved a resolution expressing the Society's sympathy with Dr. Priestley on the losses he had sustained from the sacking of his house by the Birmingham mob on 14 July. The resolution was not carried, but in the following year, 1792, the reformers – headed by Joseph Priestley, jun., the doctor's son, and Thomas Cooper, the Radical who later became a prosperous lawyer and slave-owner in the U.S.A. – showed their independence by forming the Manchester Reading Society or the 'Jacobin Library', as it was nicknamed.[60]

There were also many flourishing schools, both secular and Sunday,[61] in Manchester by 1800, and the town was frequently visited by itinerant lecturers, mainly on scientific subjects. In addition the Manchester College of Arts and Sciences had been established in 1783, although it did not fulfil the hopes of its founders.[62] The stirrings and controversies of the 1780s and the 1790s indicate that Manchester had crossed the threshold of intellectual maturity.

NOTES

This paper is reprinted from the *Bulletin of the John Rylands Library*, Vol.42, No.1, September 1959, pp.40–60.

1. Quoted by J. Lee in *Maps and Plans of Manchester and Salford, 1650 to 1843* (1957), pp.10–11.
2. A.P. Wadsworth and J. de L. Mann, *The Cotton Trade and Industrial Lancashire, 1600–1780* (1931), pp.509–11, Appendix A: 'The Growth of Manchester'; Dr. J. Aikin, *A Description of the Country from thirty to forty miles round Manchester* (1795), pp.155–7; P. Mantoux, *The Industrial Revolution in the eighteenth century* (1928), pp.365–6.
3. Dr. Thomas Henry, 'Observations on the Bills of Mortality for the towns of Manchester and Salford', *Memoirs of the Literary and Philosophical Society of Manchester*, iii (1795), 160.
4. Henry, op. cit., iii, 161–2.
5. Aikin, op. cit., p.157. See also W. Brockbank, *Portrait of a Hospital, 1752–1948* (1952), p.213, Appendix III: 'Population of Manchester'.
6. *Archives Nationales*, Paris, T 591: 4 et 5.
7. H.T. Crofton, 'The Scots and Manchester after the '45', *Trans. Lancashire and Cheshire Antiquarian Society*, xxvi, 1908 (1909), 65–95; W.H. Chaloner, 'John Galloway (1804–1894) ...', ibid., lxiv (1954), 93–4 (reproduced as Ch. 6 of the present volume).
8. E.M. Brockbank, *Sketches of the Lives and Work of the Honorary Medical Staff of the Manchester Infirmary ... 1752 to 1830* (1904), passim.
9. Henry, op. cit., 163–4. Henry gives the triennial figures for the whole period 1765–85. The baptisms for 1786 and 1787 were 2,219 and 2,256 respectively and the burials 1,282 and 1,761 respectively (ibid. p.173). The bills of mortality for the *township* of Manchester from 1580 to 1832 are printed in E. Baines, *The history of the County Palatine and Duchy of Lancaster* (edn. of 1868 by J. Harland), i, 346–8. The last year in which they show an excess of burials over baptisms is 1766. Baines stated in 1836 that they had been 'extracted from the registers of the Collegiate Church to the year 1821; and subsequent to that time from those registers and the register of the Rusholme Road Cemetery combined'. He went on: 'There are also funerals at other churches and chapels in the town, fluctuating from 500 to 1,000 a year' (op. cit., p.348, n.2). For criticisms of these and the Parish Register Abstract figures for Manchester see Barbara Hammond, 'Urban death-rates in the early nineteenth century'(*Economic History*, no.3, Supplement to the *Economic Journal*, Jan. 1928, pp.419–28 and esp. pp.424–6).
10. Aikin, op. cit. p.157.
11. Wadsworth and Mann, op. cit. pp.355–78.
12. J.L. and B. Hammond, *The Skilled Labourer, 1760–1832* (1920), pp.287–9.
13. Op. cit. pp.203–5. On the use of one distinctive variety of potato as fodder see the article by the author of *The History and Social Influence of the Potato* (1949), R.N. Salaman (1875–1955), 'The Ox-Noble Potato: a Study in Public-House Nomenclature', *Trans. Lanc. and Ches. Antiq. Soc.*, lxiv – 1954 (1955), pp.66–82, with the first two footnotes added by Chaloner as editor. For the growth of the wholesale trade in foodstuffs in the nineteenth century see H.B. Wilkinson, *Old Hanging Ditch: its trades, its traders and its renaissance* (1910), passim, and J.T. Slugg, *Reminiscences of Manchester fifty years ago* (1881), passim.
14. Quoted in G.H. Tupling, 'The turnpike trusts of Lancashire', *Mem. and Proc. Manchester Lit. and Phil. Soc.*, xciv (1952–3), 2.
15. T.S. Willan, *River Navigation in England, 1600–1750* (1936), pp.30, 37–8, 59–61.
16. H. Clegg, 'The third Duke of Bridgewater's canal works in Manchester', *Trans. Lanc. and Ches. Antiq. Soc.*, lxv (1955), 92.

17. V.I. Tomlinson, 'Salford activities connected with the Bridgewater Canal', *Trans. Lanc. and Ches. Antiq. Soc.*, lxvi (1956), 53–5.
18. Clegg, op. cit. pp.94–5. The canal was not, as is often stated, opened throughout to Manchester in 1761.
19. Op. cit. p.205.
20. *The Entrepreneur: papers presented at the Annual Conference of the Economic History Society ... 1957*, 1957 (Research Centre in Entrepreneurial History, Harvard).
21. E. Baines, *History of the Cotton Manufacture in Great Britain* (1835), p.215; Charles Wilson, 'The entrepreneur in the Industrial Revolution in Britain', *History*, xlii, no.145 (June 1957), 108. Little has been published on the history of Manchester banking since L.H. Grindon's *Manchester Banks and Bankers* (1877), but mention should be made of T.S. Ashton's article on 'The Bill of Exchange and Private Banks in Lancashire, 1790–1830', *Econ. Hist. Rev.*, xv (1945), 25–35.
22. Aikin, op. cit., p.158; [James Ogden,] *A Description of Manchester* (1783), p.46.
23. W.H. Chaloner, 'Robert Owen, Peter Drinkwater and the early factory system in Manchester, 1788–1800', *Bulletin of the John Rylands Library*, xxxvii (1954–5), 82–94 (and Ch. 8 of the present volume).
24. There had been an attempt by a Mr. Gartside about 1758 to drive swivel-looms by water power at Garratt Hall (Aikin, op. cit., pp.175–6; Wadsworth and Mann, op. cit., pp.301–2).
25. Aikin, op. cit., pp.176–7; T.S. Ashton, *Iron and Steel in the Industrial Revolution* (1924), pp.80–1, 102; F.S. Stancliffe, *John Shaw's, 1738–1938* (1938), pp.69–70 (Wm. Sherratt), pp.87–8 (James Bateman). Some details about the Griffin Iron Foundry, Swan Street, Manchester, set up in the 1780s as a branch of a Derbyshire firm, are given in P. Robinson's *The Smiths of Chesterfield: a history of the Griffin Foundry, Brampton, 1775–1833* (Chesterfield, 1957), p.43. The early history of engineering in Manchester has recently been discussed in detail by A.E. Musson and Eric Robinson, 'The Early Growth of Steam Power', *Economic History Review*, 2nd ser., xi (April, 1959), 418–39.
26. Chaloner, 'John Galloway ...', *Trans. Lanc. and Ches. Antiq. Soc.*, lxiv (1954), 103–4. According to Galloway, Brodie was the 'maker of a new stove for ships, and had a large connection, especially with Government'.
27. Aikin, op. cit., p.176. This is a reference to the brown-paper mill of Smith and Inglis at Throstle Nest, Agecroft (D.C. Coleman, *The British Paper Industry, 1495–1860* (1958), p.197; Chaloner, op. cit., p.96).
28. Aikin, op. cit., p.178.
29. The evidence concerning Albert's activities is conveniently summarised in W.O. Henderson, *Britain and Industrial Europe, 1750–1870* (1954), pp.46–7.
30. John Scholes, 'Manchester Foreign Merchants, 1784–1870' (MS., Manchester Central Reference Library).
31. *The Court Leet Records of the Manor of Manchester* (ed. J.P. Earwaker), ix (1889), p.261.
32. *D.N.B.* vol. xlix.
33. Op. cit., p.184.
34. Op. cit., p.191.
35. B. Keith Lucas, 'Some influences affecting the development of sanitary legislation in England', *Econ. Hist. Review*, 2nd ser., vi, No.3 (April 1954), 290–6.
36. A. Redford, assisted by I.S. Russell, *History of Local Government in Manchester*, i (1939), 100–1, 157–8, 192–3, 200–1.
37. Redford and Russell, op. cit., pp.206–7.
38. T. McKeown and R. G. Brown, 'Medical Evidence related to English population changes in the eighteenth century', *Population Studies*, ix, no.2 (Nov. 1955), 119.
39. F.S. Stancliffe, 'The birthplace of the Manchester Royal Infirmary', *Trans. Lanc. and Ches. Antiq. Soc.*, vol. lxi for 1949 (1951), 35–42; W. Brockbank, *Portrait of a Hospital, 1752–1948* (1952), p.18.
40. Brockbank, op. cit., p.10.

41. Ibid., pp.18, 26–7.
42. Ibid., p.31.
43. Ibid., p.28.
44. Henry, op. cit., iii, 167–8.
45. M.C. Buer, *Health, Wealth and Population* ... (1926), pp.139–48.
46. *The Works ... of Thomas Percival, M.D.* (4 vols., 1807), iv, 5–7.
47. Sir J. Drummond and A. Wilbraham, *The Englishman's Food* (1957), pp.149–60, 271–6; *The Works ... of Thomas Percival, M.D.*, iv, edn. of 1807, 354–62.
48. Anon, 'The putrid fever at Robert Peel's Radcliffe Mill', *Notes and Queries*, cciii (Jan. 1958), 26–35; broadsheet in Chetham's Library reporting meeting of Manchester committee 'for the relief of the sick poor afflicted with the epidemic fever', 12 Dec. 1794.
49. E.P. Hennock, 'Urban sanitary reform a century before Chadwick?', *Economic History Review*, 2nd ser. x, No.1 (Aug. 1957), 113–16.
50. *Peterloo* (1958), p.3. Mr. L.S. Marshall, *The Development of Public Opinion in Manchester, 1780–1820* (Syracuse, 1946) must be used with caution. Even if it were admitted that Manchester may have been culturally under-developed in 1800, extenuating circumstances might be pleaded – the rapid growth of the new industrial community and the defective education of some, but not all of the new men who were rising to the top.
51. D. Read, '*Manchester News-Letter*, a discovery at Oxford', *Manchester Guardian* (31 Aug. 1956). See also *Manchester Review*, viii (Winter, 1957–8), 124.
52. G.A. Cranfield, *A handlist of English Provincial Newspapers and Periodicals, 1700–1760*, Cambridge Bibliographical Society, monograph no.2 (1952), pp.12–14; R.C. Jarvis, 'The Rebellion of 1745 ...', *Trans. Lanc. and Ches. Antiq. Soc.*, xlvi (1941–2), 124–8; xlvii (1943–4), 47–50; G.R. Axon, 'Roger and Orion Adams, printers', *Trans. Lanc. and Ches. Antiq. Soc.*, xxxix (1921), 108–24; *Collectanea relating to Manchester and its Neighbourhood ...*, ii, ed. J. Harland (Chetham Soc., lxxii (1868), 102–20; *Manchester Mercury* 24 Jan. 1804 (obituary of Harrop); F. Leary, 'History of the Manchester Periodical Press' (MS., c.1897, Manchester Reference Library).
53. Harland, op. cit., p.106. A second *Manchester Journal* appeared between 1754 and 1756 (Cranfield, op. cit., p.14).
54. Harland, op. cit., p.109. Harland complained: 'Nothing is more difficult to trace than the deaths of newspapers.'
55. Ibid., pp.110–14.
56. C. Roeder, 'Beginnings of the Manchester Post-Office', *Trans. Lancs. and Ches. Antiq. Soc.*, xxii, 28–34, 39–42; K. Ellis, *The Post Office in the Eighteenth Century*, pp.32, 99; Howard Robinson, *The British Post Office* (1948), p.215. It is quite wrong to imagine that there was no penny post until 1840. There were dozens of local penny posts in operation before Rowland Hill's reform.
57. A. and N. Clow, *The Chemical Revolution* (1952), p.189.
58. W.H. Brindley, 'The Manchester Literary and Philosophical Society', *Journal of the Royal Institute of Chemistry* (Feb. 1955), 62–9; E.M. Fraser, 'Robert Owen in Manchester, 1788–1800', *Mem. and Proc., Manchester Lit. and Phil. Soc.*, lxxxii (1937–8), 35–40.
59. Pauline Handforth, 'Manchester Radical politics, 1789–1794', *Trans. Lanc. and Ches. Antiq. Soc.* lxvi (1956), 87–106; F. Knight, *The Strange Case of Thomas Walker* (1957).
60. W.E.A. Axon, *Handbook of the Public Libraries of Manchester and Salford* (1877), pp.61–2.
61. For the Sunday schools, see A.P. Wadsworth, 'The first Manchester Sunday Schools', *Bull. John Rylands Library*, xxxiii (1950–1), 299–326.
62. H. McLachlan, *Warrington Academy: its history and influence* (Chetham Soc., cvii (N.S., 1943), 123–4.

10

The Birth of Modern Manchester

In 1700–50 Manchester stood on the threshold of a period of extraordinary expansion, which established the city almost as a rival to London in the determination of national fiscal policy. This expansion depended a good deal on improved communications. Situated at the confluence of the Rivers Irk and Irwell, the latter a major tributary of the Mersey, Manchester was already the natural road centre of southeast Lancashire and north-east Cheshire. In the 1720s and 1730s the work of rendering the Mersey and Irwell navigable up to Hunt's Bank under an Act of Parliament passed in 1721 was completed. This Act had been solicited by members of the chief trading families and wholesale drapers in the area – John Lees, of Clarksfield, Oldham, Joseph Byrom and James Lightbowne. Then in 1737 seven landowners and merchants from the Manchester area obtained a second act empowering them to deepen Worsley Brook down to its junction with the Irwell. Some, if not all, of this second set of 'undertakers' seem to have been connected with the Company of Proprietors of the Mersey and Irwell Navigation, but the scheme did not materialise, and a plan put forward by a group of Manchester businessmen in 1753–4, i.e. five years before the Duke of Bridgewater's successful project, also came to nothing.

This period also witnessed the beginning of organised road improvement. Lancashire in the seventeenth and eighteenth centuries was notorious for its bad roads, supplemented by paved causeways, raised above the level of the fields, just wide enough for horses but too narrow for wheeled traffic. Improvement began, as far as the Manchester area was concerned, in the early eighteenth century. It is significant that the first road in Lancashire to be placed under the administration of a turnpike trust was the stretch from Manchester to Stockport, forming part of the Manchester to Buxton trust set up in 1725. In 1732 the Manchester–Ashton-under-Lyne–Mottram road was turnpiked, to be followed three years later by the Manchester–Oldham–Austerlands road into Yorkshire. In 1738 a local historian wrote that there were causeways 'everywhere about Manchester ... of a common breadth and kept in good repair by the extraordinary care of the proper officers'. From the 1730s to the 1760s no further turnpiking took place in the Manchester area, but from the latter decade until the beginning of the railway age there was great activity in road improvement throughout south-east Lancashire and north-east Cheshire. The story of the third Duke of Bridgewater's canal (1759–61), which brought his Worsley coal to Castlefield in the heart of Manchester by 1764, has frequently been told. By reducing the price of coal and increasing the town's supplies, it made Manchester a more comfortable place to live in. But the extension of the Duke's canal across north Cheshire to Runcorn on the Mersey, opened throughout in 1776, proved to be economically more important. Not only did this extension enable Manchester to draw on a wider area for food supplies, e.g. potatoes from Ormskirk and Frodsham, but it also linked the Manchester area to the Midlands market via the Grand Trunk canal and provided a means of importing West Indian and American cotton more cheaply into south-east Lancashire via Liverpool.

The Worsley pits did not supply all Manchester's coal. In the reign of James I the coal consumed in Manchester already amounted to more than 10,000 tons per annum and came chiefly from the manor of Bradford, east of the town and now a part of the city. The main Bradford colliery was greatly developed in the 1760s, and Dr. Aikin noted in his *Description of the Country from 30 to 40 miles around Manchester* (1795):

The supply of coals to Manchester is chiefly derived from the pits about Oldham, Ashton, Dukinfield, Hyde, Newton, Denton etc. ... The supply from the Duke of Bridgewater's pits at Worsley is less considerable, although a very useful addition for the poor.

The activities of the eighteenth-century merchants and manufacturers who directed the Manchester area's textile industries and marketed their products have not yet been investigated in great detail, although it was mainly through their efforts and those of their agents that the official value of British exports of cotton goods rose from practically nothing in 1751 (£46,000) to £200,000 by 1764, and to nearly £5$\frac{1}{2}$ million by 1800, a figure almost equal to that for woollen and worsted cloths, linen, ribbons, and mixed cloths of linen and cotton. In 1739 a historian of the town noted that the industrious and frugal Manchester textile dealers were always 'contriving and inventing some thing new to improve or sell off their goods'. In social ambitions they differed little from the English merchant class generally, as the successful ones often ended by investing their money in land as the owners of old family estates in the neighbourhood sold off their patrimonies. Early in the eighteenth century those merchants who organised the manufacture of cloths in the town and its surrounding region had been called 'linen drapers', but as the eighteenth century progressed they became known as 'merchants' or 'manufacturers', specialising in checks, fustians or, later, cotton velvets. By the mid-1750s the largest of the mercantile and manufacturing houses appear to have been those in the check trade, of whom the Touchet family is the best known, as the result of the activities of Samuel Touchet, M.P. (d. 1773), who rose to be a London merchant and Government financier. William Radcliffe, in his *Origin of Power Loom Weaving* (1829) stated that as late as 1800 'all the great [Manchester] merchants were manufacturers with scarcely an exception', i.e., they still employed domestic workers over a wide area. They might also be dealers in raw materials – cotton, wool, linen warps – and finishers, undertaking to get the cloths bleached, dyed or printed. From the 1760s onwards the larger merchants concentrated on selling in the London and overseas markets, and after the boom in machine cotton spinning from the early 1780s, they were joined by the precursors of the many foreign merchants, whose activities added a strong cosmopolitan element to Manchester life, and had made it even by 1800 'in every respect ... one of the commercial capitals of Europe'. The home market, with the exception of the counties of the South East served by London, fell into the hands of the 'middle class of manufacturers and petty chapmen'. The Manchester and Salford directories of 1773 and 1781 show clearly the importance the two towns had already gained as the centre of the finishing processes. By 1780 most of the production of the 'country' textile manufacturers was passing through the hands of the Manchester merchants and the large Bolton warehouses were deserted; the Manchester calenderers (cloth pressers) seem to have supplied most of the warehousing space until the great warehouse building boom of the 1820s.

From the 1770s the boom in cotton associated with the great spinning inventions and the beginnings of the factory began to alter the town and the trade of Manchester in an astonishing fashion. The first cotton spinning factory in Manchester, containing a water frame, appears to have been built in the early 1780s by Sir Richard Arkwright, in partnership with two local men, Simpson and Whittenbury. It stood on Shudehill, and was noteworthy because a Newcomen-type steam pumping engine supplemented the power of its water-wheel, replenishing the reservoir by pumping back into it the water which had already flowed through the wheel. Some of the large wholesale merchants, such as Peter Drinkwater(d. 1801), and Samuel Oldknow of Stockport and Mellor, invested the profits of trade in the new industrial equipment, but many of the new factory industrialists of the 1780s and the 1790s (e.g. Robert Owen, John Kennedy and James McConnel) did not begin as merchants, but as manufacturers of textile machinery. The merchant middlemen now added to their functions that of supplying machine-made yarn, although the great master cotton-spinners never became dependent on them as did the smaller 'commission spinners'. The perfection of the power-loom (c. 1800–30) brought about the addition of the weaving sheds to many cotton spinning mills and the creation of 'mixed firms' which had less need of the yarn merchant. By 1802 there were 52 spinning mills in Manchester; by 1830, 99. In the 1820s roughly one quarter of the cotton spindles in the United Kingdom were within the township boundaries and in 1827 Manchester and Stockport between them accounted for half the power looms in the country.

During the same period Manchester's Tuesday market for textiles began to attract manufacturers from the smaller cotton towns of Lancashire. In 1800 Manchester was still largely 'a town of little dealers and manufacturers who bought unbleached fabrics in Bolton, dyed them and then hawked them on horseback from market to market'. By 1820 these men had increased greatly in wealth and economic importance and were advertising in the press for commissions to finish goods either for the home trade or for overseas markets. Their success stimulated the expansion of warehouse capacity, particularly in the 1820s. In 1820 only 126 warehouses were listed on the township's ratebooks, but nine years later the number had increased to nearly one thousand. The new warehouse district was only a few hundred yards from the Collegiate Church (now Manchester Cathedral), and, according to a contemporary observer, Sir Robert Peel, senior, had initiated this development.

The mechanisation of cotton spinning created a demand for textile machinery-making and engineering industries. The successive issues of the Manchester and Salford directories reveal a striking increase in the number of engineering firms and textile machinery makers between 1781 and 1800. Skilled artisans practising trades which had existed for centuries, such as joiners, turners and clockmakers, began to advertise themselves as shuttle makers, loom makers etc.; millwrights, i.e. water-mill engineers, became more numerous, and from 1772 onwards the terms 'engineer' and 'engine maker' appear in local newspaper advertisements. Some of the early master cotton-spinners either started their careers as machine makers or maintained engineering sections in their mills, but the large firm which specialised (if that is the correct word where products were so numerous) in engineering and foundry work now made its appearance. Such an establishment was that founded by James Bateman in the late 1780s in partnership with William Sherratt. This concern, with its main works in Salford, operated blast furnaces at Dukinfield and probably built more steam engines for Lancashire firms than did Boulton and Watt. There were by

1795 at least five other considerable foundries in Manchester and Salford; in addition pig iron, castings and other iron work had to be imported into the district from Yorkshire, the Midlands and North Wales. By 1815, with the rapid increase in the application of steam power to factory production and the adoption of the power loom, the cotton industry in the area was completing the initial phase of its phenomenal expansion, which was to reach its peak just a century later.

Some idea of the phenomenal rate of expansion of the town may be gauged from the growth in the population of Manchester in the late eighteenth century. Estimates made about 1717 give figures of 10,000 for the population of Manchester and 2,500 for that of Salford. By 1758 the township of Manchester alone, according to a local census, contained 17,000 souls, and fifteen years later (1773–4) 24,386. By Christmas 1788 the estimated figure for Manchester stood at nearly 43,000, and when the first official census was taken in 1801 there had been a further rise to well over 70,000. This increase can be traced to a number of causes: better supplies of food after the 1750s as the result of better communications, immigration from Scotland, Ireland and the surrounding countryside, improved medical services (Manchester Royal Infirmary was founded in 1752 and St.Mary's lying-in hospital in 1790) and a high birthrate. Reliable evidence about the local death rate in the eighteenth and early nineteenth centuries is difficult to come by.

Local government, meanwhile, had developed very slowly as compared with local industry. Up to 1765 the township of Manchester's status, as Defoe remarked, was indeed that of a village – it was governed by the Court Leet of the lords of the manor, the Mosley family. Every year the Court Leet chose unpaid officers who administered such municipal services as existed at the time – the borough-reeve (a kind of mayor but with little executive power, except that he alone could convene public meetings), the day police, the market lookers or inspectors, the scavengers, and so on. As the Court Leet met only twice a year long periods sometimes elapsed before offenders were summoned before it. Yet the early eighteenth-century alternative to this system was to have an oligarchical municipal corporation which might try to control the town's economic expansion in its own narrow interest, and would not necessarily take a wider view of its sanitary functions than the Court Leet. Dr. Aikin summed up late eighteenth-century opinion when he remarked: 'With respect to *government* it [Manchester] remains an open town, destitute (probably to its advantage) of a corporation, and unrepresented in Parliament'.

In 1765, however, local reformers secured the passage of the Manchester and Salford Police Act, which set up a body of Cleansing and Lighting Commissioners empowered to provide more adequate local government services. If the influential inhabitants named in the act had used their statutory powers more vigorously they could largely have superseded the Court Leet, but they did not, and things went on much as before, in spite of the passing of a second local Improvement Act in 1776. By the 1780s there was much discontent with the Court Leet, which had in many of its functions become 'sluggish and inactive', and the setting up of the Manchester and Salford Police Commissioners by a third act in 1792 marked the first substantial step towards a recognisably modern system of local government. At first the new Police Commissioners did little to justify their existence. They had the power to light and cleanse the streets, and to maintain a police force during the hours of darkness, but not until the first decade of the new century did the Commissioners, animated by a new spirit of enterprise, begin to exercise their functions with vigour and in a spirit of public service.

In the home of *laissez-faire* the Police Commissioners created an early example of municipal socialism by starting to manufacture the new illuminant, gas, at first for the purpose of lighting their own offices (1807), and later for the lighting of the streets and the supply of private consumers (1816). The large gasworks which they erected in 1817 proved a financial success from the start, and the Commissioners used the gas profits to defray other municipal expenses such as those incurred for paving and refuse disposal.

Dissatisfaction with the system of local government in Manchester grew very rapidly during the 1830s. There were heavy arrears of paving and refuse disposal on the books of the Police Commissioners. The Court Leet continued to exist, but there was a growing reluctance in the 1820s and 1830s to accept office under this Court. One prominent citizen who refused to serve in 1837 had to pay a fine of £200. No member of the Court Leet or of the Police Commission was a justice of the peace, and a chronic lack of co-ordination between the administration of justice and the administration of the public services existed. The desire for more resident magistrates who would be actively concerned in the town's affairs was one of the forces behind the struggle of 1837–8 for the incorporation of Manchester as a municipal borough under the Municipal Reform Act of 1835. This Act did not create any new municipal corporations, with the exception of Stockport; it merely reformed the old ones. It did, however, make provision for the creation by Royal Charter of new boroughs with elected councils, and separate benches of magistrates, provided sufficient local inhabitants of standing petitioned the Crown to that effect. So Richard Cobden and his fellow-Radicals got up such a petition in 1837, and in the following year Manchester received a charter of incorporation. It took a further eight years before the structure of local government was rationalised. The Police Commissioners continued in existence and did not surrender their functions, and their gas works, until 1841. The police forces of the Court Leet (the day police), the Police Commissioners (the night police), and the new Borough Council remained separate until 1841–2, when a Government Commissioner amalgamated them and handed a unified force over to the new Corporation. The Court Leet itself came to an end only in 1846, when the Corporation purchased from Sir Oswald Mosley for £200,000 the lordship of the manor, the manorial records and the right to hold markets and take tolls. Finally, in 1851 the Corporation purchased the property of the Manchester and Salford Waterworks Company, which had been formed in 1809 to take over and extend the waterworks operated by the lord of the manor. The status of a city was conferred on Manchester in 1853.

By the 1830s Manchester had become the metropolis of a manufacturing region which drew the bulk of its most important raw material, cotton, from the U.S.A., and the new railways had begun to simplify and speed up the processes of manufacturing and merchanting. From 1830 the railway joined Manchester to Liverpool – the first large British towns to be linked by the new method of communication – and by 1837–8 Manchester was linked with Birmingham and London by the opening of the Grand Junction and the London and Birmingham companies' lines. The first shorter route to the South, via Stockport and Crewe instead of via Newton-le-Willows on the Liverpool and Manchester line, came in 1842.

In 1844 an observer noted that towns such as Bolton, Bury, Rochdale, Oldham, Ashton, Stalybridge, Hyde and Stockport were to be regarded as the manufacturing parts of one great town:

> If we take our station in Market Street, Manchester, at the west-end of which is the Exchange, we are immersed in the heart of the system. We have around us the wholesale warehouses and offices wherein is transacted all the business between the dealers, the manufacturers, the spinners, the bleachers, the calico-printers, etc., whether of Manchester or of any of the surrounding towns. One street especially, viz., Mosley Street, presents a curious index to the whole arrangement. Here almost every house is occupied in the way stated; no manufactures are carried on, no retail shops exhibit the manufactured goods, but every house and almost every floor of every house constitutes the business establishment of some large manufacturing firm ... A bargain is struck, say, for 10,000 pieces of calico, as per sample, and this may be done in a small room between the manufacturer and the dealer, while the goods are perhaps at that moment being manufactured at Bolton, or Ashton, or Stockport.

Manchester businessmen and industrialists connected with the cotton trade found it increasingly profitable to concentrate their activities and those of their employees in textile merchanting, the finishing processes, such as dyeing and bleaching and the manufacture of textile machinery. Even Disraeli, whose social background and political ideals were not those of the manufacturing North, but who nevertheless recognised power and true achievement when he saw them, had to admit that Manchester was 'rightly understood, as great a human exploit as Athens'.

In the late 1820s Britain imported on the average 100,000 tons of raw cotton a year; by the late 1830s the figure had doubled, and in 1849 no less than 346,000 tons came in, valued at about £15 millions. The North West and the other cotton spinning districts of Great Britain were selling increasing quantities of cotton cloth and yarn overseas. For the years 1835–40 the average annual value (in official figures) of British cotton manufactures exported stood at just under £24 millions, compared with less than £6 millions for woollen and worsted exports, and about £20 millions for all other exports. In Sir John Clapham's words:

It is not surprising that Britain's foreign trade presented itself almost as a problem in cotton, or that Manchester claimed a great share in the determination of the commercial – and industrial and social – policy of the country.

Although the doctrines of Free Trade did not originate in Manchester – they had been enunciated by Thomas Tooke in the famous petition of the London merchants to Parliament in 1820 – the successful campaign against the Corn Laws of 1828 and 1842 was conducted by an organisation, the Anti-Corn Law League, which had its headquarters in Manchester. In the conditions of the late 1830s and the early 1840s the Corn Laws became symbolic of the whole obsolete tariff structure, and the vital character of the part played by Manchester men and Manchester ideas in the struggle against tariffs on imported foods and foreign manufactured goods received due recognition in the House of Commons on February 20th, 1846, when Disraeli put the phrase 'the Manchester School' into general circulation for the first time as a collective description of the forces which had triumphed over those who favoured the maintenance of Protection for British agriculture and industry.

The merchants, industrialists and 'the intelligent workingmen' of the cotton districts were driven by inescapable facts to adopt Free Trade principles and assume the natural leadership of the movement. What was happening in Manchester was also happening over much of the industrial North. The industrial North needed regular supplies of food at moderate prices for its expanding population, food which British farmers were becoming less and less able to supply in adequate quantities at reasonable prices. The population of Great Britain grew from 12,597,000 in 1811 to over 18,000,000 in 1841; in the 1840s it was increasing at the rate of over 200,000 a year. As Britain became decade by decade more industrialised, with a diminishing percentage of her people engaged in food production, increased imports of food became necessary.

To the merchants and industrialists of the North and Midlands, and especially those of Manchester, it seemed as though Parliament's restrictions on the free import of wheat and other foods were creating both semi-famine conditions and unemployment in Britain, particularly during the economic depression of 1837–42. In 1838, a year of heavy unemployment and distress in the factory districts, the price of corn soared to levels reminiscent of 1811–12 and the 'Luddite' food-riots. The advocates of free trade in corn argued that the impoverished farmers and landowners of the corn-exporting regions of Europe, unable to secure a regular outlet for their grain surpluses because of the British duties on imported corn, could not afford to buy British manufactured goods.

That this analysis of the situation, calling for the adoption of what may be described in modern terms as a policy of full employment through Free Trade, was to a large extent a just one is suggested, to take one example, by the expansion of British exports to the Eastern Mediterranean after the repeal of the Corn Laws in 1846–9. By 1855 the dominions of the Sultan of Turkey imported more Manchester piece-goods than all the European countries combined, and in 1856 the chairman of the Manchester Chamber of Commerce felt able to say:

As to cottons in Alexandria, we have no rivals and mainly by reason of the increase of our grain trade ... there has been a large increase in our exports of cotton to that place.

An Anti-Corn Law Association had been formed in London in 1836, and on March 16th, 1838, C.P. Villiers (1802–98), M.P. for Wolverhampton from 1835 until his death, had moved the first of his series of annual motions in the House of Commons calling for an inquiry into the working of the Act of 1828. It was not, however, until a few months after the preliminary meeting held to form the Manchester Anti-Corn Law Association on September 24th, 1838 that the movement assumed a mass character. One of the seven men who attended this inaugural meeting was Archibald Prentice, editor of the Radical *Manchester Times*, who published a two-volume history of the League in 1853. Alderman Richard Cobden (1804–65), fresh from his part in the struggle for the incorporation of Manchester as a municipal borough, who later became the chief spokesman of the League in Parliament, joined the Association before the end of October. Cobden's friend,

John Bright (1811–89), the Quaker cotton-spinner from Rochdale, who developed into the League's most powerful and popular public speaker, had joined earlier in the month.

On December 20th, 1838, the Manchester Chamber of Commerce, under the influence of Cobden and his associates, approved a petition to the House of Commons calling for the removal 'of all existing obstacles to the unrestricted employment of industry and capital', and in March, 1839, a Manchester conference of delegates from local Anti-Corn Law Associations decided to form an Anti-Corn Law League with its headquarters in Manchester. The League adopted a policy of total and unconditional Corn Law Repeal which estranged it from the Whig Government in power at the time, but the repealers soon began to influence the composition of the House of Commons by promoting the return to Parliament of R.H. Greg, of Styal, a cotton manufacturer and a member of the Association, as a representative of Manchester (September, 1839). In the General Election of 1841, the repealers put a number of candidates in the field, especially in the industrial North. Seats were won from both Whigs and Tories and the strength of the League in Parliament, both in numbers and ability, was considerably enhanced. Cobden was returned as M.P. for Stockport, Dr. (afterwards Sir) John Bowring for Bolton. Bright joined the group in 1843 as M.P. for Durham.

The League was the first political organisation to use modern methods of propaganda. The merchants and industrialists of the North and Midlands raised enormous subscriptions to finance its work – on the completion of the struggle in 1846 Cobden alone received a gift of £75,000 in recognition of his services. Besides voluntary workers, the League maintained a body of paid speakers who toured the country stirring up, not only the masses in the towns, but the farmers and labourers in the countryside. The League tried with some success to split the agricultural interest, by representing Protectionist landowners as the enemy of the farmers and Protectionist farmers as the enemy of the labourers. It published millions of books, pamphlets and handbills on the subject of Free Trade and the Corn Laws, and the quality of the literary opposition to the League was feeble. After 1840 the League was able to use a cheap and convenient channel of distribution for its literature – Rowland Hill's penny post. Anti-Corn Law dances were held, Anti-Corn Law songs sung and Anti-Corn Law poetry read and recited. An Anti-Corn Law bazaar, held in the Theatre Royal, Manchester, from January 31st to February 10th, 1842, was, according to Prentice, more in 'the character of a great Art Exposition than a mere bazaar.' Together with a larger one held in Covent Garden, London in May 1845, this bazaar can claim some share in the ancestry of the Great

Exhibition of 1851. Although modern historians are inclined to discount the importance of the part played by the Anti-Corn Law League in securing the repeal of the Corn Laws in 1846–9, there can be no doubt that Peel himself was strongly influenced by Cobden's forceful exposition of Free Trade principles in Parliament.

In the early nineteenth century Manchester gained notoriety not only as the exemplar of factory industry but also as the 'mainspring' of all the working-class movements of the time. Clubs of operative cotton spinners and skilled craftsmen had existed since the 1790s and earlier. There was a particularly widespread strike of cotton spinners in the Manchester area in 1810, and as early as 1818 there was an attempt to organise a 'general union of trades' or 'Philanthropic Hercules' with its headquarters in the town. In 1830 John Doherty, after forming a temporarily powerful National Union of Cotton Spinners, established a far more ambitious National Association for the Protection of Labour, with delegate meetings covering a variety of trades, again based on Manchester, but this organisation faded away in 1832. In the late 1830s and early 1840s, the Socialist or 'communitarian' theories of Robert Owen, who had managed cotton factories in Manchester in the 1790s, gained many adherents and an Owenite Hall of Science was erected in 1839 as a centre for socialist propaganda and other working-class activities. The Chartists of Manchester were numerous and vocal; they included many adherents of the 'physical force' theory. It is clear from the working class agitations of 1837–45, and especially the Plug Plot riots of August 1842, when the town was for a short time almost at the mercy of a mob of demonstrators from the surrounding factory districts, that numerous trade clubs existed among the skilled artisans, particularly those in the building trades. In 1838 the Manchester carpenters, for example, opened their Carpenters' Hall. In 1845 the 'United Trades' of Manchester made a fleeting appearance, and in 1853–4 Ernest Jones, the Chartist barrister, attempted to organise a nation-wide 'Labour Parliament', which held its first (and last) general assembly in March 1854 in Manchester with between 30 and 40 delegates. Side by side with this ephemeral organisation existed the Trades Defence Association of Manchester (1854), which was apparently a local trade union body with soberer and more limited aims. Between 1858 and 1867 about a dozen permanent trades councils were established in the cities and large towns of Britain and the present Manchester and Salford Trades Council traces its history back to this period, being founded in 1866. Two years later, on the initiative of the Manchester and Salford Trades Council, the first Trades Union Congress of the present series was held in the city. Manchester and

Salford can therefore claim to have played a vital part in shaping the modern British system of industrial relations.

During the 1850s and 1860s Manchester's economic links with the cotton region were further strengthened by the construction of a comprehensive railway network, with the city as its centre. This facilitated the circulation of heavy goods traffic but it was not until the construction of tramway systems from the 1880s onwards that public passenger traffic in the area began to assume its modern mass character. Although some of the great departmental stores which have made Manchester the great shopping centre of south-east Lancashire and north-east Cheshire, e.g., Lewis's (1880), date back to the mid-nineteenth century, the city's pre-eminent position in this sphere was not finally assumed until the coming of cheap public and private motor transport in the 1920s and 1930s. The Co-operative Wholesale Society has had its headquarters in Manchester since its foundation in 1863, with the result that the city is now the distributive, and in some cases the manufacturing, centre for an important sector of the nation's retail trade.

During the Cotton Famine of 1861–5 Manchester, with its numerous agents and warehousemen who found 'half trade at treble prices' more profitable than full employment at normal rates, did not suffer so acutely as those of its satellite towns which were dependent to a greater degree on the employment afforded by the actual manufacturing processes of the cotton industry. The spinning and weaving of cotton had largely disappeared from the centre of the city by the 1880s, although it continued to be important in north-east Manchester, but by then probably about three quarters of all the cotton yarn spun in the United Kingdom and an even larger proportion of the cotton cloth produced were sold in the city.

Allied industries became more important as the century went on. For example, Manchester played an important part in the early history of the British rubber industry. For a time Charles Macintosh (1766–1843), a Scots manufacturing chemist, made his patent rubberised waterproof cloth in Glasgow, but in 1824 he decided to set up a new factory in Manchester in partnership with R.W. Barton and the brothers J. and H.H. Birley, cotton spinners and manufacturers. In Manchester many improvements were introduced, of which the most important proved to be the machine for spreading the rubber solution on to the cloth. Between 1826 and 1834 Macintosh was forced to establish a partnership with Thomas Hancock (1786–1865) of London, the second most important name in early rubber technology, to manufacture garments and other articles made from waterproof materials and to retail them direct to the public. This was necessary in order to break down the resistance of the tailors to the introduction of the new fabric. By 1839 the Macintosh–Hancock factory employed between 200 and 600 hands (an indication that the demand for 'Macintosh cloaks' was highly seasonal) and its domination of the scene is clear from the fact that it consumed 250,000 lb. of raw rubber a year out of annual British imports of just under 320,000 lb. Other Manchester rubber manufacturing firms date from this early period – David Moseley and Sons, founded in 1833, J. Mandleberg and Co. (1850) and P. Frankenstein and Sons (1852). Today the factory of the Dunlop Rubber Company stands on the site of the original Macintosh factory of the 1820s.

Manchester's economy did not, however, depend entirely on the cotton and related trades, even in the mid-nineteenth century. Surprisingly enough, occupations connected with the woollen and worsted trades continued to provide considerable employment in the Manchester area until the early twentieth century. The manufacture of textile machinery and stationary steam engines forms the oldest surviving branch of Manchester's engineering industry and by the 1850s such names as Mather and Platt, Sharp Roberts, and Galloways were famous throughout Western Europe. The greatest Manchester engineer of the mid-nineteenth century was undoubtedly Sir Joseph Whitworth (1803–87), whose armament and precision instrument-works, originally established in Chorlton Street in 1833, and moved to Openshaw in 1880, heralded the future importance of Manchester's machine-tool industry. Whitworth, famous for his production of a perfectly plane surface, suggested a 'scheme for standardizing screws, screw threads and other mechanical essentials' which was widely adopted in British workshops by 1860. His experiments in a specially constructed shooting gallery at Fallowfield in 1855 showed how defective the Army's Enfield rifle was and led him to produce both small arms and cannon, using a special 'Whitworth' steel. Manchester engineering firms were among the first to make and use Bessemer steel in the 1860s and 1870s. In 1897 Whitworths, which had been joint-stocked in 1874, was amalgamated with Sir W.G. Armstrong & Co. of Newcastle-on-Tyne. Under the impact of the depression in the iron and steel trades in the 1920s the steel interests of Armstrong–Whitworth, Vickers of Barrow and Cammell Laird of Birkenhead were merged to form the English Steel Corporation, the whole of the small tools and tool steel business carried on by these firms being concentrated at Openshaw.

Locomotives have been made in Manchester since 1831. By the mid-nineteenth century not only were there railway company workshops belonging to the Manchester, Sheffield and Lincolnshire at Gorton, to the London and North Western at Longsight and to the Lancashire and

Yorkshire Company at Newton Heath, but C.F. Beyer and Richard Peacock had begun in 1854 to manufacture locomotives both for home and overseas lines at Gorton. Owing to its success in pioneering and exporting the Garratt locomotive in the period after 1914 this firm has an international reputation and is now the sole survivor of the Manchester locomotive builders of the nineteenth century.

In the early nineteenth century there was comparatively little specialisation by product in engineering, and most engineering works could swiftly be adapted to turn out whatever kind of capital equipment was in briskest demand. Later, firms tended to concentrate on specialities. For example, the Atlas works of Sharp, Roberts and Co. (Sharp, Stewart and Co. from 1852), which had concentrated on self-acting mules in 1825–34, became world-famous for locomotives before it was closed down and the firm's activities transferred to Glasgow shortly after its amalgamation with the Clyde Locomotive Co. in 1888. Similarly Galloways, of Knott Mill and Ardwick, after building the first Manchester locomotive in 1831, specialised in boiler production at their Hyde Road works after 1872. Some famous Manchester engineering firms, after a glorious life, met with disaster. The Ancoats bridge-building, steam engine and boiler works established in 1817 by the celebrated William Fairbairn (1789–1874), in partnership with James Lillie, and carried on by his sons after 1853, had to be wound up shortly after the death of its founder 'owing to a depression in trade'.

The Census of 1921 showed that Manchester's textile machinery industry was the second most important in Lancashire, employing 6,445 persons, as compared with Oldham's 13,493 and Bolton's 4,715. Just as some Manchester-born engineering firms, such as Craven Bros., manufacturers of machine tools, established in 1853, and now at Reddish, have migrated from the city, so others founded outside have either entered the city or been absorbed within it as Manchester's boundaries were extended. Mather and Platt, the largest of the Manchester engineering firms, provides an example of the latter tendency. Originally founded in the 1830s in Salford, Mather and Platt began to transfer their business to the Park Works at Newton Heath in 1901. Under the energetic leadership of Sir William Mather the firm did a heavy export trade in textile machinery, particularly with Russia, and also manufactured fire-fighting apparatus. In 1893 the management took the revolutionary but successful decision to introduce the eight-hour day, thus becoming the first large engineering works in the Manchester area to do so.

During the world-wide 'Great Depression' of 1873–96 alarming symptoms of local economic stagnation became apparent. During the early 1880s observers noted that more warehouses were unoccupied than at any period since the hard times of 1836–42, and the city of Manchester was said to contain as many empty houses as there were inhabited ones in the whole borough of Stockport. The city's rateable value showed only a modest rise between 1880 and 1890, in contrast to the rapid increases of earlier decades. The merchants and industrialists of Manchester reacted vigorously against the threat of falling profits and sagging prices; they proved once again that the price of economic progress is heavy and continual capital investment. The British cotton industry of the nineteenth and early twentieth centuries provided the most spectacular and extreme example of the international division of labour, and Manchester's existence as one of the economic capitals of the world depended primarily on the cheap transport of cotton and cotton goods in and out of south-east Lancashire. As the 'Great Depression' deepened the necessity to cheapen transport costs became ever more urgent. Liverpool dominated the Mersey, and Liverpool interests levied what Manchester men considered to be excessive charges for their services in organising the import trade in raw cotton. In addition, the railway companies serving the Lancashire cotton towns seem to have taken advantage of their quasi-monopolistic position to charge high rates on goods traffic, particularly as they controlled the old canal system. The answer to this was to make Manchester a port by constructing a ship canal through the North Cheshire plain. The Manchester Ship Canal project originated in a meeting held at the Didsbury house of Daniel Adamson the engineer in 1882, but it not only met with violent and protracted opposition from Liverpool and local railway interests but also aroused 'the powerful antagonism of the merchant aristocracy of Manchester many of whom were, it seems, committed to the support of steamship lines sailing from Liverpool'. In spite of this coalition, the Company secured its Act of Parliament in 1885, and with the heavy financial backing of Manchester Corporation this 'great national work' was ready to be opened by Queen Victoria on New Year's Day 1894, after setbacks and miscalculations which eventually raised the capital outlay to £15 million.

The effect of the Ship Canal on the economic life of Manchester was all the more remarkable in that its completion coincided with the end of the 'Great Depression'. Constructed at a time when rates of interest and prices of raw materials were low, the Ship Canal stood ready to give Manchester the advantage of the general increase in British overseas trade which started in the late 1890s and continued until 1914. By 1910 Manchester had become the fourth port in the United Kingdom in terms of the value of traffic handled, and roughly one-seventh of the total raw cotton consumption of Lancashire was arriving via the Ship Canal.

The manager of the Ship Canal Company until 1896 was the energetic Marshall Stevens (1852–1936), who soon saw that the new port needed equipping with the latest facilities. He resigned his post as manager to become managing director of the first British trading estate, Trafford Park Estates Ltd., and took an active part in companies formed to build Manchester's grain elevators, port warehouses and cold storage plants. The Ship Canal has preserved to the Manchester area all those industries such as corn milling, meat processing and papermaking which tend under modern conditions to die out in inland areas and to flourish in the larger ports.

Unlike Liverpool, Manchester had coal close at hand, although it could only be won with increasing difficulty by the deep-mining techniques developed to an increasing extent throughout the late nineteenth century. By 1881 coal had been won from Ashton Moss colliery, Audenshaw, at a depth of 2,688 ft. and coal was raised from Pendleton colliery in 1904 from 3,483 ft., then a record depth for Great Britain. In the late 1920s the two Bradford pits, by then within the city boundary, raised about 250,000 tons a year and employed about 1,200 men. These coal supplies facilitated the establishment and growth of Manchester's important chemical industry, which is most heavily concentrated in the north-eastern districts of the city. It was no accident that in 1857 Dr. F. Grace Calvert founded a factory for the production of carbolic acid from coal tar near Bradford colliery. Messrs. Levinstein Ltd. had been producing sulphuric acid and naphthalene at Blackley since 1865, and this district today appropriately enough contains the headquarters of I.C.I.'s Dyestuffs Division. By 1914 the Clayton Aniline Dye Co. of Manchester was one of the few British firms engaged in putting Sir William Perkin's discovery of the secret of producing synthetic dyes from coal tar to commercial use, and the painful revelation of Britain's inferiority to Germany in this branch of industrial technology disclosed by the outbreak of the First World War resulted in State regulation of the dyestuffs industry in 1920. This ensured increased activity in Manchester dyeworks during the depressed inter-war years.

Since the 1880s new branches of engineering have arisen out of the bell-wire and battery industry and the needs of the electric tramway and lighting systems. W.T. Glover Ltd., cable manufacturers, for example, started as bell wire makers in Salford, and moved to Trafford Park at the turn of the century. In 1908 an observer remarked: 'the experiment is being tried of establishing generating stations for supplying electricity to works situated miles away. Mills are already run by electric power and have long been lighted by this luminant'. Not only did entirely new businesses come into existence, such as the British Westinghouse Electric and Manufacturing Co. (now 'Metrovick'), an

American concern which established itself in Trafford Park in 1900–2, but older local firms, such as Mather and Platt, extended their activities to the new sphere and began the manufacture of electrical machinery and equipment. During his visit to the U.S.A. in 1882 Sir William Mather met Edison and arranged to manufacture the Edison dynamo in Lancashire, where it was greatly improved by Drs. J. and E. Hopkinson.

The gradual triumph of the motor-car from the 1890s onwards further modified the structure of Manchester's industry, and by 1914 Manchester engineers were producing many types of petrol-driven vehicles. In particular Belsize and Crossley cars, made at Clayton and Openshaw respectively, were finding a rapidly expanding market. Crossley and Co. had originally started as manufacturers of gas engines. In the 1920s Manchester seemed to be on the point of developing into a motor-car manufacturing centre large enough to rank with Birmingham and Coventry. Unfortunately the Ford Motor Company, which had built a works at Trafford Park in 1911–12, decided to transfer the seat of its operations to Dagenham, Essex, in 1929. It is interesting to note that Sir Alliott Verdon-Roe began building aeroplanes in an old mill off Great Ancoats Street in the years before the 1914–18 war, although the firm which bears his name no longer operates in Manchester, but in nearby Chadderton. In the Fairey Aviation Co. the area possesses a representative of the most spectacular development in the modern engineering industry. The story of Manchester's engineering achievement during and after the Second World War remains largely unwritten, since only a few of the larger firms have published detailed accounts of their part in the war-effort and in the period of transition.

Not all Manchester's industries are carried on solely in factories. In 1907 a Manchester Corporation official reported that there were over 4,000 persons in the city who worked in their own homes for employers in the ready-made clothing trade. This appeared surprising 'in a place which, in world-wide estimation, is in a special degree historically and comparatively associated with the factory system'. The clothing trade, then located chiefly in the Strangeways and Cheetham Hill district, was based on the sewing-machine rented by the out-worker from the middleman-employer at about 1s. 6d. per week. It was primarily a Manchester industry because in the satellite cotton towns ample alternative sources of employment for women existed. By the 1930s there were more clothing workers in Manchester than in Leeds, the classic centre of the industry, although the Manchester clothing factories and workshops concentrated on blouses and light dresses for women rather than the heavier men's tailoring for which Leeds is famous. By the 1930s, too, there had been a considerable extension of the factory system, although the largest Manchester establishments were much smaller than the giants of Leeds, and seldom employed more than 300 persons. A good deal of 'home work' still exists, and appropriately enough the production of rainwear is an expanding Manchester speciality.

By reason of its diversified economy, Manchester, although badly hit by the decline in British exports of cotton piece goods between 1914 and 1938, escaped the full force of the general depression which afflicted the old industrial districts of Britain dependent on coal, iron, steel and shipbuilding during the same period. Manchester's importance as a financial centre, with the largest provincial bank clearing, two independent banks (the District and the C.W.S.), its companies specialising in the insurance of industrial plant, has grown rather than declined during the last fifty years, while the Manchester wholesale produce markets serve a constantly growing region round the city. The city's heavy industrial contribution to the winning of the Second World War and the comparative ease with which the transition to an unsettled peace-time economy was effected reveal Manchester's adaptability and indicate that its citizens may look forward to a second century as a city with some hope.

NOTE

'The Birth of Modern Manchester' is reprinted from C.F. Carter (ed.), *Manchester and its Region* (British Association, 1962).

BIBLIOGRAPHY

A.P. WADSWORTH and J. de L. MANN, *The Cotton Trade and Industrial Lancashire, 1600–1780* (1931).

A. REDFORD assisted by I.S. RUSSELL, *The History of Local Government in Manchester*, 3 vols. (1939–40).

A. REDFORD and others, *Manchester Merchants and Foreign Trade:* Vol.I, 1794–1858 (1934); Vol.II, 1850–1939 (1956).

D. READ, *Peterloo: the Massacre and its Background* (1958).

D. READ, *Press and People, 1790–1850: opinion in three English cities* (1961).

D.G. BARNES, *History of the English Corn Laws from 1660–1846* (1930).

N. McCORD, *The Anti-Corn Law League, 1838–1846* (1958).

L. FAUCHER, *Manchester in 1844: its present condition and future prospects* (1844).

F. ENGELS, *The Condition of the Working Class in England* (trans. and ed. W.O. Henderson and W.H. Chaloner, 1958).

W.O. HENDERSON, *The Lancashire Cotton Famine, 1861–1865* (1934).

H. CLAY and K.R. BRADY (eds.), *Manchester at Work* (1929).

A. BRIGGS, *Friends of the People: the Centenary History of Lewis's* (1956).

S. and B. WEBB, *The History of Trade Unionism, 1666–1920* (1920).

W.H. CHALONER, 'Manchester in the latter half of the eighteenth century', *Bulletin of the John Rylands Library*, Vol. 42, No.1, Sept. 1959, pp.40–60 (and Chapter 9 of the present volume).

A.E. Musson and E. Robinson, 'The origins of engineering in Lancashire', *Journal of Economic History*, June 1960, pp.209–33.

A.E. Musson and E. Robinson, 'The early growth of steam power', *Economic History Review*, 2nd ser., Vol.11, No.3, 1959, pp.418–39.

A.E. Musson and E. Robinson, 'Science and industry in the late eighteenth century', *Economic History Review*, 2nd ser., Vol.13, No.2, 1960, pp.22–44.

R. Smith, 'Manchester as a centre for the manufacture and merchanting of cotton goods, 1820–30', *University of Birmingham Historical Journal*, Vol.4, 1953, pp.47–65.

R. Smith, 'The Manchester Chamber of Commerce and the increasing foreign competition to Lancashire cotton textiles, 1873–1896', *Bulletin of the John Rylands Library*, Vol.38, No.2, March 1956, pp.507–34.

J.S. McConechy, 'The economic value of the Ship Canal to Manchester and district', *Trans. Manchester Statistical Society*, Session 1912–1913, pp.1–126.

W.H. Brindley (ed.), *The Soul of Manchester* (1929).

11

Manchester's Historian. A Memoir of Arthur Redford, 1896–1961

Arthur Redford, one of the leading figures in the development of modern economic history, was born at Droylsden near Manchester on May 25th, 1896, the third and youngest child of Arthur Redford (1865–1922), cotton self-actor minder, and his wife Martha (née Street), cotton reeler (1859–1925). Arthur Redford senior later became an overlooker, moving house rather frequently in the years before the first World War, so that young Redford acquired a wide experience of working-class life in Ashton-under-Lyne, Audenshaw, Oldham and Failsworth as well as in Droylsden. He received part of his elementary education at Salem School, Lees Brook, Oldham, and later (c. 1906–8) attended Moorside Council School, Droylsden. From there he entered the Oldham Education Authority's municipal secondary (i.e. grammar) school. He was 'top boy' during the sessions 1910–11 and 1911–12, besides being a promising and versatile athlete. In 1912, having gained an Oldham Education Committee University scholarship of £60 per annum, he entered the Honours School of History in the University of Manchester, where he came under the influence of the great T.F. Tout, graduating with first-class Honours in 1915 after specialising in medieval history. In his third year he was in residence at Dalton Hall. His B.A. thesis on 'The climax of mediaeval Ireland: the administration of Ireland under Edward II', submitted in 1915, has since been much in request by other scholars working in the same field. On the results of his final examination he was awarded a graduate scholarship and took the degree of M.A. in 1916.

During his undergraduate days the family fortunes reached a low ebb (his father in 1914 bought a run-down grocer's shop and general store in Failsworth which did not do well) and at one time Redford seriously considered the possibility of abandoning his university course. Fortunately his father's circumstances seem to have improved somewhat before his death in 1922.

In 1915 Redford joined the Army, and served with the 13th Battalion, the Manchester Regiment, in the Eastern Mediterranean. He was soon commissioned and after a period in the line on the Salonika front, was appointed to serve on the General Staff in Greece and Asia Minor (1917–19), in which capacity he brought to London the official news of the Bulgarian armistice. A by-product of his war experiences is to be found in an unpublished MS on the history of the Balkan peasantry (c. 1920).

On demobilisation he decided to return to Manchester University to take the honours course in the School of Economics and Political Science and was awarded a first-class degree and the Langton Fellowship in 1920. In his second period at Manchester he came under the spell of Professor George Unwin, holder of the first chair of Economic History to be established in Britain. Unwin's imaginative and creative approach to the subject inspired Redford, although he was critical of the master's difficult lecturing style. During the sessions 1920–1 and 1921–2 he worked under Unwin's supervision on a thesis for the newly-established Ph.D. degree on the subject 'The Migration of Labour in England in 1800–50', for which he was awarded the doctorate in 1922.

In 1922 he accepted a temporary post as lecturer in economic history in the University of Liverpool and two years later was appointed Sir Ernest Cassel lecturer in commerce at the London School of Economics. While in London he married Miss Lucy Ashton, Professor T.S. Ashton's sister, an honours graduate of the English School at Manchester, by whom he had two sons. Mrs. Redford died in 1955. Shortly after Unwin's death in 1925, Redford was made Reader in Economic History in the University of Manchester and twenty years later was given the Chair.

Redford's *Labour Migration in England, 1800–1850*, published in 1926 and based on his Ph.D. thesis, was a pioneering study of this aspect of the Industrial Revolution, and was undoubtedly his most original work. The meticulous scholarship for which he was renowned is here most clearly evident. In 1926–7 he helped to form the Economic History Society and was one of its first council members. In 1931 he published the *Economic History of England, 1760–1860*, and a revised edition was published in 1960. Another of his works was *Manchester Merchants and Foreign Trade*, published in 1934, to which he added a second volume in 1956. He was chosen by the city authorities to write the *History of Local Government in Manchester*, which was completed in three volumes between 1939–40. In 1940 volume I of this work was named by the First Edition Club of London and New York as one of the fifty outstanding books of 1939.

Redford was first and last a Mancunian. The main work of his career was to put Manchester on the map both in its region, in his massive *History of Local Government in Manchester*, and in the sphere of world trade, as evidenced by the activities of its merchants. He was a stimulating teacher, and following Unwin's example, associated many young scholars with himself in his researches. After his promotion to the Chair of Economic History in 1945, he was responsible for the impressive expansion in the teaching of economic history which took place to meet the needs of the post-war generation. In early life he seems to have been extremely and warmly disputatious, and although he later mellowed somewhat in this respect, his general outlook tended to be one of cautious pugnacity.

When he decided in the early part of 1961 to retire, he could justly feel that his life's work, of establishing the subject as one of the main pillars of both historical and economic studies, had been achieved. And this he accomplished under a heavy burden of illness and bereavement. At the same time he always retained a cheerful friendliness and a fund of sage advice.

NOTE

This Memoir has been compiled from information kindly supplied by Mr. Timothy Redford, Mr. Maurice Harrison, Director of Education for Oldham, Mr. Herbert Nuttall of Hollinwood, and from obituary notices which appeared in *The Times* and *The Guardian* newspapers. It has been reprinted from the second edition of A. Redford, *Labour Migration in England 1800–1850* (Manchester University Press, 1964), pp.xv–xvii.

BIBLIOGRAPHY OF THE MAIN WRITINGS OF ARTHUR REDFORD

1. *Labour Migration in England, 1800–1850* (1926; 2nd rev. ed., 1964).
2. 'Some problems of the Manchester merchant after the Napoleonic Wars', *Trans. Manchester Statistical Society*, Session 1930–1, pp.53–87.
3. *The Economic History of England, 1760–1860* (1931, 2nd rev. ed., 1960).
4. 'The emergence of Manchester', *History*, Vol. XXIV, No.93, June 1939, pp.32–49.
5. (Assisted by Miss I.S. Russell) *The History of Local Government in Manchester* (3 vols., 1939–40).
6. *Manchester Merchants and Foreign Trade, Vol.I, 1794–1858* (1934), by students in the Honours School of History in the University of Manchester and Arthur Redford.
7. *Manchester Merchants and Foreign Trade, Vol.II, 1850–1939* (1956) (assisted by Brian W. Clapp).
8. 'Portrait of the founder' (a short biography of John Owens (1790–1846), the founder of Owens College), *Manchester Guardian*, 1 Aug. 1946.
9. 'Historia económica e social (1940–1941)' (*Revista Portuguesa de História*, Vol.III, Coimbra, 1947, pp.363–70).

PART FOUR

SOCIAL ASPECTS
OF THE
INDUSTRIAL REVOLUTION

12

Working-class History and Middle-class Historians: the Webbs, the Hammonds and the Coles

How very difficult it is for the well-to-do to lead the very poor towards the promised land.

> Beatrice Webb, quoted by Malcolm Muggeridge,
> *Punch*, April 18, 1956, p.463.

Social questions are the vital questions of today: they take the place of religion.

> Beatrice Webb, *My Apprenticeship* (1926), p.149.

It is a bad case of the occupational disease so common among high-strung men and women who come out of a conservative environment into proletarian politics. *By continuously talking to another class in the language they think that class speaks instead of in their own vernacular* they deceive themselves and create distrust in their audience.

> Beatrice Webb's Diaries, 1924–1932, pp.96–7,
> 14 May 1926, apropos of the activities of Susan
> Lawrence (1871–1947) during the General Strike.

The purpose of this paper is to take a look at the three great partnerships which did so much from the 1890s onwards for the study of economic and social history – Sidney Webb (1859–1947) and Beatrice Webb (1858–1943), J.L. le Breton Hammond (1871–1949) and Barbara Hammond (1872–1961) and G.D.H. Cole (1889–1959) and Margaret I. Cole (1893–1980). The members of these partnerships all wrote extensively, persuasively and influentially on various topics of working-class history, but they were all from the middle classes, and, indeed, all but one from the upper strata of the middle class. And although they all delved into working-class history only one of them – Beatrice Webb – had any intimate contact with working-class life over any considerable period of time. Yet Beatrice Webb, curiously enough, was the most unsympathetic of the six in her attitude towards the workers whom she wished to help.

When one states that they had little direct contact with manual workers, one must make an exception in favour of domestic servants. It is doubtful whether any of the three partnerships could have functioned efficiently without domestic help. Beatrice Webb in particular was very proud of the two maids she kept, and boasted that in nearly forty years' tenancy of 41, Grosvenor Road, Westminster, she and Sidney had employed only five separate servants. They even took 'the devoted Emily' Wordley, her parlour maid, on holiday with them. For example, their Margate lodgings in 1902 were made 'quite homely' by Emily.[1] It is interesting to note that as early as 1911 G.K. Chesterton summed up Mrs Webb as follows:

Nor can I at this moment think of a single modern woman writing on politics or abstract things, whose work is of undisputed importance; except perhaps Mrs. Sidney Webb, who settles things by the simple process of ordering about the citizens of a state, as she might the servants in a kitchen.[2]

It is significant that Mrs Webb, although she had many religious doubts and engaged in spiritual wrestling, remained an Anglican; in the words of Bertrand Russell: 'as a socialist she preferred the Church of England because it was a State institution.'[3]

Both the Webbs and the Hammonds lived ascetic, careful lives in the Victorian middle-class tradition. 'Monotonous' and 'execrable', as well as 'plain' and 'wholesome', were the adjectives used by visitors to describe the food served at the Webbs' table, and their cold mutton became a by-word. Meals were bolted down so that Beatrice could have extra time for cross-examining her guests.[4] An article in *The Manchester Guardian* entitled 'Centenary reflections on Beatrice Webb, not all of them flattering' noted 'the lack of warmth (actual and metaphorical) in the Webbs' household'.[5]

Their guests found other things lacking. Kingsley Martin, the former editor of the *New Statesman*, tells of a visit to the Webbs in their celebrated house in Grosvenor Road:

After lunch I asked Webb, who looked a little surprised, if I could use the lavatory. Harold Laski and I walked away together [after lunch]. Harold declared that my request had been an extraordinary act of courage which no one had ever dared perform before in the Webb household. He said that the week before he had dined there with Ramsay MacDonald, and that he and the premier had had to make use of a timber yard on the way home.[6]

Perhaps the best general description of their later household at Passfield Corner, Liphook, Hants, is by Mr Malcolm Muggeridge, who wrote in a review of *Beatrice Webb's Diaries, 1924–1932:*

One of the most arrogant, cruel, and, in her own odd way, fascinating women I have ever known was Beatrice Webb. She lived with her consort, Sidney, a minute, bearded and rather pitiable figure, in a considerably enlarged cottage near Liphook, waited upon by two excellent Scottish maids, and with for a companion an odious dog called Sandy. At week-ends a great variety of visitors descended upon the house and talk was incessant. Mrs Webb took a leading part (she had a way of saying 'lower classes' with a short 'a' which suggested an attitude of mind pretty remote from the more revivalistic aspects of the Labour Movement),[7] and Sidney would chip in as required. I never heard him disagree with her, but, with the best will in the world he might make some observations not wholly to her taste. Then she would say 'Don't be silly, Sidney', and that was the end of the matter. ... In the afternoons she went to lie down, but Sidney was instructed to take exercise, since this, like light breakfasts, was considered to be good for his health. He was no great walker, and what happened on the occasions when I accompanied him was that he found a convenient hayrick, lay down on it, spread a handkerchief over his face and enjoyed a quiet nap. Then on awakening, he would hurry back to the house, thereby getting into a sufficient sweat to suggest that he had covered the three miles or so which Mrs Webb considered adequate.[8]

It is not surprising that J.M. Ludlow once, by a Freudian slip of the pen, referred to Sidney and Beatrice as 'Mr. and Mrs. Potter.'[9]

When the systematic study of economic history began in the 1860s and 1870s its first practitioners naturally came from the comfortable middle classes – Thorold Rogers, Archdeacon William Cunningham and Arnold Toynbee. Owing to the nature of the educational system of Victorian England this state of affairs was inevitable: persons of working-class and lower middle-class origin who had had even a grammar school education were few, and fewer still had been to university or university college before the full effects of the Education Acts of 1902 and 1918 began to be felt. Historians were therefore recruited almost entirely from the upper strata of the middle classes, because no one in the working classes possessed the necessary technical skills for pursuing historical research and writing history in the academic sense.

The few examples which we possess of studies in economic history written by genuine members of the working class (and not by those who 'adopted' the working class and working-class causes) are either in the nature of autobiographical studies or chronicles of events, e.g. Alexander Somerville, *Autobiography of a Working Man* (1848); G.J. Holyoake's *The History of Co-operation in England* (2 vols., 1879); Lloyd Jones's *The Life, Times and Labours of Robert Owen* (4th edn.1905); W.J. Davis, *The British Trades Union Congress: History and Recollections* (1910); William Kiddier, *The Old Trade Unions from Unprinted Records of the Brushmakers* (1st edn. 1930, 2nd revised edn. 1931).[10]

Therefore the 'old guard' – the Webbs, the Hammonds and the Coles – tended to write economic and working-class history very much from the top floor of the social structure. The first notable exception to this was George Unwin (1870–1925). His father, Edward Unwin, a railway clerk, kept a public house, the Daw Bank Vaults, and later a grocer's shop, in Stockport. George left school at the age of 13 and took a clerical job with a firm of local hatmakers. This he held for nearly seven years. After three years attending Cardiff University College in order to read for a London University external degree (1890–3), thanks to a scholarship and the generosity of an uncle, Unwin won a classical scholarship offered by Lincoln College, Oxford, where he spent the years 1893 to 1897. Unwin spoke feelingly at this time of 'the present iniquitous system by which Oxford is monopolized by the middle and upper classes'.[11]

Unwin eventually made his breakthrough by means of an appointment in 1899 as secretary to Leonard H. Courtney (1832–1918), a Radical M.P. to whom he had been introduced by Mr and Mrs Webb (Courtney was the husband of Beatrice's sister Kate).[12] This post Unwin held until his appointment in 1908 as lecturer on economic history in Edinburgh University, from whence he moved to Manchester in 1910. These details about Unwin are mentioned merely as a foil – Unwin, although deeply interested in the subject, did not write much working-class history. Most of his published writings are on fiscal and business history.

THE WEBBS

I now propose to discuss each of the six partners in turn. Beatrice was the youngest of the nine daughters[13] of Richard Potter, a wealthy Victorian entrepreneur, and acted for a considerable period, in the beginning as secretary to her father and latterly, as general manager of his affairs. She was the most notable product of the system of education elaborated by that mid-Victorian philosopher, Herbert Spencer; in her early youth she was something of a social butterfly, and at one time it seemed likely that Joseph Chamberlain would marry her.[14] She became, however, increasingly interested in social work and, to give her credit, Beatrice did endeavour to secure first-hand experience of working-class life. First she stayed with distant but humble relatives of the Potter family who were cotton operatives at Bacup. Here she stayed under the disguise of 'Miss Jones, farmer's daughter, near Monmouth' who had come to Lancashire 'to see town life and manufactures'[15], from November 1883 to March 1884. She seems to have enjoyed herself, 'The people are wonderfully friendly,' she wrote[16] – but 'Of course the living is trying to anyone unaccustomed to a farinaceous diet'.[17] She made later visits to Bacup between 1886 and 1889 and the pages from her autobiography which describe the Bacup episode are of great value for students of the late nineteenth-century Lancashire working class.

Mrs Webb also came into direct contact with the workers in their everyday life by doing work for the Charity Organization Society and for her cousin Charles Booth's survey of London life and labour. In 1888, while engaged on Charles Booth's survey, she undertook to secure evidence of the 'sweating' system in the East End of London by getting employment in several ready-made clothing workshops as a 'plain trouser hand'.[18] While employed in one of these workshops she overheard the proprietor remark to his wife:

'She's [i.e. Beatrice Potter's] no good at the sewing: if I keep her I will put her to look after the outworkers – she's got the voice and the manner to deal with that bloody lot.'[19]

In 1887 Beatrice appeared on the platform at a dockers' meeting in the Tabernacle, Barking Road, Canning Town. Ben Tillett wrote:

I was one of the speakers, but neither I nor any of the other people on the platform appeared to have made a very satisfactory impression upon our rather aristocratically prejudiced visitor; she was young, clever, much petted by the intellectuals of the older generation; undoubtedly sincere, anxious to help, but somewhat condescending.[20]

Sidney James Webb (1859–1947) 'came from a social stratum well below that of the Potters'.[21] His mother kept a retail shop for ladies in Cranbourn Street, Leicester Square, London and continued to keep it after her marriage in 1854 to Sidney's father, an accountant by profession. Sidney went to a private middle-class school and to schools in Germany and Switzerland, but at the age of fifteen entered the office of a colonial broker. He continued his education at night school, however, and this enabled him to pass one of the entrance examinations to the Civil Service in 1878. He rose rapidly in the Civil Service and was called to the Bar in 1885. Then, in 1891 he resigned from the Civil Service to live on what he had saved and by journalism. By this time he had become one of the leading members of the Fabian Society.[22] Bertrand Russell summed Sidney Webb up as follows: 'He was somewhat earnest and did not like jokes on sacred subjects such as political theory.'[23]

Of Beatrice's conversion to Fabianism Bertrand Russell writes:

When she became interested in Socialism she decided to sample the Fabians, especially the three most distinguished, who were Webb, [G.B.] Shaw and Graham Wallas. There was something like the judgment of Paris with the sexes reversed, and it was Sidney who emerged as the counterpart of Aphrodite.[24]

So in 1892 Beatrice and Sidney married, to form a formidable partnership which lasted over fifty years. Beatrice wrote:

We opened Our Partnership with certain assets. An unearned income of £1000 a year, and a liking for the simple life, ensured unfettered freedom in the choice of a career.[25]

At least Beatrice dignified their union by the name of partnership, but as her nephew Colonel Richard Meinertzhagen wrote:

Aunt Bo wanted a slave, not a master or even a partner, though she subsequently exaggerated her marriage with Sidney into a partnership. In Sidney she found what she wanted – a slave and a secretary. It was an ideal marriage.[26]

Without Sidney she would nevertheless have remained an erratic amateur. He disciplined her energies and taught her to analyse and arrange her findings, although he himself appeared to be completely colourless and intellectually uninteresting:

Despite outward appearance, he dominated even Beatrice. Without him she would have been only an interesting personality. With him, she won a place in Westminster Abbey.[27] Sidney Webb is the key to the story, and it is a key which will never be turned.[28]

In this partnership Sidney was the research worker, the writer and systematiser, Beatrice the organiser and 'contact-woman':

Skill in social intercourse was my special gift ... I could insinuate myself into smoking-rooms, business offices, private and public conferences, without arousing suspicion ... in those days ... to be a woman and, therefore, at the start-off, not taken seriously, yielded better innings, whether through cross-examination, disguised as light conversation, or by a happy-go-lucky acquisition (by guile, not theft) of confidential documents.[29]

and

Born and bred in the world of big business of two continents, I had, as a young girl, dashed about the outer ring of London 'society', spent week-ends at the country houses of bankers and brewers and, more rarely, in the homes of county magnates. In these delectable places, I had associated with men of science and distinguished ecclesiastics; with Cabinet Ministers and leading lawyers, with 'society' dames and university dons.[30]

Bertrand Russell has some interesting comments on her arrogance. She once told Bertrand Russell that she considered herself to be 'the cleverest member of one of the cleverest families in the cleverest class of the cleverest nation in the world'.[31] Russell goes on to give an amusing account of a dinner party which Beatrice and Sidney Webb gave on February 7, 1905 to among others, the then Conservative Prime Minister, A.J. Balfour, i.e. the most powerful man in the most powerful empire in the world. Poor Balfour had to listen to 'a lecture from Mrs. Webb on "the first principles of Government, for beginners"; at least that would have been an appropriate title for her dinner-table discourse.'[32]

The Webbs' first task was the writing of a pioneer *History of Trade Unionism*, first published in 1894 and reissued in a revised edition in 1919–20.[33] This book is still the most detailed full-scale historical account in one volume of the British trade union movement and only recently has it come under serious criticism from a new generation of scholars.[34]

The partnership did not work unaided. In January 1892 they engaged F.W. Galton,[35] a bright young man of 24, as their secretary. He had been the secretary of the highly-skilled Manchester-based trade union of silver crest engravers, and in the course of 1892 Beatrice spent a good deal of time training him in historical research on trade union and co-operative documents.[36] On July 2nd 1892 she commented:

Galton drudges away in the board room of the [Leeds] Co-operators ... at the minutes etc. of local societies. He works very hard but he needs more training. Sidney is indulgent [to him] ... I have to be critical.[37]

Galton remained with the Webbs until 1898; and in 1899 they decided to write the history of English local government in order to establish 'a science of society'[38] and looked around for another secretary and research assistant, whom they found in Frederick Herbert Spencer, an elementary school teacher whose father had been a mechanic in Swindon railway works.[39] In the following year they engaged a second research assistant, Miss Amy Harrison, co-author with B.L. Hutchins of that classic work *A History of Factory Legislation* (1903, new edn. 1966). Eventually the Webb partnership employed as many as five research assistants. This was indeed 'Research Magnificent.' Some of Beatrice's comments read like communiqués on the progress of a battle:

Spencer, Mildred Sturge and I spent a week over the St. Pancras vestry minutes. We have taken on Mildred Sturge, a Newnham graduate, as a sort of paid apprentice. She is not able, but accurate and painstaking. An expedition to Norwich to start a Miss Watson on the Norwich records ends our autumn campaign. Next week we go to Plymouth for the Christmas recess to undertake the records there (Dec. 14th, 1899).[40]

Or in October 1905:

Five days' hard grind at MS. records of the Bristol Corporation of the Poor, and Municipal Corporation; encouraging Mrs Spencer with my presence and leaving her to finish.[41]

Mrs Webb was indeed a good trainer of servants.

By 1906 the number of secretaries was down to four and as she explained to Sir Julius C. Wernher, the South African millionaire

My husband and I have all the wealth we could possibly make use of without diminishing our delightful happiness. Four private secretaries on £1000 a year: a fifth would break me down.[42]

In spite of these researches into the history of provincial local government, she remained contemptuous of the efforts of the provinces to educate themselves, instead of looking to London, Oxford and Cambridge. Her diary for May 22nd 1906 contains the following entry:

... Sunday with Sir Charles Eliot, late Governor of East Africa and now Principal of Sheffield University ... Poor Sir Charles ... has taken on a wholly uncongenial task. To be more or less subordinate to a second-rate town council, to be organizing lectures by fifth rate professors for clerks and unemployed young women, is somewhat riling to a distinguished diplomatist and bureaucrat of the Empire.[43]

Yet posterity's verdict on Mrs Webb has become increasingly critical since her death in 1943. The writer of the anonymous article in the *Manchester Guardian* on the centenary of her birth noted her 'disregard for human liberty'. In Beatrice's opinion, 'the just and tidy organisation of human society was more important than the happiness of the individuals composing it'.[44]

It will come as no surprise to learn that the Webbs supported the war of 1899–1902 against the two Boer Republics, on the grounds that the future belonged to large organisations like the British Empire. Beatrice had, in fact, become a worshipper of efficient organisation, and her dislike of those members of the working class who acted for themselves without reference to their benevolent middle-class patrons increased. Let us see what she thought in 1895 of some miners' leaders whom she met in Derbyshire:[45]

The Angel, Chesterfield, Nov. 12, 1895; Away on one of my investigating tours. Attended a Derbyshire Miners Council meeting ... a stupid, stolid lot of men characterized by fair mindedness and kindliness – but oh! how dense! The officials are the ordinary good type, hardworking, narrow minded, whiskey drinking, self-complacent persons, excellent speakers on the question of Miners' Trade Unionism, and competent negotiators, but stupid, stupid, stupid like the men. Is it the abnormal quantity of whiskey these good fellows drink – without getting drunk – that deadens their intelligence – or is it brainwork carried on by an uncultivated and untrained mind that exhausts all the intelligence? How can one fear anything but unmitigated Conservatism from the English Democracy? The miners' radicalism is largely traditional, made up of allegiance to the [Liberal] Party that gave them the vote. Of course there remains the fact that their real interests are on the side of Economic Collectivism and sooner or later they will, I suppose, perceive it in a dim sort of way. But it will have to be dinned into them – and they will depend exclusively on middle-class leadership for years to come.[46]

Yet thirty years later she expressed a rather different opinion concerning 'the intuitive decision of the unthinking multitude who if left alone to feel their way for themselves are by no means such fools as some people think'.[47] It is hardly surprising that the canny trade union politicians of the 1920s and 1930s tended to leave the Webbs very much alone, in spite of Beatrice's patronising efforts to teach the wives of Labour M.P.s in the Parliament of 1919–22 the niceties of middle-class deportment by means of her Half-Circle Club.[48]

The centenary article in the *Guardian* provoked a protest from Lord and Lady Simon of Wythenshawe, who appeared shocked that anyone should dare to criticise Beatrice.[49] But this in return brought what can only be described as a counterblast from no less a person than Lady Konradin Hobhouse, the wife of one of Beatrice's nephews, who was just as critical of her as Mr Malcolm Muggeridge is. Lady Hobhouse wrote:

Aunt Bo ... despised the working classes with all the zest of her admirable Victorian middle-class upbringing. She disliked their fecklessness, their good nature, and the way they stood up for each other when in trouble.[50]

If Mrs Webb ever possessed a supply of the milk of human kindness it dried up completely under the influence of her visits to Stalin's Russia in the 1930s, where she saw the dictatorship over the proletariat in full operation.[51] The Webbs visited Lady Konradin one day after their Russian visit:

I had asked the headmistress of one of our local secondary schools, who had been on an extensive tour down to the Ukraine, to come and meet them ... The headmistress mentioned her horror at finding her party at a station where several cattle trucks [full] of 'enemies of the state' had been pulled up at a siding on their way to Siberia. 'Very bad stage management', said Aunt Bo severely. 'Ridiculous to let you see them; the English are always so sentimental!' At which the headmistress, rather shocked, said, 'But Mrs Webb, they were starving and held out their hands for food – they were in a pitiable condition.' 'I know', the great one replied, 'but you can't make an omelette without breaking eggs.'[52]

To quote Mr Malcolm Muggeridge again: 'In the end it was power she cared for, and only power';[53] and to quote Russell again: 'Both of them were fundamentally undemocratic, and regarded it as the function of a statesman to bamboozle or terrorize the populace.'[54]

THE HAMMONDS

Mrs Lucy Barbara Hammond (1873–1961) was born in 1873, the seventh and last child of Dr. E.H. Bradby, D.D., a notable headmaster of Haileybury. Writing was a family pastime; one of her sisters, for example, wrote a much-used textbook on the French Revolution.[55] Barbara received a private education, at Miss Dove's, St. Andrews. At Oxford, from Lady Margaret Hall, she followed up a first in classical moderations with a first in *lit. humaniores* (Greats), the first woman to do so (1896).

From 1896 to 1900 she was a Fellow of Lady Margaret Hall and in 1901 married John Lawrence Le Breton Hammond. *The Times* of November 17, 1961 ended its obituary of her with the following sentence: 'Both she and her husband were very fond of riding, and for long they kept horses for that purpose.'[56]

John Lawrence Le Breton Hammond (1872–1949) came from the same social class as his wife.[57] He was born in 1872 at Drighlington in Yorkshire, where his father, the Radical scion of a Jersey family, held a cure of souls. He was educated at Bradford Grammar School (1886–91) and went to St. John's College, Oxford, as a classical scholar. He ended his academic career in 1895 with a second in *lit. humaniores* (Greats). The chief influence on Hammond at Oxford was Sidney Ball, Fellow and tutor of St. John's, a Liberal member of the Fabian Society, with a strong interest in social reform. On leaving Oxford Hammond combined journalism with the post of secretary (1895–99) to Sir John T. Brunner (1842–1919), Liberal M.P. for Northwich (1885–6, 1887–1909) and chemical manufacturer. From 1899 to 1906 he edited the Liberal weekly, *The Speaker*, of which Brunner had been the chief proprietor. In 1907 after the absorption of *The Speaker* by *The Nation*, Lawrence Hammond was made secretary of the Civil Service Commission, a rather surprising appointment, which possibly owed something to his work for the political party in power. From 1913 onwards, with the exception of a short period of commissioned service with the Royal Field Artillery during the 1914–18 war,[58] he earned his living as a journalist and free-lance historian in partnership with his wife, their most important works on economic and social history being *The Village Labourer, 1760–1832* (1911); *The Town Labourer 1760–1832* (1917); *The Skilled Labourer, 1760–1832* (1919); *Lord Shaftesbury* (1923); *The Age of the Chartists, 1832–1854* (1930); *The Bleak Age* (1947) (a revised abridgement of *The Age of the Chartists*); *Life of C.P. Scott* (1934); *Life of James Stansfield* (1932); and *Gladstone and the Irish Nation* (1938). In general it may be said that, while *The Village Labourer* has been the most influential of their works, it has also been historically the most permanently misleading[59] in its account of the enclosure movement of the eighteenth and early nineteenth centuries. It has been called 'the greatest work of historical fiction in the English language'. *The Skilled Labourer* is probably the best book of the five: by 1919 the Hammonds had learnt a good deal about history and the methods of historical research. In their work in the Home Office Papers the Hammonds, like the Webbs, employed research assistants, and one of them let them down rather badly by not making complete transcripts of material.[60] In their celebrated controversy of the 1920s with Sir John Clapham on the question of working-class standards of living between the 1790s and 1850 they came off second best, relying too much on fine writing, moral indignation and irrelevant comparisons with ancient Greece and Rome, and not enough on statistics, otherwise they might have noted the defects in Silberling's cost-of-living index (1779–1850) on which Sir John Clapham relied for his victory in the controversy. Silberling's index was later heavily criticised.[61]

THE COLES

George Douglas Howard Cole (1889–1959) was the only son of George Cole of Ealing. Educated at St Paul's School, he entered Balliol as a classical Exhibitioner in 1908 and from 1912 to 1919 held a prize fellowship at Magdalen. For a short time he was in charge of the teaching of philosophy at Armstrong College, Newcastle-upon-Tyne, but this experience of life in the industrial North seems to have been his only one, and subsequently he never seems to have been much further away from the South of England than Birmingham, living mainly in London (Hendon) and Oxford after his appointment as Reader in Economics at Oxford in 1925. For a time after the 1914–18 war he was an official of the Amalgamated Engineering Union, and it is possible that this episode in his career is referred to in one of his obituary notices, where it is stated that he 'had a considerable hand in drawing up a constitution for one trade union – not, it must be said, entirely happily for standards of work-a-day efficiency'.[62]

Although appointed by Ramsay MacDonald to membership of the Economic Advisory Council during the Labour Government of 1929–31, Cole never acquired any great influence in Labour politics at the highest level. He quarrelled with Ernest Bevin soon after 1931 in the matter of the Society for Socialist Inquiry and Propaganda and, partly as the result of this, had little direct contact with any of the leading figures in the Labour Government of 1945–50, 'which made little or no use of his services and – to his own annoyed disillusionment – showed few signs of ever wanting his advice on any matter of importance'.[63] His intellectual resources were never as weighty as those of the Webbs, and the trade union side of the labour movement was now perhaps a little less susceptible to patronage by well-meaning members of the middle classes. By the 1940s trade unionism had become 'a massive organisation with resources and alliances that made it both less dependent on and more suspicious of the intellectual free-lance with its future mapped out for it'.[64]

The following are Cole's chief contributions to working-class history: *The Life of William Cobbett* (1st edn. 1927, 3rd edn. 1947); *Robert Owen* (1925) – a short rehash of Podmore's longer study; *A Short History of the British Working Class Movement* (3 vols., 1925–7); *The Common People 1746–1938* (1st edn. 1938) – with Raymond Postgate, who wrote most of it; *Chartist Portraits* (1941); *A Century of Co-operation* (1945); *Attempts at General Union: a study in British Trade Union History, 1818–1834* (1953).

Of these, *The Life of William Cobbett* is undoubtedly his best and most original book. Much of his work is marred by a more than average number of small slips and an insufficient grounding in original research.[65] Hugh Gaitskell has given us an amusing and significant portrait of Cole, who was 'less intellectual and more emotional' than is generally realised. Describing walking tours with Cole in the 1920s, Gaitskell wrote:

We walked in Southern England ... Like George V, Douglas never cared much for 'abroad'. I emphasise *Southern* England. I do not recollect his showing much enthusiasm even for Yorkshire dales, Welsh mountains, Cheviot Hills, or Scottish Lochs. But he loved Southern England, especially the Home Counties ... He was not even a little Englander – really a little Southern Englander.
I made one other discovery about Douglas during these walks. At the time it rather shocked me ... I discovered how much more he hated the Liberals than the Tories. This came out vividly when we were walking past the grounds of Highclere Estate near Newbury (which belongs to the Earl of Carnarvon). At this point Douglas, to my astonishment, launched into a panegyric of the English aristocracy. It might not have been wholly serious, but it did, I think, reflect a certain nostalgia for pre-industrial Britain.[66]

Cole married in 1918 Margaret Isabel Postgate (1893–1980) daughter of J.P. Postgate, Professor of Latin at Liverpool University, and sister of Raymond Postgate, co-author with G.D.H. Cole of the successive editions of *The Common People* (1938), and sole author of *The Good Food Guide* (1951), the knowledge and circulation of which amongst the British common people can hardly be extensive or really necessary.[67] Educated at Roedean and Girton, Cambridge, Mrs Cole obtained a first class in the Honours Classics Tripos. For 20 years from

1961 she remained the sole surviving member of the three partnerships
of which we are hardly likely to see the equivalent again.

NOTES

This essay appears here in print for the first time. The text is based on a lecture which was
delivered to various historical societies between 1960 and 1981.

1. *Our Partnership* (ed. B. Drake and M.I. Cole, 1948), pp.33 and 172.
2. *The Victorian Age in Literature* (1911), p.91.
3. B. Russell, *The Autobiography of Bertrand Russell, 1872–1914* (1967), pp.76–7.
4. M. Muggeridge, review of *Beatrice Webb's Diaries, 1924–1930* (ed. M.I. Cole,
   1956) in *Punch*, 18 April 1956, pp.463–4.
5. *Manchester Guardian*, 23 Jan. 1958, p.7. The Hammonds, too, were 'fresh air
   fiends' (another way of describing carefulness or meanness with domestic fuel).
   This was part of the medical regimen prescribed for Mrs Hammond, in whom a form
   of tuberculosis had been diagnosed in about 1905. It did not prevent her from living
   to the age of 88 and outlasting her husband by 12 years.
6. K. Martin, *Father Figures* (1965), p.115, quoted in the *Times Literary Supplement*,
   20 Jan. 1966.
7. Cf. Lady Konradin Hobhouse's complaint that the Webbs' stress on the need for
   regimentation has given an unfortunate direction to the Labour Party, away from
   the romantic and human side of social reform (*Manchester Guardian*, 4 Feb. 1958).
   Konradin Huth Jackson Hobhouse (1896–1964), the daughter of the banker
   Frederick Huth Jackson (1863–1921), married one of the 27 nephews of Beatrice
   Webb. Cf. B. Russell, *The Autobiography ... 1872–1914* (1967), p.79: 'indubitably
   the British Labour Party would have been much more wild and woolly if [the
   Webbs] had never existed.'
8. *Punch*, 18 April 1956, pp.463–4.
9. N.C. Masterman, *John Malcolm Ludlow* (1963), p.264.
10. See also the 10 autobiographies by working men listed in W.H. Chaloner and R.C.
    Richardson, *Bibliography of British Economic and Social History* (1984), p.135.
11. Quoted by R.H. Tawney in the introductory memoir to *Studies in Economic
    History: the Collected Papers of George Unwin* (1927), p.xix. For further bio-
    graphical details see T.S. Ashton's introductory 'Note on George Unwin' in G.
    Unwin, *Industrial Organization in the Sixteenth and Seventeenth Centuries* (2nd ed.,
    Cass, 1957), pp.xi–xvi.
12. J. Ramsay MacDonald served his apprenticeship to politics as secretary (1888–92)
    to a Liberal tea magnate, Thomas Lough (1850–1922) who was M.P. for Islington
    1892–1918, and a friend of the Webbs (Elton, *The Life of James Ramsay Mac-
    Donald (1866–1919)*, 1939, pp.57–9; *Our Partnership*, pp.332–3, 514). And as we
    shall see later J.L. Hammond had a similar experience.
13. Malcolm Muggeridge wrote: 'Mrs. Webb once remarked to me, with a zest her
    dedication to the cause of Socialism could not abate, that at one point all her
    brothers-in-law had incomes of not less than £20,000 a year' (foreword to R.
    Meinertzhagen, *Diary of a Black Sheep*, 1964, p.vi). The sizes of estate left by the
    members of the partnerships are interesting, even after allowance has been made
    for the change in the value of money. Sidney Webb left £59,420 in 1947 but J.L.
    Hammond left only £12,797 in 1949. G.D.H. Cole had been left by his father in 1936
    £80,858, which with consols at 3% would have generated a steady income of £2,700
    per annum. Cole himself left £46,617 in 1959 while Raymond Postgate left £24,980
    in 1971 and Mrs Cole £137,957 in 1980.
14. On the four years' obsession with Chamberlain (1883–87) see P. Fraser, *Joseph*

Chamberlain (1966), pp. 112–29, 'Chamberlain and Beatrice Webb'.

15. *My Apprenticeship*, Vol. I, pp. 178–9 (Pelican edn., 1938).
16. *Ibid.*, p. 194.
17. *Ibid.*, p. 194.
18. *My Apprenticeship*, Vol. II, 367.
19. M.I. Cole, *Beatrice Webb* (1945), p. 33.
20. *Memories and Reflections* (1931), p. 109. It is only fair to say that Tillett added: 'But I would not write a word in criticism of this brilliant and devoted woman.' For Beatrice Webb's account of this meeting, see *My Apprenticeship*, Vol. II, pp. 354–5 (Pelican edn., 1938).
21. M.I. Cole, *op.cit.*, p. 45.
22. For Sidney Webb's work in the Fabian Society see E.R. Pease, *History of the Fabian Society* (1st edn 1916, 2nd edn 1924, 3rd edn 1963) and M.I. Cole, *The Story of Fabian Socialism* (1961). For a critical review of the latter see *Past and Present*, No. 21, April 1962, pp. 78–80.
23. *The Autobiography* ... pp. 76–7. Russell was an adept at pulling Mrs Webb's leg. He suggested to her that she liked the Japanese only because they were efficient and sanitary and read the Webbs' books but she disliked the Chinese because they were dirty and insanitary. Whereupon 'Mrs Webb got very angry. Sidney, as usual, refused to be drawn' (K. Martin, *Father Figures*, 1966, p. 115).
24. *The Autobiography* ..., p. 77.
25. *Our Partnership*, p. 12.
26. R. Meinertzhagen, *Diary of a Black Sheep* (1964), pp. 120–1.
27. The transfer of the ashes of the Webbs to Westminster Abbey took place on 12 December 1947 when there were 229 Fabians in the House of Commons, or 58% of Labour M.Ps., and ten in the Cabinet, including Beatrice's nephew as Chancellor of the Exchequer. M.I. Cole, *The Story of Fabian Socialism* (1961), 301.
28. A.J.P. Taylor, *The Observer*, 5 Nov. 1967. However Webb, the ex-civil servant, by then ennobled as Lord Passfield, was a failure as Colonial Secretary in the Second Labour Government: 'he was carried on the shoulders of a Civil Service saturated with anti-Semitism' in his handling of the Palestine mandate troubles (Meinertzhagen, *op.cit.*, p. 72).
29. *Our Partnership*, pp. 12–13.
30. *Ibid.*, p. 13.
31. Russell, *op.cit.*, p. 77.
32. Russell, *op.cit.*, p. 176. Note Russell's opinion of Balfour: 'He is quite obviously weak, obviously without strong feelings, apparently kindly and not apparently able; at least I saw nothing I should have recognised as showing ability, except his tact, which probably is the main cause of his success' (*ibid*).
33. *The History of Trade Unionism* was reprinted in 1896, 1902 and 1911. The enlarged edition of 1920 lacked the bibliography, compiled by R.A. Peddie, included in the six editions of 1894–1911. The book was translated into at least six foreign languages: it was published in Dutch in 1894, in German in 1895 and 1906, in Russian in 1889, in Italian in 1900 and in Japanese in 1920. The Webbs never wrote the book on trade unions in the twentieth century which they had projected as a sequel to their work of 1894. Sidney also published *The Story of the Durham Miners, 1662–1921* and was elected M.P. for the Seaham division of Durham (1922–29). Georges Sorel and Gabriel Tardé both thought that Sidney Webb's reputation was exaggerated: Tardé even dismissed him as a worthless scribbler. See G. Sorel, *Reflections on Violence* (1950), pp. 141–2.
34. On 27 Jan. 1962 the Society of Labour Historians held a one-day conference on 'The Webbs as historians of trade unionism' during which they came under heavy criticism from Dr V.L. Allen, Mr A.E. Musson and Mr Hugh Clegg. See summary report in the *Bulletin of the Society for the Study of Labour History*, No. 4, Spring 1962, pp. 4–9.
35. F.W. Galton (1867–1952).
36. *Our Partnership*, pp. 27–8.

37. *Ibid.*, p.30.
38. *Ibid.*, p.170. The project was eventually completed in 9 volumes by 1929.
39. *Ibid.*, pp.153–4 and p.525.
40. *Ibid.*, p.163.
41. *Our Partnership*, p.180. Mrs Spencer was Amy Harrison, who had married F.H. Spencer (1871–1946). The Webbs elaborated their own research technique and, typically, wrote a whole book about it, *Methods of Social Study* (1932). In practice they seem to have made the same untidy chaotic notes as other research workers. Their interpretation of administrative history has evoked criticism. Max Beloff discovered when writing his own first book, *Public Order and Popular Disturbances 1660–1714* (1938) that the Webbs' history of local government was based upon a premise for which there was no evidence at all, viz. that the Revolution of 1688–89 marked a new beginning in local government, a mistake inevitably arising from 'their total lack of intellectual foundations'. See Beloff's review of *The Letters of Sidney and Beatrice Webb* (1978).
42. *Our Partnership*, p.347.
43. *Our Partnership*, p.342. Sir Charles N.E. Eliot (1862–1931), Vice-Chancellor of Sheffield University (1905–12).
44. *Manchester Guardian*, 23 Jan. 1958.
45. This passage from her diary was not reproduced in *Our Partnership*. In 1900 Beatrice Webb dismissed the working class as 'stupid, and in large sections sottish, with no interest except in racing odds' – *Our Partnership* (1948), p.195 and p.337. In 1927 she lectured the General Secretary of the Trades Union Congress 'somewhat in the manner of a schoolmistress, dealing with a slow-witted pupil'. Lord Citrine, *Men and Work. An Autobiography* (1964), p.269.
46. Quoted in P.P. Poirier, *The Advent of the Labour Party* (1958), p.269.
47. *Beatrice Webb's Diaries, 1924–32*, p.97 (14 May 1926). See, however, her comments of 7 June 1917: 'The Trade Union movement has become like the hereditary peerage, an avenue of political power through which stupid untrained persons may pass up to the highest office if only they have secured the suffrages of the members of a large union. One wonders when able rascals will discover this open door to remunerative power' (*Beatrice Webb's Diaries, 1912–24*, p.89).
48. For the Half-Circle Club, founded in 1920, see *Beatrice Webb's Diaries, 1912–1924* (ed. M.I. Cole and B. Drake, 1952), pp.200 and 208–11. A rather patronising footnote in *Beatrice Webb's Diaries, 1924–32* (1956) described its purpose as being 'to groom Labour women and Labour men's wives for social life' (p.4n). See also Jennie Lee, *My Life with Nye* (1980), pp.70–71.
49. *Manchester Guardian*, 29 Jan. 1958. In 1948 a radio broadcast by Malcolm Muggeridge on Beatrice Webb's Journal evoked a protest to the governors of the B.B.C. See John Bright-Holmes (ed.), *Like it Was. The Diaries of Malcolm Muggeridge* (1981), p.280 (18 June 1948).
50. *Manchester Guardian*, 4 Feb. 1958.
51. Jennie Lee, *op.cit.*, p.71: 'It was treated as a great joke among sophisticated Communist officials when the Webbs got out their notebooks wherever they went, and wrote down, uncritically, everything they were told.'
52. *Manchester Guardian*, 4 Feb. 1958.
53. *Punch*, 18 April 1956, p.463. For the change in the Webbs' attitude to the Soviet Union, see Marcel Liebman, 'Fabianisme et Communisme: les Webb et l'Union Soviétique' (*International Review of Social History*, Vol.V, 1960, pp.400–23 and Vol.VI, 1961, pp.49–73) and the same author's 'The Webbs and the new Civilisation' (*Survey*, London, No.41, April 1962, pp.58–74). See also S.R. Letwin, *The Pursuit of Certainty* (1965), pp.373–6. The Webbs had no knowledge of Russian nor had most of the reviewers of their book, which Norman Stone described in 1983 as 'the silliest book ever written on that subject [Russia under Stalin]'. Malcolm Muggeridge on his last visit to his aunt was permitted to view the portrait of Lenin which Stalin had presented to her. Lighting from below 'seemed to bring out the Mongolian cruelty of his high cheek bones and slit eyes. Mrs Webb, I

could see, was in a state of exaltation: and I reflected then, in one of those moments of almost agonising illumination which come so very rarely, that I was witnessing the final prostration of Victorian high-mindedness before the naked brutality of our time' (*Sunday Times*, 24 Feb. 1963; *Punch*, 18 April 1956, p.463).

54. B. Russell, *Autobiography*, p.79.

55. The eldest sister, Elizabeth Dorothy Bradby (1861–1927), published *A Short History of the French Revolution, 1789–95* (1926 and 1932).

56. See also the *Guardian*, 17 and 20 Nov. 1961 (appreciation by R.H. Tawney). This interest dated from Hammond's service in the field artillery during the Great War.

57. See R.H. Tawney, 'J.L. Hammond, 1872–1949' in the *Proceedings of the British Academy 1960*, Vol.XLVI, pp.267–94.

58. He was discharged on medical grounds.

59. See R.A.C. Parker, *Enclosures in the Eighteenth Century* (1960) and W.H. Chaloner, 'Bibliography of Work on Enclosure, the Open Fields and related Topics' in the *Agricultural History Review*, Vol.II, Aug. 1954, pp.48–52.

60. A.A.W. Ramsay, 'A socialist Fantasy' (*Quarterly Review*, Vol.252, No.499, Jan. 1929, pp.32–65), J.L. and B. Hammond, 'A socialist Fantasy: a Reply' (*op.cit.*, Vol.252, No.500, pp.272–92) and 'A socialist Fantasy, the last Word' (*op.cit.*, Vol.253, No.501, pp.113–17). Other early critics included M.D. George in 1925, H.W.C. Davis in 1925 and W.H. Hutt in 1926.

61. T.S. Ashton, 'The Standard of Living of the Workers in England, 1790–1830' in F.A. Hayek (ed.), *Capitalism and the Historians* (1954), pp.146–7.

62. *Guardian*, 15 Jan. 1959. For a sketch of the newly-wed Coles in November 1918 see *Beatrice Webb's Diaries, 1912–24 op.cit.*, pp.135–6. 'Cole, who is from the intricate convolutions of his subtle brain to the tips of his long fingers an intellectual and an aristocrat is becoming disillusioned about the labour leaders' (p.136).

63. *Guardian*, 15 Jan. 1959.

64. Ibid.

65. See, for example, Arthur Redford's review of *Attempts at General Union* (1953) in *Economic Journal*, Vol.LXIV, No.254, June 1954, pp.394–5.

66. In *Essays in Labour History in Memory of G.D.H. Cole* (ed. A. Briggs and J. Saville, 1960), pp.12–13.

67. See Mrs Margaret Cole's reminiscences *Growing up into Revolution* (1948), particularly pp.80–1 and 103–4, and the entry under Raymond Postgate in *Who's Who* for 1961. Raymond Postgate (1896–1971) was the great-grandson of a Scarborough builder and wrote *The Builders' History* (1923) as well as a biography of his father-in-law, George Lansbury (1951).

13

1989: 1688 or 1789?

In 1989, no doubt, the French people and government will rightly commemorate the bicentenary of their French Revolution, as they celebrated its centenary in 1889. We know that in 1788 local, if not nation-wide, celebrations of England's Glorious Revolution of 1688–89 took place, but little or nothing was done to commemorate its bicentenary in 1888 (it was probably too soon after Queen Victoria's jubilee festivities of the previous year). Will there be enough enthusiasm and historical imagination to launch a commemoration of the ter-centenary of the accession of William and Mary in 1988? The Revolution settlement is, after all, the nearest we have to a British constitution. Popular understanding of it should be fostered at a time when there is a sustained, if as yet somewhat unconcerted, attack on its principles. (Glorious has in recent years been written derogatorily as 'Glorious', as though to cast doubt on the description.) What changes have occurred in the intellectual climate to damp down interest in the political upheavals of the late seventeenth century, once so beloved of British writers and politicians?

FROM GLORIOUS TO 'GLORIOUS'

The answer is to be found in the seduction of our intellectuals, and particularly academic intellectuals, by the radical appeal of the vague French ideals of liberty, equality and fraternity, and by the spread of Marxist ideas, fostered unwittingly by a tolerant State itself through the recent expansion of higher education and subsequent infiltration. The abstract and emotional principles of the French Revolution have never been received or adopted in Britain, which has its own traditions of freedom to set against 'liberty'. The pursuit of 'equality' is a will-o'-the-wisp, in spite of the preachments of R.H. Tawney. As a Frenchman[1] put it, the spirit of equality is widespread among children and immature adults – while 'fraternity', if not based on the family or the close association of the voluntary society or club, is nebulous nonsense.

Fortunately for British political progress and stability the Revolution of 1688–89 was bloodless, but instead of rejoicing, modern revolutionary intellectuals find it a cause for disappointment and suspicion, because it appears to disprove one of their favourite justifications for revolutionary violence and judicial murder: 'you can't make omelettes without breaking eggs.' Modern left-wing intellectuals have found consolation in their espousal of the so-called 'English Revolution of 1640–60' (it used to be called the Puritan Revolution before radical scholars 'went off religion', or adopted the new one of Marxism). This has been one of the fastest growth-points of historical research since the late 1930s and the heyday of the Left Book Club.

LOCKE AND 'POSSESSIVE INDIVIDUALISM'

At the same time the Revolution Settlement of 1688–1714 and the Whig interpretation of history which held sway for the following two hundred years have been under increasing criticism. (Professor Herbert Butterfield's *The Whig Interpretation of History*, which laid the debate open to popular interest for the first time in 1931, now seems rather thin and inadequate.) John Locke (1632–1704), once the revered political philosopher of the Williamite settlement, has now become the object of modern radical attack, and it is not difficult to see why. Locke was a stubborn defender of private property: 'The great and chief end ... of men's uniting into commonwealths, and putting themselves under government, is the preservation of their property.' Property, to which man had a natural right, was defined by Locke in a wide sense as 'life, liberty and estate'. How, without men of property and independent means, could private individuals stand up against the powerful State? This 'doctrine of possessive individualism' is, of course, a dangerous doctrine in the opinion of our latter-day collectivists, who consider it to be subversive of the foundations of the Socialist state and an affront to doctrinaire egalitarianism. Hence their general reluctance to support the movement for a new Bill of Rights to serve as a fundamental guarantee of British freedoms, and to replace the Bill of Rights of 1689[2] which the passage of three centuries has now rendered inadequate to protect the liberties of the subject.

Modern radical antipathy to the Glorious Revolution has now extended to the Hanoverian succession, Sir Robert Walpole and eighteenth-century Whiggery. The latest exponent of this hostility is Mr E.P. Thompson, who now sounds more like a Jacobite,[3] rather than the Jacobin[4] we all thought he was, in his harking back to a mythical Stuart paternalism. In a curious article in *The Times Literary Supplement* of 1973, followed by a full treatment in a book published two years later, he launched a furious denunciation of an Act of Parliament of 1723 passed against deer-stealers, cattle-maimers, armed gangs of poachers and vandals operating in the Royal Forests. It is little wonder that the latest historian of early Hanoverian England, Dr W.A. Speck, remarks:

The view that a ruling-class ideology found expression in laws to protect property is most tendentiously expressed in E.P. Thompson, *Whigs and Hunters: the Origin of the Black Act.*[5]

FROM PATERNALISM TO FREEDOM

The liberating influence of the ideas of philosophers such as John Locke and Bernard Mandeville and economists such as Sir James Steuart and Adam Smith during the eighteenth and early nineteenth centuries led directly and indirectly to the decline in the enforcement or the legal abolition of many obsolete restrictions on free enterprise in economic life. These had for the most part been imposed during the so-called period of Tudor and Stuart paternalism, not so much because of sympathetic royal interest in 'the condition-of-the-people question', as from a desire to foster the stability of the two dynasties by trying to remove possible causes of public riot and disorder. Examples of this type of restrictive legislation were the regulations affecting the internal wholesale trade in corn outside the public markets and between different areas of the kingdom, fixing statutory prices and weights for various sorts of bread (the Assize of Bread),[6] the cumbrous and ineffective county machinery for fixing, at Quarter Sessions, the maximum rates of wages in a variety of occupations (the Statute of Artificers, 1563), and the restrictions on the numbers and conditions of artisan apprenticeship. By the mid-1820s all these had not merely fallen into desuetude but had been swept away by Parliament.

Throughout the eighteenth century and particularly after the South Sea Bubble of 1719–20, monopolistic practices and enterprises tended to be looked upon by Parliament and public opinion with caution and grave suspicion. Long before 1800 foreign visitors had been marvelling at the remarkable freedom of British economic life, in comparison with the pettifogging systems of bureaucratic control which hampered businessmen and industrialists in, say, France, Russia and Prussia. There can be little doubt that this atmosphere of economic freedom contributed to the rapid development and productive triumphs of the Industrial Revolution in Britain.

The espousal of French Revolutionary ideas by English poets, extremist dissenters and political publicists in the 1790s is richly documented, thanks to Tawney's friend P.A. Brown, whose book *The French Revolution in English History* (1918) has not yet been super-seded, although increasingly inadequate. A considerable literature now exists on the subject, on the whole uncritically sympathetic to the mixed bag of idealists, fellow-travellers and crackpots whose 'sufferings' have been lovingly researched by successive generations of scholars since the beginning of the twentieth century. So the curious situation has developed that a large segment of the British intelligentsia sympathises with the conscious and unconscious dupes of authoritarian régimes against which successive British governments fought long, bloody, and ultimately successful wars between 1793 and 1815. British admirers of Napoleon continued to believe in the essential peacefulness of his aims and, what was more, the essential wickedness of the British government, and to hamper the prosecution of the war right up to the news of Waterloo.

Like the radical disappointment with the bloodless character of the Revolution of 1688–89, a similar sense of disappointment can be traced in the writings of historians and others, who, taken with the violent character of the French and subsequent revolutions, seem to regret there was no bloody Jacobin revolution in Britain during the period 1790–1830, alleged to have witnessed 'the making of the English working class'. Reviewers have pointed out the unusual frequency with which the word 'bloody' occurs in E.P. Thompson's *The Making of the English Working Class*, first published in 1963. This book has given birth to a host of disciples and would-be imitators. What does this new wave of revolutionary thinkers hope for the British state in the closing years of the twentieth century?

NOTES

'1989: 1688 or 1789?' is reprinted from *The Coming Confrontation. Will the Open Society survive to 1989?* (Institute of Economic Affairs, 1978), pp.31–40.

1. An eminent social and economic historian, in a private conversation with the writer.
2. In David Ogg's words, the Bill of Rights of 1689 'reaffirmed what had been asserted by the great medieval jurists, that the king (i.e. the executive) is subject to law; and that for many of his most important acts, there must be the consent of those (whether *magnates* or parliament) who could claim to speak on behalf of the nation' (*England in the Reigns of James II and William III*, 1965 edn., p.243). Ogg's short account of the Bill (pp.241–5) should be supplemented by Jennifer Carter, 'The Revolution and the Constitution', in G. Holmes (ed.), *Britain after the Glorious Revolution, 1689–1714*, Macmillan, 1969, pp.39–58.
3. 'Alexander Pope and the Windsor Blacks', *The Times Literary Supplement*, 7 Sept. 1973, pp.1,031–3.
4. A reading of *The Making of the English Working Class* shows very clearly what our forefathers would have called his 'Jacobinical' views.
5. *Stability and Strife: England, 1714–1760*, Edward Arnold, 1978, p.294.
6. W. Duncan Reekie, *Give Us This Day* ..., Hobart Paper 79, IEA, 1978. The Assize of Bread involved the fixing of the price of bread and the sizes of loaves by the Justices of the Peace.

READING LIST

Sir Herbert Butterfield, *The Whig Interpretation of History* (1931), Penguin, 1973.
C.B. Macpherson, *The Political Theory of Possessive Individualism: Hobbes to Locke*, O.U.P., 1964.
R.C. Richardson, *The Debate on the English Revolution*, Methuen, 1977.
David Ogg, *England in the Reigns of James II and William III*, O.U.P., 1955.
J.R. Jones, *The Revolution of 1688 in England*, Weidenfeld and Nicolson, 1972.
Maurice Ashley, *The Glorious Revolution of 1688*, Hodder & Stoughton, 1966.
G. Holmes (ed.), *Britain after the Glorious Revolution, 1689–1714*, Macmillan, 1969.
H.T. Dickinson, *Liberty and Property: political ideology in eighteenth-century Britain*, Weidenfeld & Nicolson, 1977.
J.H. Plumb, *The Growth of Political Stability in England, 1675–1725*, Macmillan, 1967.
W.A. Speck, *Stability and Strife: England, 1714–1760*, Edward Arnold, 1978.
E.T. Lean, *The Napoleonists: a study in political disaffection, 1760–1960*, O.U.P., 1970.
J.R. Western, *Monarchy and Revolution: the English State in the 1680s*, Weidenfeld & Nicolson, 1972.

14

The Skilled Artisans during the Industrial Revolution, 1750–1850

During the discussions arising out of the renewed controversy of the past few years on the standard of life of the working classes during the Industrial Revolution there has been a tendency to group all wage-earners together in an undifferentiated mass. The Germanic concept of the *Lumpenproletariat*, with its opprobrious connotations, has gradually, and perhaps unwittingly, been extended to cover the whole of a very varied economic category. Little has been said about what is called, according to the writer's political views, either 'the aristocracy of labour' or 'the back-bone of the working class', namely the skilled artisans and their apprentices. These men, members of the working class just as much as their less fortunate brothers, have had a poor press in a world increasingly fascinated by mass production, the assembly line, computers and other substitutes for skill and laborious craftsmanship, a world also increasingly egalitarian, prone to see in superior excellence (save in the world of sport) an unjust advantage enjoyed by one human being over another.

The gulf between the artisans and mechanics on one hand and the semi-skilled and labourers on the other, and the wide variety of living standards inside the working class during this period may be illustrated by examining 19 working-class family budgets collected in 1841 – a year of depression – by William Neild, mayor of Manchester, and recorded in the *Journal of the Statistical Society of London*. The families inhabited Manchester and Dukinfield, a small cotton town nearby, and the budgets give weekly income and expenditure. The most prosperous of the 19 families was that headed by a machine printer. His household of nine persons had a total weekly income of 87s., or 9s. 8d. per head. The second most prosperous family was that of a millwright, a skilled artisan, whose household numbered ten, and who had a total weekly income of 90s., or 9s. per head. The poorest family was that of a mechanic's assistant, i.e., a semi-skilled labourer, with 7 persons in his household living on a total income of only 16s., or 2s. 4d. per head. The most prosperous family spent 12.4% of its income on bread, whereas the poorest family spent no less than 33%.[1]

A few of these skilled artisans have left us intimate accounts of their living and working conditions. Samuel Bamford (1788–1872) depicted life in the household of his uncle, a weaver of fine silk and cotton cloths at Middleton near Manchester during the period of the Napoleonic Wars.[2] Thomas Dunning (1813–94) of Nantwich in Cheshire described his life as a shoemaker in the late 1820s and early 1830s,[3] while William Lovett (1800–70) wrote of his seven years' servitude to rope-making and his subsequent practice of the trade of cabinet-maker without any formal apprenticeship.[4]

Less well known are Christopher Thomson's *The Autobiography of an Artisan* (1847) and *A Journeyman Engineer* [Thomas Wright], *Some Habits and Customs of the Working Classes* (1867). By combining the information given in these works with material from other sources it is possible to show that the skilled craftsmen as they existed in the 1770s and 1780s – the printers, millwrights, woolcombers, hatters, brush-makers and a host of others ('the old artisans') – were joined during the next fifty or sixty years by new recruits, from the better paid occupations created by the technological changes of the Industrial Revolution. For example, in the cotton industry, there were the mule, or fine, spinners,[5] and in engineering the mechanics (the 'new artisans'), who are soon found adopting the trade customs of the 'old artisans'. In this way the new skills were grafted on, as it were, to the older occupational groups, with a consequent partial merging of interests. It has been estimated by E.J. Hobsbawm that this 'labour aristocracy' formed 'perhaps 15% of the adult male working class'.[6] This may possibly be an underestimate. The phrase itself seems to have been first coined by the Chartist barrister Ernest Jones, who wrote in his *Notes to the People*, 1851–52, Vol. I, p. 511: 'Of all aristocracies, the aristocracy of labour has been the most fatal to the people' – a curious comment from a member of a profession which has always operated and benefited from the closest of 'closed shops'.

The older skilled trades were still very numerous in England even as late as 1851, a fact which is often overlooked, because attention has been concentrated on the newly-mechanised industries, of which the outstanding example was the cotton industry. With increasing population, and the rising national income generated by an expanding economy, there was a growing demand for all sorts of goods which continued to be produced entirely or largely by hand – dwelling houses, clothing, boots and shoes, cutlery, printing, bookbinding, etc., etc. The following figures will illustrate the point: the whole cotton industry of Great Britain employed between 375,000 and 400,000 men, women and children (including handloom weavers) in 1831, but there were about 203,000 adult male artisans in the building trades, and 133,000 adult boot and shoe makers and menders.[7] Trade clubs were numerous among these two categories of worker.[8]

The skilled workers were well aware of their superior status and artisans often treated mere labourers with contempt. Alexander Somerville, writing of his experiences in a Scots quarry in 1830, stated: 'The masons were intolerable tyrants to their labourers ... the privileges of masons were not to be questioned by labourers.'[9] Hobsbawm gives later examples of artisan contempt for labourers.[10] Conversely, this distinction between the possessors of a trained skill and the mass of the unskilled was also well understood among those members of the working class who had not been 'brought up to a trade'. In 1847 William Dodd, the factory cripple patronised by Lord Ashley, gave a fascinating account of the English class structure for the benefit of American readers, in which he distinguished no less than eight classes in English society. Of these the skilled artisans were fifth down the social scale:

> 5th. The higher order of Mechanics, known as 'skilled laborers', (from their being obliged to pay large fees, and to serve an apprenticeship of seven years to the trade which they follow,) shopkeepers, etc., compose this class. Generally speaking, they are an industrious and intelligent class, and are sufficiently remunerated for their services to enable them to bring up their families in a respectable manner, and to lay by something for the comforts of old age.'[11]

Dodd contrasted the comparatively comfortable lot of the artisans with that of the sixth class:

> 6th. This class comprehends a great number of individuals who get their living by the 'sweat of their brow', but who are not required to serve seven years at their trade or calling. Manufacturing, agricultural, and many other kinds of laborers, come under this head. This class is a hard-working, ill-paid, and ill-used set of human beings; frequently dying with every symptom of premature decay, at from 35 to 50 years of age.[12]

As far as England and Wales were concerned, Dodd was right in seizing upon apprenticeship as the institution which distinguished the artisan from the unskilled or semi-skilled labourer.[13] Therefore, if we can show that the custom of apprenticeship was well maintained during the period 1750–1850, it would suggest that artisans in general were adapting themselves successfully to the new society born of the Industrial Revolution, and also maintaining that limitation on recruitment which fortified their bargaining power.

In 1750 apprenticeship was governed partly by the Statute of Artificers (sometimes misnamed 'of Apprentices') passed in 1563 during the early years of the first Elizabeth, and partly by custom operating through the common law. In brief, the Statute of Artificers made apprenticeship compulsory on artisans, with a general servitude of seven years for young recruits. Subsequently the operation of the Act was modified in various ways, mainly by legal decisions in the

Courts. The most important of these decisions, in 1615, laid down that the Act only applied to the 61 trades mentioned by name in the apprenticeship clauses of the statute.[14] In spite of this limitation, the seven years' apprenticeship was widely considered as the ideal to be aimed at in trades not covered by the Act. It was possible for attorneys to draw up legally enforceable indentures binding an apprentice to serve a master for seven years in any trade, and the evidence suggests that this was a widespread custom. During the eighteenth century the growing 'trade clubs' or 'trade societies' of journeymen craftsmen almost invariably placed the maintenance of an efficient apprenticeship system in the forefront of their aims, allegedly as a safeguard to the consumer, but obviously as one means of restricting the number of trained journeymen and thereby increasing the bargaining power of the members of the craft. Even after the obligation to serve an apprenticeship was abolished by statute in a particular trade, as in the case of the hatters (1771), the trade clubs of the journeymen hatters succeeded in maintaining customary apprenticeship.[15] It is clear that there was increasing insistence on a seven years' apprenticeship by the English trade clubs in the first decade of the nineteenth century, when sharp rises in the cost of living due to the Napoleonic Wars made it imperative to safeguard the craftsman's standard of living. The Liverpool shipwrights' trade society, according to its printed rules of 1800, enforced apprenticeship rigorously. The Thames caulkers' society demanded that every new member admitted must produce his indentures (1810), and in 1809 the Old Amicable Society of Woolstaplers actually lengthened the term of servitude for apprentices from five to seven years.[16] The minute book of the London Society of Bookbinders for 1807–11 reveals that most of the Committee's time was taken up in examining the credentials of applicants for membership. Their apprenticeship indentures were carefully examined for evidence of date and for falsification of dates.[17]

Christopher Thomson, who was born on December 25th, 1799 at Hull, noted that during the later stages of the Napoleonic Wars everyone who intended to 'make a man of himself' was struggling to get into the well-paid war-flushed trades.[18] His father, a shipwright, accordingly apprenticed young Christopher to the trade of shipwright at the end of 1811 or the beginning of 1812. Thomson complained later of the ignorance of his fellow-apprentices:

Our average number of apprentices was about fifteen ... We had also another class of apprentices, more dangerous if possible, than the younger ones – these were up-grown men at the time of their being articled to the trade. The impulse given to our business by the lengthened continental war, induced our employers to take persons as apprentices, who had already attained their majority; for advanced age and physical ability were expected to yield good per centage for their extra wages. They were generally well paid, having eighteen and twenty shillings per week; some of them received more wages at the latter part of their service, as apprentices, than they could realize as journeymen. This class of men-apprentices, was principally from remote towns and villages, and ... were called 'Johnny Raws'...[19]

Up to 1814, when the apprenticeship clauses of the Act of 1563 were repealed, trade clubs, particularly in the London area, employed an attorney to conduct prosecutions in the law courts on charges of illegal apprenticeship. There is evidence that by August 1812 the trade clubs of London, with some participation from the provinces, had formed a joint Committee, consisting of two delegates from each club, to draw up a petition to Parliament for the stricter enforcement of apprenticeship. This petition eventually contained 32,000 signatures, of which half had been collected outside London. An interesting feature of this movement is the identity of interest revealed between the small masters and their employees, for about 2,000 (1 in 16) of these signatures were those of *master* craftsmen. A second petition promoted by the trade clubs in 1813 contained nearly 63,000 signatures. This agitation failed completely, however, and Parliament not only refused to tighten up the existing legislation but also in 1814 repealed the apprenticeship clauses of the Act of 1563.[20]

On the surface this looks like a defeat for the artisans, but the available evidence suggests that the struggle to maintain the institution of apprenticeship still went vigorously on and was, to some extent, successful, although experience varied from union to union. Let us take, for example, the printing trade, the members of which formed one of the largest artisan groups in London in the early nineteenth century. The history of the English printers' trade clubs or 'chapels' both in London and the provinces up to 1850 is very largely the history of a long but not always successful struggle to prevent an influx of newcomers to the trade who had not served the customary apprenticeship. The journeymen printers were at once the most intelligent and the most highly paid members of the artisan class. The historians of the London Society of Compositors state, with regard to the apprenticeship problem, that 'the journeymen [printers] never achieved much success' between 1788 and 1815.[21] Fortunately the printers were saved from the worst consequences of this increase in their numbers by the growing demand for all forms of printed material in an increasingly literate age. After the re-establishment of the London Society of Compositors on a stable footing in 1848, the new union was eventually able to restrict entry to the trade severely. In the provinces the experience of the printers' trade clubs was roughly the same (the

Northern Typographical Union, 1830–44, the National Typographical Association, 1845–48).[22] An interesting example of the conflicting political and economic interests of the working class in this period is provided by the disputes between the Chartist leader, Feargus O'Connor, and the printers' unions both in Yorkshire and London. In the 1840s this friend of the workers was denounced by the printing unions as an unfair employer in his newspaper publishing business (*The Northern Star*) and there were bitter complaints that an excess of apprentices was employed on a journal which ostensibly supported the claims of labour.[23]

In addition, the old trade clubs passed on the tradition of seven years' apprenticeship to the new unions built up in the mid-nineteenth century. The engineers attached great importance to the seven years' servitude, and, when the famous 'new model' union, the Amalgamated Society of Engineers, was founded in 1851 out of three smaller trade clubs, the continuity between the Tudor concept of an 'ordered society' and the aims of the nineteenth-century artisans was demonstrated. The preface to the rules of the chief constituent body of this amalgamation, printed in 1845, expresses very clearly the hierarchic, professional pride of the skilled engineer:

> The youth who has the good fortune and inclination for preparing himself as a useful member of society by the study of physic, and who studies that profession with success so as to obtain his diploma from the Surgeons' Hall or College of Surgeons, naturally expects, in some measure, that he is entitled to privileges to which the pretending quack can lay no claim; and if in the practice of that useful profession he finds himself injured by such a pretender, he has the power of instituting a course of law against him. Such are the benefits connected with the learned professions. But the mechanic, though he may expend nearly an equal fortune and sacrifice an equal proportion of his life in becoming acquainted with the different branches of useful mechanism, has no law to protect his privileges.[24]

The youthful engineer was thereupon urged to join his union, which aimed at securing the same protection for his trade against interlopers as was enjoyed by the professional classes.

The carpenters and joiners of London in 1851 numbered 23,000 – the largest of the London crafts. Only 10% of this number were under 21 years of age, which would seem to indicate that the apprenticeship customs of this trade were exercising a restraining power on the influx of new apprentices.[25] It is significant that in 1860 the Amalgamated Society of Carpenters and Joiners was formed from this occupational group on the model of the Amalgamated Society of Engineers, with almost the same rules.

It is clear, then, that apprenticeship placed the skilled craftsmen in a strong position to resist attacks on their living standards, and even to improve those standards during the classic period of the Industrial Revolution.

Legal restrictions on the operation of trade clubs must now be considered. The acts of Parliament against conspiracies or combinations of workmen in particular trades passed in the eighteenth century were supplemented in 1799 and again in 1800 by two General Combination Acts, which prohibited all associations of workmen for the purpose of raising wages and shortening the hours of labour. This legislation was directed almost entirely against the artisans, for the trade clubs originated mainly with them, rather than with the new cotton spinners. Combinations of unskilled or semi-skilled workmen remained extremely rare, although not unknown, until the 1870s. Nevertheless modern research has shown that the trade clubs of skilled artisans survived and flourished both clandestinely and openly during the first quarter of the nineteenth century, often thinly disguised as friendly societies, which had been legalised and regulated by an Act of Parliament in 1793. All the evidence goes to show the very real power which trade clubs exercised in the workshops and on constructional sites during the period of legal repression. For example, when the young engineer William Fairbairn applied for a job on the building of the future Waterloo Bridge in London in 1810, he was told by the foreman that he must join the millwrights' society before he could start, as it was a case of 'no ticket, no job'.[26]

There is a good description of the organisation of the millwrights in the late eighteenth century by John Rennie (1761–1821), the famous engineer, whose son wrote:

> They were a particular class of skilled workmen embodied into a special Guild or Craft for making machinery, and they would not upon any account admit any man to work with them unless they [sic] had been apprenticed for the same number of years to a master millwright as themselves, and it must certainly be admitted that they were a very superior body of workmen, not only good workmen but good engineers competent to direct others and to superintend mechanical work. They were highly paid, receiving 7/– per day besides extra time. If the masters tried to employ anyone who had not served seven years they struck work and would not return until he had been discharged. They had a committee who examined indentures on pay [Saturday] nights. They were powerful because they were in short supply.[27]

The woolcombers, who formed the aristocracy of the worsted workers, numbered between 50,000 and 60,000 in the 1790s. They earned high wages and were also stated to be 'strongly impregnated with political doctrines of the democratic school'.[28] One rule of the woolcomber's trade clubs or societies laid it down that only a woolcomber's eldest son could be apprenticed to the occupation. Some indication of their power is given by the fact that during the period

1799–1824, the woolcombers' trade clubs held a national congress at Coventry in 1812, without Government interference. The Home Office was informed of the intended congress, and the law officers of the Crown were asked to advise as to a prosecution. They replied: 'These combinations are mischievous and dangerous, but it is very difficult to know how to deal with them.'[29] Francis Place attributed the improvement of the conditions of London artisans during the Napoleonic Wars partly to the higher wages obtained through trade club activities and strikes, wages which they were for the most part able to maintain during the peace which followed.[30]

The artisans of the period had another means of exercising control over their economic fate. The trade clubs of the eighteenth and early nineteenth centuries did not provide 'static' unemployment pay. They expected their unemployed members to look actively for work and possessed an institution which took surplus craft labour off the market temporarily and at the same time acted as a form of unemployment pay. This was the tramping system, which dates from at least 1700 in the case of the Devon woolcombers. By 1800 it was common to all artisan trade clubs.

Briefly, the artisan who wished to leave town, whether unemployed or not, received a document certifying that he was a member of the club. This he presented to the local secretary or relieving officer in the 'lodge house' or 'club house' or 'house of call' of the strange town – generally a pub – receiving in return supper, lodging, perhaps beer, and a tramp allowance. If there was work to be found he took it.[31] The 'house of call' was in effect an unofficial labour exchange. If there was no work he tramped on. Should he find no permanent work, the artisan would eventually return to his home town, having made the grand tour of all the society branches. Among the compositors in the 1850s the grand tour was 2,800 miles, among the brush-makers in the 1820s 1,200 miles. Naturally tramping, romantic though it sounds, could be an unpleasant experience, and the tramping artisan always ran the risk of degenerating into a tramp in the modern sense.

The Socialist thinker J.F. Bray (1809–97), who served his seven years to a printer in Yorkshire (1822–9), has left us a vivid description of his experiences on tramp in 1830–2 (in the third person):

He conceived the idea of the necessity for industrial reforms while wearily plodding from town to town in search of work as a 'tramp'. He constantly met the tailor, the shoemaker, the weaver and other workmen, all 'tramps' looking for employment and all in need of the things which his fellow-tramp could produce. Walks of twenty to thirty miles a day, half fed and a shelter in some low lodging house where vermin prevented sleep was enough to set any man to thinking of the causes of these miseries.[32]

The number of artisans going on tramp remained high until the middle years of the nineteenth century, after which it declined both absolutely and relatively, even during the 'Great Depression' of the last quarter of the century, when we should expect to find an increase.

The friendly societies, characteristic institutions of the nineteenth century, were built up mainly by the artisans, together with small shopkeepers and other members of the lower middle classes, in order to provide themselves with some security against the poverty resulting from sickness and death as an alternative to the official poor law system. The first of these societies were founded in the early eighteenth century and it is estimated that by 1815 the total membership of friendly societies was about one million. There was a particularly steep rise in the membership in the so-called 'Hungry Forties', and by 1850 a membership figure of one and a half millions had been reached. These institutions fostered thrift and discouraged drunkenness, at least in the nineteenth century. In Clapham's words, they encouraged 'what modern Moscow calls a bourgeois ideology'.[33]

Without doubt there were artisans who failed to maintain their position in the face of competition from machinery, and the handloom weavers form a case in point. In the 1820s and 1830s handloom weavers in woollen, worsted, cotton, silk and mixed fabrics numbered about 250,000.[34] But it should be remembered that they were not a homogeneous group – they ranged from the skilled silk weavers, who still tried to enforce a seven years' apprenticeship, down to the Irish immigrants in Lancashire who were learning how to weave plain calicoes in three weeks in 1818.[35] There were other artisans who grasped their chances and became entrepreneurs, sometimes on a small scale, sometimes on a large scale, like the hundreds of building craftsmen from North Wales who became master builders in the Liverpool area after 1800.[36] An interesting example from N.E. England concerns William Boutland Wilkinson (1819–1902), who was apprenticed on October 3, 1833 to Robert Robson, master plasterer of Newcastle upon Tyne, for a period of seven years; he was to receive 3s. per week for the year 1833–34, rising by annual increments of one shilling to 9s. per week in the final year 1839–40. Wilkinson became an innovator in the use of concrete for building purposes and a director of the Newcastle and Gateshead gas and water companies.[37] It should never be forgotten that during the Industrial Revolution economic mobility and openings for the new entrepreneur were greater than ever before, and inside the working class the artisans, both of the old and the new groups, were the best fitted to make the most of their opportunities.

There is clearly a need for more statistical information on a number of points. It is extremely hazardous even to guess at the approximate number of skilled artisans in any particular occupation before the census of 1841. Did advancing industrialisation during the early nineteenth century lead to an increase or to a decrease in the *percentage* of skilled workers in the total labour force, i.e., was there a relative as well as an absolute increase in their numbers? The manuscript Census Enumerators' returns for 1851 and 1861 (the later ones are not yet generally available to students) could be used to estimate the numbers of skilled artisans, or rather artisans claiming to be skilled, in particular localities, and these estimates might be checked against the very full local directories which were published in mid-nineteenth-century England.[38]

NOTES

'The Skilled Artisans During the Industrial Revolution, 1750–1850' was a pamphlet published by the Historical Association in 1969, being No.15 in the *Aids for Teachers* series. It is now out of print.

1. W. Nield, 'Comparative statement of the income and expenditure of certain families of the working classes in Manchester and Dukinfield in the years 1836 and 1841', *Journal of the Statistical Society of London*, Vol.IV, 1841, pp.320–34. Nield's dietaries have recently been critically examined in the light of modern nutritional knowledge by J.C. McKenzie ('The composition and nutritional value of diets in Manchester and Dukinfield, 1841', *Transactions of the Lancashire and Cheshire Antiquarian Society*, Vol.72, for 1962, 1965, pp.123–40), with results on the whole favourable to the 'optimists'.
2. *The Autobiography of Samuel Bamford*, ed. W.H. Chaloner, Vol.1, 1967, pp.98–105.
3. 'The Reminiscences of Thomas Dunning ...' (*Trans. Lancs. and Cheshire Antiquarian Society*, Vol.LIX, 1947, pp.85–130).
4. W. Lovett: *Life and Struggles of William Lovett in his pursuit of bread, knowledge and freedom*, ed. 1920.
5. For the interesting attempt in 1829 by the cotton spinners' union to restrict entry to their craft by insisting that only 'sons, brothers, or nephews of spinners, or masters' poor relatives' should be instructed in spinning, see N.J. Smelser, *Social Change in the Industrial Revolution*, 1959, p.237.
6. 'The British standard of living, 1790–1850', *Economic History Review*, 2nd ser., X, Aug. 1957, p.50. The basis of Hobsbawm's estimate is not indicated.
7. Clapham, *Economic History of Modern Britain*, Vol.I, pp.72–3, 169.
8. Shoemakers were notorious for their Radical politics and supplied many prominent recruits for the Chartist movement of 1838–48 (M. Hovell, *The Chartist Movement*, 1925, p.210).
9. *The Autobiography of a Working Man*, ed. J. Carswell, 1951, p.86.
10. 'The labour aristocracy in nineteenth-century Britain', *Democracy and the Labour Movement*, ed. J. Saville, 1955, p.204.
11. An Englishman [William Dodd], *The Laboring Classes of England*, Boston, 1847, pp.9–10.
12. Dodd, *op.cit.*, p.10. Dodd's *Narrative of the Experience and Sufferings of William Dodd, a factory cripple* (1841) should also be noted.
13. It is curious that E.J. Hobsbawm in his article on 'The labour aristocracy in 19th-century Britain' (*Democracy and the Labour Movement*, ed. J. Saville, 1955,

pp.201–39), ignores this characteristic of artisan life.

14. E. Lipson, *The Economic History of England*, Vol.III, 1934, pp.279–83. See also O. Jocelyn Dunlop, *English Apprenticeship and Child Labour: a history*, 1912, and Margaret G. Davies, *The Enforcement of English Apprenticeship, a study in applied mercantilism, 1563–1642*, 1956. Miss Dunlop exaggerates the decline of apprenticeship, and neglects the importance of trade clubs and trade unions, in the eighteenth and nineteenth centuries. See also R.A. Bray, *Boy Labour and Apprenticeship* (1912).

15. Lipson, *op.cit.*, p.291; Phyllis M. Giles, 'The felt-hatting industry, c.1500–1850, with particular reference to Lancashire and Cheshire', *Trans. Lancs. and Cheshire Antiquarian Society*, Vol.LXIX, 1959, pp.104–32.

16. T.K. Derry, 'The repeal of the apprenticeship clauses of the Statute of Artificers [in 1814]', *Economic History Review*, Jan. 1931, p.70. But about 1820, Lovett tells us, the London Cabinet-Makers' Society insisted only on a five-year apprenticeship (Lovett, *op.cit.*, p.30).

17. E. Howe and J. Child, *The Society of London Bookbinders, 1780–1951*, 1952, p.83.

18. *The Autobiography of an Artisan*, 1847, p.56.

19. *Op.cit.*, p.73.

20. Derry, *op.cit.*, pp.67–87.

21. E. Howe and H.E. Waite, *The London Society of Compositors (re-established 1848)*, 1948, p.66. See also the companion volume of documents, *The London Compositor ... 1785–1900* (ed. E. Howe), 1947.

22. A.E. Musson, *The Typographical Association* (1954).

23. Musson, *op.cit.*, p.83.

24. Preface to *Rules of the Journeyman Steam-Engine, Machine-Makers, and Millwrights' Friendly Society*, edition of 1845 (quoted by S. and B. Webb, *History of Trade Unionism*, ed. 1920, p.218).

25. Clapham, *Economic History of Modern Britain*, Vol.I, p.568. For the successful restrictions on hours and the entry of apprentices imposed by the Sheffield trade clubs – saw makers, fork and table knife makers, grinders, joiners, tool makers – in the early 1840s, see S. Pollard, *Labour in Sheffield*, 1959, pp.69–70.

26. J.B. Jefferys, *The Story of the Engineers* (1946), p.12. For the Combination Acts see M.D. George, 'The Combination Laws reconsidered' (*Economic History*, supplement to the *Economic Journal*, No.2, May 1927, pp.219–28) and M.D. George, 'The Combination Laws', *Economic History Review*, April 1936, pp.172–8; A. Aspinall, *The Early English Trade Unions* (1949) – documents from the Home Office Papers in the Public Record Office from 1791 to 1825; R.Y. Hedges and A. Winterbottom, *The Legal History of Trade Unionism* (1930).

27. C.T. Boucher, *John Rennie, 1761–1821 – The Life and Work of a Great Engineer*, p.94.

28. John James, *History of the Worsted Manufacture*, 1857, p.559. On the question of working-class radicalism, see G.A. Williams, *Artisans and Sans-Culottes* (1968), and E.P. Thompson, *The Making of the English Working Class* (2nd, rev. ed., 1968). The critical comments on Thompson's book (references on pp.916–39) should be carefully studied.

29. Clapham, *Econ. Hist. Mod. Brit.*, Vol.I, p.205. See also J.L. and B. Hammond, *The Skilled Labourer, 1760–1832* (1920), pp.195–204.

30. MS. 'Trade Unions Condemned, Trade Clubs Justified', 1834, British Museum Add. MSS. 27, 834, fols.51, 63.

31. E.J. Hobsbawm, 'The tramping artisan', *Economic History Review*, 2nd ser., Vol.III, No.3, 1951, pp.299–300.

32. M.F. Jolliffe, 'Fresh light on John Francis Bray', *Economic History*, Vol.III, No.14, Feb. 1939, p.241; J.F. Bray, *A Voyage from Utopia* (ed. M.F. Lloyd-Pritchard, 1957), p.8. Bray's account should be compared with Charles Manby Smith's *The Working Man's Way in the World*, ed. E. Howe, 1968, which originally appeared in the 1850s, and is now republished by the Printing Historical Society.

33. Clapham, *Economic History of Modern Britain*, Vol.II (1932), p.473. See also

Vol.I, pp.295–8, 588–9. Mr. P.H.J.H. Gosden's book, *The Friendly Societies in England, 1815–75*, 1961, provides a standard history of the movement during this period.

34. D. Bythell, 'The hand-loom weavers in the English cotton industry during the Industrial Revolution: some problems', *Economic History Review*, 2nd ser., Vol.XVII, 1964.

35. A. Redford, *Labour Migration in England, 1800–1850*, 2nd edn., 1963, p.42.

36. J.R. Jones, *The Welsh Builder on Merseyside* (1946), *passim*.

37. Wilkinson MSS, kindly communicated by Mrs. M. Wasteneys Smith, Riding Mill, Northumberland.

38. See Clive Day, 'The distribution of industrial occupations in England, 1841–1861', *Trans. Connecticut Academy of Arts and Sciences*, Vol.XXVIII, March 1927, pp.79–235 and H.D. Fong, *Triumph of Factory System in England*, 1930. For the directories see Jane E. Norton, *Guide to the National and Provincial Directories of England and Wales ... published before 1856* (1950).

15

The Hungry Forties

... stories assumed to be familiar are apt to become good
nesting places for legend. Until very recently, historians'
accounts of the dominant event of the nineteenth century,
the great and rapid growth of population, were nearly all
semi-legendary; sometimes they still are. Statisticians had
always known the approximate truth; but historians had too
often followed a familiar literary tradition. Again, the
legend that everything was getting worse for the working
man, down to some unspecified date between the drafting of
the People's Charter and the Great Exhibition, dies hard.
The fact that, after the price fall of 1820–1, the purchasing
power of wages in general – not, of course, of everyone's
wages – was definitely greater than it had been just before
the revolutionary and Napoleonic wars, fits so ill with the
tradition that it is very seldom mentioned, the work of
statisticians on wages and prices being constantly ignored by
social historians. It is symbolic of the divorce of much social
and economic history from figures that, in a recent enquiry
into the fortunes of one group of trades, the tradition of
decline appears in the text, some corrective wage figures in
an appendix, and the correlation nowhere.[1]

Like 'the Industrial Revolution' and 'Luddism', the phrase 'Hungry
'Forties' has become part of the mental stock-in-trade of politicians,
journalists and the general public, and in the process has acquired a
mythical significance.[2] What is the history of the phrase, and how far is
it a just description of the decade between 1840 and 1850?

There is little evidence that the phrase was current in the 1840s. It has
been suggested that Richard Cobden used it in one of his public
speeches, but it does not come into his *Speeches on Questions of Public
Policy*, edited by John Bright and J.E. Thorold Rogers in 1878. Neither
does the phrase appear in Arnold Toynbee's *Lectures on the Industrial
Revolution of the Eighteenth Century in England* (1884), nor in the new
preface written in 1892 by Friedrich Engels for the first edition of *The

Condition of the Working Class in England in 1844, to be published in this country. It was used, however, in a circular letter dated February 6, 1904, and sent to the press by the publisher, T. Fisher Unwin, a son-in-law of Cobden and an active Radical publicist. Like most active Liberals of the time, Unwin found himself conducting vigorous Free Trade counter-propaganda against Joseph Chamberlain's Tariff Reform campaign in general and against the registration duties imposed on imported wheat and flour in 1902, by Hicks Beach, the Conservative Chancellor of the Exchequer, in particular. Unwin's letter ran as follows:

Sir, – Some time since I read in the press a letter from Lord Rosebery suggesting that those who remembered the miseries of Protection should lose no opportunity of telling their fellow-countrymen their experiences. He went on to say that in his judgment it was clearly a duty they all owed their country, and their testimony would be of far more avail than the speeches, however eloquent and persuasive, of a younger generation, and that if they would stand on platforms and testify with regard to the facts of Protection, they would render an inestimable service at the present time.

I trust that many have carried out his suggestion on the public platform, but it occurs to me that there must be many who are in possession of private documents and diaries, illustrative of the bad old times, or who, from age and experience, might prefer rather to write down in simple language their recollections and experiences. Tradesmen's bills and private house-keeping accounts of the 'Hungry Forties' would also be of interest and useful for comparative study. Some interesting documents of the kind have already appeared in the public press, and, as I am making a collection of such documents, I should esteem it a great favour if any of your readers would contribute any they may possess. I can promise that if I receive a good response to this suggestion I will publish the results in volume form in the interests of the cause of Free Trade, which all your readers, I feel confident, have much at heart. Let me add that any documents addressed to my care will be copied and returned if desired.

I am, sir, yours truly,
T. FISHER UNWIN

11, Paternoster Buildings, London, E.C.
6th February, 1904[3]

Lord Rosebery's letter to the press referred to by Unwin has not been traced, but on October 13, 1903 he made a speech in Sheffield which indicates the trend of his thoughts in the direction of the 1840s:

Your fathers must have told you, and, if not, if they be with you, ask them, what the condition of things was in this country when protection was rampant and ruling. I do not think the new policy will get a single vote from any man here of sane mind, and still less from any woman, who recollects the year 1846. No one who remembers the days of protection will ever again give a vote to bring that curse back upon us.[4]

Later in 1904 Unwin published a selection of the heart-rending material received as a result of his appeal under the title of *The Hungry Forties: Life under the Bread Tax: descriptive letters and other testimonies from contemporary witnesses,* with an introduction by his wife, Mrs Jane Cobden Unwin, daughter of the great Free Trader.[5] In view of the great improvement in working-class conditions which had taken place over the previous sixty years, and especially during the so-called 'Great Depression' of 1873–96,[6] it is not surprising that the old people who wrote to Unwin retained some highly unpleasant memories of the 1840s. Most were the sons and daughters of agricultural workers, and some of them ranged over the 1820s, 1830s and even the 1850s in the search for harrowing details.

For example, the reminiscences of Richard Rigg, born in 1804, tell of hard times from the years of the Regency onwards, and especially after 1826, when he and his wife were 'half-starved'. In the 1830s, however, Rigg secured a job as a navvy on the earthworks of the London and Birmingham railway and did not mention the 1840s as times of special distress.[7] At the other extreme, a Miss Benjafield wrote of the Crimean War of 1854–6 as being a period when 'the [agricultural] poor were in great distress,' and another correspondent, Edward Cook, born as late as 1844, confirmed this, at any rate as regards the parish of Icklingham in Suffolk. He stated that until he reached the age of eighteen, i.e. up to 1862, 'my belly had not been properly filled eighteen times since I was weaned from my mother's breast'.[8]

The general impression which emerges from Unwin's compilation is of a labouring class, particularly in the countryside, constantly hungry for bread and meat from the opening years of the nineteenth century until well into the 1860s.[9] This unsatisfied craving for meat is the main reason for the prevalence of poaching and sheep-stealing in England during the early nineteenth century. In most families the only forms of meat consumed in any quantity appear to have been pork and bacon, and those mainly on Sundays. The wheaten bread and flour available were frequently of poor quality; rye bread apparently remained in common use throughout the mid-nineteenth century and unwilling resort had frequently to be made to the particularly revolting barley bread, notorious for the severity of the heartburn it could inflict on the consumer.[10] On the other hand, the evidence collected together in *The Hungry Forties* suggests that agricultural workers of the mid-nineteenth century ate a good many potatoes, together with what amounted to a surfeit of fresh vegetables – turnips, swedes, beans, cabbages and onions. This probably saved them from widespread starvation and malnutrition.[11] Even in particularly hard times turnips and swedes could always be stolen at night from the fields. As a natural consequence, fresh vegetables were heartily despised among the poor of the countryside, and even Brougham Villiers, writing a postscript to *The Hungry Forties* in 1904 – some years before the vitamin theory of nutrition had been enunciated – spoke with scorn of their place in diet:

> The prominent part that swede turnips played in the diet of the people will probably strike most readers with horror. Here, indeed, we come to a food basis on which it seems impossible that healthy life can be maintained. ... The turnip is the last refuge of desperate poverty, for as long as there is any money with which to buy food, it is almost certain to be spent on something better.[12]

The phrase 'Hungry Forties' is not to be found in the original *Oxford English Dictionary* (1884–1928), but was added in the *Supplement and Bibliography*[2] (1933) with a note dating its first appearance as being in 1904. It is also significant that, whereas the phrase does not occur in the tenth edition of the *Encyclopaedia Britannica* (1902), the eleventh edition (1910) contains the following statement under the entry on 'Forty': 'The period just before the repeal of the corn laws in the United Kingdom is frequently alluded to, particularly by the free trade school, as the "hungry forties". ...'[13]

No earlier use of the phrase 'Hungry Forties' than T. Fisher Unwin's has so far been discovered, and it is significant that one of his correspondents, H. Cole (born in 1834) of Hayling Island, Hants, wrote: '... the "Hungry Forties," as you term them, ...'[14] which suggests that it was, at any rate, not widely known in 1904, if at all. Since that date it has become part of English literature, and few text-books of English political, economic and social history can have been published in the last fifty years which do not contain the phrase.

So much for the history of the phrase. How far is it a just description of the decade between 1840 and 1850? The classic statement of the case against 'The Hungry Forties' is that of Sir John Clapham. Briefly, in his paper 'Corn Laws Repeal, Free Trade and History',[15] he pointed out that the 1840s in England – excluding any consideration of Ireland – were, to judge by the average price of the four-pound loaf in London, no hungrier than the 1830s or 1850s. The average price of the four-pound loaf in London in the 1820s was 10d.; in the 1830s 9d.; from 1841 to 1845 8¼d. At the height of the Irish Famine in 1847 it rose to 11½d., but the average price for 1846–48 was only 9d. In the 1850s it was about 8½d. Sir John Clapham admitted that there was a relatively difficult period in 1838–42, years of unemployment and a growing burden of pauperism, general economic crisis, Chartism, the agitation against the new Poor Law, and the Plug Plot riots.

The 'hunger-propaganda' of the Anti-Corn Law League has doubtless been responsible in part for the growth of the general impression that the 1840s constituted a decade of especial suffering for the working class. The Anti-Corn Law agitation gained its first successes, like Chartism, in the crucial period of 1838–42. Indeed, in the course of its campaign the League initiated considerable research into economic conditions in 1842, and the report of its committee appointed to inquire into the effects of the Corn Laws on the nation's trade, commerce and manufactures described a gloomy state of affairs when presented to a general meeting of League deputies early in 1843:

> There is alleged on all hands a considerable falling off in the demand for labour; and as a necessary consequence there appears a very general and serious decline in their [sic] rate of wages. Certainly a reduction of the amount of employment is not understated at 20 per cent. In the rate of wages there is a signal reduction, the combined effect of which is – a less command of the necessaries and comforts of life of nearly two-fifths, compared with their means in 1834, 5 or 6. ...
> Consumption of Animal Food. – The falling off in the consumption of butcher's meat is testified in all the reports made to this committee. The decrease is variously stated at from 20 to 60 per cent.[16]

The distress of these years, combined with the tragedy of the potato crop failure and the famine in Ireland (1845–7) have served to obscure the fact that the period from the end of 1842 until 1847 was marked by general prosperity and trade revival.[17] Peel's tariff reforms began to make their influence felt on the economy and the hectic construction which characterised the railway boom kept hundreds of thousands of labourers and skilled craftsmen busy. Tooke wrote:

> The complaints of want of employment for agricultural labourers would probably have been even louder and more frequent ... than they were, had not a new demand for field labour gradually arisen during the summer and autumn of 1844, from the construction of new railways, consequent on the speculations of that year. This additional demand does not seem to have had much effect upon the purely agricultural districts, whence, chiefly, the complaints were heard, until the beginning of 1845; but after that period these districts appear to have shared completely the renewed activity previously displayed elsewhere.[18]

The contrast between the early 1840s and the prosperous middle years of the decade (and incidentally, the sharp difference between the groups inside the working class in different parts of England) is well brought out in the reminiscences of Thomas Wood (1822–1880), which have only recently come to light. He does not mince his words – he had first-hand experience of the hard times in the early 1840s. But in the summer of 1845 he tramped into Lancashire and got work at a good wage with Messrs. Hibberts, Platts, textile machinery makers, of Oldham, with whom he remained a year:

> The men among whom I worked were wicked and reckless. Most of them, gambled freely on horse or dog races. Numbers brought a day's food with them

and nearly all their breakfast, which was despatched with celerity when betting books were produced and bets made. There were very few who took care of their money, fewer still who went to a place of worship or regarded the Sabbath in any other light than as a holiday. Their mode of living was different to the homely manner I had been accustomed to. Flesh meat, as they called it, must be on the table twice or thrice a day. A rough and rude plenty alone satisfied them. The least pinching, such as I had seen scores of times without a murmur, and they were loud in their complainings about 'clamming' ... While the population, generally, were bent on their own pleasure, in which dog racing and dog fighting by expensively-trained animals formed a large part, there were some who shone conspicuously by every grace that adorns the Christian. ... I came to the conclusion that Oldham ordinary people would give up or leave home to go singing in the street when their income was reduced to a level on which Yorkshiremen brought up their families respectably.[19]

An examination of the treatment accorded to the period in a popular survey, G.D.H. Cole and R.W. Postgate's *The Common People*,[20] which has enjoyed a wide circulation since the first edition was published in 1938, indicates the power of a phrase to lull the critical faculties. Chapter XXIV is entitled 'the Hungry 'Forties' and contains just over eighteen pages,[21] eleven of which are devoted to the Bank Charter Act, the legal evolution of the joint stock company during the early nineteenth century, and the railway booms of the 1830s and 1840s. Four pages deal with the rapid advance of urbanisation and its effect on town populations. The examination of wage- and price-series which alone can form a basis for discussing the fundamental facts of the 'condition-of-the-people' question in the 1840s occupies less than four pages.[22] After summarising the remarkable statistics of British economic growth between 1832 and 1850,[23] the authors go on to ask and answer the question: 'How, during this period of exceedingly rapid capitalist expansion, did the working classes fare? The evidence is irresistible that they fared very ill.'[24] They then quote G.H. Wood's figures estimating the average weekly wages in Lancashire and Cheshire cotton factories at 9s. 9d. in 1833, 10s. in 1836, 9s. 7d. in 1840, 10s. 1d. in 1845 and 9s. 6d. in 1850. Figures are also given for a number of other trades:

Mr. Wood's general wage indices, taking 1832 as 100, show increases by 1850, in engineering to 104, in shipbuilding to 106, in building to 109, and in the Huddersfield woollen industry to 105. In printing the wage level remained unchanged, except for levelling up in a few low-wage areas; and in cotton it dropped by 7 per cent.[25]

These, of course, are only money rates and take no account of changes in the cost of living. Messrs. Cole and Postgate, taking the average of 1828–32 as a basis, point out that the cost of living, as measured by Silberling's index of retail prices, rose 8 per cent. above the basis in 1838–42, and then *fell* 6 per cent. *below* the basis in 1842–47, and to 17 per cent. *below* in 1848–50.[26] Their two conclusions are:

It is plain, on the basis of these figures, that the worst sufferings of the working classes were in the years between 1838 and 1842. ... By 1850 falling prices had substantially advanced the real wages of most sections of the working class, except the agricultural labourers; but this benefit did not begin to be felt until after 1842.[27]

Not much remains, therefore, of the 'Hungry Forties.' And the statistics of consumption of certain popular stimulants show an upward tendency during the middle years of the decade, increasing proportionately faster than the population:[28]

	Tobacco Consumption (in million lbs.) in the United Kingdom	Tea Consumption	Rum Consumption (in million gallons) in the United Kingdom.
1842	22·2	37·4	2·10
1843	23·0	40·3	2·10
1844	24·6	41·4	2·20
1845	26·2	44·2	2·47
1846	26·9	46·7	2·68
1847	26·7	46·3	3·33
1848	27·3	48·7	2·99

The consumption of sugar, too, expanded rapidly between 1840 and 1850, aided by falling world prices caused by growing production in the East and West Indies:[29]

Year	Sugar and Molasses retained for Consumption.	Average Consumption of each person.
	lb.	lb.
1834	4,204,411	18·31
1835	4,349,582	19·21
1836	3,922,901	16·58
1837	4,349,453	18·83
1838	4,286,782	18·38
1839	4,047,616	17·18
1840	3,764,710	15·28
1841	4,208,324	17·65
1842	4,068,331	16·76
1843	4,196,865	17·11
1844	4,359,473	17·59
1845	5,091,304	20·33
1846	5,457,154	21·57
1847	6,045,121	23·64
1848	6,427,234	24·88
1849	6,287,217	24·12

Montague Fordham seems to have come very near to the truth when he wrote in 1932:

... towards the end of the [nineteenth] century some ingenious mind invented a new, and from the free traders' point of view a priceless, myth: 'The Story of the Hungry Forties' ... But the so-called 'Hungry Forties' were not in Britain a time of special poverty or of specially high prices of food. There was, in fact, only one year of dear food in the forties, when wheat went up to over 100s. a quarter and bread to about 1s. a four-pound loaf; that, curiously enough, was in 1847, substantially a free-trade year.[30]

INDEXES OF WHOLESALE AND RETAIL PRICES, 1820–1860

Date.	Silberling Retail 1790 = 100	Silberling Wholesale 1790 = 100	G. H. Wood Retail 1850 = 100	Jevons and Sauerbeck (as linked by Layton and Crowther) Wholesale 1900 = 100
1820	132	124	—	172
1	115	117	—	157
2	100	114	—	147
3	111	113	—	148
4	113	106	—	147
5	128	118	—	172
6	111	103	—	150
7	110	101	—	150
8	108	97	—	135
9	106	94	—	132
1830	108	93	—	135
1	111	95	—	137
2	109	94	—	130
3	107	97	—	125
4	102	97	—	130
5	99	100	—	133
6	111	112	—	143
7	111	102	—	140
8	118	104	—	140
9	123	111	—	153
1840	121	108	—	145
1	116	103	—	142
2	106	94	—	125
3	94	86	—	118
4	96	87	—	115
5	97	88	—	123
6	100	88	—	123
7	116	93	—	130
8	97	84	—	113
9	86	80	—	107
1850	83	84	100	107
1	—	—	97	110
2	—	—	97	108
3	—	—	106	123
4	—	—	122	138
5	—	—	126	133
6	—	—	126	137
7	—	—	119	142
8	—	—	109	127
9	—	—	107	128
1860	—	—	111	132

Source: see note 31 for columns one and two, note 32 for column 3 and note 33 for column four.

NOTES

'The Hungry Forties' was a pamphlet published by the Historical Association in 1957, being No.1 of the *Aids for Teachers* series. It is now out of print.

1. Sir John Clapham, *Economic History of Modern Britain. The Early Railway Age, 1820–1850* (1926), preface to the first edition, p.vii.
2. For the most recent discussion of 'the Industrial Revolution' and 'Luddism' by modern historians see Sir George N. Clark, *The Idea of the Industrial Revolution* (Glasgow, 1953) and Dr E.J. Hobsbawm, 'The Machine Breakers', *Past and Present*, Vol.I, No.1, 1952, pp.57–70.
3. This letter was printed, for example, in the *Manchester Guardian* of 9 Feb. 1904, and also appeared in *Reynolds News, The Christian World, The Methodist Times* and *New Age*.
4. *The Times*, 14 Oct 1903, page 5, col.3.
5. The book proved extremely popular and an edition priced at one penny only was published in 1912.
6. See H.L. Beales, '"The Great Depression" in industry and trade', *Economic History Review*, Vol.V, No.1, Oct. 1934, pp.73–4; Sir John Clapham, *Economic History of Modern Britain*, Vol.III, pp.464–7. Of working-class conditions during the period 1886–1900 Sir John Clapham commented: 'Grandfather might talk of the hungry 'forties, and you thanked God you had not been young with grandfather.'
7. *The Hungry Forties ...* (first edn., 1904), pp.63–4.
8. *Op.cit.*, pp.102–11, 162. Cook ended his letter: 'Perhaps some will think my case an exceptional one. To such I might say, "No, by no means; ours was better than many as my father always brought his wages home, whereas some of the men spent part of theirs at the village pub."' (Spelling corrected.)
9. For the very spare diet of a Lancashire weaver even before the Cotton Famine – a dish of ham and eggs was an Easter Sunday luxury – see 'The Diary of John Ward of Clitheroe, weaver, 1860–64', ed. R. Sharpe France, *Transactions of the Historic Society of Lancashire and Cheshire*, Vol.105, 1953, p.160.
10. *The Hungry Forties*, pp.261–2 (on 'the terrors of barley bread').
11. On the nutritional adequacy, by modern standards, of a diet largely composed of potatoes, see K.H. Connell's remarks in *The Population of Ireland, 1750–1845* (1950), pp.151–6. Mr Connell is careful to stress the monotony of such a diet.
12. *The Hungry Forties*, p.263.
13. Vol.X, p.279. It has been pointed out that on page 281 of Canon Henry Scott Holland's *A Bundle of Memories* (1915) the following anecdote, dating from the 1890s or 1900s occurs: 'Those members of the Christian Social Union who used to creep in to our monthly meetings would often see there, in the early days of our London branch, a bent figure sitting ... And now and again, when some pink, youthful, cheerful Psalmist, such as Mr (C.F.G.) Masterman (1874–1927), had plunged us into the abyss of despair, the old man would rise ... and bid us cheer up. "You young fellows have never seen the Hungry Forties ...".' The old man was J.M. Ludlow (1821–1911), but we have only Canon Scott Holland's memory to vouch for the actual use of the phrase by Ludlow. I am indebted to Mr D.S. Colman of Shrewsbury for this reference.
14. *The Hungry Forties*, p.144.
15. Read to the Manchester Statistical Society on 10 Oct. 1945.
16. *Manchester Guardian*, 4 Feb. 1843, p.5, col.6.
17. For a detailed survey of economic conditions during these years see A.D. Gayer, W.W. Rostow and A.J. Schwartz, *The Growth and Fluctuation of the British Economy 1790–1850* (1953), pp.276–341.
18. T. Tooke, *A History of Prices*, Vol.IV, p.58.
19. Thomas Wood, *Autobiography* (privately published – 1936), pp.14–15 (available

[in 1957] from Miss Dorothy Wood, Brontë Hall, Beckett Park, Leeds, 6. Price 1/3d).
20. Page references are to the second edition of 1946, *The Common People, 1746–1946*, 'enlarged, brought up to date and largely rewritten'. The publishers then described it as 'the sole authentic history of the British people that has been written for the common reader since J.R. Green'.
21. Pp.291–309.
22. *Op.cit.*, pp.302–6.
23. For example, the number of seamen employed in the mercantile marine rose from 138,000 in 1832 to 193,000 in 1850: pig iron production soared from 700,000 to 2,350,000 tons in the same period, and coal output from about 26 million tons to about 60 millions.
24. *Op.cit.*, p.302.
25. *Op.cit.*, p.303.
26. *Op.cit.*, pp.303–4.
27. *Op.cit.*, p.304.
28. Gayer, Rostow and Schwartz, *op.cit.*, Vol.I, p.338.
29. G.R. Porter, *Progress of the Nation* (edn. of 1851), p.543. Compare Lord John Russell in *Hansard's Parliamentary Debates*, Vol.99, col.733. See also Gayer, Rostow and Schwartz, *op.cit.*, Vol.2, pp.856–7 for the fall in sugar prices between 1840 and 1848 and the consequent sharp rise in total imports.
30. M. Fordham, *Britain's Trade and Agriculture* (1932), pp.28–9. For material progress among the working classes in the 1840s see also W.R. Greg, 'England as it is', *Edinburgh Review*, Vol.XCIII, Jan.–April 1851, pp.305–39, reprinted in his *Miscellaneous Essays* (2nd ser., 1884), pp.136–92. The article is a review of William Johnston's pessimistic *England as it is ...* (1851).
31. N.J. Silberling, 'British prices and business cycles, 1779–1850' in *Harvard Review of Economic Statistics*, 1923.
32. From Sir Walter Layton and G. Crowther, *An Introduction to the Study of Prices* (3rd edn. 1938), p.273.
33. Layton and Crowther, *op.cit.*, Chart 1.

BIBLIOGRAPHY

Sir John H. Clapham: *An Economic History of Modern Britain*, Vols.I and II (1926 and 1932).

Sir E. Llewellyn Woodward: *The Age of Reform, 1815–1870* (Oxford History of England), 1938, pp.58–60, 113–19.

D.G. Barnes: *A history of the English Corn Laws from 1660–1846* (1930) (contains a bibliography of pamphlets).

C.R. Fay: *The Corn Laws and Social England* (1932).

R.L. Schuyler: *The Fall of the Old Colonial System: a study in British Free Trade, 1770–1870* (1945).

Cambridge History of the British Empire, Vol.II: *The Growth of the New Empire, 1783–1870* (1940), Ch.XI: 'The Movement towards Free Trade, 1820–1853', by C.R. Fay.

Sir John H. Clapham: 'Corn Laws Repeal, Free Trade and History', *Transactions of the Manchester Statistical Society*, 1945.

K.H. Connell: *The Population of Ireland, 1750–1845* (1950).

G. Kitson Clark: 'The repeal of the Corn Laws and the politics of the forties', *Economic History Review*, second series, Vol.IV, No.1, 1951, pp.1–13.

G. Kitson Clark: 'The electorate and the repeal of the Corn Laws', *Transactions of the Royal Historical Society*, 5th series, Vol.I, pp.109–26 (1951).

G. Kitson Clark: 'Hunger and politics in 1842', *Journal of Modern History*, Vol.XXV, No.4, Dec. 1953, pp.355–74.

Archibald Prentice: *History of the Anti-Corn Law League* (1853), 2 vols.

Mark Hovell: *The Chartist Movement* (1918).

G.L. Mosse: 'The Anti-League: 1844–1846', *Economic History Review*, Vol.XVII,

No.2, 1947, pp.134–42.

A. Redford: *Manchester Merchants and Foreign Trade, 1794–1858* (1934), esp. chaps.X and XI.

T.S. Ashton: 'The origin of the Manchester School', *The Manchester School*, Vol.I, No.2 (1930–31), pp.22–27.

F.E. Hyde: *Mr. Gladstone at the Board of Trade* (1934).

Derek Walker Smith: *The Protectionist Case in the 1840s* (1933).

G.M. Trevelyan: *The Life of John Bright* (1913).

J.E.T. Rogers (ed.): *Speeches on questions of public policy, by the Rt. Hon. John Bright, M.P.* (1869).

John Morley: *The Life of Richard Cobden*, 2 vols. (1881).

John Bright qnd J.E.T. Rogers (ed.): *Speeches on questions of public policy by Richard Cobden, M.P.* (1878).

W.O. Henderson: 'Charles Pelham Villiers', *History*, Vol.XXXVII, No.129, February, 1952, pp.25–39.

A member of the Cobden Club (ed.): *The Free Trade Speeches of the Rt. Hon. Charles Pelham Villiers, with a political memoir*, 2 vols. (1883).

For Peel see works listed in Woodward: *op.cit.*, pp.615, 618, and the Earl of Rosebery: *Sir Robert Peel* (1899) – reprinted in his *Miscellanies, literary and historical* (1921).

16

Mrs Trollope and the Early Factory System

Mrs Frances Trollope, the mother of Anthony Trollope the novelist, is not generally associated with the North of England and its cotton industry, although her now rather rare novel, *The Life and Adventures of Michael Armstrong, the Factory Boy*, which appeared in twelve shilling parts during 1839–40,[1] purports to be an exposure of the worst horrors of the Industrial Revolution in the expanding textile districts. The illustrations to the book, engravings by Auguste Hervieu, R.W. Buss, and Thomas Onwhyn,[2] have considerable period charm, being sometimes sentimental and sometimes horrific, in the early Victorian manner.

Mrs Trollope's first book, *Domestic Manners of the Americans* (1832),[3] published when she was over fifty years of age, was based on her unfortunate experiences in the U.S.A. of the late 1820s. She arrived in Cincinnati during 1828 with the plan of establishing her son Henry in business as the proprietor of a grandiose department store, a project which failed miserably and forced her return to England in 1831. *Domestic Manners of the Americans* showed that she had a genius for depicting vulgar people, and proved an immediate best-seller. Readers and critics in the U.S.A. were furious at her indictment of American society, but the powerful anti-American and conservative elements in Britain and Western European society rejoiced. The new literary lioness followed this unexpected good fortune with a forced stream of novels and travel books, for she was a liberal spender as well as an industrious writer, having a large family and an unpractical, ailing husband to support.[4]

By the late 1830s, in her search for fresh and profitable subjects, Mrs. Trollope discovered the agitation for further factory legislation which was then proceeding in Britain. She therefore determined, in her own words, 'to drag into the light of day, and place before the eyes of Englishmen, the hideous mass of injustice and suffering to which thousands of infant labourers are subjected, who toil in our monster spinning-mills' (*Michael Armstrong*, p.iii). Her well-attested affection for children and her general humanitarian outlook coincided happily with her interests as a professional novelist.[5] It should be remembered that a Factory Act, which regulated the employment of children and young persons in textile mills, had been passed in 1833. The increasingly effective administration of the provisions of this act by paid inspectors was stamping out the worst abuses in the factories before Mrs Trollope took any interest in the subject. But by 1836 the supporters of the Short Time movement in the manufacturing towns of Lancashire, Yorkshire, and the Midlands, inflamed by the speeches of demagogues such as the Rev. Joseph Rayner Stephens of Ashton-under-Lyne and Richard Oastler of Yorkshire, 'the King of the factory children', were pressing for the ten-hour day.[6] Lord Ashley, however, the recognised leader of the movement in the House of Commons, counselled caution. Agitation and discussion continued spasmodically throughout 1838 and 1839, when abortive factory bills were before Parliament. The question of factory reform, in its manifold aspects and with its powerful humanitarian appeal, seemed to Mrs Trollope an excellent basis for another best-seller. *Michael Armstrong*, therefore, forms part of that general reaction against novels about high life ('the silver fork school') which was in train by 1839, partly as a result of Carlyle's influence.[7]

Mrs Trollope went about the collection of background material with characteristic efficiency. From Lord Ashley she obtained a sheaf of introductions to 'a rather strange assortment of persons',[8] and set off *incognita* on 20 February 1839 'by the mail train' from London to Manchester on the recently opened railway, accompanied by her eldest son, Thomas Adolphus.[9] He proved 'useful to her in searching for and collecting facts in some places where it would have been difficult for her to look for them', and after her death he claimed, by implication, joint authorship of *Michael Armstrong* with his mother (T.A. Trollope, pp. 8–9). The first instalment (in which there was little that needed first-hand experience of the North) was already on its way from the publisher to the bookshops by the time Mrs Trollope arrived in the North of England. The *Northern Star* of Leeds, Feargus O'Connor's Chartist newspaper, noted approvingly in its issue for Saturday, 2 March 1839:

This lady is taking the right way to write the truth about 'The Factory Boy.' She has been spending some time in the neighbourhood of Manchester, making her own observations upon the real state in which 'The Factory Boy' exists. She is determined not to have her judgement warped, but to see all the sides of his case for herself.... She has introductions to the rich and to the poor; and she seems determined to avail herself of these opportunities of making herself mistress of the whole question *pro* and *con*. We may differ from the lady on many points; but we cordially award to her the meed of our praise for the pains she is now taking thoroughly to understand the case of the poor wretch whom she has chosen as the hero of her next romance.   (p.4)

In Bradford the Trollopes met John Wood, a philanthropic worsted spinner, whose firm employed three thousand hands (T.A. Trollope, pp.8–9, 11). Wood and his partner, William Walker, were strong supporters of the ten-hours agitation. At Wood's residence they were also introduced to another local champion of the factory children, the Rev. G.S. Bull, the Anglican incumbent of Bierley, who appears in *Michael Armstrong* under the thin disguise of 'Parson Bell of Fairly' in Yorkshire.[10] In Manchester itself they met the pioneer trade-unionist John Doherty,[11] by then earning a living as 'a small bookseller, of Hyde's Cross'. T.A. Trollope described him as 'an Irishman, a Roman Catholic, and a furious Radical, but a *very* clever man' (T.A. Trollope, p.10). With much difficulty he persuaded Doherty to dine with Mrs Trollope, but while at table Doherty's excitement was 'so great and continuous that he could eat next to nothing'. But of all their informants Richard Oastler, 'the Danton of the movement', made the greatest impression (T.A. Trollope, p.10). The rabble-rousing Stephens, whom they heard preaching in his chapel at Stalybridge on Sunday, 24 February,[12] on the text of 'the cruel and relentless march of the great Juggernauth, Gold', did not completely justify his great reputation.[13]

The effects of these experiences can easily be traced in *Michael Armstrong*. The tale centres around the imaginary Lancashire factory town of Ashleigh, and the narrative reflects the conditions of the 1820s. From the description given of it, Ashleigh appears to have been situated somewhere in the Ashton–Stalybridge–Stockport area.[14] The villain of the novel is a coarse, preposterous monster, Sir Matthew Dowling, 'the proprietor of many cotton-mills.' He is fabulously wealthy: 'throughout the whole line of that Golconda country, which, being the busiest of the manufacturing districts, is probably the richest in the world, there was not anyone who could vie in wealth with him' (*Michael Armstrong*, p.2). Naturally he opposes factory legislation, fears strikes, overworks his miserable operatives, and is worried about trade unionist activities at 'The Weavers' Arms' public house. Oddly enough, by a curious transposition, the description of Dowling's appearance and physique tallies very closely with that of Oastler as given by T.A. Trollope (pp.12–13).

Sir Matthew is trapped by his social ambitions into adopting a miserable ten-year-old factory boy, Michael Armstrong, from his Brookford spinning mill. But Michael spends only a short time as a member of the numerous family at Dowling Lodge. Sir Matthew soon becomes embarrassed by the presence of 'the factory brat,' and appren-

'Love Conquered Fear': Michael meets his brother Edward in Sir Matthew
Dowling's mill (*Michael Armstrong* (1840), facing p.82)

The scene re-engraved fourteen years later as frontispiece to John C. Cobden's *The White Slaves of England*

tices him for a period of eleven years' servitude to his friend Elgood Sharpton, Esq., of Thistledown House, Derbyshire. Sharpton owns the grim and dreadful Deep Valley Mill on Ridgetop Moor in the same county, an establishment so secluded that it was 'hardly possible to conceive a spot more effectually hidden from the eyes of all men' (*Michael Armstrong*, p. 180). In the dismal Deep Valley apprentice-house 'hundreds of little aching hearts' (p. 181) languish, often competing with the pigs for swill, sometimes trying to escape, and dying off in dozens from fever. It is here that the influence of Doherty becomes apparent. In 1832 Doherty had reprinted as a pamphlet John Brown's celebrated *Memoir of Robert Blincoe*, originally published in 1828, which described the sufferings of a pauper apprentice, first in a cotton-mill at Lowdham near Nottingham, and then at Litton Mill, near Tideswell in Derbyshire.[15] This second mill was owned by Ellice Needham (i.e. 'Elgood Sharpton') of Highgate Wall, near Buxton in Derbyshire. As described by Blincoe, the setting of Litton Mill, 'at the bottom of a sequestered glen, and surrounded by rugged rocks, remote from any human habitation',[16] answers completely to that of Deep Valley Mill, and indeed, Mrs Trollope explained in a footnote: 'The real name of this valley (which most assuredly is no creation of romance) is not given lest an action for libel should be the consequence. The scenes which have passed there and which the following pages will describe, have been stated on authority not to be impeached' (p. 180). T.A. Trollope's statement about the novel, 'What we are there described to have seen, we saw' (p. 9), seems to be, to say the least, exaggerated.

The secret of how Michael Armstrong succeeded in escaping from the clutches of Elgood Sharpton to take part in the famous York meeting of factory reformers on Easter Monday, 24 April 1832,[17] and of the surprising sequel to the adoption of his brother Edward by a young, beautiful, but orphaned cotton heiress, Miss Brotherton, must be left to those who wish to browse in the diffuse jungle of this early Victorian novel. Mrs Trollope's publisher, Henry Colburn, paid a 'long price' for *Michael Armstrong*, and did not complain, so that it presumably sold well. But it was not one of the more popular of her novels, and, as T.A. Trollope remarked: 'Novel readers are exceedingly quick to smell the rhubarb under the jam in the dose offered to them' (pp. 7–8). A hostile reviewer in the *Statesman* saw in the repeal of the Corn Laws the cure both for the social degradation of the workers and the economic difficulties of the millowners:

Whatever be the literary merits of *Michael Armstrong* (and we confess we see none, it is one of the dullest and heaviest productions we have ever been doomed to read) it should at once be consigned to oblivion as an exaggerated statement of the vices of a class, and a mischievous attempt to excite the worst and bitterest feelings against men, who are, like other men, creatures of circumstances, in which their lot has been cast ... we can see no more utility in a gross exaggeration or invidious exposure of the faults of these, than in the coarse and violent abuse oftentime passed out upon the landowners. Both parties are for the most part the victims of their own ignorance; and the first and most pernicious fruit of that ignorance is the corn laws ... Their repeal is the most effectual step to that protection [of 'infant labourers against sensualised parents and unthinking masters']. It would make land cheaper, wages better, healthier cottages and gardens more attainable and the necessity for parents sending their children to work less irksome. Until this be done, the landowners are quite as blameable as the manufacturers for the wrongs done in the 'monster spinning mills.' But we abominate abuse of the landowner as we do the counsel of the 'torch and dagger'; we think the author of *Michael Armstrong* deserves as richly to have eighteen months in Chester Gaol as any that are there now for using violent language against the 'monster cotton mills.'[18]

As an account of factory conditions in general *Michael Armstrong* cannot be said to justify the praise given to it by some historians.[19] The *Statesman* was not alone in its hostile criticism, and towards the end of 1839 Frederic Montagu published a counterblast in the form of a novel with the striking title of *Mary Ashley, the Factory Girl, or Facts upon Factories*. *Michael Armstrong*, however, found high favour among the members of the Chartist movement, which enjoyed its period of greatest influence and violence in 1839–40. Mrs Trollope wrote in a private letter shortly after its publication: 'between ourselves, I don't think any one cares much for 'Michael Armstrong' – except the Chartists. A new kind of patrons for me!' (F.E. Trollope, p.301). In public the Tory-minded authoress was quick to disown her new supporters, for she wrote in the preface to the collected parts:

it is grievous to see misguided and unfortunate men pursuing a course which must necessarily neutralize the efforts of their true friends. When those in whose behalf she hoped to move the sympathy of their country are found busy in scenes of outrage and lawless violence, and uniting themselves with individuals whose doctrines are subversive of every species of social order, the author feels that it would be alike acting in violation of her own principles, and doing injury to the cause she wishes to serve, were she to persist in an attempt to hold up as objects of public sympathy, men who have stained their righteous cause with deeds of violence and blood.

(pp.iii–iv)

It is a tribute to Mrs Trollope's feelings that the mediocre literary success of *Michael Armstrong* did not prevent her from publishing in 1842–43 *Jessie Phillips: a Tale of the Present Day* on the theme of the harshness with which the Poor Law Amendment Act of 1834 was administered in some parts of the country.

One of the illustrations in *Michael Armstrong* had a curious later history. It purports to show a scene during a tour of Dowling's Brook-ford Mill, when the sleek, well-dressed and adopted Michael Arm-strong greets his younger brother Edward, who is still at work as a child labourer. In 1853 or 1854 this touching scene was redrawn to serve as the frontispiece of John C. Cobden's muckraking work, *The White Slaves of England, Compiled from Official Documents*.[20] Cobden directed his attack mainly against the 'feudal' British aristocracy, but industrialists also came in for strong criticism on account of their 'treatment of the laboring classes in the factories and coal mines of Great Britain'. Some of his phrases have a familiar ring: 'The poor [in Britain] are every year becoming poorer, and more dependent upon those who feast upon their sufferings; while the power and wealth of the realm are annually concentrating in fewer hands, and becoming more and more instruments of oppression' (p.6). The author quoted Mrs Trollope's *Michael Armstrong* and Charles Dickens' *Oliver Twist* approvingly as evidence of English social conditions, and expressed his indebtedness 'to the publications of distinguished democrats of England, who have keenly felt the evils under which their country groans' (p.7).

The late Humphry House, in *The Dickens World* (Oxford, 1941), warned against the temptation to make uncritical use of Charles Dickens' novels as sources for the social and economic history of his times.[21] It is suggested that this caution has a wider application. While the careful examination of fictional incidents based on the social and economic life of a writer's age will undoubtedly throw light on that author's mind and working methods, it can never be a substitute for a study of the original historical sources themselves.

NOTES

This article is reprinted from *Victorian Studies*, December 1960, pp.159–66.

1. Published by Henry Colburn, Great Marlborough Street, London, pp.viii + 387. The first part appeared on 26 Feb. 1839 (*Northern Star*, 2 Mar. 1839, p.1).
2. Onwhyn (d. 1886) executed 'illegitimate' illustrations to Dickens' works in 1837–38 (*DNB*).
3. There is an excellent edition of *Domestic Manners of the Americans*, ed. Donald Smalley (New York, 1949).
4. Perhaps the best short analysis of the reasons for Trollope senior's lack of success in life is given by Smalley, pp.xiv–xv, lxii. See also Anthony Trollope, *An Auto-biography*, ed. Michael Sadleir (Oxford, 1923), pp.6–7, 10–14, and Sadleir, *Trollope: A Commentary* (London, 1933), pp.70–73.
5. See also Sadleir, pp.92–94, and L.P. and R.P. Stebbins, *The Trollopes* (London, 1946), pp.97–98.
6. For Stephens, see J.T. Ward, 'Revolutionary Tory: the Life of Joseph Rayner Stephens of Ashton-under-Lyne (1805–1879)' in *Transactions of the Lancashire*

MRS TROLLOPE AND THE EARLY FACTORY SYSTEM 251

and *Cheshire Antiquarian Society*, LXVIII (1959), 93–116, and for Oastler, Cecil Driver, *Tory Radical: the Life of Richard Oastler* (New York, 1946).

7. Kathleen Tillotson, *Novels of the Eighteen Forties* (Oxford, 1954), pp.73–88.

8. T.A. Trollope, *What I Remember* (London, 1887), II, 8.

9. F.E. Trollope, *Frances Trollope: Her Life and Literary Work from George III to Victoria* (London, 1895), I, 300–1; *Northern Star*, 2 Mar. 1839, p.4.

10. *Michael Armstrong*, pp.198–211, 319–24; see J.C. Gill, *The Ten Hours Parson* (London, 1959).

11. T.A. Trollope, p.8. For Doherty's importance in the working-class movements of the time, see Sidney and Beatrice Webb, *The History of Trade Unionism, 1666–1920* (London, 1920), pp.107, 117–8, 121, 124 and G.D.H. Cole, *Attempts at General Union: a Study in British Trade Union History, 1818–1834* (London, 1953), *passim*.

12. *Northern Star*, 2 Mar. 1839, p.4.

13. T.A.Trollope, pp.12–13. During Stephens' service Oastler mounted the pulpit and gave out the verses of a hymn, which the congregation sang after him.

14. There is a description, dating from the early 1840s, of these three cotton towns in Friedrich Engels, *The Condition of the Working Class in England*, ed. W.O. Henderson and W.H. Chaloner (Oxford, 1958), pp.52–3.

15. See A.E. Musson, 'Robert Blincoe and the Early Factory System' (*Derbyshire Miscellany*, I [Feb. 1958], 111–17), which gives the fullest and most reliable account of Blincoe and this pamphlet, and J.D. Chambers, *The Vale of Trent, 1670–1800* (Cambridge, 1957), pp.60–2.

16. John Brown, *A Memoir of Robert Blincoe* (Manchester, 1832), p.32.

17. *Michael Armstrong*, pp.312–14. For the York meeting, see B.L. Hutchins and Amy Harrison, *A History of Factory Legislation* (London, 1907), pp.51–2, and Driver, ch.xiv, 'The Pilgrimage to York'.

18. Quoted in the *Bolton Free Press* of 22 Feb. 1840. I am indebted to Mr. Rhodes Boyson for this reference. The Rev. J.R. Stephens was sentenced to eighteen months' imprisonment in Chester Gaol at the Chester Assizes of August 1839 for having used seditious and inflammatory language. The *Athenaeum* of 10 Aug. 1839 attacked *Michael Armstrong* bitterly and searchingly on much the same lines while the parts were still being issued.

19. See, for example, J.L. and B. Hammond, *Lord Shaftesbury* (London, 1936), p.173; Sadleir, p.93; F.D. Klingender, *Art and the Industrial Revolution* (London, 1947), p.132; Driver, pp.403–4. For a more critical and less sentimental examination of the subject of factory conditions and working-class welfare in early nineteenth-century England, se W.H. Hutt, 'The Factory System of the Early Nineteenth Century' in *Capitalism and the Historians*, ed. F.A. von Hayek (London, 1954), pp.160–88; N.J. Smelser, *Social Change in the Industrial Revolution* (London, 1959); the introduction (pp.xi–xxxi) to Engels, *The Condition of the Working Class in England*, ed. Henderson and Chaloner; R.M. Hartwell, 'Interpretations of the Industrial Revolution in England, Part I', *Journal of Economic History*, XIX (1959), 229–49; and A.J. Taylor, 'Progress and Poverty in Britain, 1780–1950: a Reappraisal', *History*, XLV (1960), 16–31.

20. Published by Miller, Orton and Mulligan, of Auburn and Buffalo. By 1854 it had reached its second edition and fifth thousand.

21. See, in particular, ch.i, 'History' (pp.18–35) and pp.92–105 (the Poor Law, with particular reference to *Oliver Twist*). See also William O. Aydelotte, 'The England of Marx and Mill as Reflected in Fiction', *Journal of Economic History*, VIII (1948), Supplement, 42–58.

17

Trends in Fish Consumption

It might be expected that fish would form an important article of diet for the inhabitants of an island kingdom situated in temperate latitudes, endowed with many rivers and strategically based on a shallow Continental shelf. The difficulty, however, is to obtain any quantitative idea of fish consumption and the following paper is an attempt to indicate some of the evidence for the eighteenth and nineteenth centuries and at the same time to indicate what changes occurred in the supply of, and demand for, fish in Great Britain.

EIGHTEENTH-CENTURY FRESHWATER FISHING

Let us first consider fresh-water fish. Generally speaking fish of all kinds was held in lower esteem than the flesh of beasts and birds,[1] and the illegal taking of fish from rivers above tidal limits attracted neither the same attention nor the same harsh penalties as the taking of game.[2] In country districts easily accessible lakes, rivers and streams, as yet unpolluted to any great degree by deadly industrial effluents, must have provided fish as an important supplement to diets largely based on cereals or potatoes or both. The deliberate cultivation of fresh-water fish in ponds, popularly supposed to have died out in the sixteenth century with the suppression of the monasteries, continued in fact into at least the late eighteenth century. For example, on 25 May 1747 the Corporation of Leicester, which owned extensive fishing rights in the River Soar, ordered 'that a Stew be made in such part of the Corporation Water as Mr Mayor shall think most proper for the keeping of fish in'.[3] In 1764 nets were provided 'for Mr Mayor for the time being for Fishing the Corporation waters'.[4] Other references indicate that pike provided the main produce.[5] Again, in his *Description of the Country from Thirty to Forty Miles round Manchester* (1795), Dr John Aikin stated in his account of Manchester's food supply: 'Many ponds and old marl-pits in the neighbourhood are well stored with carp and tench, and pike and other fresh water fish are often brought to market.'[6]

One locality provided a fresh-water speciality which was sent as far as London. About 1681–84 Daniel Fleming wrote that Coniston Water in the Lake District produced

> many Pikes or Jacks, Bass or Perch, Trouts, Eels, & Charrs; w[hi]ch last ... is much esteemed and valued, being sold here for ye most part at Two Pence apiece and many Charr-Pies being yearly in Lent (when this fish is in Season) sent unto London & other distant Places.[7]

Clearly it is quite impossible to assess the quantitative importance of fresh-water fish in the national diet in the eighteenth and nineteenth centuries, but such indications as these suggest that, at least in rural districts and small towns, it was not negligible. It almost certainly became of relatively less importance after about 1825–50, with the progressive pollution of industrial rivers. This period coincided, however, with the beginning of the great increase in sea fish supplies.

EIGHTEENTH-CENTURY SEA FISHING

More precise information about the British sea fisheries is available, partly because the preservation of sea fish involved a greater use of salt, an article of diet which was taxed from the reign of Elizabeth I until 1825 and partly, because from the sixteenth century onwards various schemes were put forward, and some actually carried into effect, for increasing fish exports.

The deleterious effects of the salt tax on the levels of fish consumption among the poorer classes became a more and more frequent cause of complaint as the eighteenth century wore on. For example, in 1785 Thomas Fennings, a fisherman at Harwich, told the Select Committee on the British fisheries

> that if they had salt duty-free, it would be of great service to the poor, as they could salt a great number of small fish, which they are now obliged to throw away, not being able to get them to a market before they stink – that sometimes they throw away their whole voyages, amounting to two or three hundred score of fish, which they could cure, and bring to market, if salt was allowed duty-free.[8]

An Act of 1785 went some way towards meeting criticisms of the salt duty by abolishing the import duty levied on herrings cured at sea for home consumption.[9]

Technical innovations in the eighteenth century, leading to quicker and larger catches, better preservation and more expeditious landings, appear to have been few and are difficult to trace. One that is reasonably well documented was the adoption from about 1770 by the Harwich fishermen of 'long-line' fishing (as distinct from hand-line fishing) for the larger species of fish, and especially cod:

... the information came from an Englishman that had been employed in the Dutch service ... and was employed by a smack owner to fit out a vessel with long lines.[10]

The cost of installing this new equipment in a vessel might be as much as £40, and as the result of its adoption the British long line fishing for cod on the Dogger Bank was almost equal to the Dutch by the mid-1780s.

The rise, and sometimes the 'decay', of local fisheries await systematic investigation. Most of what is known, for example, about the fishing in the Irish Sea, carried on from Liverpool, the Lancashire coast and the Isle of Man, comes from the *Report* of 1798 on the British herring fisheries.[11] Little is known about the rise of Fleetwood in Lancashire from obscurity in 1800 to the position of the fourth largest fishing port in the United Kingdom by the 1930s. The rise of Harwich as a fishing port in the eighteenth century was spectacular – in 1715 only three smacks operated from Harwich; by 1735 the number had increased to thirty and by 1774 was 62.[12] However, by the end of the century Harwich had declined, and by 1852 only five smacks were operating from it. Revival came in the third quarter of the nineteenth century with the coming of the railway from London.[13] Similarly Yarmouth, after enjoying prosperity in the first three-quarters of the eighteenth century, declined during and after the War of American Independence, only to revive in the nineteenth century.

The general impression received from a study of the various local fisheries is one of immense annual fluctuations in the shoals and the catches, leading to sharp alternations of glut and scarcity. The figures for red herrings entered for home consumption in the port of Yarmouth between 1739 and 1782 show extraordinary annual variations, the two worst years being 1760 (1.98 million) and 1782 (1.78 million) and the two best years 1757 (21.5 million) and 1773 (15.5 million).[14]

Another example is that of the Cornish pilchard fishery. By the end of the eighteenth century there were two main pilchard fisheries off Cornwall, one carried on from St. Ives on the north coast and the other on the southern coast from Mount's Bay eastwards to Devon.[15] The surplus of these maintained the population in 'rude plenty':

During the season, great quantities [of pilchards] at each Fishery, are given away fresh, or sold at a low price; they are cured at home by the poorer people; and what is more than adequate to the consumption of the family, is retailed out, and becomes, with potatoes, the chief support during the winter months, of the poorer classes, and particularly of the miners of Cornwall. – Their distress is ever complicated with that of the Fishery ... on failure of the Pilchard, they can have no substitute equally cheap or adequate to their wants.[16]

The supply for an average family for a winter was about 1,000 pilchards, if they could afford the salt; the difficult time of the year in Cornwall in the period 1780–1830 was not, however, the autumn pilchard season, when gluts frequently occurred, but the spring and early summer when both grain stocks and stocks of cured pilchards were at a low ebb.[17] In fact in the autumn of 1812 and again in 1813 west Cornwall farmers were carting the pilchard catches direct from the beaches of St Ives and Mount's Bay to their fields, using them as manure for better grain and potato crops.[18]

THE GROWTH OF BUSINESS ENTERPRISE

The fishery schemes of the seventeenth and eighteenth centuries were normally conceived not with a view to increasing the home consumption of fish but with the object of paying for imports or to bring gold and silver into the realm by exporting fish, or of training a potential naval reserve of seamen or simply in order to obtain various Government bounties on fish exports or fishing vessels.[19] As Dr Malcolm Gray has so happily expressed it:

The fishery, an industry of majestic vessels and widespread markets, lay deep in the mercantilist consciousness. Did not the Dutch for two centuries bestride Northern Europe with their great fishing fleet and its products? The Dutch herrings came from eastern coastal waters of Britain, from the Shetlands down to East Anglia ... and the annual progress of their fleet was an affront to national pride.[20]

Unfortunately, these projects 'of building for the herring fishery a massive sea-going fleet that would tour the west coast, as did the Dutch the east'[21] did little more at first than spoil the efforts of local fishermen. Two of these schemes may be briefly noticed. The Society for the Free British Fishery, set up by Act of Parliament (23 Geo. II, cap. 24) and Royal Charter in 1750, was a London based joint-stock company with a nominal capital of £500,000, the purpose of which was the building of herring buses (decked vessels of between 20 to 80 tons burthen), which were to catch, sort, gut and barrel herring under the superintendence of 'Danish skippers lately arrived from Holland'. Swift tenders were to take the barrels from the buses operating off the Shetlands and later off East Anglia to West European ports. The State guaranteed both an annual interest of 3 per cent on the subscribed capital of the company and an annual bounty on vessels actually built and maintained in this fishery. The project eventually collapsed and was sold up in 1772, although in 1755 the company had cured 70,000 barrels of herring at Yarmouth and Lowestoft, of which 18,000 were for home consumption.[22]

The second joint-stock company, the British Society for extending the Fisheries and Improving the Sea Coasts of this Kingdom, was of rather a different kind. It had a nominal capital of £150,000 and came into existence partly as a result of the publicity generated by the Parliamentary inquiries of 1785 and partly as a result of the activities of George Dempster (1732–1818), of Dunnichen near Forfar. Dempster was M.P. for Forfar 1784–90, a pioneer advocate of the use of ice in the transport of fresh salmon from Scotland to London.[23] The Society did not undertake fishing directly but arranged for and encouraged improved curing facilities in the Western Highlands, particularly at Ullapool on Loch Broom, where an extensive tract of land was purchased.

The fishery in the Shetlands and the west coast of Scotland operated under many handicaps, apart from the uncertainty as to which lochs the shoals would enter and whether the number of fish so entering would be large or small. The local male inhabitants, often in debt to the lairds, were not specialised fishermen, as many of them held crofts. No large urban markets existed to stimulate that 'spirit of improvement' which the entrepreneurs and politicians of the eighteenth and early nineteenth centuries considered so desirable:

> As there are no great towns on those coasts [of the Western Islands], which could furnish a ready market for fresh fish, no men follow that employment as a business, the people on the coast only going out from time to time to catch as many as serve their own families when they want them. They are therefore extremely unexperienced fishermen. ...[24]

The Customs collectors of this region frequently considered that the inhabitants of the Western Islands were unenterprising, oppressed, indolent and too addicted to smuggling, which proved more profitable if not more exciting than fishing – the Orcadians, for example, were labelled as 'these lazy islanders'. There were exceptions – the inhabitants of Lewis dried ling and cod for sale in considerable quantities.[25]

The general picture is of seas swarming with fish which remained largely unharvested not only because the industry lay in the hands of small men who lacked the capital but also because a low but adequate standard of living could be achieved without regular work:

> ... those poor people [the Shetlanders] at present live mostly upon tea, fish and barley bread ... there are an amazing quantity of fish about the Shetland Islands, particularly Cod, Ling and Tusk, there are also a great quantity of Coal Fish, on which the people can live without bread.[26]

By the 1780s signs of rapid change existed. The pull of the growing industrial markets of the Lowlands and even of the London market began to make itself felt. The Collector of Customs at Isle Martin, on the west coast of Scotland, reported in 1785 that

Mr Cuming, a merchant in Inverness ... lately made a contract with Sir Hector Mackenzie of Gairloch, for all the Cod caught by his tenants at 2d each, and he has erected store-houses &c for curing them at Gairloch. In Lent 1783 Mr Cuming took out a ticket from the Custom house at Isle Martin for 2,000 Cod − these he acknowledges cost him sixpence each by the time they were laid down in Billingsgate market, London, and he sold them there at eighteen pence each.[27]

When Henry Beaufoy, M.P., Chairman of the British Society for extending the Fisheries, toured the west coast of Scotland in 1786 or 1787 he found similar signs of economic awakening. On Isle Martin, on Loch Broom, a partnership from Liverpool had erected 'extensive works for the cure of herrings'; on the island of Ternera a few miles away 'houses for the cure of large quantities of herrings have been erected by a Company of Scotch Gentlemen, who also wish to be purchasers to a large amount,' and finally at Loch Inver north of Loch Broom a similar establishment had been built 'by a Company in the Isle of Man'.[28] Shortly afterwards the British Society voted £720 to Robert Melville for the erection of smoking houses for cod and herring at Ullapool.[29] The greatest progress was, however, to be made on the east coast of Scotland rather than on the west.

In 1785 the Collector of Customs at Aberdeen had stated that

if proper vessels were employed that could go from ten to thirty leagues from the coast, there is not a doubt but their success would be very great, as there is vast abundance of Cod and Ling on that coast, and as large shoals of Herrings come from the north in the months of July and August, a most beneficial fishery may be expected from them.[30]

This prophecy proved correct and from about 1800, fishermen operating from the coasts of Caithness, Moray and Aberdeen carried through what has been called a 'revolution' with 'new boats considerably larger than the fishing craft of the west' which were able, by doing a nightly turn, to reach the deep waters and to break the regularly passing shoals. These fishermen were themselves only small capitalists, but were helped financially by the town merchants. Between 1800 and 1850 the annual catch of herrings by Scots fishermen rose from less than 100,000 barrels to about half a million.[31] The breakthrough which had been dreamed of for centuries had occurred.

An exception to the export-centred schemes is provided by a plan which gave rise to what must be one of the earliest pieces of market research in British economic history. The Restoration topographer, John Adams, barrister of the Inner Temple, stated in 1680:

'Tis now about eight years since I was at Mr Lloyd's of Llanvorda, in Shropshire, who then Designing a Fishery on the Coast of Wales, I endeavor'd to compute what Sale he might make in the Neighbouring Markets, by Projecting a Specimen, wherein making Aberdovey, a Village on the Coast of Merionithshire, the first Landing-place, I set down all the Markets within an hundred Miles, and entered the Distances between them in figures ...[32]

Unfortunately nothing further is known of this scheme, but it shows that the inland transport of fresh or lightly salted fish over long distances was not thought to be impossible. A hundred years later, however, considerable improvements in inland transport had been made, by the turnpiking of roads and the development of a speedier coach service. On 12 February 1786 the Rev. F. Shepherd of Brixham in Devon could write the following to John Rolle, MP.:

In the last year there were sent from Brixham alone to London, 500 machines load [i.e. 500 coach-loads] of different fish; the prime cost on the beach, upon an average, £13 per load, amounting to £6,500. The like quantity was sent to Bath and Bristol (of which Turbot is by far the most valuable article) besides a vast quantity carried on horses, &c. into every market town and village in the county.[33]

It is clear from the Report of the Select Committee on the British Channel Fisheries of 1833 that similar supply networks radiated from the fishing ports of Folkestone and Hastings, covering the whole of Kent, including towns so near to the Thames as Maidstone, Chatham, Rochester, Faversham and Canterbury, as well as a large part of East Sussex.[34] The North Kentish towns were in a very favourable position for they also received fish from vessels putting in at Gravesend and Barking.[35] The supply of fish to London from the S.E. coast was, however, said to be hampered by turnpike tolls.[36] The fish was distributed in large luggage vans pulled by four or six horses, according to the load.

In time of local gluts, the poor benefited. William Breach, a fishmonger at Hastings, was asked at the inquiry of 1833 whether the poor of Hastings lived much on fish. He replied:

At this time they would be very bad off at Hastings if it was not for the fish; our fishermen are very liberal, and no poor tradesman goes down [to the harbour] and asks for a bit of fish and goes away empty handed ... if they have any to spare.[37]

In the early 1830s the disposal of local gluts of fish by steam boat was still in an experimental stage and one witness stated:

It would be difficult to get a steam vessel round from Hastings [to Billingsgate] as quick as you could come by land, and there would be a loss occasioned by it.[38]

FISH FOR LONDON

Let us now examine the supply of fish to London, which was particularly important as the largest urban concentration in the country and because it lay very close to the Continent. No foreign fishing vessel was allowed to land any sort of fish in Great Britain except turbot, eels, lobsters and sturgeon. Of these only eels paid a duty. Nevertheless between the end of the Napoleonic Wars in 1814–15 and 1833 the French, Dutch and Belgian fishermen gradually became bolder and bolder in their contraventions of the spirit of this general prohibition. To an increasing extent they fished in the Channel, in the Thames Estuary and in the North Sea to supply the London area and sold their catches to British vessels called 'carriers' or 'hatch-boats'. Payment was made on the spot in gold sovereigns. These carriers, after collecting the catches in baskets from a number of vessels, both British and foreign, would then sail to Billingsgate. (By 1833 few British boats which had actually caught fish came any further up the river than Gravesend.) The crews of the carriers had the reputation of being hard, violent characters even by the standards of the sea – 'a set of boisterous, blustering men', according to one witness – and therefore well fitted for hard bargaining with foreign fishermen.[39] The French were particularly active in this illegal traffic, their vessels, generally of between 40 and 60 tons, being at least double the size of the general run of British fishing smacks. In 1832 some French vessels came so close inshore at Broadstairs that spectators on shore 'could see them shift the basket from one vessel to the other'.[40]

The customs revenue suffered no loss when these illegal cargoes of fish were declared to be 'British caught', as no revenue could possibly arise from a product the import of which was banned; the officers of the Customs appear to have ignored this traffic and legal action against it by private individuals was difficult and unrewarding.[41] There can be no doubt therefore that a substantial and increasing proportion of the fish coming into London during the early nineteenth century was supplied by foreign fishermen.

A control in the estuary attempted to even out the flow to Billingsgate. As soon as the fishing vessels arrived off the Nore a customs officer noted the time of the arrival and allowed each vessel so many days in which to send the fish to London.[42]

There are numerous indications scattered through the *Report* of 1833 that the supply of fish available for the growing population of London was increasing. It was estimated that in 1799 2,500 tons of fish reached Billingsgate by water from the Dogger and North Sea, or about 5 lb. per head per annum. This is probably an under-estimate of total supplies to

London; for example, it excludes the considerable overland supplies, although the Revolutionary and Napoleonic Wars had certainly reduced the amount available. After 1815 fish prices at Billingsgate fell considerably, one sign of increasing supplies, and by 1823 the estimated supply of fish reaching Billingsgate by water had risen to 12,000 tons.[43]

As supplies increased, people got more choosy. So many plaice were caught in the early nineteenth century that this fish, an eighteenth-century delicacy, fell in social esteem. Michael Myers, a fishmonger in the City, said that he had been in the trade since about 1803 and considered that there had been 'a great increase' in supply, combined with a growing fastidiousness on the part of poor purchasers: 'It is a mistaken idea that a poor person will eat anything; they are more dainty than the first gentleman in the country.' In 1825 Myers had been employed by a firm called the Fish Company which tried 'to establish a sale of fish to the poor'. He gave orders to his servants 'to sell fish at almost any price, but the poor would not buy it'. Of conditions eight years later he was able to say that his warehouseman found

more difficulty in a poor person buying a bit of fish than a rich man, because if he had 100 mackerel to sell [at the end of the day] he would not get rid of them, but if he had eight or ten salmon to sell, he could get rid of them immediately.[44]

INCREASING FISH SUPPLIES

Several reasons for the increase in supplies can be identified. One was the rapidly increasing use of well-vessels, i.e. specially designed fishing boats in which the catch could be kept alive during the voyage home. A larger supply of fresh fish, as distinct from salt fish, was an improvement from the dietary point of view. This appears to have been a Dutch innovation of the seventeenth century, but its first recorded intro-duction to Britain appears to have been at Harwich in 1712, where it was used in the North Sea cod fishers.[45] The use of the well-vessel spread to the Thames estuary, when it proved to be one of the factors in the rising prosperity of the Barking fishermen[46] who ventured, both in the eighteenth and early nineteenth centuries, as far afield as Iceland. There are frequent references to the activities of the Barking smacks supplying London in the *Report* of 1833. The Barking fishermen even colonised Ramsgate in the nineteenth century.[47]

An extension of this device was the use of live-fish boxes or chests. At Grimsby, for example, cod were taken out of the well-vessels and placed in wooden chests which could hold about forty large cod. There were apertures round the chests so that they could be kept under water in the dock, and a reserve of between ten and twenty thousand live cod was constantly available at Grimsby from this source during the season

from October to January after the coming of the railways, which seem
to have benefited the fish supply to the interior of the country even
more than that to Billingsgate.[48]

Another innovation making for better supplies of fish came from the
increasing use of ice in fish preservation. In 1817 7,206 one hundred
pound boxes of iced salmon from the Scottish rivers Dee and Don were
despatched to London. By 1838 a regular steamboat service was taking
the iced salmon to Edinburgh and London.[49] In this way the fish could
be kept fresh for between six to ten days, depending on the weather.

The icing of white fish at sea was pioneered by Samuel Hewett of
Barking (1797–1871) who gave evidence before the Committee of
1833. His fishing firm, founded in 1764, had previously initiated the
procedure of fishing in organised fleets under an admiral, pooling the
catch daily and sending it direct to Billingsgate in a 'carrier'. Hewett
organised the farmers for miles around Barking to flood their fields at
the onset of winter in order to collect the ice as a regular crop:

Local farmers for miles around used to flood their fields in the winter, and
collect the ice as a regular crop. Watchers were employed in various areas of the
Thames marshes to see that as the ice was formed on ditches and canals it was
not disturbed by skaters, etc. It was cut and carted to a warehouse at Barking;
2,000 to 3,000 men, women and children were engaged in gathering it in.
Although the first supplies of thin ice were usually available in mid-November,
heavy frosts did not normally set in until after Christmas, when it was hoped to
lay in sufficient to last until the following November. As much as 10s to 15s was
sometimes paid for a cart-load of about 30 cwt of ice at the beginning of the
season, when it was particularly valuable, decreasing as the season went on to
4s at the end. The ice-house, situated in Abbey Road, then known as Fisher
Street, was about eighteen feet underground and had walls eight feet thick.
There was storage capacity for about 10,000 tons, so that probably getting on
for twice this quantity was used annually, allowing for wastage. The thin sheets
stuck together in the store under pressure.[50]

Imports of ice from Norway also began in the period 1800–25.[51]

New fishing grounds, too, contributed their quota. A large new
oyster bed was discovered in mid-channel between Shoreham and Le
Havre after the Napoleonic Wars.[52] When it is considered that the
annual street sale alone of oysters in London about 1850 was 124
millions, normally at 4 a 1d, the importance of this new source to the
diet of London cannot be overlooked.[53] The total of oysters landed at
Billingsgate in a year then was nearly 500 millions.

More important was the discovery of the 'Great Silver Pits' in the
North Sea sixty miles from the mouth of the Humber. There is a dispute
as to who discovered them – claims are made for the fishermen of
Brixham, William Sudds of Ramsgate, and Hewetts of Barking. There
can be no disputing, however, that they were discovered at some time

between 1837 and 1843 and that they were very rich – in the early days only cod, soles, turbot, brill and halibut were kept by the fishermen, the rest of the catch (plaice, haddock, whiting, ling, etc.) being thrown back into the sea as offal.[54] The type of trawler used in the Channel and the Irish Sea had to be improved and fishing gear and methods adapted to the more turbulent fishing grounds of the North Sea.

It is in the light of these developments that the well-known accounts of fish consumption in London during the late 1840s and early 1850s must be read: Henry Mayhew's *London Labour and the London Poor*, vol. I, 1851[55]; the chapter on 'Billingsgate and the fish supply' in George Dodd's *The Food of London* (1856),[56] and the anonymous *Quarterly Review* review article of 1854 generally referred to as 'The London Commissariat'.[57]

Mayhew was much impressed with the number of herrings eaten by the poorer classes of London – an estimated 875 million were sold in the streets annually, at an average price of 4 for a penny. The number landed at Billingsgate both fresh and barrelled totalled 1,225 millions.[58] Mayhew stated:

The rooms of the very neediest of our needy metropolitan population always smell of fish; most frequently of herrings. So much so, indeed, that to those who, like myself, have been in the habit of visiting their dwellings, the smell of herrings, even in comfortable homes, savours from association, so strongly of squalor and wretchedness, as to be often most oppressive. The volatile oil of the fish seems to hang about the walls and beams of the room for ever.[59]

What impressed Dodd and the anonymous author of 'The London Commissariat' was the improvement in fish supplies brought about by the new railway network: Dodd uses the phrase 'fish-train' in inverted commas as if it were a fairly new coinage in 1856:[60]

Of old nine-tenths of the supply came by way of the river, the little that came by land being conveyed from the coast, at great expense, in four-horse vans. Now the railways are day by day supplanting smacks, and in many cases steamers; for by means of its iron arms, London, whilst its millions slumber, grasps the produce of every sea that beats against our island coast, and ere they have uprisen it is drawn to a focus in this central mart. Thus every night in the season the hardy fishermen of Yarmouth catch a hundred tons (12,081 yearly), principally herring, which, by means of the Eastern Counties Railway, are next morning at Billingsgate. The South-Western Railway sends up annually, with the same speed, 4,000 tons of mackerel and other fish, the gatherings of the south coast. The North-Western collects over night the 'catch' from Ireland, Scotland and the north-east coast of England, and adds to the Thames-street mart 3,578 tons, principally of salmon, whilst the Great Northern delivers to the early morning market, or sometimes later in the day, 3,248 tons of like sea produce. The Great Western brings up the harvests of the Cornish and Devonshire coasts, chiefly mackerel and pilchards, to the amount of 1,560 tons in the year; and the Brighton and South Coast conveys the incredible number of 15,000 bushels of oysters, besides 4,000 tons of other fish. Nearly one-half in fact of the fish-supply of London, instead of following as of old the tedious route of the coast, is hurried in the dead of night across the length and breadth of the land to Billingsgate.[61]

There is little wonder that by the 1850s the old Elizabethan Billingsgate market had become inadequate and had to be replaced from August 1852 onwards by a new and more spacious building, of which the architect was J.B. Bunning.[62]

TABLE, SHOWING THE QUANTITY, WEIGHT, OR MEASURE OF THE FOLLOWING KINDS OF FISH SOLD IN BILLINGSGATE MARKET IN THE COURSE OF THE YEAR (c. 1850).

Description of Fish	Number of Fish	Weight or Measure of Fish	Proportion sold by Costermongers
WET FISH		lbs	
Salmon and Salmon Trout (29,000 boxes, 14 fish per box)	406,000	3,480,000	One-twentieth
Live Cod (averaging 10 lbs each)	400,000	4,000,000	One-fourth
Soles (averaging ¼ lb each)	97,520,000	26,880,000	One-fifteenth
Whiting (averaging 6 oz. each)	17,920,000	6,720,000	One-fourth
Haddock (averaging 2 lbs each)	2,470,000	5,040,000	One-tenth
Plaice (averaging 1 lb each)	33,600,000	33,600,000	Seven-eighths
Mackerel (averaging 1 lb each)	23,520,000	23,520,000	Two-thirds
Fresh Herrings (250,000 barrels, 700 fish per barrel)	175,000,000	42,00,0000	One-half
Fresh Herrings (in bulk)	1,050,000,000	252,000,000	Three-fourths
Sprats	—	4,000,000	Three-fourths
Eels from Holland .. ⎱(6 fish		1,505,280	One-fourth
„ England and Ireland⎰per 1 lb)	9,797,760	127,680	One-fourth
Flounders (7,200 quarterns, 36 fish per quartern)	259,200	43,200	All
Dabs (7,500 quarterns, 36 fish per quartern)	270,000	48,750	All
DRY FISH			
Barrelled Cod (15,000 barrels, 50 fish per barrel)	750,000	4,200,000	One-eighth
Dried Salt Cod (5 lbs each)	1,600,000	8,000,000	One-tenth
Smoked Haddock (65,000 barrels, 300 fish per barrel)	19,500,000	10,920,000	One-eighth
Bloaters (165,000 baskets, 150 fish per basket)	147,000,000	10,600,000	One-fourth
Red Herrings (100,000 barrels, 500 fish per barrel)	50,000,000	14,000,000	One-half
Dried Sprats (9,600 large bundles, 30 fish per bundle)*	288,000	96,000	None
SHELL FISH			
Oysters (309,935 barrels, 1,600 fish per barrel)	495,896,000	—	One-fourth
Lobsters (averaging 1 lb each fish)	1,200,000	1,200,000	One-twentieth
Crabs (averaging 1 lb each fish)	600,000	600,000	One-twelfth
Shrimps (324 to the pint)	498,428,648	192,295 gals.	One-half
Whelks (224 to the ½ bushel)	4,943,200	24,300 ½ bus.†	All
Mussels (1,000 to the ½ bushel)	50,400,000	50,400 „	Two-thirds
Cockles (2,000 to the ½ bushel)	67,392,000	32,400 „	Three-fourths
Periwinkles (4,000 to the ½ bushel)	304,000,000	76,000 „	Three-fourths

* Costermongers dry their own sprats.

† The half-bushel measure at Billingsgate is double quantity – or, more correctly, a bushel.

(From H. Mayhew, *London Labour and the London Poor*, Vol. I, 1851, p. 63. Mayhew compiled this table from information furnished 'by the most eminent of the Billingsgate salesmen'.)

FISH CONSUMPTION OUTSIDE LONDON

Apart from London little is as yet known about the supply of fish to the industrial cities and large towns of Britain in the nineteenth century. The latest large-scale study of Birmingham, the most inland of our great cities, reveals only the bare facts that a fish market had been established there by about 1791 and that a wholesale fish market was opened in 1869 and extended in 1883.[63]

At Manchester the fishmarket seems to have been well supplied with sea-fish for an inland town, even in the early 1790s, for Aikin reported as follows:

> With fish, Manchester is better provided than might be expected from its inland situation. The greatest quantity of sea-fish comes from the Yorkshire coast, consisting of large cod, lobsters and turbots, of which last, many are sent even to Liverpool, on an overflow of the market. Soles chiefly of a small size, come from the Lancashire coast. Salmon are brought in plenty from the Rivers Mersey and Ribble, principally the latter.[64]

Clearly a system of transport by fast coaches and vans from the Yorkshire coast, similar to that already noted as operating from the Cinque ports and Brixham, must have existed.[65] In 1857 Manchester Corporation opened a large wholesale fish market at Shudehill, although nothing is known of the quantities passing through it or of its commercial organisation.

In the case of Liverpool the only significant piece of information discovered so far is that salt cod was 'until recently a customary Sunday dish amongst working-class families' in that city, a custom which must go back to the eighteenth century and earlier.[66]

Miss Janet Blackman's article on the food supply of Sheffield in the nineteenth century, however, gives some illuminating details about the improvement in fish supplies to the town which followed the construction in the 1840s of what later became the Manchester, Sheffield and Lincolnshire Railway.[67] The railway company resuscitated and developed the ancient fishing port of Grimsby from 1848 onwards. Fish landed there in the earlier part of the century had been largely used for fertiliser. By 1863 numerous fishing vessels had been attracted to Grimsby from other ports; in that year there were 70 trawling smacks and 43 live cod smacks fishing out of Grimsby, but by 1873 the numbers had risen to 248 and 82 respectively. At the same time a rapid increase in the average size of vessel took place. Landings of fish rose from 1,500 in 1856 to 31,000 in 1872, excluding fish shipped in carriers direct to Billingsgate. In 1858 the Manchester, Sheffield and Lincolnshire Railway offered Grimsby fish merchants free railway tickets when they went on business journeys securing orders.[68] It is not surprising to find that a new wholesale fish market had to be built at Sheffield under the

Market Act of 1872, as the town had gradually become a centre of redistribution for the vast markets of the West Riding and Lancashire.[69]

FRIED FISH

Finally we come to the fried fish industry in the nineteenth century. It is not known how long this activity has been a commercial one, but the large-scale frying of fish for retail sale may date back to Chaucer's time. The frying of fish in oil or fat, beside cooking it, also arrests and camouflages decay temporarily; the rise of the trade in the early nineteenth century was essentially a response to the increased availability of fish, especially plaice, soles, haddock, whiting, flounders and herrings, at Billingsgate, i.e. in Cutting's words it was a method of 'fish saving'. Dickens in *Oliver Twist*, published in 1837–8, mentions 'a fried-fish ware house'[70] in Field Lane, Fagin's quarter, in phrases which suggest that these establishments were part of the normal neighbourhood components of the central London rookeries. Madame Rachel, the notorious and fraudulent beautician of mid-Victorian times, kept a fried-fish shop in the 1850s near to the present site of the London School of Economics (Vere Street in Clare Market).[71] According to Mayhew[72] the number of itinerant street sellers of fried fish in Central London varied from 250 to 350, apart from stall-keepers who sold it only on Saturday nights and perhaps Monday nights. One such seller told Mayhew that a liberal allowance of oil 'will conceal anything'; a good deal of the fried fish sold came from fishmongers' end-of-the-day stocks. By 1851 one tradesman in Cripplegate had installed 'a commodious oven which he had built for the frying, or rather baking, of fish' in order to go into the wholesale business and cook fish for some of the retailers.[73] This may, indeed, have been one of the 'warehouses' which Dickens had in mind. One costermonger selling fried fish told Mayhew that sales were best in a gin-drinking neighbourhood, 'for people hasn't their smell so correct there'.[74]

In mid-Victorian times fish frying expanded alongside the frying of chipped potatoes, and soon iron founders and engineers began to manufacture coal grates and ranges which would mitigate the nuisances to which wholesale fish-frying in open pans gave rise. A vivid and nauseating description of early fish frying is quoted by Cutting.[75]

It has been suggested that the high proportion of women and girls employed in the Lancashire cotton industry, leading to a dearth of domestic labour in working-class houses, led to the adoption of fish and chips as a ready made meal,[76] but the historical process whereby fish and chips became associated seems to be obscure and certainly complicated.

Today a large percentage of fish and chip frying ranges are manufactured in Lancashire, and the oldest surviving firm engaged in the business, Faulkner and Co., restaurant engineers, of Hollins Road, Oldham, founded in 1862, is believed to have started by manufacturing ranges solely for chip frying between about 1870–75. They were supplied to local tripe dressers who installed them at the rear of their shops. A Mrs 'Granny' Duce, who had had a shop or chain of shops selling chips at first in one of the West Riding towns and later at High Wycombe, Bucks, since 1854 (the firm is still in existence), started ordering ranges from Faulkner and Co. in the 1880s. It is claimed that Mrs Duce was the first person to fry chips for public sale and this may well be so.[77] The custom is said to have been introduced from France. It is significant that Mayhew does not mention chip-sellers in his classic work of 1851. The firm of John Rouse (Oldham) Ltd., founded by John Rouse (d. 1921) in 1880, claims to be the firm which popularised the joint sale of fish and chips. Rouse was an Oldham cotton mill engineer who devised a fish and chip frying range on wheels called the 'Dandy' with a long chimney resembling that on the 'Rocket'. From this vehicle he sold fish and gave away chips with them at Oldham's Tommyfield market, in a successful attempt to popularise the combination.[78] Such were the humble origins of a trade which provides balanced meals to an industrialised population and accounts today for one quarter of all the fish consumed in the country.

NOTES

'Trends in Fish Consumption' is reprinted from T.C. Barker, J.C. MacKenzie and J. Yudkin (eds.), *Our Changing Fare* (MacGibbon and Kee, 1966), pp.94–114.

1. H. Mayhew, *London Labour and the London Poor* (1851), vol.8, p.78. In 1833, John Goldham, Yeoman of the Waterside and Clerk of Billingsgate Market under the Corporation of London, stated, 'The lower class of people [in London] entertain the notion that fish is not substantial food enough for them, and they prefer meat; but at times, when mackerel and herrings become very cheap, they eat a great deal of them' (*Report of the Select Committee on British Channel Fisheries*, Parl. Paper 676, of 1833, p.94, q.1704).
2. For the game laws see J.L. and B. Hammond, *The Village Labourer 1760–1832*, (1911), pp.184–99, and two articles by Chester Kirby, 'The English game law system', *American Historical Review* (1932–33), Vol.38, pp.240–62 and *Journal of Modern History* (1932), Vol.4.
3. G.A. Chinnery (ed.), *Records of the Borough of Leicester* (1965), Vol.V, p.62.
4. *Ibid.*, p.213.
5. *Ibid.*, pp.52, 111.
6. P.205. The volume was compiled in the early 1790s.
7. *The Memoirs of Sir Daniel Fleming*, ed. W.G. Collingwood, *Cumb. and Westm. A.A. Soc.* Tract Series, No.XI (1928), pp.83–4. I am indebted for this reference to Dr Joan Thirsk.

8. *1st Report from the Select Committee appointed to inquire into the State of the British Fisheries,* 11 May 1785 in *Reports from Committees of the House of Commons* (1803), Vol.X, p.12. The duty on English salt used for fish curing at this time was 7s per bushel, on foreign salt 10s per bushel of 84 lb.
9. For the salt tax, see E. Hughes, *Studies in Administration and Finance, 1558–1825* (1934).
10. *1st Report* (1785), *op.cit.,* p.21.
11. *Report on the State of the British Herring Fisheries,* 1798. Reports from Committees of the House of Commons (1803), Vol.X, pp.250–2, 263–5.
12. *1st Report* (1785), *op.cit.,* p.21.
13. C.L. Cutting, *Fish Saving* (1955), p.208.
14. *3rd Report* (1785), *op.cit.,* p.61.
15. See John Rowe, *Cornwall in the Age of the Industrial Revolution* (1953), pp.262–304.
16. *Report from the Committee, appointed to inquire into the State of the Pilchard Fisheries,* 26 April 1785, in Reports from Committees of the House of Commons (1803), vol.X, p.4.
17. Rowe, *op.cit.,* p.283.
18. Rowe, *op.cit.,* p.283.
19. For early fishery schemes see W.R. Scott, *The Constitution and Finance of English, Scottish and Irish Joint-Stock Companies to 1720* (1910–12), 3 vols.
20. *The Highland Economy, 1750–1850* (1957), pp.108–9.
21. *Ibid.,* p.109.
22. Cutting, *op.cit.,* pp.94–5. For the origins and vicissitudes of the project see J.M. Mitchell, *The Herring* (1864), pp.193–211.
23. Cutting, *op.cit.,* pp.97, 214. Mitchell, *op.cit.,* pp.219–21.
24. *3rd Report* (1785), *op.cit.,* Appendix, Dr James Anderson, p.81.
25. *Ibid.,* pp.139–40.
26. *Ibid.,* p.24.
27. *Ibid.,* p.140.
28. *The Substance of the Speech of Henry Beaufoy, Esq., to the British Society for extending the Fisheries* ... (1788), pp.36–7.
29. Cutting, *op.cit.,* p.97.
30. *3rd Report* (1785), *op.cit.,* p.140.
31. Gray, *op.cit.,* pp.158–60.
32. John Adams, *Index Villaris* (1680), preface.
33. *First Report on the State of the British Fisheries,* 1786 (Reports from Committees of the House of Commons, Vol.X, 1803, p.192, appendix). In 1817 it was stated by a Parliamentary Committee that 'all the lower ranks of society' in South Devon subsisted chiefly on fish. J.M. Mitchell, *The Herring* (1864), p.287.
34. *Report from the Select Committee on British Channel Fisheries* in Parliamentary Paper No.676 of 1833; House of Commons Papers (1833), Vol.XIV, evidence of Charles Golden of Folkestone p.46, qq.609–10, evidence of Wm. Breach of Hastings, pp.76–7, qq.1311–39. Similarly, a schoolboy travelling from Leeds to London in 1789 noted that the coach 'was so overburthened with Fish that we came all the way with six horses'. E. Hughes, *North Country Life* (1965), II, pp.321–2.
35. *Ibid.,* pp.110–1, q.2085.
36. *Ibid.,* p.76, q.1316.
37. *Ibid.,* p.76, q.1335.
38. *Ibid.,* p.87, q.1566.
39. *Report from the Select Committee on British Channel Fisheries* (1833), p.84, qq.1506–10.
40. *Ibid.,* pp.79–80, qq.1418–23.
41. See *Report* of the Select Committee of 1833, passim, and esp. evidence of Francis Tapley, pp.83–4, qq.1486–1505.
42. *Ibid.,* pp.84, 167–8.
43. Cutting, *op.cit.,* pp.207, 219.

44. *Report from the Select Committee on British Channel Fishery* (1833), p.98, q.1778.
45. Cutting, *op.cit.*, pp.118, 203–6.
46. *Ibid.*, pp.158, 204.
47. *Ibid.*, p.208.
48. *Ibid.*, p.211.
49. *Ibid.*, p.216.
50. *Ibid.*, p.222.
51. *Ibid.*, pp.223–4.
52. G. Dodd, *The Food of London* (1856), p.361.
53. H. Mayhew, *op.cit.*, Vol.I, p.78.
54. Cutting, *op.cit.*, pp.220–1.
55. *Ibid.*, pp.61–78 and 163–70.
56. *Ibid.*, pp.330–6.
57. *Quarterly Review* (June–September 1854), Vol.95, pp.271–308. The author of the article is identified in the *Wellesley Index to Victorian Periodicals* (1966), I, p.378 as Andrew Wynter (1819–76), physician: the article itself is reprinted in *Curiosities of Civilisation* (1860).
58. Mayhew, *op.cit.*, p.63.
59. *Ibid.*, p.62.
60. Dodd, *op.cit.*, p.344.
61. 'The London Commissariat', p.273.
62. Dodd, *op.cit.*, pp.346–8. See also Dodd's remarks on the unsuccessful attempt to set up a rival to Billingsgate at Hungerford in 1831 (p.346).
63. *Victoria County History of Warwick* (1964), p.251.
64. *Description of the Country from Thirty to Forty Miles round Manchester* (1795), pp.204–5.
65. It is known, too, that in 1833 Yarmouth herrings were sent in considerable numbers to 'Yorkshire, Liverpool and Lancashire' (*Report* of 1833, p.135).
66. Cutting, *op.cit.*, p.182.
67. Janet Blackman, 'The Food Supply of an Industrial Town', *Business History* (1963), Vol.V, no.2, pp.93–4.
68. Cutting, *op.cit.*, p.234.
69. Blackman, *op.cit.*, p.94.
70. Chapter XXVI.
71. F. Boase, *Modern Biographical Dictionary* (1892; rep. Cass, 1965), vol.III, p.3. Clare Market was also well known as the location of a celebrated street seller of hot eels (Mayhew, *op.cit.*, p.160).
72. Mayhew, *op.cit.*, pp.165–70.
73. *Ibid.*, p.166.
74. *Ibid.*
75. Cutting, *op.cit.*, p.241. For the popularity of fried fish in home cooking, see James Greenwood, *Journeys through London* (1867).
76. *Ibid.*
77. Private communication from Mr J.K.W. Faulkner, to whom the author is grateful. The White Fish Authority has assisted local celebrations in 1965 of the centenary of the 'fish and chip partnership' but the evidence for this is not clear, *Guardian*, 17 Sept. 1965.
78. See anon, 'The History of the House of John Rouse (Oldham) Ltd', *Fish Trades Gazette*, 18 July 1936. The author wishes to thank John Rouse (Oldham) Ltd. for information about the firm's history. See also correspondence in *Sunday Times*, 5, 12 and 19 June 1960. There are two other manufacturers of fish-frying ranges in the Oldham area: James Stott and Co. (Engineers) Ltd of Royton and G. Mallinson and Sons, Ltd of Crossbank Street, Oldham.

PART FIVE

MONETARY STANDARDS
AND
IMPERIAL TRADE

18

Currency Problems of the British Empire, 1814–1914

Only rarely do economic historians pay much attention to the numismatic side of their subject, and conversely, writers on numismatics frequently either ignore completely the social and economic background of the coin series with which they are dealing or present a few scraps of history with such naivety and inaccuracy that economic historians become suspicious of their competence even in the numismatic field. Philip Grierson's plea, made in 1948, for the 'more perfect marriage of numismatics and history'[1] seems to have been largely ignored.[2] This contribution is an attempt to show how the two disciplines may be combined, particularly as the use of coinage was one of the most effective ways in which the people were brought into everyday contact with the State and educated in the practicalities of economic and financial life. Indeed, it is safe to say that the educative power of money has been greater than that of all the popular textbooks on economics ever written.[3]

It has often been pointed out that the so-called 'British empire', a convenient phrase which had no legal meaning, covered a diversity of territories even in 1814, territories which contained peoples with widely differing cultures and standards of living. Between 1814 and 1914 the collection of imperial territories became even more heterogeneous, ranging from the headhunters of Borneo and Sarawak to representatives of such ancient civilisations as the Chinese of Hong Kong and Wei-hai-wei and the subtle Greeks of Cyprus.

THE ORIGINS OF THE GOLD SOVEREIGN STANDARD

In 1814 no uniform system of currency existed in the empire, but from 1816 to 1821 two powerful unifying forces existed: first, a newly equipped Royal Mint on Tower Hill in London and, secondly, the British gold standard and its monetary expression, the British gold sovereign or 20s piece (£1 sterling). The spread of the sovereign as an international unit naturally aided the growth of the economic power of the City of London in the century of the *Pax Britannica*. Other countries showed their faith in the gold standard by allowing British sovereigns to circulate freely instead of striking their own gold coins in sufficient quantity, e.g. Chalmers stated in 1893, '... the gold currency of Portugal consists mainly of British sovereigns'.[4] As late as 1920 it could be said of the land-locked republic of Bolivia, high in the Andes: 'British sovereigns and Peruvian gold are the only coins accepted to an unlimited extent at a fixed value of B[oliviano]s 12.50.'[5]

The adoption by the second Lord Liverpool's government of a gold standard between 1816 and 1821 was not, as has sometimes been suggested in the textbooks, a far-seeing move, but rather a measure to restore Sir Isaac Newton's eighteenth-century gold standard system, which had been rudely interfered with by the liquidity crisis of 1797 and the consequent suspension of cash payments. After 1797 Britain managed with a paper currency and gold guineas circulated at a varying premium in terms of paper pounds.[6]

Under the terms of Lord Liverpool's[7] Coinage Act of 1816 (56 Geo. III, c. 68) the new gold unit or sovereign (20s) was to replace the old guinea (21s), last struck in 1813. These sovereigns weighed 'five penny-weights, three grains 2740/10,000 troy weight of *standard* gold', i.e. they were to be 22 carat (fine or pure gold is 24 carat), and were to be legal tender to any amount.[8] Private persons could have their gold bullion freely coined into sovereigns at the mint at the rate of £3 17s 10½d per standard ounce (or £4 4s 11d per fine ounce).

Sovereigns and half-sovereigns were accordingly put into circulation in 1817. Under the terms of the Act provision was also made for a badly needed coinage of sixpences, shillings, half-crowns (2s 6d) and crowns (5s) at the rate of 66s sterling silver, i.e. 92.5 per cent fine, to the pound troy (12 oz). These remained the standards of weight and fineness of the British silver coinage until 1920. By the end of 1817 £2.5 millions' worth of the new silver coins had been minted and put into circulation, but they were not legal tender for debts of more than 40s. The Act also provided that after a date to be proclaimed it should be lawful for any person to bring any quantity of silver bullion to the mint and have it coined at the rate of 62s to the pound troy; the remaining 4s out of the pound troy was to be taken by the mint for its trouble. It was clearly the intention of the framers of the Act that there should be a free coinage of gold side-by-side with an almost free coinage of silver. The proclamation was, in fact, never issued, and the country was thereby saved from the confusions of a so-called bimetallic standard.

The successful restoration of a gold standard and the maintenance of the new silver currency in circulation depended on the price of silver remaining below 5s 6d per standard or sterling ounce (i.e. 66s per lb troy). Above this price there would be a temptation to melt down or export the new silver currency. In fact in 1815 the price of silver had fluctuated between 5s 9d (low) and 6s 9½d (high) per standard ounce, but had then fallen rapidly in 1816 to between 4s 11½d and 5s 4½d per ounce. Only in 1818 did silver reach 5s 6d for a short period, and until 1872 it fluctuated within very narrow limits around 5s per ounce, so that although the new British silver currency of the nineteenth century became a subsidiary token currency, it contained very nearly its face value in silver until the great fall in the value of silver began after 1872.

It should be borne in mind that until the 1870s a gold standard of the British type was regarded as unusual. Only one major financial power, the Netherlands, followed Great Britain's example after the Napoleonic wars, and so strong was the belief in the stability of silver that even the Dutch switched from what was practically gold monometallism to silver monometallism in 1847, because her statesmen believed

it had proved disastrous to the commercial and industrial interests of Holland to have a monetary system identical with that of England, whose financial revulsions, after the adoption of the gold standard, had been more frequent and severe than in any other country.[9]

Even in Britain all statesmen did not regard the question of the standard as a settled issue. In 1826, after the liquidity crisis of 1825, Huskisson actually proposed that the government should issue silver certificates which would be full legal tender. In 1828 the banker Alexander Baring gave it as his opinion that the gold standard, far from being the cause of Britain's commercial prosperity, was a hindrance to it, as it tended to isolate her from those countries which were on a silver basis, i.e. most of the rest of the world.[10] Even as late as 1844 Peel introduced a clause into the Bank Charter Act allowing the Bank of England to hold up to a quarter of its metallic reserves, against which notes could be issued, in the form of silver bullion.[11]

Most of the sovereigns – possibly as many as two-thirds – struck at the Royal Mint between 1816 and 1914 were exported. For example, in the ten years 1852–61, busy years for the London mint, 58,495,000 sovereigns were struck, but no fewer than 37,505,000 were exported. During the seven years ending 31 December 1910, another busy period for the mint, 104 million sovereigns were struck, but during the same period 86 millions were exported or withdrawn for remelting as being too light. It is estimated that of the 460 million sovereigns issued since the accession of Victoria in 1837 only 120 million were still in circulation in Great Britain and Ireland in 1914.[12]

THE EMPIRE OF THE RUPEE

While Great Britain struggled to maintain a gold standard with some difficulty the East India Company, on the other side of the world, was moving inexorably towards a silver standard. Like any other benevolent despotism of the eighteenth century the court of directors had begun to reform, to concentrate and to simplify the administrative arrangements, and among them the currency systems, of the diverse territories under its control. The basic currency unit of the Mughal empire had been the silver rupee, which, considering the political anarchy of eighteenth-century India, differed remarkably little in weight and silver content from mint to mint. The company had minted currencies under licence from the Mughal emperors and lesser native rulers since the 1670s, and by 1800 controlled a considerable number of mints in its three presidencies of Bombay, Calcutta and Madras.[13] The guidelines of reform were laid down by the court of directors of the company in a despatch dated 25 April 1806 which expounded theory and then fixed a new rupee of account:

It is an opinion supported by the best authorities, and proved by experience, that coins of gold and silver cannot circulate as legal tenders of payment at fixed relative values ... without loss; this loss is occasioned by the fluctuating value of the metals of which the coins are formed. A proportion between the gold and silver coin is fixed by law, according to the value of the metals, and it may be on the justest principles, but owing to the change of circumstances gold may become of greater value in relation to silver than at the time the proportion was fixed, it therefore becomes profitable to exchange silver for gold, so the coin of that metal is withdrawn from circulation; and if silver should increase in its value in relation to gold, the same circumstances would tend to reduce the quantity of silver coin in circulation. As it is impossible to prevent the fluctuation in the value of the metals, so it is also equally impracticable to prevent the consequences thereof on the coins made from these metals ... To adjust the relative values of gold and silver coin according to the fluctuations in the values of the metals would create continual difficulties, and the establishment of such a principle would of itself tend to perpetuate inconvenience and loss.

The court then laid it down that 'silver should be the universal money of account [in India], and that all ... accounts should be kept in the same denominations of rupees, annas and pice ...'.[14] The new rupee was to be of the gross weight of 180 grains troy, of which 15 grains were to be base metal alloy, so that the company's new rupee would contain 165 grains troy of fine silver and be eleven-twelfths fine.

The court of directors wished not merely to rationalise the currency of its Indian possessions but also to facilitate the transfer of money or 'supply' between the three presidencies, for although each presidency had its own fiscal system and mints, yet they depended upon one another for the finance of their deficits, and the money coined at the mints of one presidency was not legal tender in the territories of the other two; e.g on 9 April 1824 the Bombay government had been forced to issue a proclamation declaring rupees of 1819 minted at Farrukhabad in Bengal as legal tender within its territories in order to facilitate the transfer of money from Bengal to Bombay.

But things moved slowly in the East, and not until 1835 could it be said that the directors' orders of 1806 had been carried out in their entirety. In 1818 the Madras presidency superseded its old Arcot rupee and proclaimed the new one of 180 grains troy, eleven-twelfths fine, as the standard. Bombay presidency followed suit in 1824, but in the Bengal presidency the situation was complicated by the existence of mints at Benares, Farrukhabad, Murshidabad and Sagar as well as that at Calcutta. The Benares mint was closed down in 1819, the Farrukhabad mint in 1825 and the Sagar mint in 1835, but the Bengal presidency was reluctant to abandon its 'heavy' *sicca* rupee (192 grains troy, eleven-twelfths fine, i.e. containing 176 grains of fine silver) and wished, like Bombay and Madras, to continue coining gold mohurs (fifteen-rupee pieces) at a fixed ratio to the silver rupee:

At the end of 1833, therefore, the position was that the Court desired to have a uniform currency with a single standard of silver, while the authorities [i.e. the governments of the three presidencies] in India wished for a common currency with a bimetallic standard.[15]

The India Act of 1833 setting up a unitary Government of India was followed by the passing of a Currency Act (xvii of 1835) overruling the wishes of the presidencies, and finally fixing the silver rupee weighing 180 grains troy, and containing 165 grains troy of fine silver, as the common currency and sole legal tender throughout the Indian territories of the East India Company. Dies for the Indian mints at Bombay, Calcutta and Madras now came from the London mint, and the new standard rupees of 1835, although struck in the name of the East India Company as agent for the imperial government, bore for the first time the head of a British monarch, William IV. The Government of India's Act XIX of 1861 set up a Department of Paper Currency, modelled on the British Bank Charter Act of 1844, to issue State paper money, but the average note circulation for 1882–91 was only 15.74 million rupees, i.e. around £1 million.[16]

The need for safeguarding the overland route to India via Egypt, the extension of British power in India itself and later the emigration of Indian merchants and labourers led to a rapid expansion of the 'Empire of the Rupee' after 1835. Ceylon, which had become a British Crown colony after 1801, continued for a time on the old Dutch colonial standard, in which the rix-dollar (*rijks–daalder*), valued at 1s 6d British, was divided into 192 doits or 48 stuivers. In 1825 the British sterling system was introduced for government accounts, and at various dates between 1828 and 1842 the London mint coined, first, copper half farthings and then quarter farthings for circulation in Ceylon. Silver 1½d pieces were also struck between 1834 and 1862. These minute coins were designed to replace the old Madras silver fanams, twelve of which passed for 1s 6d. or one rix-dollar.

In spite of all this the pull of the rupee area to the north prevailed. Rupees imported from Madras formed so large a proportion of the local monetary circulation that the governor of Ceylon issued a proclamation in 1836 rating the East India Company's rupee at 2s sterling, and although Ceylon government accounts continued to be kept in sterling until 1869, the Indian rupee was formally adopted as the currency unit between 1869 and 1872, with a series of distinctive Ceylon subsidiary coins at the rate of 100 cents to the rupee, and ranging in value from fifty cents to a quarter of a cent.[17]

In Aden, annexed by Britain in 1839 and administered by the East India Company and the Government of India successively, the Indian rupee, with its fractional subsidiary pieces, became the local monetary unit. In the neighbouring imamate of Muscat and Oman the Indian rupee became the money of account shortly afterwards, and from 1894 the Imam began to issue his own one-twelfth and quarter annas.

The enterprise of Indian traders in East Africa was reflected in the adoption by the Sultan of Zanzibar of a coinage system based on 192 pysa (pies) to the Indian rupee, and the striking of copper quarter annas and silver rials equal to two Indian rupees in 1882. In 1888 the Imperial British East Africa Company put into circulation from its offices in Mombasa (Kenya) bronze quarter annas and silver rupees struck at Ralph Heaton & Sons' private mint at Birmingham, and after the declaration of East Africa as a British protectorate the striking of bronze quarter annas bearing the head of Queen Victoria began in the year of the diamond jubilee. From 1905 the Indian rupees circulating in East Africa were supplemented by distinctive fractional coins of fifty, twenty-five, ten, five, one and half cent at the rate of 100 cents to one rupee. Between 1909 and 1921 the government of Italian Somaliland formally acknowledged the fact that its territory formed part of the rupee area by striking a coinage based on 100 besa to the silver 'rupia'. To the south the German East African Company found it convenient to adopt the rupee unit in 1890 for its local currency in Tanganyika (German East Africa), coining bronze one-pesa (i.e. quarter anna) pieces from 1890 to 1892, silver one-rupee pieces of Indian standard from 1890, quarter and half rupees from 1891 and a few two-rupee pieces in 1893 and 1894. These, however, bore distinctive German legends and the portrait of the emperor Wilhelm II and were manufactured in Berlin, not in Bombay.[18] The 'Empire of the Rupee' ceased to hold sway south of Tanganyika, a fact made quite clear by a *cri de coeur* from the diary of Sergeant Pearman of the 3rd (King's Own) Light Dragoons, who sailed home from Karachi to England with his regiment in 1853. The troopship put in at Cape Town to take on fresh water and stores:

I went on shore with others to change our rupees into English money; but at the Cape they were two pence less value to us than in India, but we had to lose it. In India the rupee is to the soldier 2s 0½d but at the Cape they would only give us 1s 10½d for the rupee, and in England 1s 9½d for the rupee, so they had us all ways.[19]

When the British occupied the Ile de France in the Indian Ocean in 1810 and restored its Dutch name of Mauritius they found the pre-1792 French currency system in operation and indeed in 1822, under British sovereignty, pieces of twenty-five and fifty sous were issued for the island in billon (base silver heavily alloyed with copper). In so far as the British government can be said to have had any settled policy for colonial currency immediately after the Napoleonic wars it found expression in the striking in the London mint in 1820, for circulation in Mauritius, of the so-called silver 'anchor' money, bearing the name and titles of George IV in denominations of a half, a quarter, one-eighth and one-sixteenth of a dollar, and designed to provide change for the Spanish American 'pillar' dollars or pieces-of-eight (8 reales) which circulated universally in the West Indies and north America, over wide areas in west Africa and in various places bordering on the Indian Ocean, in south-east Asia and Australia.[20] The experiment was repeated in 1822, when the same four denominations of 'anchor' money were struck for circulation in the West Indian islands. They do not appear to have been popular, and no further strikings were made.[21] The large-scale emigration of Indian labourers to Mauritius for work on the sugar plantations reinforced the already strong links with mainland India, particularly as a class of Indian traders developed, and the Indian rupee, with its subdivisions, became the everyday unit of currency. Chalmers noted in1893 that for a time the opening up of Australia and the gold discoveries there from 1851 onwards 'threatened to make gold permanently the standard in Mauritius, but the opening of the Suez Canal in 1869, whilst dealing a heavy blow at the commerce of the colony, swept the island back into the Indian "currency area" ...'[22] A Mauritius order-in-council and a subsequent proclamation of 12 August 1876 made the Indian rupee the only legal tender unit and, as in Ceylon, the government of Mauritius ordered fractional coins (20c, 10c, 5c, 2c and 1c) to be struck in Britain from 1877 to 1897 and from 1911 to 1924 onwards at 100 cents to the rupee. The Indian rupee also circulated in the Seychelles group of islands to the north.[23]

On the other side of the Indian Ocean the independent kings of Burma, Mindon Min (1852–78) and Thebaw (1878–85), had issued copper, silver and gold coins in anna/rupee denominations even before the country was occupied by the government of India. Their silver 'peacock' rupees (1852, 1880) were approximately of the same size, weight and fineness as the Indian rupee, and indeed their advanced workmanship suggests a product of Western technology.[24] With the annexation of Burma in 1885 and the substitution of Indian currency for King Thebaw's, the 'Empire of the Rupee' reached almost its greatest extent – from the south-western frontiers of China on the banks of the river Mekong in the east to the eastern borders of the Belgian Congo in the west, from Mauritius in the south to the borders of Afghanistan and Tibet in the north. Large quantities of Indian rupees went through the Himalayan passes into central Asia and the outlying parts of the Celestial Empire. Even inside the Chinese empire the Tibetan government issued in 1903 large numbers of silver coins struck in Szechwan which were nothing more than Chinese-style copies of the genuine rupee bearing the familiar features of the Empress of India.

THE EXTENSION OF THE STERLING AREA AND THE GOLD DISCOVERIES IN AUSTRALIA AND SOUTH AFRICA

After the failure of the 'anchor' money of 1820 and 1822 to become popular enough to create a continuing demand for further strikings, and the survival of the gold standard after the crisis of 1825, the British Treasury and mint worked to spread the use of the sterling system in various ways. One means of furthering this was by issuing small-value coins for colonial circulation which fitted into the monetary system of the mother country.[25] An early example of this method was the issue from 1827 onwards of a one-third farthing coin for Malta in substitution for the local unit of Sicilian origin known as the grano (grain), although 2.8 million silver 120-grani pieces (dollar size) struck by the defunct Kingdom of the Two Sicilies continued to circulate in Malta until they were repatriated, largely by Maltese government action, in 1885. Similarly the silver 1½d piece of 1834 for Ceylon already mentioned was exported to the West Indies, where it served as a substitute for the Spanish American silver quarter real, together with a new silver 3d piece or half real. An identical silver 3d piece was issued for Malta in 1840.

The second means was the order-in-council of 23 March 1825.[26] This had been preceded by a long and detailed Treasury minute of 11 February of the same year[27] detailing the various currency systems of the British colonies and possessions, where other ranks (but not officers) in some of the British army stations had been complaining through their paymasters that they were paid not in British sterling coin but largely in Spanish dollars at army-fixed rates which were often of long standing and therefore inequitable. This led directly to the order-in-council of 23 March 1825 approving a directive of the Lords Commissioners of His Majesty's Treasury that:

... His Majesty's troops serving in the several British colonies and possessions abroad should, in certain cases, be paid in British silver and copper money; and that, with a view of securing the circulation of such money in those colonies, it would be expedient that an Order in Council should be issued declaring that in all those colonies where the Spanish dollar is now, either by law, fact, or practice, considered as a legal tender for the discharge of debts, or where the duties to the Government are rated or collected, or the individuals have a right to pay, in that description of coin, that a tender and payment of British silver money to the amount of 4s 4d should be considered as equivalent to the tender or payment of one Spanish dollar ...

In theory the sterling system prevailed in Australia from the first landings in Botany Bay in 1788, but in practice the local media of exchange consisted of a strange medley of British and foreign coins, mutilated and countermarked Spanish American silver dollars ('holey' dollars), receipts for stores supplied to the army commissariat and bills of exchange on the British Treasury. Finally in 1822 the unmutilated Spanish American silver dollar was recognised as the ordinary standard. Rated at 5s in local sterling, it was deliberately overvalued to keep it within the colonies until 1825, when the home government insisted on the establishment of a sterling standard and called down the exchange value of the dollar to 4s 4d in current British money.[28] As the economies of the Australian colonies expanded, British currency was imported in larger quantities, but it tended to flow back to Britain whenever the Australian colonies had an unfavourable trade balance, and for a period in the mid-nineteenth century large issues of copper and bronze penny and halfpenny tokens minted in Birmingham were issued by shop-keepers and others in the rising Australian cities.[29] Not until 1910, nine years after the Act of 1901 setting up the Commonwealth of Australia, did a separate Australian silver and bronze currency (bronze pence and halfpence, silver 3d 6d, 1s and 2s pieces) issue from the London mint.[30]

The discovery of gold in New South Wales and Victoria in 1851 and the subsequent gold rushes both transformed the monetary system of Australia and strengthened the British gold standard. Within two years of the discoveries the British government had decided to set up a branch mint at Sydney and had sent out young W. Stanley Jevons, soon to be a world-renowned economist, as one of the two deputy assay masters. Production of Sydney sovereigns began in 1855, so that diggers who had been receiving only about £3 per ounce for their produce could now receive around £4. In 1856 3 million ounces were produced; with continuing finds a second branch mint was set up at Melbourne in 1872, and a third at Perth in Western Australia in 1899. The only other branch mint which operated between 1814 and 1914 was that at Ottawa, which struck the comparatively small number of 627,834 sovereigns between 1908 and 1921.[31] Between 1855 and 1926 the Sydney mint struck over 149 million sovereigns, the Melbourne mint over $147\frac{1}{4}$ millions between 1872 and 1931, and the Perth mint over 106 millions between 1899 and 1931.[32] Although much of the Australian gold went direct to Britain, particularly before the Melbourne mint was opened, it is clear that a large number of the sovereigns found their way into the hoards, melting pots and jewellery of India. Jevons wrote in 1865:

Asia, then, is the great reservoir and sink of the precious metals. It has saved us from a commercial revolution, and taken off our hands many millions of bullion which would be worse than useless here ... it relieves us of the excess of Australian treasure.[33]

Professor S.B. Saul, looking at the problem from a different angle, and after remarking that Indian imports of bullion reached their height at over £16 million in the financial year 1859–60, goes on:

These imports of bullion tended therefore to neutralise the import of capital, since to a considerable extent they were merely used for hoarding, and so made no contributions at all to economic growth.[34]

Attempts have been made to suggest that the importance of hoarding has been exaggerated, but the official figures show that net imports of gold and silver into India between 1850 and 1886 were as in Table 1.[35]

TABLE 1

NET IMPORTS OF GOLD AND SILVER INTO INDIA, 1850–86

	£ million sterling		
	Gold	Silver	Total
1850–9	18	52	70
1860–9	59	101	160
1870–9	18	50	68
1880–6	28	50	78

Source. M.G. Mulhall, *The Dictionary of Statistics* (London, 4th edition, 1899), p.309.

This unproductive salting away of potential currency by India may have damped down the rise in the general level of world prices during the 'golden age of Victorian prosperity', but the process continued unabated during the world depression of prices between 1873 and 1896, and therefore must have contributed to the economic malaise felt by businessmen and farmers in the Atlantic economy, even though, as Professor Saul has stressed, they may well have been *malades imaginaires*. It is interesting to note how the critics of the British Raj in India play down these unhealthy economic habits of the Indian peasants, and fail to draw the conclusion that in this, as perhaps in other ways, the poverty of the Indian masses was largely self-induced. Britain is often accused of having operated a drain of bullion etc. from India; it would be nearer to the truth to say that India in the nineteenth century was to a large extent parasitic as regards bullion, capital and brains on the advanced industrial nations of Western Europe, and particularly on Britain.

At the Cape of Good Hope the old Dutch rix-dollar was superseded as the unit of account by British sterling after the order-in-council of 23 March 1825. No special coins were struck, but British currency was imported into the South African colonies throughout the nineteenth century. The discovery of gold in the Transvaal and the Orange Free State from 1886 onwards assured for 'Great Britain and the gold standard world of the late nineteenth century ... the gold supplies necessary to their economy'.[36] When the South African Republic (the Transvaal) ordered its first considerable coinage[37] from 1892 onwards the British monetary system served as the model as to the denominations, weight, fineness and size (bronze penny, silver 3d, 6d, 1s, 2s, 2½s, 5s pieces, with gold 10s and £1 pieces).[38] The coins themselves, however, bore the stern, unsmiling effigy of President Paul Kruger, and in the denominations from 2s upwards the coat of arms of the republic. The imperial authorities allowed this Boer currency to remain in circulation after the peace of Vereeniging in 1902 and even extended its use to the whole of South Africa.[39] A South African branch of the Royal Mint was set up at Pretoria in 1922, and began to strike sovereigns in 1923.

THE FALL IN THE VALUE OF SILVER AFTER 1872

After 1872 the average price of silver per British standard ounce, i.e. 92.5 per cent fine, began to fall from $5s\ 0\frac{5}{16}d$ to $2s\ 11\frac{5}{8}d$ in 1893, reaching a trough in 1902 at $2s\ 0\frac{1}{16}d$. A slight recovery occurred subsequently, but in 1914 its price was only $2s\ 1\frac{5}{16}$d. Never before in recorded history had the price of silver in relation to gold fallen so far and so rapidly. From time immemorial the value relationship between one ounce of silver and one ounce of gold had varied (except in Japan) between the limits of 10 : 1 and about $15\frac{1}{2}$: 1.[40] The movements had been secular ones, but now, after only three decades of sagging silver prices, the ratio was down to 39 : 1. The nations of Western Europe, valuing stability, now began to see virtues in the distrusted British gold standard, and hastened to adopt more or less similar monetary arrangements.[41] The myth of the so-called automatic gold standard began to spread.[42] The depreciation of the rupee in terms of gold-based currencies stimulated exports of Indian manufactured goods, foods and raw materials, particularly in cases where peasants and British planters grew cash crops for the markets of the West, but it added greatly to the difficulties of the government of India and the Indian railway companies, which had to acquire large amounts of sterling with which to make payments in London. How long it took the Indian masses to find out that their hoarded silver was rapidly losing its purchasing power cannot be known, but the Indian money changers, merchants and bullion dealers of Bombay must have discovered this disconcerting fact soon enough, and switched out of silver into gold. Daniell, writing about the Indian monetary position in the early 1880s, stated:

The sovereigns of the Royal and of the Australian Mints are to be bought in every large town in the country, and are daily quoted in the exchange tables published in the capitals ... Sovereigns can be said to circulate in India in the sense that they daily change owners ... In times of pressure, French, Turkish, American, and Russian gold coins are brought to the mints to be melted and assayed.[43]

It is not proposed here to discuss the bimetallic controversy, except to note that between the 1870s and 1890s the USA and France, owing to inadequate currency arrangements, which no longer bore any relation to the relative market prices of gold and silver, were both encumbered with very large stocks of silver. The silver lobbies in these two countries proved powerful enough to make possible the calling of three international monetary conferences 1878 (Paris), 1882 (Paris) and 1892 (Brussels), the basic object of which was to persuade Great Britain to relieve France and the USA of the consequences of their own mistakes by taking measures to support the falling price of silver. Fortunately official opinion in Great Britain remained not only unconvinced but actively hostile to any schemes which would clearly have placed burdens on the British taxpayer.[44] In 1893 the government of India closed its mints to the free coinage of silver into rupees by repealing sections 19–26 inclusive of the Indian Coinage Act, XXIII of 1870, which laid the obligation on its mint masters to coin all silver brought to their mints. The rupee circulation of India was adequate and the rupee was still legal tender. At the same time a government notification was issued under the Indian Paper Currency Act of 1882 directing that Indian government currency notes would be issued to all applicants in return for gold at the rate of fifteen rupees to £1 sterling. After some fluctuations between 1893 and 1898 the rupee settled down at a sterling value of 1s 4d,[45] and in 1899 British sovereigns were declared legal tender. A further notification of 1906 laid it down that rupee notes would be issued only against British sovereigns and half sovereigns.[46] These measures, which in effect constituted a gold exchange standard with an internal currency mainly of silver, enormously extended the area of influence of the British gold sovereign, the circulation of which was becoming more usual over wide areas of India by 1914. Notes, too, from five rupees upwards, were more widely issued. Keynes gives an account of currency flows inside India at this period which can hardly be bettered.[47]

THE FAR EASTERN POSSESSIONS, 1814–1914

The Straits Settlements to 1862

In the late eighteenth century the East India Company paid for its purchases of tea, silks and porcelain from China in silver bars, the Spanish American silver dollars to which reference has already been made, and, later, in opium. Between 1800 and 1842, however, a considerable outflow of bullion took place from China to India in payment for the increasing imports of Indian-produced opium. In 1837 the merchant William Jardine wrote from Canton, 'Without sycee [silver bullion] or gold as remittance to India we should never be able to get on.'[48] The Chinese were very particular about the kinds of Spanish American dollar they would accept. Birley Worthington & Co. of Shanghai wrote to Rathbone Bros. & Co. of Liverpool in 1854 requesting the despatch of dollars, but insisting that they must be those of Charles IV of Spain, particularly those struck in Mexico City:

avoiding *Ferdinands or other descriptions* at any price whatever. The favourite Dollar is the one with the letters $\overset{\circ}{m}$ after the word Rex on the reverse side and there is also a dollar of Carolus IV with ọ in the same place on the coin[49] which, being here at a discount of 20 per cent, must of course be avoided.[50]

From the 1820s the 'pillar' dollar was joined by the various silver dollars struck by the newly independent republics of South America, and particularly by Mexico; the Mexican mints maintained a fineness roughly equivalent to that of the old Spanish dollar until the last years of the regime of President Porfirio Diaz in 1909–10![51] These South American pieces also circulated over a wide area of south-east Asia and Oceania. The Chinese had no silver dollar-size coin until 1890; their *tael* or *liang* was a weight of pure silver, not a coin, ideally 583·3 grains.[52] As late as the 1890s Chalmers noted:

The old 'Carolus', or 'Pillar Dollar' of Spain is to this day the standard coin in certain of the neighbouring Malay and Siamese–Malay States. In Achim and in the States of Raman, Lege, Patari and (to a less extent) Kelantan, none but pillar dollars are accepted by the natives.[53]

In the period after the end of the Napoleonic wars the British government placed the Straits Settlements (Penang, Malacca and Singapore) under the control of the East India Company, and in 1826 the company declared the heavy *sicca* rupee of Calcutta to be the official currency of these territories, but with little practical effect in view of the public faith in the Spanish American dollar. The need for small change was met after 1814 by Dutch copper doits intended for circulation in Indonesia. These doits were equal in diameter to, but thinner than, a British farthing of the period. After 1824 these tokens flooded the market places of Singapore, Pulu Penang (Prince of Wales Island) and Malacca. They were then imitated by local merchants, who placed orders in Birmingham and London and imported vast quantities of tokens of similar size known as 'kepings' or 'kapangs'. They arrived from Britain in casks, each cask containing about 100,000 kapangs and weighing about 500 lb.[54] In 1833 only fifty casks of kapangs were imported into Singapore. In 1835 the value of imported kapangs amounted to 13,754 dollars (merchandise value) and in 1842 114,030 dollars' worth was imported. After a slump from 1843 to 1845 the value of imported kapangs was back at 103,287 dollars in 1846. From 1849 only the numbers imported are known – 42·4 millions in 1849, 23·7 millions in 1851. Importation ceased after 1853. The extraordinary fact emerges that there was no stable relationship between the kapang and the silver dollar: quotations for the kapang varied from as low as eighty to as high as 1,600 to the dollar: 'On the same day in the same bazaar, two different dealers would be paying and receiving tokens or doits at different rates.'[55] The ceaseless fluctuation and uncertainty associated with this wretched unofficial currency must have inflicted hardship on the inhabitants of the British settlements and their hinterlands. Attempts in 1825 and 1842 to introduce the company's copper pieces (half annas, pice, etc) failed, and the East India Company reluctantly accepted defeat in 1845 by striking its own quarter, half and one-cent pieces for the Straits Settlements, to pass at the rate of 100 cents to the Spanish and Mexican dollar. The new government of India repeated this series of coins in 1862 and, to judge by the large numbers of them which survive, the issues must have been very numerous and popular.

The Hong Kong dollar, 1866–68: the mint that failed[56]

The island of Hong Kong was ceded to Great Britain by the emperor of China in 1841, and naturally continued to feel the pull of the Chinese silver area. On 29 March 1842 the governor of Hong Kong, Sir Henry Pottinger, issued a proclamation making all the following coins legal tender for bazaar (i.e. retail) trade in the colony: Spanish, Mexican and other silver dollars, the East India Company's rupee, and Chinese brass cash at the rate of 288 cash to the British shilling; a second proclamation of 27 April 1842 made Mexican dollars and dollars of the South American republics legal tender for large-scale mercantile transactions. The home government, which wished to extend the circulation of British sterling coins, showed displeasure at Pottinger's proclamations, and the result was a third proclamation, of 28 November 1844, containing a tariff of the sterling equivalents of various pieces, e.g. the Indian rupee was to circulate as 1s 10d British, Mexican and other dollars at 4s 2d, etc. In spite of a later proclamation of 27 April 1853 settling the British gold sovereign as the legal base of the currency, Mexican dollars continued to reign supreme in the local circulation, a fact recognised by another proclamation of 9 January 1863. Distinctive Hong Kong bronze cents, rated at 100 to the dollar, were struck from 1863 onwards, and a rival to the Chinese cash was prepared in the shape of a mil, or one-tenth of a cent. These mils proved unacceptable to the local Chinese and had to be largely remelted. The home government, however, accepted a proposal from the governor to set up a branch of the Royal Mint in Hong Kong, principally with the object of coining a British dollar capable of competing with Mexican and other pieces in the Far East. It was to have a weight of 416 grains and a standard of 90 per cent fine silver. Between May 1866 and May 1868 over two million dollars of this type were coined, dated 1866, 1867 and 1868, but the Hong Kong mint made a heavy loss on these and the minor coins it produced. A short-sighted home government refused to underwrite any further losses, and the mint had to close. The new Japanese government set up as a result of the restoration of 1868 bought the redundant but up-to-date Hong Kong mint machinery for its new mint at Osaka, planned as part of the westernisation of Japan.

The questions remain: given the initial losses, should the British have persevered? Or was it unreasonable when the London mint was pushing the British sterling currency, including the expensive gold sovereign, for very small direct gains on a large capital outlay, to expect the British and colonial taxpayers to underwrite the introduction of a new silver unit in competition with the Mexican mints and the prolific American silver mines?[57] It is noteworthy that after 1868, when the Hong Kong government obtained its silver five-, ten-, twenty- and fifty-cent pieces as required from the London mint, that these became very popular on the south China mainland and formed 'a standard silver currency' until after 1889, when the modernisation of the Chinese mints began,[58] with the opening of the Canton mint, equipped with machinery by Ralph Heaton & Sons of Birmingham. In this instance, as so often in the late nineteenth century, British statesmen and officials seem to have lacked the imperial vision. Additional evidence that the 1866–8 experiment should have been persevered in is provided by the second and more successful attempt in 1895 to promote a British silver dollar in the Far East as the result of a shortage of Mexican dollars and the recommendation of the Imperial Currency Committee of 1893. An imperial order-in-council of 2 February 1895 authorised the striking at the mints of Bombay and Calcutta of a dollar bearing a standing frontal figure of Britannia (weight 416 grains, 90 per cent fine). These were to be issued from Hong Kong. In the end this British dollar proved very popular and continued to be struck until 1935, by which time over 100 million had been put into circulation. The fact that the South Chinese paid the British dollar the compliment of forging it extensively in good silver suggests that these pieces filled a widespread need in south-east Asia at a time when supplies of Spanish and Mexican dollars were beginning to fail.

The Straits Settlements, 1867–1914

As from 1 April 1867 the Straits Settlements were transferred from the government of India to the Colonial Office. Up to this time the Straits Settlements government accounts had been kept in rupees, but in the year of transfer the governor issued an ordinance repealing the statutes making the rupee legal tender and declaring that as from 1 September 1867 'the dollar issued from Her Majesty's Mint at Hong Kong, the silver dollar of Spain, Mexico, Peru and Bolivia, and any other silver dollar to be specified from time to time by the Government in Council, shall be the only legal tender'.[59] In 1889 the Straits Commissioners of

Currency were brought into being by ordinance No. 4 of that year. They were empowered to issue government currency notes from one dollar upwards, but their function was to economise on the use of silver dollars by printing high-value notes, and they did not in fact put out one-dollar notes until 1905.[60]

We have seen that a shortage of Mexican dollars developed in the early 1890s and ended in the issue of an imperial British silver dollar from Hong Kong. The Imperial Currency Committee of 1893 had touched briefly on the question of establishing a gold standard in the Straits Settlements, and in 1897 the Singapore chamber of commerce, unsettled by the continuing fall in the price of silver, appointed a sub-committee 'to enquire into the local currency with the view of calling the attention of the Government to the question of converting the Straits currency to a gold standard'.[61] The Straits government found that considerable differences of opinion existed among the British community, and nothing was done. In 1902 the price of silver reached its trough (the silver dollar, originally 4s 2d sterling, had by then fallen to 1s 7d). The Singapore chamber of commerce again approached the Straits government on the matter of establishing a fixed exchange rate, and the upshot was the appointment of the Straits Currency Committee, which produced a scheme for establishing a gold exchange standard on the lines of that operated by the government of India. A new Straits Settlements dollar was suggested, designed eventually to oust the Mexican and the new British dollars of 1895 from circulation, and this should be rated at a fixed number to the gold sovereign, as was the Indian rupee.

Accordingly the Straits Settlements Coinage Order of 25 June 1903 laid it down that a new Straits Settlements dollar weighing 416 grains and 90 per cent fine, to be coined in the Indian mints, should be the new unit; when supplies arrived they were to be declared the sole legal tender. The first batch of the new dollars arrived in late September 1903. They were declared legal tender on 3 October, and after that date the further import of British and Mexican dollars into the Settlements was prohibited. Conversely, the export of the new coins was prohibited.[62]

Unfortunately for the Straits Settlements government the price of silver began to improve somewhat after 1902, by which time the dollar had sunk to 1s 6⅝d sterling as against the pre-1872 norm of 4s 2d, and as the currency committee had not recommended any definite exchange value for the new dollar the government now had the task of divorcing the exchange value of the dollar *vis-à-vis* the gold sovereign from its bullion content. It has been estimated that by November 1904 some 35 millions of the new Straits dollar were in circulation, and all rival dollars had been demonetised. Finally, in January 1906 the government decided to fix the value of its dollar at 2*s* 4*d* sterling, and on 22 October 1906 a Straits Settlements order-in-council made the sovereign legal tender in the colony at the rate of seven sovereigns to sixty Straits dollars. This remained the rate up to 1914. In 1905 the Straits Commissioners of Currency issued one-dollar notes for the first time, although they had had the power to do so since their creation by ordinance No. 4 of 1889.

The slight improvement in the price of silver between 1902 and 1906 forced the Straits government to issue a dollar with less silver in it in order to minimise the risk of melting down. Accordingly the government announced on 11 February 1907 the issue of smaller dollars of the pattern of 1903 (312 grains weight, 90 per cent fine, i.e. 25 per cent lighter), without recalling the heavier dollars of 1903–5.

The new policy had repercussions far outside the Straits Settlements, for the new gold-exchange standard dollar became the unit not only for the Federated and Protected Malay States but also for North Borneo, where the British North Borneo Company had begun issuing subsidiary one-cent and half-cent coins in 1882–5, followed later by some cupro-nickel and silver denominations; for the sultanates of Labuan and Brunei, and for Sarawak, where Rajah James Brooke issued bronze cents, half cents and quarter cents for the first time in 1863, supplemented during the long reign of his nephew and successor Rajah Charles Brooke by silver pieces up to fifty cents (1868–1917).[63] The realm of the silver dollar had now fallen indirectly to the empire of the gold sovereign.

THE WEST INDIES AND BRITISH GUIANA

During the nineteenth century the small-scale economies of the West Indian possessions, in comparison with the large-scale economies of the East Indies, declined relatively, and in some cases absolutely, in importance in the imperial scheme. Throughout the British West Indian islands in 1814 the Spanish American silver dollar and its fractions reigned supreme, supplemented by the Spanish gold doubloon (equal to eight scudi or sixteen dollars) and the Portuguese gold johannes of 6,400 reis or four escudos. The fractions of the dollar were sometimes the original coins (often pierced or counter-stamped) of four and two reales and one, half and quarter real, the pistareen or two-real piece being particularly popular; sometimes the dollar itself was cut into segments and the segments or 'bits' counter-stamped to circulate as small change. Needless to say, great confusion could be caused to trade and finance by local methods of coin mutilation and local shortages.[64]

A device frequently adopted in order to prevent the outflow of dollars from any particular island or group of islands was to rate the Spanish dollar in a purely *local* sterling currency, e.g. the dollar would be accepted at a value of anything from 6s 8d to 10s currency in local retail transactions, when its real value in international trade was, say, 5s British sterling. This represented a form of devaluation of local goods and services which attracted merchants and specie to the particular islands and territories resorting to this device.

The order-in-council of 23 March 1825 establishing British sterling as the standard was brought into operation in Jamaica and the other Caribbean islands for the purpose of introducing British silver and copper coins into general colonial circulation. The immediate effect of this differed from colony to colony. Between 1825 and 1828, for example, the Army Commissariat Department introduced £35,000 in British silver and copper into Jamaica. The copper proved extremely unpopular and failed to circulate because the general population was in the habit of using silver and gold only; the British sterling silver was promptly revalued for everyday use in local currency terms at 1s 8d to the British shilling, which was equated with the quarter dollar or pistareen. On 7 September 1838 the order-in-council of 23 March 1825 was revoked, as far as the West Indian and the American colonies were concerned; the dollar and the doubloon were called down to 4s 2d and 64s sterling respectively and British silver coins declared legal tender to any amount. It was at this point of time that Jamaica and the Bahamas decided to adopt the British sterling system permanently – a sign, as Chalmers put it, of the 'rapidly widening "currency area" of Great Britain'.[65]

The only exception to the rule of the Spanish dollar was in British Guiana (Berbice, Demarara and Essequibo), where the Dutch guilder standard still obtained (three guilders = sixty stivers = one dollar). Rather surprisingly, the British mint served British Guiana well, and as late as 1832–6 a complete coinage series from three guilders downwards was struck, bearing the effigy of William IV. In 1839, however, three guilders were officially rated at 4s 2d sterling. Not until 1836 did the home government begin to replace the Dutch system by introducing the imperial 'Britannia' silver 4d piece (the groat or joey) to circulate throughout the Caribbean possessions. This piece was also legal tender in Great Britain. In British Guiana it passed as a quarter guilder, and considerable quantities were struck for most years until 1856. The 'Britannia' groat was struck again in 1888, and from 1891 a distinctive British Guianan–West Indian silver 4d piece was introduced, the remains of the old guilder currency having been demonetised in the previous year. By 1914 the other British coins circulated freely, as well as the 4d piece, except that, in common with the other Caribbean colonies, the imperial bronze coins were not popular.

This unpopularity accounts for the fact that in 1869–70 the governor of Jamaica persuaded the imperial government to allow the coinage of special farthings, halfpence and pence for Jamaica in cupro-nickel, the first time that this new coinage alloy had been used in the British empire. These proved very popular.[66] Owing in part to the low standard of living, British silver 3d pieces and the curious silver 1½d piece originally struck for Ceylon also proved popular in Jamaica, fresh supplies of these being called for and struck in 1860 and 1862.[67]

Spanish American dollars ceased to circulate to any considerable extent after about 1850, but when the price of silver began to fall after 1872 these types of dollar, now joined by French five-franc pieces, started to flow back into circulation again and the island legislature had to pass a law, No. 8 of 1876, finally demonetising the dollar and its subdivisions. After this date pounds, shillings and pence, and particularly the shilling, became established as the standard of value in Jamaica, although in popular speech terms originating in the days of the double standard survived – a shilling was still a 'mac' or 'maccaroni' (quarter dollar or pistareen), and a 'mac and fipence' meant 1s 3d British sterling because fivepence was the Jamaican currency rating of the smallest silver coin circulating in the island, the half real, approximately equal to the British threepenny piece.

The only complete exception to the use of sterling in the British West Indies was British Honduras, where in 1855 the legislature passed an Act, 18 Vic., c. 16, whereby public accounts were to be kept in dollars and reales or rials (amended to dollars and cents in 1864), although a sample taken in 1870 revealed a strange medley of coins in actual circulation – British silver pieces, Spanish, Mexican, Colombian and Guatemalan dollars and fractions, and United States half and quarter dollars. The gold circulation consisted of Spanish doubloons and British sovereigns.[68] Foreign silver coin flowed in after the beginning of the fall in the price of silver after 1872, and by 1876 all full-weight gold coins had been drained out of the colony. In 1885 a public meeting in Belize, the capital, decided, with two dissentients, against adopting the British sovereign as the standard; an excellent example of the non-chauvinistic character of British economic 'imperialism' is provided by a royal proclamation two years later which, issued under an order-in-council of 15 September 1887, declared the Guatemalan silver dollar to be the standard of value and allowed the circulation of six other foreign dollars. Bronze British Honduras cents bearing the head of Queen

Victoria, which had been first struck in 1885, were to be legal tender up to fifty cents. In effect British Honduras was under a regime similar to that obtaining at the time in Hong Kong, i.e. silver monometallism.[69] This state of affairs did not last for long. As Pridmore comments under the year 1894:

This silver standard dollar was soon upset by the disturbances in the gold-price of silver and it became necessary for the colony to adopt the gold standard. Accordingly the previous legislation was repealed and by local ordinance No.31 of 1894, the gold dollar of the United States of America was made the standard of value.[70]

It then became necessary to have a range of fractional coins, and as the coins of Canada were also subsidiary to the US gold dollar the new coins of 1894 for British Honduras (50c, 25c, 10c, 5c and 1c) were made to correspond to those of Canada in denomination, weight and fineness.[71]

A partial exception to the use of British sterling as the standard was in Trinidad, where a strange confusion reigned for most of the period from 1814 to 1914. By Governor Sir Ralph Woodford's proclamation of 14 September 1814 the Spanish American silver dollar bore the high valuation of 10s in local currency, and the gold doubloon (normally £3 4s British sterling) was rated at £8 local currency. The imperial government tried to impose the British sterling system from 1825–6 onwards, but the attempt remained fruitless for many years, since British sterling coins were bought up in exchange for dollars and doubloons, which were somewhat overrated in British sterling values at the new local valuations of 4s 4d and 69s 4d respectively. They were then shipped back to London at a small profit. The Trinidadians petitioned the Crown on three occasions for their own distinctive currency. On the final occasion in 1834, when the United States of America reformed its currency system and overvalued silver, so that neighbouring States were stripped of small silver change, the British government sent out a supply of silver 3d pieces, which were immediately shipped back to London as being 'unsuitable and not such as required'.[72]

Following the cheapening of gold in terms of silver after the discoveries in California (1848–9) and in New South Wales and Victoria (1851) silver dollars began to disappear from Trinidad. The way was paved for the rapid introduction of British token silver coins between 1850 and 1852, and in 1853 United States gold coins were declared legal tender; this was followed by a similar declaration with respect to Sydney sovereigns in 1866. Curiously enough, neither US gold dollars nor British sovereigns circulated to any great extent, but in practice the United States dollar was regarded as the current unit, and valued at 4s 2d. Chalmers wrote of Trinidad in 1893:

As no ordinance has ever been passed in this island prescribing sterling denominations of account, (i) private persons continue to reckon in dollars and cents, whilst (ii) in the government offices accounts are kept both in £ s d and in $ currency.[73]

With the exceptions of British Honduras and Trinidad, the British possessions in the Caribbean had been brought within the sterling area by 1914, and the pieces of eight and doubloons largely relegated to the melting pots and the museums.

WEST AFRICA

The first British coinage struck for west Africa, and incidentally the first imperial decimal series, consisted of the Sierra Leone Company's silver dollar of 1791 and its subdivisions at 100 cents to the dollar, struck at Matthew Boulton's Soho mint. This dollar bears witness to the popularity of the Spanish American dollar and 'bits' down the west coast of Africa (although the Sierra Leone dollar contained $30\frac{2}{3}$ grains less of fine silver),[74] and also owed something to the adoption of the dollar/cent system by the newly independent United States of America. North America, the West Indies and west Africa can therefore be considered as one currency area at the beginning of the nineteenth century. In Sierra Leone the Spanish American dollar was rated at 5s local currency. The British 'anchor money' of 1820 and 1822 seems to have been acceptable, but fifths and quarters cut from pieces of eight continued to circulate. 'Cut quarters' were even made legal tender in Sierra Leone by a proclamation of 6 December 1834. An attempt was then made to introduce British silver coins, beginning with $1\frac{1}{2}d$ and 3d pieces in the same year, followed by the higher denominations shortly afterwards, so that in January 1839 it proved possible to call in, demonetise and melt down the 'cut money'.[75] As in the West Indies the order-in-council of 1825 imposing the British currency system was eventually revoked in 1843, 'so far as respects Her Majesty's colonies and possessions at Sierra Leone, the River Gambia and Cape Coast, and elsewhere on the western coast of the continent of Africa', and a list of acceptable foreign coins with their British sterling equivalents was published. This reveals an almost identical state of affairs to that obtaining in the West Indies – doubloons, Spanish and Mexican dollars (4s 2d), French twenty-franc gold pieces and silver five-franc pieces ($3s\ 10\frac{1}{2}d$) were declared legal tender. As there was no legal tender limit on the French five-franc pieces, which had become undervalued in gold terms in France, these gradually ousted all the gold coins in circulation. Attempts to call the Sydney sovereign into circulation failed in 1867 and 1871. By 1879–80, with the continuing depreciation of silver, Sierra Leone and the Gambia had passed rapidly on to a silver standard. By this time, however, the French had in 1873 moved away from a simple bimetallic system, and the five-franc piece was worth a little more than its silver content. In 1874–5, too, Belgian and Swiss five-franc pieces and Italian five-lira pieces had been made legal tender in Sierra Leone by order-in-council. British gold and silver tended to be kept in hoards rather than in circulation.[76]

On the Gold Coast a somewhat similar situation obtained up to 1880, except that, as the country produced some gold, gold dust was used by weight as currency, the ounce representing £3 12s, and one-sixteenth of an ounce, or 'ackey', representing 4s 6d sterling, approximately a dollar.[77] British silver proved acceptable only if unworn and bearing the head of Queen Victoria. In 1880 the demonetisation ordinance was passed to stem the inward flood of cheapening Mexican dollars, and the same ordinance also demonetised French five-franc pieces and Dutch two-and-a-half guilder pieces. United States gold coins and Spanish American doubloons were recognised as acceptable currency at fixed prices in sterling. The foundation in 1894 of the Liverpool-based Bank of British West Africa Ltd, with a monopoly of the importation of new British silver coins from the Royal Mint, led to a rapid increase in the use of British currency.[78] Of the British coins the silver 3d piece was most extensively used in retail trade. Gold dust and nuggets were demonetised on 12 April 1899.

An unusual feature of Gold Coast currency was the use of curved copper 'manillas' as small change. They were imported from Liverpool for a century and a half, and passed as the equivalent of about 3d sterling each until withdrawn during 1948.

Finally, between 1907 and 1912 the West African Currency Board was set up to unite Nigeria, the Gold Coast, the Gambia and Sierra Leone for monetary purposes. The basic unit was the British £, but the board issued no piece of greater value than a silver 2s; silver shillings, sixpences and threepenny pieces were issued, supplemented by cupro-nickel coins for 1d, $\frac{1}{2}d$ and $\frac{1}{10}d$, with central holes, at first issued for circulation in Nigeria only. By 1939 the normal unit of monetary calculation had become the shilling.

THE CANADAS, THE MARITIME PROVINCES AND NEWFOUNDLAND

As in the West Indies, the Spanish American dollar provided the basis of the everyday currency of British North America in 1814 and reigned unchallenged until 1825, although a few worn French silver crowns (*écus*) of the pre-1792 monarchical issues remained in circulation until the 1830s. The Spanish American dollar was rated at 5s local or 'Halifax', i.e. Nova Scotia,[79] currency and the British gold guinea (21s sterling) at 23s 4d in Halifax currency.[80] Small change was provided by the Spanish two-real piece (quarter dollar or 'pistareen'). After the order-in-council of 1825 the British crown piece (5s) was rated at 5s 9d Halifax currency and the British shilling at 1s 2d. This made the British sovereign worth 23s, and at this price it was eagerly bought up with local currency for re-export to Britain, via New York, where it stood at a heavy premium, in part settlement of the USA's chronic trade deficit with the United Kingdom. In 1828 it was reported that 'the circulating medium of the two provinces [of Upper and Lower Canada] is paper; British coin is never seen and except among the Canadians below Quebec, rarely a silver dollar. Specie cannot swim so near the engrossing gulf of the American paper circulation.'[81] It should be borne in mind that for the first three-quarters of the nineteenth century the United States dollar, far from being a 'hard' currency, was more often than not a 'soft' currency, partly because of this trade deficit, the existence of excessive issues of paper money and the fact that the United States mint was bound by bimetallic rules which from time to time led to monetary confusion affecting neighbouring countries.[82]

Copper change in the Canadas was supplied by large issues of private tokens for 1d and ½d ordered by shopkeepers, merchants and bankers in Upper and Lower Canada (united after 1840 as the Province of Canada), and in the Maritime Provinces. The revocation of the 1825 order-in-council in 1838 in so far as it related to the British possessions in North America and the West Indies removed one obstacle to the adoption of the United States dollar/cent system in the Canadian public accounts, which became law in 1857. The second step, again for the Province of Canada, was also taken in 1857 when the governor-in-council approved the report of a committee of the executive council on the currency question which made possible the striking, under letters patent dated 10 December 1858, of one-cent, five-cent, ten-cent and twenty-cent coins (the twenty-five-cent piece was substituted for the twenty-cent piece in 1870, in conformity with the US quarter dollar). Nova Scotia, New Brunswick and Prince Edward Island adopted the dollar/cent system for their currencies in 1859–60, 1860 and 1871 respectively, after futile attempts to enforce the order-in-council of 1825 and to secure adequate supplies of British currency.[83] About the same time these provinces put into circulation coins of various denominations in cents. Shortly after confederation in May 1867 the parliament of the new Dominion of Canada declared that it was desirable that the Canadian currency should remain of the same value as that of the United States, and two Acts passed in 1868 and 1871 translated this wish into law: United States gold coins were to circulate concurrently with the British sovereign, which was rated at $4·86⅔. Chalmers noted in 1893:

The *metallic* currency is, therefore, on an exclusively gold basis, and consists almost entirely of eagles [$10 pieces] and other United States gold coins. British sovereigns occur at Halifax, where British troops are stationed, and an Imperial dockyard has been established. But ... gold is rarely seen in circulation in the Dominion, its place being taken by Bank and Dominion notes ... If gold is required (e.g. by individuals going to England) it is obtained from a bank.[84]

The establishment of a branch of the Royal Mint in Ottawa in 1908 which began to strike not only the Canadian fractional coins but also British sovereigns (from 1908), and Canadian five- and ten-dollar pieces (1912–14) marked the beginning of full Canadian monetary independence from Britain.[85]

By 1914, with the exception of Canada, Hong Kong, Trinidad and British Honduras, the countries and possessions of the British empire were firmly anchored, either directly or indirectly, to the standard of the gold sovereign, which had become, like the gold stater of Alexander the Great, the Roman silver denarius and the Maria Theresa dollar, one of the great international monetary units of history. This sterling area had come into existence by a strange mixture of accident and design, aided not only by British economic predominance in the world but also by the unpredictable and extraordinary cheapening of silver after 1872, which made this metal increasingly unreliable as a standard of value. The gold sovereign and the *Pax Britannica* had provided the twin bases for a century of unprecedented world economic expansion.

NOTES

'Currency Problems of the British Empire, 1814–1914' appeared in B.M. Ratcliffe (ed.), *Great Britain and her World: Essays in Honour of W.O. Henderson* (Manchester University Press, 1975), pp. 179–207.

1. *Numismatics and History* (Historical Association, London, 1951), p. 18.
2. Notable exceptions are: F.C. Spooner, *The International Economy and Monetary Movements in France, 1493–1725* (Cambridge, Mass., 1972); J.D. Gould, *The Great Debasement: Currency and the Economy in mid-Tudor England* (London, 1970); J.K. Horsefield, *British Monetary Experiments 1650–1710* (London, 1960); M-H. Li, *The Great Recoinage of 1696–9* (London, 1963); Sir A.E. Feavearyear, *The Pound Sterling* (1st edition, Oxford, 1931; 2nd edition revised by E.V. Morgan, London, 1963); S.J. Butlin, *Foundations of the Australian Monetary System, 1788–1851* (Sydney, 1953).
3. The standard work on the subject, reprinted in 1972, is still Robert Chalmers, *A History of Currency in the British Colonies* (London, 1893), with three chapters by

C.A. Harris of the Colonial Office. It has a chapter on India, and Chalmers, who was at the Treasury, printed many key official documents (pp.414–65). An earlier work, James Atkins, *The Coins and Tokens of the Possessions and Colonies of the British Empire* (London, 1889), is still of some value. H.W.A. Linecar, *British Commonwealth Coinage* (London, 1959), and L.V.W. Wright, *Colonial and Commonwealth Coins* (London, 1959), are also useful. In 1960 F. Pridmore issued part I of his thorough guide, *The Coins of the British Commonwealth of Nations to the end of the reign of George VI, 1952* (London). Part I lists the coins and tokens of British territories in Europe, eg. Gibraltar, Malta and Cyprus; part II (Asian Territories, excluding India) followed in 1962, and part III (Bermuda, British Guiana, British Honduras, and the British West Indies) in 1965. These are referred to in footnotes as Pridmore, parts I, II and III. Further parts are promised. For miscellaneous datings, etc, see W.D. Craig, *Coins of the World, 1750–1850* (Racine, Wis., 1st edition, 1966), and R.S. Yeoman, *A Catalog of Modern World Coins, 1850–1964* (Racine, Wis., 8th edition, 1968), will be found invaluable.

4. *Op. cit.*, p.396.

5. National Bank of South Africa, Ltd., *Income Tax; Weights and Measures; Stamp Duties; Coinage* (London, 1920), p.318. In addition, Keynes reported in 1912–13 that a large proportion of the currency in Egypt and the Sudan consisted of British sovereigns.

6. E. Cannan, *The Paper Pound of 1797–1821* (London, 1919).

7. The first Lord Liverpool was a currency expert, famous for his *Treatise on the Coins of the Realm* (London, 1805, reprinted in 1880).

8. Feavearyear, *op. cit.*, 1st edition, pp.196–9. These were the 'little shillings', as distinct from previous shillings struck at 62s to the pound troy, so wrongheadedly denounced by Cobbett, whose understanding of financial matters was minimal. Silver 4d pieces (the unpopular 'Britannia' groats) were added in 1834, the silver 3d piece in 1834, and the silver florin or 2s piece in 1849.

9. *Report of the US Silver Commission* (1876), p.68, quoted in B.R. Ambedkar, *The Problem of the Rupee* (London, 1923), pp.27–8. Needless to say, once the price of silver began to fall in the 1870s, the Dutch mint, which had stopped striking silver 1 guilder pieces in 1866, ceased to strike silver 2½ guilder pieces (approximately 5s) – the last being coined in 1874 – and in 1875 resumed the striking of gold 10 guilder pieces after an interval of twenty-two years. In 1877 the Netherlands adopted the first, rather crude, gold exchange standard of the modern type: J.M. Keynes, *Indian Currency and Finance* (1971 edition, London), pp.22–3.

10. Evidence of Baring before the Committee for Coin (1828), *Parl. Papers, C.31* of 1830.

11. Section iii of 7 & 8 Vict. c.32 (text in T.E. Gregory (ed.), *Select Statutes, Documents and Reports relating to British Banking*, vol.I, 2nd impression (London, 1964), p.131).

12. Sir G. Duveen and H.G. Stride, *The History of the Gold Sovereign* (London, 1962), pp.92–3.

13. B.B. Misra, *The Central Administration of the East India Company, 1773–1834* (Manchester, 1959), pp.105–7, and B.R. Ambedkar, *The Problem of the Rupee* (London, 1923), pp.1–48. See also K.N. Chaudhuri (ed.), *The Economic Development of India ... 1814–58* (Cambridge, 1971).

14. Ambedkar, *op. cit.*, p.9. Prior to the 1870s the rupee was equivalent to about 2s sterling. One rupee = 16 annas; 1 anna = 4 pice. There was also a smaller unit, the pie, of which there were three in 1 pice, twelve in 1 anna and 192 in 1 rupee.

15. Ambedkar, *op. cit.*, p.21.

16. Ambedkar, *op. cit.*, pp.55–6.

17. Pridmore, part II, 1962, pp.32–4. This early adoption of the decimal system in Ceylon was in part due to the influence of Sir Hercules Robinson, governor 1865–72, who had previously been governor of Hong Kong when the decimal system was adopted in that colony.

18. R.S. Yeoman, *op. cit.*, pp.202–3. For later developments, including the establish-

ment of the East African Currency Board in December 1919, see D. Vice, 'The florin coinage of British East Africa', *Numismatic Circular*, London, vol.82, May 1974, p.192.
19. Marquess of Anglesey (ed.), *Sergeant Pearman's Memoirs* (London, 1968), p.114.
20. Cf. the eulogy of the Spanish pillar dollar by the governor of New South Wales, Sir Thomas Brisbane, in 1822: 'that invaluable coin, which has for centuries been disseminating its benefits over every other portion of the earth ... a coin which from the extension of its circulation over every part of the commercial globe may justly be defined as the money of the world. ... Like the ocean that surrounds our continent, a grand circulating medium assisting to waft to every part of the world the various products of her diversified climates. Driven, indeed, from the United Kingdom by her monies of sterling denomination it still however maintains all its pre-eminence in every one of her colonies. Confined in its advantages to no faith, kindred, or government. I refer you ... to those sterling benefits it has for ages been bestowing on the British and Protestant North American Colonies; on the French and Papal Canadas; on Mohammedan India; and on the whole world.' *Sydney Gazette*, 30 Aug. 1822, quoted in S.J. Butlin, *op. cit.*, pp.143–4.
21. Sir John Craig, *The Mint: a History of the London Mint from A.D. 287 to 1948* (Cambridge, 1953), p.381.
22. Chalmers, *op. cit.*, p.360. British silver coins flowed in between 1851 and 1860 as the price of sugar rose in Europe; *ibid.*, p.367.
23. A distinctive coinage (100 cents to the rupee) was issued for the Seychelles only from 1939 onwards. The Andaman and Nicobar Islands in the Eastern part of the Indian Ocean also used the rupee unit, as they were part of the Indian empire.
24. It has recently been shown that they were in fact struck at the mint of Ralph Heaton & Sons at Birmingham (*Coins*, X, 7, July 1973, p.12).
25. Craig, *op. cit.*, pp.380–2.
26. Full text in Chalmers, *op. cit.*, p.425.
27. Full text in Chalmers, *op. cit.*, pp.417–24.
28. S.J. Butlin, *op. cit.*, pp.30–49 and ch.VI, 'The dollar standard'.
29. A. Andrews, *Australian Tokens and Coins*, 1965.
30. New Zealand currency history parallels that of Australia to some extent. At first Spanish silver dollars circulated, although New Zealand was on sterling. In the middle years of the nineteenth century there were private issues of bronze tokens for 1d and ½d as in Australia. British silver and bronze circulated in New Zealand until the issue of separate New Zealand subsidiary coins in the early 1930s; P. Blakeborough, *The Coinage of New Zealand, 1840–1967* (1966) [*sic*].
31. Duveen and Stride, *op. cit.*, p.96.
32. Morrell, *op. cit.*, pp.200–312; see Duveen and Stride, *op. cit.*, pp.94–6. For the effect of the opening of the Sydney and Melbourne mints on Australian banking policy see E.A. Boehm, *Prosperity and Depression in Australia 1887–1897* (Oxford), pp.233–4. There is a valuable table of estimates of Australian exports and imports of gold and silver coin for the years from 1885 to 1897 on p.307 of the same book. The Australian mints also issued 'gold bullion ... for export to India in the form of gold bars of the weight of 10 oz.' (National Bank of South Africa, *Income Tax. Weights and Measures. Stamp Duties. Coinage, British, Colonial and Foreign* (London, 1920), p.244).
33. W.S. Jevons, *Investigations in Currency and Finance*, ed. H.S. Foxwell (1884), p.137.
34. *Studies in British Overseas Trade, 1870–1914* (Liverpool, 1960), pp.205–6. J.A. Mann (*The Cotton Trade of Great Britain* (London, 1860), pp.78–9) remarked on the heavy silver drain to India in the late 1850s and the need for a government of India note issue.
35. C. Daniell (*The Gold Treasure of India* (London, 1884), pp.95–6) estimated that up to 1882 gold stocks in India amounted to more than £212 millions, i.e. two and a half times the gold then in circulation in Great Britain. For a modern critique of the 'drain' theory, see Tapan Mukerjee, 'Theory of economic drain: impact of British

rule on the Indian economy, 1840–1900', in K.E. Boulding and T. Mukerjee (eds.), *Economic Imperialism: a Book of Readings* (Ann Arbor, Mich., 1972), pp.195–212. To some extent the hunger of the Indian peoples for gold was satisfied from home production in the years before 1914. The successful exploitation of the Kolar goldfield by the Mysore Gold Mining Company and Goldfields of Mysore Ltd from 1880 onwards using the new cyanide process, raised India from seventh among the world's gold producers in 1887 to fifth during 1889–93. In 1894 India produced 6 tons of gold worth £800,000 (Nancy Crathorne, *Tennant's Stalk* (1973), pp.138–41; M.G. Mulhall, *Dictionary of Statistics* (4th edition, 1899), p.739; *Encyclopaedia Britannica*, 1911 edition, XII, p.195).

36. D.A. Farnie, 'The mineral revolution in South Africa', *South African Journal of Economics*, 24, 2, 1956, p.128. See also W.P. Morrell, *The Gold Rushes* (London, 1940), ch.IX, 'The diamonds of Kimberley and the gold of the Rand'.

37. T.F. Burgers, president of the Transvaal 1872–7, had issued gold £1 pieces in 1874, but only 837 were struck.

38. A. Kaplan, *The Coins of South Africa* (3rd edition, 1965). Significantly, however, the Transvaal coins were struck in Germany.

39. It was not withdrawn and demonetised until the 1940s, even though an adequate distinct South African currency had been issued since 1923 from the Pretoria mint. The everyday circulation of the old Transvaal currency must have contributed towards keeping alive the spirit of Afrikaner nationalism.

40. Daniell, *op. cit.*, pp.83–98.

41. Ambedkar, *op. cit.*, pp.73–6.

42. Keynes was suspicious of the concept as early as 1913, when he wrote: 'To illustrate how rare a thing in Europe a perfect and automatic gold standard is, let us take the most recent occasion of stringency – November 1912' (*Indian Currency and Finance*, 2nd edition (London, 1972), p.17). The myth of the automatic gold standard has been exposed by A.E. Bloomfield, *Monetary Policy under the International Gold Standard, 1880–1914* (New York, 1959), and A.G. Ford, *The Gold Standard, 1880–1914; Britain and Argentina* (Oxford, 1962). See also M. de Cecco, *Money and Empire: the International Gold Standard, 1890–1914* (Oxford, 1975).

43. Daniell, *op. cit.*, p.102.

44. Ambedkar, *op. cit.*, pp.135–44. There had been an international monetary conference in Paris in 1867. For the whole subject of the international monetary conferences, see H. Higgs (ed.), *Palgrave's Dictionary of Political Economy*, vol.II, reprint of revised 2nd edition, 1925–6 (New York, 1963), pp.783–7.

45. Compton Mackenzie, *Realms of Silver: One Hundred Years of Banking in the East* (London, 1954), pp.184–6. The stabilisation of the rupee at 1s 4d sterling had the advantage of making one anna equal in value to one penny sterling.

46. Keynes, *op. cit.*, pp.4–8.

47. Keynes, *op. cit.*, pp.29, 36–7. H.F. Howard stated, in his *India and the Gold Standard* (Calcutta and London, 1911), p.iii, that the decision of 1893 was 'a great practical experiment in the direction of the establishment of a Gold Exchange Standard'.

48. M. Greenberg, *British Trade and the Opening of China, 1800–42* (Cambridge, 1954), p.199. See also pp.vii, 49, 141–2, 159.

49. This was the mint mark of Santiago, Chile.

50. Sheila Marriner, *Rathbones of Liverpool, 1845–73* (Liverpool, 1961), p.176. See also Greenberg, *op. cit.*, p.159, n.2.

51. The standard Mexican dollar contained 377 grains of pure silver and was 90·27 per cent fine. A sample of 11,846 Mexican dollars assayed at the London mint in 1891 revealed that on average the silver content was 90·16 per cent (Chalmers, *op. cit.*, pp.393–4.

52. W.F. Spalding, *Eastern Exchange, Currency and Finance* (4th ed. London, 1924), pp.412–20.

53. *Op. cit.*, pp.392–3. Chalmers noted that the Malays, 'like the Arabs of North Africa

... call these coins *"cannon* dollars" mistaking the Pillars of Hercules for the recognised pioneers of European civilisation'.

54. Most, if not all, of these kapangs were made at Boulton's Soho Mint, near Birmingham, where they were popularly known as 'cock money' from the emblem they bore on the obverse side (P.E. Razzell and R.W. Wainwright, *The Victorian Working Class: Selections from Letters to the 'Morning Chronicle'* (London, 1973), p.310). The most detailed study of the 'cock money' is to be found in F. Pridmore, *Coins and Coinages of the Straits Settlements and British Malaya ... 1828–1853* (London, 1968), pp.68–143.

55. Pridmore, part II, p.150.

56. The Hong Kong series has recently been made the subject of a monograph, R. Hamson, *Regal Coinage of Hong Kong* (Hong Kong, n.d., ? 1969). The best modern account of Hong Kong's currency in the nineteenth century is to be found in F.H.H. King, *Money and Monetary Policy in China, 1845–95* (Cambridge, Mass., 1965), pp.166–88 and *passim*.

57. The US Mint introduced a silver trade dollar for the Far East weighing 420 grains, and 90 per cent fine, in 1873 and continued to strike it until 1885. It did not prove very successful.

58. Pridmore, part II, p.277. A good summary of modern Chinese currency history is to be found in R.D. Thompson, *Coinage of Kwangtung, China* (Hong Kong, 1971), pp.7–9.

59. Spalding, *op. cit.,* p.163. Straits Settlements subsidiary coins (bronze and silver up to 50c) were afterwards obtained from the Royal Mint in London.

60. Spalding, *op. cit.,* pp.168–9.

61. Spalding, *op. cit.,* p.165.

62. Spalding, *op. cit.,* pp.165–7.

63. Spalding, *op. cit.,* pp.165–9; Mackenzie, *op. cit.,* pp.189–91. Mackenzie's book, which is a history of the Chartered Bank of India, Australia and China, is based to an unspecified extent on the archives of the Bank, but contains no references, footnotes or bibliography. In its sections on currency history it appears to lean heavily on Spalding.

64. Chalmers (*op. cit.,* pp.46–149) gives an extremely detailed survey of the West Indian island currencies. Even in the largest island, Jamaica, the amount of silver coin in circulation in the 1890s was estimated to be only about £320,000 and that of notes about £160,000, at a time when the total population of the island was roughly 640,000 giving an active circulation of only 15s per head (Chalmers, *op. cit.,* p.113). For a contemporary account of Caribbean currency confusion in the mid-1820s (with tables), see F.W.M. Bayley, *Four Years Residence in the West Indies* (London, 1830), pp.63–5, 149, 224–6, 476–7.

65. Chalmers, *op. cit.,* p.27.

66. Chalmers, *op. cit.,* p.113. The Jamaican Assembly passed a Currency Act in 1840 formally declaring the currency to be that of the United Kingdom.

67. Chalmers, *op. cit.,* p.110, n.5.

68. Chalmers, *op. cit.,* p.143.

69. Chalmers, *op. cit.,* pp.144–5.

70. Pridmore, part III (1965), p.57.

71. Pridmore, *op. cit.,* p.57.

72. Chalmers, *op. cit.,* p.120.

73. *Op. cit.,* p.122. Chalmers also stated that the British silver 3d piece ('six cents') was 'slowly creeping into use'. Most of the currency must have consisted of US coins, although British silver coins were legal tender to any amount.

74. Chalmers, *op. cit.,* p.208.

75. Chalmers, *op. cit.,* pp.209–10.

76. Chalmers, *op. cit.,* pp.210–11. The customary use of the dollar is reflected today in the Gambia's striking of 4s pieces (1966) and 8s pieces (1970).

77. The extent of the use of cowrie shells as currency in West Africa has been much exaggerated and declined rapidly after 1870 (Chalmers, *op. cit.,* p.213).

78. P.N. Davies, *The Trade Makers: Elder Dempster in West Africa, 1852–1972* (London, 1973), pp.117–22. For developments after 1907 see L.V.W. Wright, *Colonial and Commonwealth Coins* (London, 1959), pp.66–7.
79. Or as the tables of currency rates at the time put it: 'Sterling into Halifax currency, the dollar at 4*s* 6*d* [sterling] passing for 5*s* currency.'
80. Chalmers, *op. cit.*, p.183.
81. Chalmers, *op. cit.*, p.184.
82. R. Giffen, *The Case against Bimetallism* (London, 2nd edition, 1892), pp.66–7, 104.
83. The wording of the preamble to the Prince Edward Island Act of 1851 (14 Vict. c.33) asserts that 'the orders-in-council and proclamations of 1825 and 1838 had no effect in this colony' (Chalmers, *op. cit.*, p.195).
84. *op. cit.*, p.198. Newfoundland, where much trading continued to be by barter until well into the nineteenth century, had a local Newfoundland sterling currency (cf. 'Halifax' currency), but adopted the dollar/cent system between 1863 and 1872. Distinctive Newfoundland gold, silver and bronze coins were struck from 1865 until 1947 (Chalmers, *op. cit.*, pp.172–4).
85. Duveen and Stride, *op. cit.*, p.96. Symbolically, the Ottawa mint was transferred to Dominion ownership in 1931, the year in which Britain finally abandoned the gold standard. A branch mint had been established in 1862 at New Westminster to service the gold-fields of British Columbia. It got as far as striking a few sample coins before it was abandoned (Craig, *op. cit.*, p.387).

PART SIX

SELECT BIBLIOGRAPHY
OF
PROFESSOR CHALONER'S
WRITINGS

Select Bibliography
of W.H. Chaloner's Writings

I BOOKS (NOS. 1-4)

1. *The Social and Economic Development of Crewe, 1780–1923*, Manchester University Press, 1950, 326 pp., including 6 pages of bibliography, reviewed in the *Manchester Guardian*, 5 Jan. 1951, in the *Crewe Chronicle*, 6 Jan. 1951, in the *Times Literary Supplement*, 20 April 1951, 248, in the *Economic History Review*, 1951, 119–21, by W. Ashworth and in *History Today*, Feb. 1951, 78. The second edition of 1973 was reviewed in the *Crewe Chronicle*, 16 June 1973 and 25 July 1974, in *Railway World*, Jan. 1975 and in *Journal of the Railway and Canal Historical Society, Book Review Supplement* No.5, July 1975, by H.P. White.

2. *Vulcan: the history of one hundred years of engineering and insurance, 1859–1959* (1959) Manchester, Vulcan Boiler and General Insurance Co., 67 pp., including a note on sources, reviewed in *The Newcomen Bulletin*, 59, Nov. 1959, 8, by S.B. Hamilton.

3. *People and Industries*, London, Cass, 1963, 151 pp., noticed in the *Times Literary Supplement*, 3 May 1963, 330, reviewed in *History Today*, July 1963, 505–6, by D.C. Coleman, in *The Newcomen Bulletin*, 70, July 1963, 8, by J. Foster Petree, in the *Economic History Review*, 1964, 163–4, by E.M. Sigsworth and in *La Metallurgia Italiana*, 19: 2, 1964, 48–50; translated into Japanese by Y. Takei in 1967 and published as 'People at the Time of the Industrial Revolution'.

4. *National Boiler, 1864–1964: a century of progress in industrial safety* (1964), Manchester, The National Boiler and General Insurance Co., 68 pp., reviewed in *The Newcomen Bulletin*, 75, March 1965, 8, by J. Foster Petree.

II ARTICLES AND PAMPHLETS (NOS. 5–136)

5. 'The History of the Cotton Manufacture in Nantwich (1785–1874)', Nantwich, *Johnson's Almanack and Directory*, 1938, 135–48.

6. 'The Worsdells and the Early Railway System', *Railway Magazine*, Oct. 1938, 235–6.

7. 'The Horse in Modern Warfare', *The Sphere*, 30 Aug. 1941, 276.

8. 'The Reminiscences of Richard Lindop, Farmer (1778–1871), and his Account of the Township of Church Coppenhall, near Nantwich, Cheshire', *Transactions of the Lancashire and Cheshire Antiquarian Society*, vol.55–1940 (1941), 107–30.

9. 'Trade Unionism a Monopoly? Crewe Fabians Debate Combines', *Crewe Chronicle*, 26 Oct. 1946.

10. 'Business Records and the National Register of Archives', *Stockport Chamber of Commerce Journal*, vol.4: 5, Nov. 1947, 51–52.

11. *Crewe Congregational Church, 1841–1947* (1947, 22 pp.), reviewed in the *Crewe Chronicle*, 25 Oct. 1947.

12. 'Business Records as a Source of Economic History with special reference

to their selective preservation in libraries', *Journal of Documentation*, 4:i, June 1948, 5–13.

13. 'A Lost Pamphlet', *Times Literary Supplement*, 3 July 1948, 373 by Dr. Joseph Priestley (c.1787) on sick clubs and friendly societies (letter).
14. 'New Light on John Wilkinson's Token Coinage', *Seaby's Coin and Medal Bulletin*, July 1948, 306–8.
15. 'John Wilkinson as Note Issuer and Banker', *Seaby's Coin and Medal Bulletin*, Dec. 1948, 550–3.
16. 'An English Ironmaster's Visit to Sweden in 1788', *Daedalus Year Book of the Swedish Technical Museum*, Stockholm, 1948, 152–4.
17. *Bridget Bostock. The 'White Witch' of Coppenhall, near Nantwich in Cheshire, 1748–1749*, Mayor of Crewe's Charity Committee, Sept. 1948, 16 pp., a bicentenary appreciation.
18. 'The Reminiscences of Thomas Dunning (1813–1894)', *Transactions of the Lancashire and Cheshire Antiquarian Society*, vol.59–1947 (1948), 85–130, 48 pp., reprinted in D. Vincent (ed.), *Testaments of Radicalism. Memoirs of Working Class Politicians 1790–1885*, Europa Publications, 1977, 117–46.
19. 'Marchant de la Houlière's Report on Casting Naval Cannon in the Year 1775', *Edgar Allen News*, Dec. 1948 and Jan. 1949, 5 pp.
20. 'Further light on the invention of the process for smelting iron ore with coke', *Economic History Review*, II:2.N.S., 1949, 185–7.
21. 'Boulton and Watt and the Drainage of Swedish Mines, 1797', *Daedalus Year Book of the Swedish Technical Museum*, Stockholm, 1949, 119–21.
22. 'Early Iron. 3. Notes on Wilkinson', *Architectural Review*, Nov. 1949, 333, with photograph of cast-iron pulpit made at Bradley, c.1790.
23. 'The Egertons in Italy and the Netherlands, 1729–1734. With Two Unpublished Letters from Joseph Smith, Sometime H.M. Consul at Venice', *Bulletin of the John Rylands Library*, vol.32:2, March 1950, 157–70.
24. 'Builders of Industry. I. John Wilkinson, Ironmaster' *History Today*, May 1951, 63–70, followed by letters from E.J. Elliot in ibid., Oct. 1951, 79 and from M.M. Rix in ibid., Dec. 1951, 78–9.
25. 'The "Hungry Forties": The Origin of a Legend', *History Today*, July 1951, 78–9, followed by letters by D.S. Colman in ibid., Sept. 1951, 78 and by N. Masterman in ibid., Dec. 1951, 79 (letter).
26. 'Free Trade and the Corn Laws', *Manchester Free Trade Hall. Commemorative Brochure*, Heaton Mersey, Cloister Press, Oct. 1951, 4–10.
27. 'The Canal Duke: Francis Egerton, third Duke of Bridgewater (1736–1803)', *History Today*, Oct.1951, 64–70, reprinted in 3 above.
28. 'The Cheshire Activities of Matthew Boulton and James Watt of Soho, near Birmingham, 1776–1817', *Transactions of the Lancashire and Cheshire Antiquarian Society*, vol.61–1949 (1951), 121–36.
29. 'Ludwig and Alfred Mond', *History Today*, June 1952, 379–85, reprinted in 3 above.
30. 'A Century's Achievements in Engineering. Many New Fields Developed', *Manchester Guardian*, 26 March 1953, 13 ii, Manchester Centenary Supplement.
31. 'Growth of a Great Industrial and Trading Centre', *Manchester Guardian*, 26 March 1953, 13 i, Manchester Centenary Supplement.

32. 'Francis Egerton, third Duke of Bridgewater (1736–1803): a biblio-graphical note', *Explorations in Entrepreneurial History*, V:3, March 1953, 181–5.
33. 'The Cartwright Brothers. Their Contribution to the Wool Industry', *Wool Knowledge*, Summer 1953, 15–21, reprinted in 3 above.
34. 'Business Records and Local History', *Bulletin of the Society of Local Archivists*, Oct. 1953, 21–5.
35. 'Sir Thomas Lombe (1685–1739) and the British Silk Industry', *History Today*, Nov. 1953, 778–85, reprinted in 3 above.
36. 'Samuel Crompton. A Textile Bicentenary', *Manchester Guardian*, 3 Dec. 1953, 6 vi, reprinted in 3 above.
37. 'Charles Roe of Macclesfield (1715–81): an Eighteenth-Century Indus-trialist', *Transactions of the Lancashire and Cheshire Antiquarian Society*, vol.62–1950/51 (1953), 133–56, and vol.63–1952/53 (1954), 52–86 (54pp.).
38. 'Bibliography of Recent Work on Enclosure, the Open Fields, and Related Topics', *Agricultural History Review*, 2, 1954, 48–52.
39. 'Robert Owen, Peter Drinkwater and the Early Factory System in Manchester, 1788–1800', *Bulletin of the John Rylands Library*, vol.37:1, Sept. 1954, 78–102.
40. 'Sources on Historical Price Movements', *History Today*, Dec. 1954, 851.
41. 'John Galloway (1804–94), Engineer of Manchester and his "Reminiscences" ', *Transactions of the Lancashire and Cheshire Anti-quarian Society*, vol.64–1954 (1955), 93–116 (24pp.).
42. 'Krupps of Essen and British Railways', *Railway Magazine*, July 1955, 471.
43. 'Cobbett and Manchester. The First Election Address', *Manchester Guardian*, 16 May 1955, 6 vi, reprinting part of manuscript of address published in *Weekly Political Register*, 25 Aug. 1832, 453–6.
44. 'Les frères John et William Wilkinson et leurs rapports avec la métallurgie française, 1775–1786', *Actes du colloque internationale: Le Fer à travers les Ages: hommes et techniques*, Annales de l'Est, Faculté des lettres de l'Université de Nancy, Mémoire No 16, 1956, 285–99.
45. 'One of the Great Victorians – Bessemer', *Manchester Guardian*, 29 Aug. 1956, Supplement, reprinted in 3 above.
46. 'Sir Henry Bessemer (1813–1898)', *Research*, Sept. 1956, 323–8.
47. 'Writings on British Urban History, 1934–1956', *Manchester Review*, 7, Autumn 1956, 399–406.
48. 'The Stephensons and the Locomotive', *History Today*, Sept. 1956, 627–34, reprinted in 3 above.
49. 'De Lesseps and the Suez Canal', *History Today*, Oct. 1956, 680–4.
50. 'McAdam the Roadmaker. The First Cheap Road Surface', *Manchester Guardian*, 21 Sept. 1956, 8 vi, reprinted in 3 above.
51. 'The History of the Rubber Industry and the Use of Rubber', *Manchester Guardian*, 15 Jan. 1957, 8, Supplement, reprinted in 3 above.
52. 'The Early History of Gas in Britain', *Manchester Guardian*, 27 Feb. 1957, 5, Gas Supplement, reprinted in 3 above.
53. 'Methodism and Revolution', *History Today*, May 1957, 335–6 (letter).
54. 'Telford and his Bridges', *Manchester Guardian*, 9 Aug. 1957, 6 vi, reprinted in 3 above.

55. 'History of Telecommunications', *Manchester Guardian*, 24 Oct. 1957, 11, Supplement, reprinted in 3 above.

56. 'The Agricultural Activities of John Wilkinson, Ironmaster', *Agricultural History Review*, 5, 1957, 48–51.

57. *The Hungry Forties: a re-examination*, Historical Association, 1957, 1963, 11pp.

58. 'Mrs. Trollope's Cotton Mill "Exposures". Historians' Praise Unjustified?', *Manchester Guardian*, 12 April 1958, 3i.

59. 'Two Thousand Years of Paper and Paper Making', *Manchester Guardian*, 9 June 1958, 4, Supplement, reprinted in 3 above.

60. 'Cotton's Troubles of a Century Ago. A Record of Dark Days', *Manchester Guardian*, 6 Oct. 1958, 14 i, 'by our own Reporter'.

61. 'Abacus to Automation', *Manchester Guardian*, 28 Nov. 1958, Supplement.

62. 'Dr Joseph Priestley, John Wilkinson and the French Revolution 1789–1802', *Transactions of the Royal Historical Society*, vol.8, 1958, 21–40.

63. 'Writings on British Urban History, 1934–57, covering the period 1700 to the present', *Vierteljahrschrift für Sozial- und Wirtschaftsgeschichte*, 45:1, 1958, 76–87.

64. Y.V. Kovalev, 'The Literature of Chartism', *Victorian Studies*, Dec. 1958, 117–8, introduction of two pages.

65. 'History of Cement', *Manchester Guardian*, 11 March 1959, 12 ii, reprinted in 3 above.

66. 'Origins and Growth of the Canning Industry', *Manchester Guardian*, 21 May 1959, 5 i, Supplement, reprinted in 3 above.

67. 'The Birth of the Panama Canal, 1869–1914', *History Today*, July 1959, 482–92.

68. 'Manchester in the Latter Half of the Eighteenth Century', *Bulletin of the John Rylands Library*, vol.42:1, Sept. 1959, 40–60.

69. 'The Bun Penny and its Predecessors', *Manchester Guardian*, 28 Dec. 1959, 4 vi.

70. 'Mrs Trollope and the Early Factory System', *Victorian Studies*, Dec. 1960, 159–66.

71. 'Isaac Wilkinson, Potfounder' in L.S. Pressnell (ed.), *Studies in the Industrial Revolution* (Athlone Press, 1960), 23–51.

72. 'Food and Drink in British History: a Bibliographical Guide', *The Amateur Historian*, 4:8, Summer 1960, 315–19.

73. 'Arnold Whitworth Boyd, M.C., M.A. (1885–1959)', *Transactions of the Lancashire and Cheshire Antiquarian Society*, vol.69–1959 (1960), 166–8, obituary of an ornithologist, naturalist, antiquarian and *Guardian* journalist since 1933.

74. A. Redford, *The Economic History of England, 1760–1800*, second revised edition, Longmans, 1960, with a tribute by the author to Chaloner's 'abounding energy'.

75. 'The Life of Gilbert Gilpin, chief clerk at Bersham ironworks, near Wrexham, 1786–1796', *National Library of Wales Journal*, vol.11:4, Winter 1960, 383–4.

76. 'William Furnival, H.E. Falk and the Salt Chamber of Commerce, 1815–1889: Some Chapters in the Economic History of Cheshire', *Transactions of the Historic Society of Lancashire and Cheshire*, vol.112, 1960, 121–45.

77. 'La condition des artisans en Angleterre pendant la révolution

industrielle (1770–1850)', *Actes du Colloque sur l'artisanat (Besançon, 10–12 Juin 1960), Cahiers d'Etudes Comtoises*, 3, Institut d'Etudes Comtoises, *Annales Littéraires de l'Université de Besançon*, vol.45, 1961, 167–80.

78. 'The Birth of Modern Manchester' in C.F. Carter (ed.), *Manchester and its Region* (British Association, 1962), 131–46.

79. W.T. Jackman, *The Development of Transportation in Modern England* (1916), second edition, Cass, 1962, with bibliographical introduction of 19 pages; re-issued in 1966 with additional bibliography of three pages.

80. 'An early denunciation of German social democracy', *Bulletin of the Society for the Study of Labour History*, No.6, Spring 1963, 28–9, referring to Alfred Krupp (1812–87) of Essen.

81. 'Salt in Cheshire 1600–1870', *Transactions of the Lancashire and Cheshire Antiquarian Society*, vol.71–1961 (1963), 58–74.

82. 'Bricks in the Building of Britain', in *People and Industries* (Cass, 1963), 115–19, being the sole previously unpublished essay amongst the 17 in that volume.

83. T.S. Ashton, *Iron and Steel in the Industrial Revolution* (1924), third edition, Manchester University Press, 1963, with bibliographical introduction of twelve pages, re-issued in 1968.

84. 'British Miners and the Coal Industry between the Wars', *History Today*, June 1964, 418–26, reviewed by Anna N. Baykova in *Voprosy istorii*, 1965, No.1, 193–4, 'A bourgeois scholar on the struggle of the English miners'.

85. 'Problèmes humains de l'industrie britannique du charbon, 1913–46', *Charbon et Sciences Humaines*, University of Lille, 1966, 233–46.

86. 'Hazards of Trade with France in Time of War 1776–1785', *Business History*, 6:2, June 1964, 79–92.

87. 'The Stockdale Family, the Wilkinson Brothers and the Cotton Mills at Cark in Cartmel c.1782–1800', *Transactions of the Cumberland and Westmorland Antiquarian and Archaeological Society*, 64 n.s., 1964, 356–72.

88. A. Redford, *Labour Migration in England, 1800–1850*, second revised edition, Manchester University Press, 1964, with six-page preface and four-page memoir of Arthur Redford, noticed in the *Times Literary Supplement*, 7 May 1964, 401; third edition with introduction of seven pages, 1976.

89. 'The Textile Inventor John Kay' (a communication), *Bulletin of the John Rylands Library*, vol.48:1, 1965, pp.9–12.

90. 'Trends in Fish Consumption' in T.C. Barker, J.C. Mackenzie and J. Yudkin (eds.), *Our Changing Fare* (MacGibbon and Kee, 1966), 94–114.

91. E. Baines, *History of the Cotton Manufacture in Great Britain* (1835), second edition, Cass, 1966, with bibliographical introduction of ten pages.

92. M. Hovell, *The Chartist Movement* (1918), reprinted in 1966 by Manchester University Press with bibliographical introduction of seven pages; new impression in 1970 with additional bibliography of one page.

93. J. Lord, *Capital and Steam Power, 1750–1800* (1923), second edition, Cass, 1966, with corrections and bibliographical introduction of five pages.

94. Samuel Bamford, *The Autobiography* (1844, 2 vols.), third edition, Cass,

1967, with introduction of 37 pages; reviewed by E.P. Thompson in the *Times Literary Supplement*, 3 Aug. 1967, 704.

95. J. Priestley, *Historical Account of the Navigable Rivers, Canals, and Railways throughout Great Britain* (1831), second edition, Cass, 1967, with introduction of two pages; also reprinted by David and Charles in 1969.

96. N. Riches, *The Agricultural Revolution in Norfolk* (1937), second edition, Cass, 1967, with bibliographical note of two pages.

97. William Harrison, *A History of the Manchester Railways* (1882), reprinted by the *Lancashire and Cheshire Antiquarian Society*, 34 pp., 1967, including a bibliographical postscript of one page.

98. 'Francis William Webb (1836–1906) of the London and North Western Railway', *Transport History*, July 1968, 169–78.

99. 'New Light on Richard Roberts, Textile Engineer (1789–1864)', *Transactions of the Newcomen Society*, vol.41 (1968–9), 27–44.

100. 'James Brindley (1716–72) and his remuneration as a canal engineer: New evidence', *Transactions of the Lancashire and Cheshire Antiquarian Society*, vols.75/76–1965–6 (1968), 226–8.

101. A. Prentice, *The History of the Anti-Corn Law League* (1853, 2 vols.), second edition, Cass, 1968, with introduction of 18 pages.

102. 'The Anti Corn Law League', *History Today*, March 1968, 196–204, a condensation of the new introduction to A. Prentice (1968), no.93 above.

103. W. Dodd, *The Factory System Illustrated* (1841–2), third edition, Cass, 1968, with introduction of nine pages.

104. Sir George Head, *A Home Tour through the Manufacturing Districts of England in the Summer of 1835* (1836), reprinted, Cass, 1968, with introduction of three pages.

105. W. Cooke Taylor, *Notes of a Tour in the Manufacturing Districts of Lancashire* (1841, 1842), third edition, Cass, 1968, with an introduction of two pages.

106. G. Unwin, *Samuel Oldknow and the Arkwrights. The Industrial Revolution at Stockport and Marple* (1924), second edition, Manchester University Press, 1968, with preface of six pages.

107. Edwin Butterworth, *A Statistical Sketch of the County Palatine of Lancaster* (1841), facsimile reprint by the *Lancashire and Cheshire Antiquarian Society*, 1968, with introduction of one page.

108. James Scott Walker, *An Accurate Description of the Liverpool and Manchester Railway: the tunnels, the bridges, and other works throughout the line* (1830), reprint, Manchester, *Lancashire and Cheshire Antiquarian Society*, 1968, with introduction of one page.

109. John B. Edmondson, *The Early History of the Railway Ticket. A Documentary Reprint,Lancashire and Cheshire Antiquarian Society*, 1968, 20 pp. including introductory note of one page, a shortened version of 'To Whom are we indebted for the Railway Ticket System?', *The English Mechanic*, 2 Aug. 1878, 524–6.

110. 'A Note on the Origins of the "Broiler" Industry', *Agricultural History Review*, 17, 1969, 161.

111. 'Three Centuries of Emigration from England and Wales', *World Conference on Records and Genealogical Seminar, Salt Lake City, Utah, U.S.A., 5–8 August 1969*, 1–20.

112. *The Skilled Artisans during the Industrial Revolution 1750–1850*, Historical Association, 1969, 14 pp.
113. 'The Agitation against the Corn Laws' in J.T. Ward (ed.), *Popular Movements* (1970), 135–51.
114. 'Industrialisation and urbanisation, 1780–1970: Origins of the modern environment' in A.J.P. Taylor and J.M. Roberts (eds.), *History of the Twentieth Century*, VIII (Purnell 1970), chap. 115, 522–5.
115. 'Trends in fish consumption in Great Britain from about 1900 to the present day' in T.C. Barker and J. Yudkin (eds.), *Fish in Britain* (University of London, Queen Elizabeth College, Dept. of Nutrition, 1971), 83–9.
116. 'General Lud's Army' and 'The age of steam' in Alan Palmer (ed.), *Milestones of History, 5: The Age of Optimism 1803–96* (Weidenfeld & Nicolson, 1971), 20–5, 54–61.
117. C.F. Dendy Marshall, *A History of British Railways down to the year 1830* (1938), by a founder-member of the Newcomen Society, second edition, Oxford University Press, 1971, with introduction of five pages and internal corrections; reviewed in *Railway Magazine*, Nov. 1971, and in *Journal of Transport History*, 1972, 193, by Jack Simmons.
118. 'The Bitter Cry of Outcast London', *The Times Literary Supplement*, 5 March 1971, 271, letter on the Rev. W.C. Preston as the author.
119. S. Horrocks (compiler), *Lancashire Business Histories*, Manchester, Joint Committee on the Lancashire Bibliography, 1971, a Contribution towards a Lancashire Bibliography, 3, with introduction of one page.
120. 'Chaloner on Jevons', *Communication*, University of Manchester, Jan. 1972, 15–16.
121. 'Jevons in Manchester: 1863–1876', *The Manchester School*, March 1972, 73–84.
122. 'John Phillips: Surveyor and Writer on Canals', *Transport History*, July 1972, 168–72, followed the reprint in 1970 of John Phillips's *General History* by Charles Hadfield of David & Charles.
123. 'Marx: white racialist', *The Observer*, 27 May 1973, on A.J.P. Taylor's review of G. Watson, *The English Ideology* (letter).
124. 'Isaac Perrins, 1751–1801, Prize-fighter and Engineer', *History Today*, Oct. 1973, 740–3.
125. 'The Cotton Industry to 1820' and 'The Cotton Industry since 1820' in J.H. Smith (ed.), *'The Great Human Exploit': Historic Industries of the North-West*, Phillimore, 1973, 17–32.
126. *The Movement for the extension of Owen's College Manchester, 1863–73*, Manchester University Press, 1973, 23pp.
127. 'Letters from Lancashire Lads in America during the Civil War, 1863–1865', *Transactions of the Lancashire and Cheshire Antiquarian Society*, vol. 77–1967 (1974), 137–51.
128. 'Currency problems of the British empire, 1814–1914', in B.M. Ratcliffe (ed.), *Great Britain and her world 1750–1914*, Manchester University Press, 1975, 179–207.
129. 'The Rev. Charles Shaw and his anonymous *When I Was a Child* by an Old Potter, 1903: Its Influence on Arnold Bennett's Clayhanger', *Proceedings of the Wesley Historical Society*, 40, June 1975, 51–3.
130. 'A Philadelphia textile merchant's trip to Europe on the eve of the Civil War: Robert Creighton, 1856–57' in W.H. Chaloner and B.M. Ratcliffe

(eds.), *Trade and Transport*, Manchester University Press, 1977, 157–72.
131. '1989: 1688 or 1789?' in *The Coming Confrontation. Will the Open Society Survive to 1989?*, Institute of Economic Affairs, 1978, 31–40.
132. 'How Immoral were the Victorians? A Bibliographical Reconsideration', *Bulletin of the John Rylands Library*, vol.60:2, Spring 1979, 362–75, The Moses Tyson Memorial Lecture, delivered on 9 Nov. 1977.
133. 'Saddleworth and the U.S.A.' in Anne Parry (compiler), *The Saddleworth–America Connection* (Saddleworth Festival of the Arts, 1979), 9–22, reviewed in the *Saddleworth Historical Society Bulletin*, 9:2, Summer 1979, 28–9, by John Murray.
134. I. Shaw, *Views of the Most Interesting Scenery on the Line of the Liverpool and Manchester Railway* (1831), reprinted Oldham, Hugh Broadbent, 1979, with introduction of one page.
135. 'Was there a Decline of the Industrial Spirit in Britain 1850–1939?' (Dickinson Memorial Lecture), *Transactions of the Newcomen Society*, vol.55 (1983–4), 211–8.
136. 'The Rev. Terence Hope Davenport (1900–20 March 1985)', *Transactions of the Lancashire and Cheshire Antiquarian Society*, vol.83, 1985 (1985), 197.

III TRANSLATIONS (NOS. 137–147)

III : i *Translations from the German*, all with W.O. Henderson:

137. W. Schlote, *British Overseas Trade from 1700 to the 1930s*, Oxford, Blackwell, 1952 (book originally published in 1938).
138. L. Drescher, 'The Development of Agricultural Production in Great Britain and Ireland from the early Eighteenth Century', *The Manchester School*, May 1955, 153–83.
139. W.G. Hoffmann, *British Industry, 1700–1950*, Oxford, Blackwell, 1955, 2nd ed. 1965.
140. W.G. Hoffmann, *The Growth of Industrial Economies*, Oxford, Blackwell, 1958.
141. F. Pollock, *The Economic and Social Consequences of Automation*, Oxford, Blackwell, 1957.
142. F. Engels, *The Condition of the Working Class in England*, Oxford, Blackwell, 1958, 1971, reviewed in the *Sunday Times*, 9 March 1958, by Robert Blake, in the *New Statesman*, 22 March 1958, 379, by Asa Briggs, in *Marxism Today*, May 1958, 132–9, by E.J. Hobsbawm and in the *Library Journal*, 1 June 1958, 1791: second revised edition 1971; paperback edition 26 July 1980.
143. *Engels as Military Critic*, Penguin 1959. A collection of Engels's articles with joint introduction by Chaloner and Henderson.

III : ii *Translations from the French with notes:*

144. Marchant de la Houlière's *Report to the French Government on British methods of smelting iron ore with coke and casting naval cannon*, 1775 (published 1949). See entry for no.17 above.
145. (with B.M. Ratcliffe), *A French Sociologist looks at Britain: Gustave d'Eichthal and British Society in 1828*, Manchester University Press, 1977, 169 pp., Faculty of Arts Publications No.22, reviewed in *Journal of*

European History, 1979, 511–12, by L. Neal.
146. (with François Crouzet and W.M. Stern, eds.), *Essays in European Economic History, 1789–1914*, Arnold, 1969, 280 pp., 12 articles with joint preface.

IV BOOKS AND ARTICLES WRITTEN IN COLLABORATION WITH OTHER AUTHORS (NOS. 147–163)

IV : i *Books written in collaboration*

with W.O. Henderson

147. *Engels as Military Critic: articles reprinted from the Volunteer Journal and the Manchester Guardian of the 1860s*, 146 pages including introduction of 10 pages, Manchester University Press, 1959.

with A.E. Musson

148. *Industry and Technology*, London, Vista Books, 1963, 202 pp., in the series A Visual History of Modern Britain, edited by Jack Simmons.

with R.C. Richardson

149. *British Economic and Social History: a bibliographical guide*. Manchester University Press, 1976, 129 pp., reviewed in the *Economic History Review*, Feb. 1977, 182–3 by M.E. Falkus; in the *Business History Review*, Summer 1977, 257–8, by Richmond D. Williams; and in *History*, 1978, 67, by M.W. Beresford.
150. *Bibliography of British Economic and Social History*, Manchester University Press, 1984, 208 pp., a revision of the first edition with 38% more entries, 5800 instead of 4200, reviewed in *Business History*, 1985, 255–6 by D.J. Jeremy.

IV : ii *Articles written in collaboration*

with F.C. Mather

151. 'A Cheshire Mother's letters to her undergraduate son at Magdalene College (Cambridge) 1728–1729', *Magdalene College Magazine*, May 1949, 10–14.
152. 'The Basingstoke Canal. An Eighteenth-Century Enterprise in Hampshire', *The Edgar Allen News*, Vol.28: 326, Aug. 1949, 365–8.

with Alan Birch

153. 'The First Cast Iron Rails: further evidence', *Railway Magazine*, Sept. 1951, 632–3.

with W.O. Henderson

154. 'Aaron Manby, builder of the first iron steamship', *Trans. Newcomen Society*, vol.29 (1953–4, 1954–5), pp.77–91.
155. 'The Manbys and the Industrial Revolution in France, 1819–84', *Trans. Newcomen Society*, vol.30 (1955–6, 1956–7), pp.63–75.

with W.O. Henderson (continued)

156. 'Friedrich Engels and the England of the 1840s', *History Today*, June 1956, 448–56, with supplementary letter in ibid., Dec. 1956, 855.
157. 'Friedrich Engels in Manchester', *Memoirs and Proceedings of the Manchester Literary and Philosophical Society*, 1956–57, vol.98, 1–17, evoking a letter by A.E. Musson to the *Manchester Guardian*, 16 Feb. 1957, 3v, and a reply by the authors in ibid., 21 Feb. 1957, 2i.
158. 'Some Aspects of the Early History of Automation', *Research*, X:ix, Sept. 1957, 334–9.
159. 'Friedrich Engels and the England of the "Hungry Forties" ', in A. Seldon (ed.), *The Long Debate on Poverty*, Institute of Economic Affairs, 1972, pp.169–86. German translation in *ORDO: Jahrbuch für die Ordnung von Wirtschaft und Gesellschaft*, 1974, pp.261–81.
160. 'Marx, Engels and Racism', *Encounter*, July 1975, 71–6, followed by letters by R.S. Wistrich in ibid., Nov. 1975, 94, 96 and by H. Hirsch in ibid., July 1976, 94.

with J.D. Marshall

161. 'Major John Cartwright and the Revolution Mill, East Retford, Notts., 1783–1806', in N.B. Harte and K.G. Ponting (eds.), *Textile History and Economic History: essays in honour of Miss Julia de L. Mann*, Manchester University Press, 1973, pp.281–303.

with J.S. Roskell

162. 'A Charter of 1467 relating to a Burgage in the Marketsted, Manchester', *Transactions of the Lancashire and Cheshire Antiquarian Society*, vols.75/76–1965/66 (1968), 229–230, with photograph of the charter by W.J. Smith.
163. 'Miss Hilda Lofthouse, M.A., F.L.A. (1912–82)', *Transactions of the Lancashire and Cheshire Antiquarian Society*, vol.82 (1983), 157, obituary of the Chetham's Librarian, 1945–73.

INDEX